Frontier Country

EARLY AMERICAN STUDIES

Series editors
Daniel K. Richter, Kathleen M. Brown,
Max Cavitch, and David Waldstreicher

Exploring neglected aspects of our colonial,
revolutionary, and early national history and culture,
Early American Studies reinterprets familiar themes
and events in fresh ways. Interdisciplinary in character,
and with a special emphasis on the period from about
1600 to 1850, the series is published in partnership with
the McNeil Center for Early American Studies.

A complete list of books in the series
is available from the publisher.

FRONTIER COUNTRY

THE POLITICS OF WAR
IN EARLY PENNSYLVANIA

PATRICK SPERO

PENN

UNIVERSITY OF PENNSYLVANIA PRESS

PHILADELPHIA

Published by
University of Pennsylvania Press
Philadelphia, Pennsylvania 19104-4112
www.upenn.edu/pennpress

Printed in the United States of America
on acid-free paper
1 3 5 7 9 10 8 6 4 2

A catalogue record for this book is available from the Library of Congress.
ISBN 978-0-8122-4861-6

For my teachers, past and present

CONTENTS

Early American Frontiers

In January 1765, as Charles Mason and Jeremiah Dixon were busy surveying the line that now bears their names, a morbid "curiousity" led Charles to stop his work and take a journey to Lancaster, Pennsylvania. As he later recorded in his diary, it was "the place where was perpetrated last winter, the horrid and inhumane murder of 26 Indians: men, women, and children, leaving none alive to tell." Mason had to see the site of this depravity to understand it.[1]

The brutal event that drew Mason to Lancaster is now known as the Paxton Boys' Rebellion. It began in December 1763 when a group of colonists living outside of Lancaster massacred their neighbors, the Conestoga Indians, who resided on a nearby manor reserved for them by the Pennsylvania government. A couple of weeks after their initial assault, the Paxton Boys raided a building in Lancaster that housed the few surviving Conestogas, killing all alive. The murderers became rebels when hundreds of supporters joined them in a seventy-mile trek through the rough winter to Philadelphia, the colonial capital, to defend the Paxton Boys' actions and protest what they saw as the government's overly benevolent policy toward Native people. The march was likely the largest political mobilization in the history of colonial Pennsylvania.

Mason was surprised by what he found when he visited. Lancaster was not some lawless frontier outpost, but instead a bustling and vibrant inland port. Its location a few miles from the Susquehanna River, a central artery that in 1763 connected the vast interior of North America to the Atlantic, meant that the town was an important waypoint for the British Empire as it expanded west across the Appalachian Mountains. Lancaster was "as large as most market towns in England," Mason noted in his diary before leaving. He was right; it was the largest inland town in colonial America.[2]

Mason's trip took another unexpected turn a few days later when he met a fellow traveler named Samuel Smith. Smith told Mason a strange tale about Lancaster and its role in creating the border Mason was then in the business of surveying. About thirty years earlier, Smith recounted, Pennsylvania was "in open war" with Maryland over control of the Susquehanna and all lands to the west. Smith, who was the sheriff of Lancaster County at the time, controlled a militia that laid siege to the home of the leader of the Marylanders, one Mr. Cresap. In the ensuing melee, Cresap's house was engulfed in flames, one Marylander died, and the Pennsylvanians captured and jailed Cresap and many of his men. Mason seemed surprised by Smith's story of two neighboring colonies engaged in such a violent conflict. It is even more surprising that Mason was unaware of this "open war" because it had led to his current assignment. When the king heard that two of his colonies were fighting, he drew a temporary boundary between them. After a court case to settle the dispute, Mason was dispatched with Dixon to establish a permanent line.[3]

During this brief but eventful trip to Pennsylvania, Mason encountered the twin problems that plagued the British Empire on its North American frontiers in the years before the American Revolution: establishing social harmony within the empire, especially between colonists and Native Americans, and creating borders between the polities that composed the empire. While Mason and Dixon were in the midst of marking a line between colonies, imperial officials were trying to create clearer boundaries between colonial settlements and Indians. Throughout the 1760s, officers of the British Empire hoped to stabilize relations with the Indians by granting them specific territories and by opening a brisk trade with Native allies. These imperial officials envisioned a porous border—an "open road" was the catchphrase of the time—that would maintain a lasting peace by incorporating Native peoples into the empire economically while also granting them some political autonomy.

The policies meant to integrate Indians into the British Empire, however, only added to colonists' growing frustrations. The Paxton Boys epitomized this viewpoint. After living through the Seven Years' War (1754 to 1763) and Pontiac's War (1763 to 1765), colonists who had experienced this decade of strife saw Indians—all Indians, even their Conestoga neighbors—as enemies rather than friends with whom they wished to trade. They viewed imperial policies, traders, and a colonial governing elite as disconnected from—even hostile to—their needs. Where imperial officials stationed in London or the eastern seaports aimed to incorporate Indians into Britain's mercantile system and increasingly global trade, many colonists on the frontiers of the British Empire wanted to exclude Indians from the rights and privileges of the imperial system and shift political power away from the east and to the west.

The Paxton Boys' massacre of the Conestogas and subsequent march on Philadelphia was the first in a series of frontier rebellions that aimed to challenge these imperial regulations in the decades before the American Revolution. A few months after Mason's venture to Lancaster, another group of colonists calling themselves the Black Boys launched a raid on a British fort near Fort Pitt, one of the most audacious attacks on imperial authority in colonial America. Three years later, another mobilization occurred to defend Frederick Stump, a man arrested for murdering a group of Indians in an attack eerily reminiscent of the Paxton Boys.

These colonial protests against their government in the 1760s were just as important to the coming of the American Revolution as such better-known urban revolts as the Stamp Act protests and Boston Tea Party. But the cause of the western discontent was far different from that of easterners. More than a decade of living on the frontlines of war transformed the worldview of colonists on the edges of Great Britain's North American Empire. During the Seven Years' War, the countryside they inhabited, once renowned for its peace and prosperity, turned into what was increasingly called a "frontier country," an important description they had not used previously. During and after the war, people in western regions that had been called the "back parts" or "back counties" before the fighting began to refer to themselves as a "frontier people" who lived in "frontier counties." Many wrote about the traumatic process of "becoming a frontier," an event marked by profound fear, utter desperation, and an abiding hatred for those that caused these feelings. These self-described "frontier people" were civilians who had turned into unwilling combatants, and they looked to their government for the military protection they believed they deserved. When the government failed them, they looked to themselves and their neighbors for security. The perception of being a people ignored by their governments lingered after peace in 1763 and animated their actions in the years before independence.

When Mason fell into the company of Samuel Smith after investigating the Paxton Boys, he stumbled upon the second problem of imperial governance: establishing political borders in the empire. Mason's lack of awareness of the border war that led to his current appointment suggests that few people outside of these contested areas were familiar with this type of intercolonial strife. For those living in the British Empire's North American holdings, however, border conflicts between colonies were a common occurrence. From New Hampshire to the Carolinas, boundary controversies were a regular part of governing. Indeed, Smith and other combatants regaled visitors with stories of colonial conflicts decades after they occurred because they still mattered to colonists at the time, many of whom lived in similarly unstable areas.

Located at the center of Great Britain's North American holdings, Pennsylvania experienced more border conflicts than any other colony. After its clash with Maryland in the 1730s, Pennsylvania waged two separate fights in the 1760s and 1770s, one against Virginia and another against Connecticut. Unlike the Maryland War, Pennsylvania lost these later battles. By 1775, the colony—once the literal and figurative heart of North America, the home of the largest city in the colonies, and the seat of the Continental Congress that was then preparing to declare thirteen colonies independent of the empire—had collapsed. Although the colonial government claimed sovereignty over the region that we today associate with Pennsylvania, its governing authority had largely vanished. Connecticut controlled the northern third of the state, while Virginia controlled the western region. In the interior portions, groups like the Paxton Boys and Black Boys ignored their government, and many renounced their allegiance to Pennsylvania so they could help other colonies establish toeholds in areas that Pennsylvania's government claimed. The failure of the British Empire and its colonies to establish clear political borders without resorting to intercolonial warfare reveals another fundamental failure of imperial administration.[4]

Indeed, in 1776, those in Philadelphia who were rejecting the British Empire thought a great deal about the frontiers and borders of the nation they were creating. As patriots explained their reasons for declaring independence, they looked west. Thomas Jefferson noted in the Declaration of Independence that one of King George III's crimes against his colonists was encouraging Indians to launch raids "on the inhabitants of our frontiers," a reference to events that were then occurring around Fort Pitt. And when revolutionaries thought about the powers of the government they were creating, they again looked west. John Dickinson, a Pennsylvanian well versed

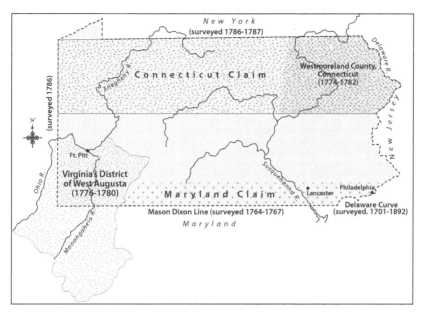

Figure 1. Pennsylvania and its contested borders. Pennsylvania fought a war against Maryland over its southern and western boundaries from 1732 to 1738. In the 1770s, Pennsylvania clashed with Connecticut and Virginia over their competing claims and lost.

in the colony's travails, made sure that the Articles of Confederation contained a clear means for states to mediate their border disputes.

But these attempts to solve the problems of the British Empire during the American Revolution beg the question: what caused the disintegration of government power in the years preceding American independence? The answer has less to do with the structure of the British Empire and its officials and more to do with, in Jefferson's words, "the inhabitants of our frontiers," people such as Samuel Smith and the Paxton Boys. Like the border wars that we should take seriously because people of the time did, we should take Jefferson's words in the Declaration of Independence seriously and try to understand what he meant by them. In fact, one of his well-chosen words connects these two problems of governing North America and helps explain the collapse of colonial and imperial rule in the west: *frontier*.

> Frontier: the border . . . which the enemies find in the front
> when they are about to enter.
>
> —N. Bailey, *The New Universal Etymological*
> *English Dictionary* (1776)

Words, like people, shape history. Words can command action, convey feelings, or encapsulate beliefs. People deploy certain words to drive events. Words are often the best—and sometimes the only—things historians have to access the past. And words, like people, possess a history. The meaning and import of a specific word may change, sometimes dramatically so. To a historian, knowing what a word meant and how its definition shifted over time can help reconstruct the way people experienced their past, show the way they used words to explain their present, and explain the course of the history these people made.

Frontier is such a word. Colonists used *frontier* to describe the world as they understood it. Specifically, a frontier in early America was a zone that people considered vulnerable to invasion, one that was created when colonists feared an onslaught from imperial rivals and other enemies. As such, it was a word that colonists used to explain their geopolitical landscape. For our purposes, an English dictionary published in 1776, the year Jefferson cited attacks on "our frontiers" as a reason to declare independence, distills the way that people thought of a frontier at the time of the American Revolution: "the border, confine, or boundary of a kingdom or province, which the enemies find in the front when they are about to enter the same."[5]

According to this definition, a version of which appeared in print at least as early as 1730, frontier zones were the opposite of how they appear in today's popular imagination. Frontiers were not areas of active expansion, exploration, and economic opportunity; they were contingent (a clear enemy threat created such zones), defensive (threatened areas required fortifications to ward off an assault), and prone to contraction (if a colony failed to adequately fortify a frontier, then the enemy would be able to push the borders of the territory inward). So defined, frontiers were often specific communities that an enemy would attack first as part of a larger invasion. Indeed, a later dictionary copied the 1776 definition verbatim and added, "thus we say, a frontier town, frontier province."[6]

As political theorists developed the idea of the early modern state, frontiers defined in this way became important parts of the larger body politic in which they existed. Frontiers were the limbs of a polity; they warded off assault and provided the first and most important protection for the heart, or capital region. The relationship between these two parts was thus based on reciprocity. While a frontier helped protect the heart, frontiers themselves depended upon the heart—the capital, the government—for sustenance and support. A diseased political body saw its frontiers wither, while a healthy political body, one that had a strong heart, sustained its limbs. As Walter Raleigh wrote in the early seventeenth century, "As health and soundness of the hands, legs, and other outward members cannot continue life, unless the heart and vital spirits within be strong and firm; so fortifications and Frontier-defences do not prevail." Such a conception of frontier crossed the Atlantic with British colonists, who adapted their language to describe their new geopolitical terrain, with officials and colonists often describing their various frontiers as "naked," "open," and "exposed," a desperate situation that demanded more military aid from the government.[7]

This reciprocal relationship, one in which those on the frontiers provided the heart of the polity with some measure of protection while those in the heart supplied the support necessary to ward off an attack, formed the fundamental contract between the government and the governed that was so important to those living in the early modern world. In fact, it was on frontiers that early modern governments were made or lost, especially colonial initiatives that projected power into North America. Benjamin Franklin expressed such an understanding when he declared in his popular pamphlet *Great Britain Reconsidered* that "the Frontier of any dominion being attack'd, it becomes not merely 'the cause' of the people immediately affected, (the inhabitants of that Frontier) but properly 'the cause' of the whole body. Where Frontier People owe and pay obedience, there they have a right to look for protection. No political proposition is better established than this."[8]

In short, *frontier* was a politically potent word in the eighteenth century. A successful frontier policy was supposed to make "frontier people" feel secure. As Franklin noted, in exchange for this security "frontier people owe and pay obedience" to their government. If the government ignored their pleas or failed to protect them against an attack, then anxiety could turn into anger so strong that it would break the bonds between the governed and the governed. As Franklin concluded, "No political proposition is better established"; it was an essential part of governing in early America.

The structure of the British Empire in North America meant that most colonies were responsible for providing for their own frontiers. In fact, most colonies passed laws from their inception to aid areas designated as such because providing security was where a colony began. Governing frontiers was thus essential to the success or failure of colonial projects. It was in these zones that colonies proved they could maintain their fundamental obligation to their constituents. If a colony could manage its frontier regions and provide the type of protection colonists sought, then the colony would secure the fundamental contract between the Crown and its peoples. From there, colonies could help establish the rest of their governing capacities and serve larger imperial aims. Such a process played out in most British colonies early in their history, as colonists waged a series of wars against their Indian neighbors or their European competitors. These colonies established militias, raised taxes to support wars, and crafted policies to strengthen frontier regions, often by encouraging more colonists to settle in them. Indeed, most colonies from their founding successfully integrated frontier policy into their governing with little controversy. They were, as William Penn described New York in 1701, "a frontier government."[9]

Pennsylvania, however, avoided a direct confrontation with a European rival or a major war with its Native neighbors for the first seventy-three years of its existence. Influenced by the pacifist ideals of its founder, William Penn, government officials took pride in their good Indian relations, often boasting that their model for colonization was superior to that of other colonies. They also benefited from their location, protected on the east by New Jersey and with New York as a buffer from French Canada. From 1681 until the 1750s, Pennsylvania flourished because it was able to win the loyalty of its colonists through peace and prosperity, providing colonists with a sense of security without warfare against Indians or European adversaries. In short, Pennsylvania lacked frontier regions because no one feared invasion. While that history makes Pennsylvania different from other British colonies in North America, it also makes the role of frontiers in early America particularly revealing.

After war with an external enemy finally came to the region in the 1750s when joint French and Indian raids attacked Pennsylvanian settlements during the Seven Years' War, many Pennsylvanians who faced such deadly incursions believed their homes in a once peaceful countryside now formed a dangerous frontier. They sought the same militarization for their communities that other British colonies had long offered their colonists. In the postwar years, the period marked by rebellions like that of the Paxton Boys, colonial and imperial officials wanted to reestablish security on former frontiers through peace with Indians and demilitarization. But colonists in the region demanded a very different policy, one more akin to the defensive and militaristic one adopted by most other colonies that continued to act as if they had a frontier region to protect. Thus, the fundamental bond between frontier people and their government began to break down in Pennsylvania as these views diverged in the 1760s. The governing crisis created on the colony's frontiers—indeed a disagreement between colonists and their colonial and imperial governments over whether the colony even contained frontiers—would only be solved by a revolution that would overthrow the colonial establishment and create a new governing contract on the terms frontier people demanded.

"Distresses of a Frontier Man"

To introduce these eighteenth-century "frontier people," let us turn to one of their most astute chroniclers, Hector St. John Crevecoeur, author of the famous work *Letters from an American Farmer.* Crevecoeur traveled throughout British North America in the 1760s and wrote about the people he met and the society he observed. Crevecoeur's perceptions were so shrewd that his book is still required reading for people seeking to understand eighteenth-century North America. As his biographers say, with little hesitation, "His writings show more detailed knowledge of American geography and life of the settlers than those of any other writer of the period." The question at the heart of his work, posed in his most famous letter, "What Is an American?" resonates still. Often overlooked, however, is the book's last chapter, titled "Distresses of a Frontier Man." His treatment of the "frontier man" provides a window into the lives of the people who form the subject of his book.[10]

"Distresses of a Frontier Man" is set at the beginning of the American Revolution. Crevecoeur's protagonist, whose name is James, lives on a farm in Carlisle, Pennsylvania. In Crevecoeur's earlier essays, the farm represented hope and opportunity. Though isolated, James nonetheless feels connected to the rest of society through his bountiful harvests that tied James's labors to the rest of the society through the market. But in the final chapter, war has turned his farm into a place of fear, desperation, and isolation, a living death. The fear of invasion looms in all that he does, and life itself becomes muted. Night is the worst time. "Whichever way" James looks, he sees "the most frightful precipices." When he looks to the mountains, he imagines "our dreadful enemy" racing down its ramparts and destroying his farm. Darkness "renders these incursions still more terrible." That is when the invasions most often come, or at least, that is when the dread of them most haunts James's imaginings. Daytime is not much better. "We never go out in the fields," James tells his friend, "but we are seized with an involuntary fear, which lessens our strength and weakens our labor."[11]

Fear interrupts the simple rhythms of life. Wracked by constant anxiety, James and his family lose their appetites and "eat just enough to keep alive." When they do find the energy to eat, "the slightest noise" disrupts meals and sends his family seeking cover. Their sleep is "disturbed by the most frightful dreams." Although James and his wife try to protect their children, every morning the young ones wake with tales of their nighttime horrors. Sometimes the howl of James's dogs stirs him from sleep and sends him running for his gun, while his wife takes the children to the cellar where they await the onslaught of Indians. "Fear industriously increases every sound" as James stands by his windows, his hands clutching his gun, expecting to receive fire at any moment: "We remain thus sometimes for whole hours, our hearts and minds racked by the most anxious suspense: what a dreadful situation, a thousand times worse than that of a soldier engaged in the most severe conflict!" Stories of "successive acts of devastation" spread through frontier homes, "and these told in chimney-corners, swell themselves in our affrighted imaginations into the most terrific ideas!" Fear more than actual warfare defines frontier society for James and his neighbors.[12]

Crevecoeur's depiction is more than mere fiction. The historical record bears out the sentiments he conveys. The emotions of that came while being holed up in their small homes, huddled around fires, fearing that an attack would come any moment, forged a distinct sense of self: a frontier people, a political identity that shaped the actions of anyone who believed that they were such a person. Treating *frontier* on its own terms gives us a way to understand how colonists and Europeans imagined the spaces they inhabited and how this imagination shaped their politics.[13]

"A Strange State of Society"

Frontiers should not be confused with our idea of borders. The two were not synonymous in the eighteenth century, though as geopolitical regions in a colony they could overlap. Frontiers appeared at moments of war to mark the colonial settlements vulnerable to invasion. And there were many different frontiers, depending on who was doing the strategizing. There were imperial frontiers that referred to the empire's holdings and could stretch across colonies and into areas not yet acquired. And there were colonial frontiers that were specific to a colony and required the attention of governors and legislatures. That is, grand strategists in England could draw clear, often contiguous lines to mark areas of expected invasion, while those tasked with governing colonies could imagine more local zones of invasion with greater specificity than those in the faraway halls of London. And finally, living on a frontier was a real experience for colonists who inhabited such zones. Sometimes these three perspectives agreed on where frontiers existed, and sometimes they did not. But even when they disagreed, there was general consensus about what a frontier was: a zone of potential, if not active, assault from an external enemy.

Borders, in contrast, were more permanent, though their specific location could be just as contested as the location of frontiers. Colonial governments, rather than the empire, most often dealt with establishing the exact location of the political borders that separated colonies from one another and distinguished between Native American land and colonial land. Colonies thus possessed many different borders that they often had to manage simultaneously. At their founding, colonial charters projected imagined borders far away from the settled coastlines. Borders, as such, were less of a concern in this earliest phase of colonization. Early maps, for instance, were often borderless. As colonies expanded, however, and came into contact with neighboring polities, often other British colonies, they began to solidify intercolonial borders. Colonies also had borders with Native American groups and with their imperial rivals that they negotiated or fought to secure, which is when frontiers and borders often overlapped.

Fixing these political boundaries between rival colonies required a distinctive type of governing. Here, colonial officials had to operate within a larger imperial framework that had its own laws and precedents for establishing jurisdiction. While colonial officials caught in the midst of a border dispute were always cognizant of the larger superstructure to which they belonged, as we shall see, during border wars they regularly ignored these laws in practice. The most distinctive part of these conflicts was the means to secure victory. While martial strength often played a role in the course of the conflict, what mattered more for victory was the ability for one of the competing colonies to appeal to the needs of local colonists and secure a loyal following that would bolster the victorious colony's governing authority. In this process of border creation, regular colonists got to pick the government they preferred and, by doing so, shape the contours of the empire through the terms of their allegiance. In the end, establishing borders, a political designation meant to create stability in the empire, fostered animosities as warring colonies adopted tactics that divided colonists, bred uncertainty, and created political disorder.[14]

When colonial border wars increased in the greater Pennsylvania region during the 1770s, the politics of frontiers, something that had been absent from previous intercolonial clashes, fused with colonial competition over borders, allowing frontier inhabitants to use their power of choice to remake the colonial and imperial governments to which they belonged. It was, as one of the people who lived at the time would later remember, "a strange state of society" in which colonists rejected the Pennsylvania model of security through peace and used colonial competition to empower the vision of a more militarized government that would come to define the future of governing American frontiers.

It is no mistake, then, that Thomas Jefferson was thinking about Indian relations on the new nation's frontiers as he penned the Declaration of Independence or that John Dickinson dedicated the longest section of the Articles of Confederation to establishing peaceful borders between the newly independent states. These two issues were a central part of the crisis of empire and among the reasons for revolution. Putting colonial competition alongside the development of "frontiers" creates a more complete—though still imperfect—picture of politics in the colonies at the very moment the British Empire in North America experienced a precipitous fall.

The politics of frontiers and border creation are the intertwined issues that form the core of this book. The story begins with Pennsylvania's founding and follows the colony's political expansion, tracing the colony's early successes in managing frontiers and border conflicts to its later catastrophic failures in both areas. Combined, the events show that the ultimate cause of Pennsylvania's collapse during the 1760s and 1770s was its inability to govern frontiers, a problem that the colony avoided during its first decades. The unstable political borders in the 1770s only exacerbated the underlying problem frontiers posed to governing Pennsylvania and the British Empire more generally. The story ends with the American Revolution, when self-described "frontier people" seized political power and remade government to do the one thing the colonial government could not: provide for frontiers.

CHAPTER 1

The Hidden Flaw

There is a fundamental principle about frontiers in the early modern world. A frontier did not exist without a government to defend it, and a government would cease to exist if it could not protect its frontiers. The developments on the eighteenth-century American frontiers, then, can only be appreciated by understanding the creation of the colonial government to which those frontiers belonged. For Pennsylvania, that founding moment came with the Frame of 1701, a document that scholars have described with many superlatives: "the most famous of all colonial constitutions," "radically democratic," "remarkably innovative," "a landmark of religious liberty," one of the "most influential documents protecting individual rights," and "comparable in the development of political institutions to the development of the wheel in transportation." In its own time, the Frame was credited with the economic prosperity that the eastern areas of Pennsylvania enjoyed for much of the eighteenth century. The colony's remarkable progress, a leading assemblyman noted in 1739, "is principally, and almost wholly, owing to the excellency of our constitution; under which we enjoy a greater share both of civil and religious liberty than any of our neighbors."[1]

There was, however, a fatal oversight in the Frame of 1701. It failed to address the issue of political expansion. Rather than creating a stable political environment, as most have assumed it did, the Frame created a formula for the colony's ultimate demise. This flaw only became apparent as the colony tried to incorporate new territory in the eighteenth century. By the time of the American Revolution, the revolutionaries who drafted a new constitution in 1776 knew of this and other problems, declaring "we are determined not to pay the least regard to the former constitution of this province, but to reject everything therein that may be proposed, merely because it was part of the former constitution." To understand how the authors of the revolutionary

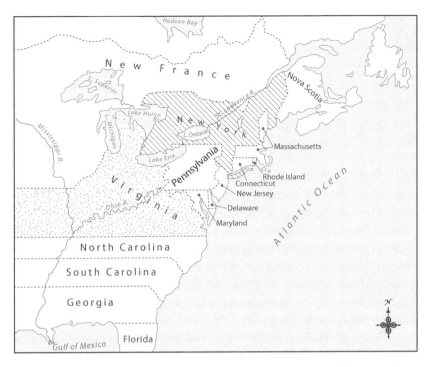

Figure 2. This map is based on a colored version of the 1755 London-printed
*A Map of the British and French Dominions in North America, with the Roads,
Distances, Limits, and Extent of the Settlements,* also known as the Mitchell Map,
named for its designer John Mitchell, a Virginia-born doctor. Pennsylvania's
boundaries in this version are farther north than they are today and include
parts of modern-day western New York, while its western border mirrors
the Delaware River. The borders appear clear on this British map, although
in practice, they were much harder to establish in the colonies. New York's
boundaries, for example, were never quite as expansive as this map depicts.

constitution of Pennsylvania came to this conclusion, we must turn to where
the seeds of this revolt were first planted: the flawed founding.[2]

"A Just, Plain, and Honest People That Neither Make War upon Others nor Fear War from Others"

For three days, the English ship *Welcome* made its course up the Delaware
River, as anxious passengers scanned the shore for signs of life. The vessel

carried William Penn and about a hundred others who had come to launch a new English colony called Pennsylvania. On the night of October 26, 1682, they came upon a clearing with a small fort and scattered houses. They had reached their destination.[3]

The boat's appearance came as a surprise to those on shore. As soon as the ship moored, several magistrates left the fort and paddled a small canoe out to investigate. Penn showed them his charter from King Charles II declaring Penn the proprietor of the land that these magistrates governed. The magistrates, appointed by the Duke of York, the previous proprietor, seemed uncertain. They took Penn's papers and told him to stay put while they went ashore to review his documents. The magistrates conferred that night. Given that Penn had sent advance agents to the colony, the magistrates' behavior was likely a performance of protocol—or at least, they wanted to ensure that the man claiming to be Penn was not an imposter. By morning, they had determined that his charter was valid and readied the ritual that would recognize Penn's power as the head of this new colony.[4]

Penn had prepared for what happened next. When he went ashore, the magistrates handed him the keys to the fort, the strongest symbol of political sovereignty in the area. Penn unlocked its door, entered, and closed the door behind him. He stood alone in the fort—now his fort—for a moment, then opened the door and walked back out. The magistrates greeted him with twigs from the forests beyond, a piece of earth, and a bowl containing river water, representations of Penn's new authority over the woods, land, and streams of this English colony.[5]

Penn's journey to the banks of the Delaware River was an arduous one. Penn, the son of a distinguished naval hero whose exploits had won the family fortune, received an education at the most elite institutions in England and on the Continent. His privilege meant that he had access to the finest things in life. Indeed, a life of indulgent complacency seemed his likely destiny. Penn, however, chose to take a different path while in his twenties. Troubled by the violent world around him, Penn became a critic of the reigning order in England. Always a searcher, he converted to Quakerism after discovering his Inner Light. He rejected the life of compliance and comfort that his father had cleared for him. Instead, he embraced the faith's tenets of individual introspection and communal harmony. Imprisoned and exiled for his beliefs, Penn fought for years to regain his stature. By 1681, Penn had won the favor of Charles II's court, and with it, the colony he would call Pennsylvania—or Penn's woods, named not for him, but for his father, Admiral William Penn, whose past service to the Crown the younger Penn had leveraged to secure a colony.[6]

The ritual Penn performed outside the fort was the culmination of his work. The "turf, twig, and water" ritual was an ancient one, dating to the days of feudalism when warring English lords needed a way to show their lieges that they had surrendered their powers to another. Now, centuries later, the tradition, known more formally as the livery of seisin, found a new purpose in the New World as a symbolic means to establish sovereignty over acquired land. Penn's acceptance of the keys and the gifts signaled the dawn of a new era. Harkening back to a lord's feudal controls over people and territory, it also showed just how much power proprietors could have in the colonies they possessed.[7]

The symbolism fit the circumstances. Charles II granted Penn a colony from the Dutch territory the Crown acquired in 1664. Charles's gift made Penn the largest landowner in the English Empire, save for the king himself. Penn's charter gave him an expanse that stretched from the Delaware River five degrees west and between the fortieth and forty-third parallels in breadth, more than twenty-five million square acres of land. Charles had carved this territory out of the holdings of his brother, the Duke of York, who held a tract of land that ran from the southern tip of modern-day Delaware all the way north, through New York City, to Canada. With the transfer of twigs, water, and earth at the fort, the Duke of York's magistrates recognized the shift of sovereignty from their previous master to their new one.[8]

The ritual also encapsulated the very peculiar nature of a proprietary government. In proprietary colonies, individuals—in this case William Penn—were vested with inordinate power. As the person who controlled the waterways, land, and woods, Penn's powers resembled those of a feudal lord. Likewise, his responsibilities were similar to those that lords had to their tenants. Penn—and, after him, his sons—would dispense land, control the courts, create governments, and form a very personal relationship with colonists based on an allegiance that resembled the loyalties tenants held toward their manorial lords. Every landowner, for instance, was to provide the proprietary with a quitrent, an annual payment given in exchange for the security and prosperity the proprietorship's good governance provided. This reciprocal relationship in which colonists gave their loyalty in exchange for protection had feudal roots, but it also mimicked the bond that knitted subjects to the English Crown in the early modern world. Indeed, it is what held all colonial governments together.

The ritual also contained an implicit statement about Penn's vision for the future of the colony. Although the colony contained only a few fledgling communities hugging the Delaware River in 1682, Penn planned for it to realize its full geographic expanse, if not within his lifetime then certainly in his descendants'. Indeed, he was well on his way before he arrived. By the time he left England, he had sold nearly 300,000 acres of land to more than 300 individuals, most of whom were fellow Quakers and many of whom were of middling means but great aspiration.[9]

Indeed, Penn kept expansion in mind in everything he designed, including his government. When Penn arrived on the banks of the Delaware, he carried two founding documents that he hoped would turn his expansionist dreams into a reality: a Frame of Government and twenty laws called "The Concessions" that would regulate the behavior of the first settlers. In the Frame, he transferred most of his political powers to his settlers by creating two legislative bodies and establishing a weak executive that he intended to grow even weaker over time. The two major governing bodies were representative bodies, the Assembly, similar in theory to a Parliament, and the more elite Provincial Council, similar to an upper House of Lords. Penn vested the Provincial Council with the power to control all facets of colonial growth. In consultation with the governor, the Provincial Council was to "settle and order the situation of all cities, ports, and market towns in every county, modeling therein all public buildings, streets, and market places, and shall appoint all necessary roads, and high-ways in the province." The Assembly, meanwhile, would grow alongside the colony to five hundred members, proportionally represented by the hundreds (an English term to define an administrative region within a county) and counties.[10]

Penn also outlined the process through which land acquisition would happen. In his "Concessions," he declared that the proprietor was the only person who could purchase land from Native Americans. He was aware that Native peoples in other colonies complained of deceptive land practices, and the strife in these colonies often frustrated English imperialists' plans for their colonial domains. Penn believed that direct negotiations between Indian groups and himself (or his representatives in his absence) would create more formalized and peaceful diplomatic protocols for acquiring land. Such procedures also reduced the chance for individuals to hold competing titles. By purchasing all land directly from Indians through formal diplomatic treaties and alliances, the transfer would thus rest on the theory of consent facilitated through diplomacy between the proprietor and Indian nations. Penn's approach to land also revealed something else about his vision for expansion. While he was willing to defer to colonists in governing settled areas, Penn's land policy meant he controlled the acquisition of all new territory.[11]

There was one thing wrong with the ritual. While Penn planned to assert his rights to all of the land outlined in his charter, he intended this growth to occur peacefully. The livery of seisin, however, occurred at a fort, a symbol of war, militarization, violence, and all the emotions such a structure conjured: fear, anger, hatred, and desperation. Penn wanted none of these things in his realm. As he promised his Indian neighbors, "The people who come with me are a just, plain, and honest people that neither make war upon others nor fear war from others because they will be just." With his designs for an ordered expansion through just treatment of Indians and good governance, Penn expected to build bridges, roads, and markets connecting people, not forts that divided. There would be no frontiers in Penn's woods.[12]

Penn knew that good relations with Native Americans were the foundation upon which his promise of peace rested. He used the Concessions to reinforce this pledge by regulating interactions between colonists and Native Americans. Penn acknowledged that disputes over trading practices had led to conflict in other colonies. In Pennsylvania, he wanted to create a means of guaranteeing open and fair trade by regulating it. He limited trading to specific areas designated as public markets, mandated that all traders receive a license through the governor, required all goods to be inspected and stamped by colonial officials to protect against fraud, and placed heavy fines on those dealing in "goods not being good."[13]

He also knew that the daily interactions of cross-cultural contact caused tensions. He thus declared that Indians should receive the same protections of the law that colonists enjoyed. If any settler wronged an Indian, Penn warned that the colonist should expect to "incur the same penalty of the law, as if he had committed it against his fellow planter." Penn seemed particularly worried that settlers might seek retribution if they felt wronged by an Indian. Penn warned that under no circumstances were settlers to take the law into their own hands, stating that colonists "shall not be his own judge upon the Indian, but he shall make his complaint to the governor of the province, or his lieutenant, or deputy, or some inferior magistrate near him." Penn also proposed a novel way to handle the inevitable conflicts that would arise between Indians and colonists: juries composed of equal numbers of Indians and colonists. Penn's goal was to create an environment of just treatment that avoided rash action.[14]

Penn's laws revealed his political acumen. He was a visionary, a theorist, and an optimist, but he was also a realist. Penn saw trade as an opportunity for both unity and friction. In theory, Penn believed fair dealing and brisk trade would help bring colonists and Indians together. In practice, he recognized that intercultural relationships were difficult and that colonists might try to defraud Indians of goods and lands. Penn the realist visionary anticipated this human inclination and saw government as the only means of safeguarding against it.

Penn applied this same foresight to controlling expansion. He envisioned developing any newly purchased land through a Land Office staffed by a Superintendent and various deputies. He would build some manors, but he would sell other land to individuals, most likely through a public auction that distributed lands fairly and evenly. All landowners would pay an annual quitrent to the proprietor for the protection and prosperity that proprietary offices provided them. The quitrent would not be onerous, but it would give Penn some compensation for his troubles and allow him to continue to develop the colony.

All of this planning would promote prosperity, peace, and stability. It was neither utopian nor cynical. Like so much else Penn had done to prepare, the plan sounded good in theory and appeared realistic from the drawing rooms in London.

"Be Soe Good and Kind a Neighbor"

Soon after arriving in his colony, Penn discovered a challenge to his expansionary vision: the imagined borders outlined in his charter conflicted with those of his English neighbors. Many of these overlapping jurisdictions existed only in the abstract because colonial settlement still hugged the eastern seaboard. No one, for instance, seemed to notice that

Virginia's claims to the Ohio River were the same as Pennsylvania's, or that Connecticut might assert ownership to parts of the territory. Such was not the case when it came to Penn's southern neighbor, Lord Baltimore, the proprietor of Maryland. Penn's charter gave Penn rights to what is today Delaware. Lord Baltimore, however, grew enraged by Penn's ownership, claiming that Marylanders already legally possessed it. Indeed, Baltimore argued that much of the land granted to Penn, including even Philadelphia, was already his. He also began to grumble that Penn's western plans interfered with his own. If Baltimore's understanding proved correct, then Penn's dreams for his colony's future would die.[15]

The dispute revealed the difficulties imperial planners faced when building an empire on a vast tract of foreign land. For those who sat an ocean away and drew lines on maps of North America, the specific location of borders looked clear and a minor detail when they saw so much open space on the parchments sitting before them. But for those whose personal wealth was tied to these lands, the ambiguities surrounding a few square miles were hard to accept. Baltimore and Penn thus marshalled legal arguments to justify their dueling claims and then looked to England for clarity.

The main sticking point in the south had to do with whether or not Europeans had settled on the southern portions of the Delaware River before English ownership. If Europeans (notably the Swedes and then the Dutch) had, then the land would have transferred to the Crown after the English defeated the Dutch in 1664 and the territory would thus be Penn's. Baltimore argued that the land was never in European hands and was rightfully his because his charter gave him the right to all undeveloped areas of the Delmarva Peninsula (the name for the spit of land that Delaware, Maryland, and Virginia now share). If Baltimore's argument won out in English courts, then Penn would lose the only waterway that provided his colony with access to the Atlantic. At stake was the future of each colony. The outcome would also shape the English Empire in this burgeoning region.[16]

The second dispute regarded the fortieth degree, or the northern border of Maryland, and proved much trickier to resolve. Here too the disagreement was over a river—this time, the Susquehanna—that both proprietors saw as a gateway to the west. Without the river, Penn worried that his western lands would become nothing more than "a dead lump of earth" because Baltimore would control all trade. Penn's charter stated that his colony's southern border was the "beginning of the fortieth degree."

According to Penn's maps, his colony started below where the Susquehanna River met the Chesapeake, giving him the entirety of the potentially lucrative river. Baltimore's charter, in contrast, contained the passage that his colony went up to "that part of the Bay of Delaware . . . which lieth under the fortieth degree." Today, such phrases may seem very specific designations, and indeed, they were meant to be exactly that. In an era of poor instrumentation and mapmaking, however, such descriptions proved troublesome. And this too was no small matter. Whoever controlled the Susquehanna would control trade with and expansion into the interior.[17]

Once Penn caught wind of Baltimore's concerns, he tried to settle their differences in a series of meetings. He asked Baltimore "to be soe good and kind a neighbour as to afford him but a back door" to his colony. Penn's friendly talk won him no favors. Baltimore appeared displeased and uninterested—if not downright hostile—at every meeting. And he had just cause. Many people at the time and quite a few historians since believed that by the letter of the law, Baltimore had a stronger case in both disputes. Penn, however, disagreed and pressed Baltimore on both fronts.[18]

Matters came to a head when Penn and Baltimore met in New Castle in August 1683. Their relations had become so poisonous that they could not even agree on how to conduct their negotiations. Penn wanted the two to adopt diplomatic protocols that resembled the way two nations negotiated treaties. He proposed that both men retire to separate houses with their respective advisers by their sides and then "treat by way of written memorials," so their words could not have "the mistakes or abuses that may follow from ill designs, or ill memory." Baltimore declined this invitation by blaming poor weather, but it was clear he had little interest in negotiating. After this failed meeting, Baltimore began issuing proclamations in the contested zone, offering more land for cheaper prices than Pennsylvania in an attempt to build a solid bulwark of loyal Marylanders who rejected Penn's authority.[19]

The race was on to see who could establish the strongest claims to the territory. Penn, realizing that Baltimore rejected Penn's own admittedly self-serving sense of neighborliness, began to adopt Baltimore's more cutthroat tactics in order to bolster his legal standing in an English court. In October 1683, just two months after the failed treaty, Penn traveled to the Susquehanna River to secure an Indian deed to this contested area. Penn's "purchase of the mouth of the Susquehanna River" was one of the shortest

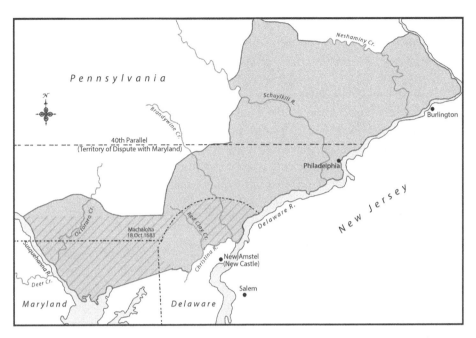

Figure 3. William Penn's first purchases of Indian lands, shown here in aggregate. One of Penn's first objectives was to secure title to the land bordering the Delaware and Susquehanna Rivers, believing that control of both arteries was essential to the future prosperity of his colony. Machaloha's grant, the approximate extent of which is noted above, overlapped with other purchases of Penn's. Penn made his purchase from Machaloha under duress, fearing that if he did not secure a claim to the land near the mouth of the Susquehanna from a Native representative, Lord Baltimore would win this valuable waterway. After Pencak and Richter, eds., *Friends and Enemies in Penn's Woods* (University Park, PA, 2004).

and vaguest of his original purchases. He purchased the land from Macha-loha, a Delaware whose right to sell it scholars have deemed "questionable." Penn ignored any doubts, however, reasoning that he could use the purchase to show that Indians invested with the original right to the land recognized his ownership. As his biographers have pointed out, Penn's purpose was "to solidify his claim and to notify the Lords of Trade," the imperial organization that mediated disputes between colonies. Driven by a feud with his neighbor and guided by his understanding of the precedents imperial officials might privilege in a case before them, Penn took the actions he believed necessary to secure his domain.[20]

Although the Susquehanna purchase instructed all settlers to "behave themselves justly and lovingly" toward the Indians, the dubious nature of the purchase suggests that when English colonies competed over land, Penn, like others, would push aside Native concerns. Indeed, such times laid bare the driving assumption of Penn's enterprise: expansion was essential to colonial success in the Middle Colonies. In this early case, Penn surrendered some of his principles to preserve his larger vision. Indeed, Penn may have considered this treaty simply a short-term expedient that did not compromise his core principles because in 1701, he negotiated a new purchase with the Conestoga Indians, the group with the strongest claim to the land he had purchased from Machaloha.[21]

"The Securitie of the Fronteers"

Penn left for England aboard the *Endeavour* in 1684 to defend his case against Baltimore. He departed feeling confident, his optimism about the future of the colony buoyed by signs of success. Just before he left, he wrote his close friend John Alloway a letter brimming with enthusiasm, bragging that Philadelphia had about six hundred people and hundreds of homes. The city supported a tavern, and colonists constructed a three-hundred-foot-long dock that jutted out into the Delaware River to accommodate the more than forty-five ships arriving annually. Penn's expansionary dreams were also coming to fruition. He boasted to another friend that Pennsylvania would eclipse its rival Maryland within seven years, and he told another with a little pride, if not vanity, "I must say, without vanity, I have led the greatest colony into America that ever any man did upon a private credit."[22]

Matters back in England gave Penn more reason for cheer. Penn and Baltimore presented their case to the Lords of Trade, the body the Crown designated to mediate such disputes. Baltimore hoped to secure the Lower Counties and receive recognition of the fortieth degree as the boundary between the two colonies. Much to his chagrin, the Lords of Trade decided largely in Penn's favor. They recognized Penn's claim to the Lower Counties, thus ensuring he had access to the Delaware River. They refused to draw the exact boundary between the Lower Counties and Maryland, however, leaving the proprietors responsible for hashing it out. Moreover, the question of the fortieth degree remained unaddressed, largely because, with

Pennsylvanian settlement still hugging the banks of the Delaware and Marylanders focusing more on their southern lands, this dispute seemed too far removed.[23]

Things then took a turn for the worse for Penn when in 1688 zones of invasion—that is, frontiers—began to appear on the geopolitical landscape of North America when England became embroiled in a war with France, known as King William's War in North America. This war was the first that the Quaker colony of Pennsylvania, founded on the principle of pacifism, had to confront. Although Pennsylvania itself was well insulated from the fighting, imperial officials expected Pennsylvania's government would aid its fellow colonies that were waging a war. For Penn, rumors circulated that he was a secret agent for the Catholic belligerent. He eventually faced charges of treason in England. The Crown, understandably, revoked his charter. Though treason was the key reason for its revocation, Penn's pacifism was also a concern. The Crown worried that a pacifist colony would fail to provide the military protection for its frontiers that was expected of its colonial governments.[24]

Indeed, the colony's wartime behavior proved that the administration's fears had merit and that frontiers were something Pennsylvanians took pride in avoiding. In 1692, the Crown wrote to Benjamin Fletcher, New York's governor who also temporarily replaced Penn as Pennsylvania's governor, instructing him that New York's neighbors should offer defensive aid. The geopolitics of frontiers drove the request. Albany was the chief frontier in England's grand imperial vision of its North American domain because it was the site at which they expected a French invasion. Without New York's successful "defence of Albany, its frontiers against the French," the Crown warned, the English colonies to the south would "not be able to live, but in Garrison." A shared concern about frontiers was thus supposed to compel colonies to cooperate. Further, the Crown's orders revealed something about life on frontiers: they were militarized zones—"garrisons" —in which people lived in constant fear of invasion.[25]

Fletcher traveled to Pennsylvania to make his case for men and money, noting that "the securitie of the fronteers" in New York depended on Pennsylvania's support. Such a request, New Yorkers believed, was a pittance compared with what they were already doing in Pennsylvania's interest because the strength of New York's frontiers secured Pennsylvania. Pennsylvania deferred, confirming for imperial officials that Pennsylvania, under its current regime, was incapable of fulfilling one of its chief responsibilities to the empire: managing frontiers. As a frustrated Fletcher wrote to the Board of Trade in 1694, "They [Quaker Pennsylvanians] will rather die than resist with carnal weapons," a sentiment that portended the fractious future of frontier politics in Pennsylvania.[26]

"Better Adapted to Answer the Present Circumstances and Conditions"

Penn eventually won his charter back in 1694 as the war wound down. He then prepared to return to Pennsylvania. Continuing strife with his personal affairs, however, kept Penn away until 1699, when he finally visited again. Penn found a much-changed colony when he arrived. In his absence, Philadelphia had undergone explosive growth and had begun to look more like a town than some small colonial outpost. There were many taverns, a courthouse, and all sorts of houses, from mansions of stone and slate to ramshackle huts. Within two years of his return, the population of the city passed two thousand souls, making it one of the largest settlements in British North America. Most of the new arrivals were Quakers attracted by Penn's promise of a refuge that protected liberty of conscience and provided a just government. The economy boomed as well. When Penn left in 1684, trade to the colony was just dribbling in. By 1699, the trickle had become a strong and steady flow.[27]

Two issues preoccupied Penn's time in the colony, both of which dealt with establishing the colony he wished to have. First, he was concerned about Indian affairs. Violence between Indians and colonists on the western fringes of settlement were fraying his once strong ties to Pennsylvania's Native neighbors. Strengthening these relations was a top priority. He did so because he wanted to keep the peace that was so important to his Quaker faith. He also knew that losing Indian allies on the Susquehanna, which seemed possible, could hurt his expansionary visions. The Indian settlement on the banks of the river was a bustling hub of trade and travel. It was here that strife seemed most pressing because Penn knew that this site, with its access to the vast interior and its trade networks, was a key part of his future plans.[28]

The Conestoga, the most influential of the many groups then residing in the Indian town, were the focus of Penn's diplomatic foray. In April, a delegation of Conestogas joined by the Shawnees, another powerful group on the Susquehanna, hiked to Philadelphia to reestablish good relations with Penn. Penn reassured his neighbors that his intentions remained unchanged. He promised that they would receive "the full and free privileges and immunities of all the said laws as any other inhabitants," extending the same protection that Penn's proprietorship gave to all colonists to include the Indians present. Penn also strengthened trade agreements and regulations. Penn's words convinced the Conestogas to agree to a deal that would last for over sixty years, only ending because the Paxton Boys killed it. The Conestoga's representatives ceded control of the eastern banks to Penn so long as they could continue to inhabit their settlement without interference. By doing so, they gave Penn even better title to the land in dispute with Baltimore, and they secured a piece of independence from colonization efforts. Penn then did a remarkable thing. To show his allies that the two were truly of "one head and one heart" who could "live in true friendship and amity as one people," he visited their community for several days, also taking time to scout out its potential as a future site for a Pennsylvania trading city.[29]

With Indian affairs on stronger footing, Penn turned to the second issue that troubled him. The government in Philadelphia had spun out of his control. In the years since he had left, the colony went through three different governments. From the moment Penn landed in 1682, colonists complained that his initial Frame with its large Assembly was too unwieldy for colonial life. In the years since Penn's initial visit, they also had grown anxious about the proprietor's powers, especially his right to collect quitrents, what they saw as a feudal form of taxation that had no place in their colony. Penn saw things differently, admitting to a friend "though I desire to extend religious freedom, yet I want some recompense for my trouble." In 1701, when Penn returned, the colony was governed by an unofficial frame of government that colonists put in place as a temporary solution after Penn's charter was returned. One of Penn's objectives on his return was to regain some control by creating a new frame of government.[30]

Penn had changed in these years as well. Most notably, he had grown more jealous of his proprietary powers as he fended off assaults on his charter and fretted about finances. He worried about what would become of his colony and of his interest in it if he ceded too much authority to the colonists who, to his eyes, seemed more interested in their private affairs than in the vision he held for the colony. Penn often expressed frustration at colonists' intransigence throughout these years—once pleading with colonists to show more deference, writing "for the love of God, me, and the poor country, be not so governmentish; so noisy and open in your dissatisfaction" and another time flippantly threatening to sell the colony to the Crown. He wanted to draft a new and official constitution that better reflected his own vision for the colony and preserved more of his proprietary authority than the previous frames.[31]

English affairs once again intruded on Penn's visit, however, and ruined his plans to draft a new frame more acceptable to him. In 1701, with still no frame agreed upon, reliable reports reached Penn that he might again lose the colony to the Crown. If there was no official governing document in place when Penn lost his charter, then the Crown could design the government any way it pleased, which certainly would have spelled the end of Penn's vision and threatened the freedom of conscience that the predominantly Quaker colonists enjoyed. While rushing to leave for England, Penn decided to let colonists design the document as they wished. He asked a select group of leading colonists to write the document "quickly." Penn did so because he knew that colonists needed a formal frame of government in place to protect them should a royal government replace a proprietary one.[32]

Penn's decision to give his colonists carte blanche produced a constitution unlike any other, though its form represented the logical culmination of the political culture that had developed within the proprietary colony. After an initial period of warm feelings toward the proprietor, colonists by 1701 saw the primary political problem in Pennsylvania as a struggle between the people and their interest and the proprietor and his prerogative. In each frame that followed Penn's first one, colonists pushed for greater power in the Assembly at the expense of proprietary authority. If anything, while Penn was away, fear of proprietary rule—if not of the proprietor himself—had lodged in the minds of most colonists, and they saw a legislature as a check against the potential for a grasping proprietorship.

The government they designed in 1701 enshrined this struggle. The Frame of 1701 went further than any other frame in empowering the Assembly. Previously, the colonial government had an upper house called the Provincial Council that exerted strong legislative powers, but the new frame transformed this body into an advisory board appointed by the governor. Instead of the bicameral structure Penn had always preferred, the colonists wanted a unicameral legislature composed of four representatives from

each county. The framers concentrated their interests in this single legislature because it would allow the people to stay united in their struggles
against a proprietor or, if Penn lost the government, a royal governor.[33]

People at the time and historians since have commended the Frame of
1701 for being innovative and democratic, and point to its longevity as a
sign of its success. It was, as its preamble declared, "better adapted to
answer the present circumstances and conditions" of colonists. But along
with significant changes, there were important continuities that historians
have missed and that left the colony ill-prepared for future circumstances.
For one thing, the proprietor still possessed an immense amount of potential power, even as the new Frame took a great deal of his immediate powers. Most of this residual power rested in the proprietor's control over
expansion. The proprietor had at his disposal a land office, a surveyor-
general, and deputy surveyors. Every landowner would need to work
through these offices to have land legally recognized. The proprietor also
continued to levy annual quitrents from landowners and could use force to
evict squatters.[34]

Aside from such strong control over land ownership, the proprietary
branch managed many of the administrative and coercive powers of the
government. The charter conferred to the proprietor enormous powers
over commerce and its regulation. The institution could collect export and
import duties and handle all licensing and fee collection, and claimed the
right to control travel on all waterways, including the sole right to license
ferries. Such revenue was not insignificant. In 1765, the income from the
collection of fees was so great that the proprietor could, if necessary, pay
for the lieutenant governor's salary without having to rely on any Assembly
support. As captain-general, the proprietor was also responsible for diplomacy with natives and military defenses in the time of war. Finally, the
proprietor appointed the judges for the Supreme Court of Pennsylvania
and, of course, the lieutenant governor, who would serve as the proprietor
in residence in Philadelphia.[35]

The proprietor's administrative power was even stronger on the local
level because of his power to appoint county officials. The county was the
main political unit of Pennsylvania. Each county had a series of offices
meant to enforce law and to provide a level of local self-government. Each
county had only two solely elective county offices: the three county commissioners and six tax assessors. When it came to county commissioners,
the proprietor often appointed the first county commissioners, but after

the county was formally established, these offices became elective. Beyond that, nearly every other office—at least ten—either was appointed directly by proprietary officials or was elective-appointive. Within the county, the proprietor directly appointed the recorder of deeds (an office, one historian notes, that was "of great significance for the daily and continuing life of the county"), the register of wills, the prothonotary, clerks of the courts, and sealer of weights and measures. The sheriff and coroner were elective-appointive because the proprietor had to select from the two highest vote getters. Notably, the Assembly had the power of only one appointment: the unpopular collector of excise. The proprietor's power to appoint these offices resided primarily in powers implied in the Frame of 1701. In previous frames, the elected Provincial Council had controlled many of these appointments, but because the Frame of 1701 did not explicitly state how each office was to be appointed, the proprietor retained the powers the council once held.[36]

The most powerful of the proprietor's local appointments was the justice of the peace. The justices convened the three major courts that handled legal disputes and law enforcement: the Court of Quarter Sessions, the Court of Common Pleas, and the Orphan's Court. Through these courts, the justices oversaw the building of roads, the punishment of crimes, the mediation of civil disputes, and the care of the poor. They also held additional appointive powers through their position on the Court of Quarter Sessions. The court appointed town constables in the same way the proprietor appointed the sheriff and all town overseers of the poor. With so many roles, most of which dealt with the enforcement of law, the justice of the peace often served as the colonial government's chief representative in areas of new settlement. The final important proprietary office on the county level was the county surveyor who was appointed by the surveyor-general, who was himself a direct proprietary appointment.[37]

All totaled, through direct proprietary appointment, elective-appointment, or appointment by proprietary institutions like the Court of Quarter Sessions, nearly every official on the county level was a proprietary office and those that were not were often elected on the local level. For the most part, the direct appointments took the form of political patronage, especially as the colony developed. Edward Shippen described the offices as "lucrative posts," and he personally benefited from his close alliance with the proprietorship. In fact, many justices of the peace held concurrent offices, providing for a very healthy salary. Even the elective-appointive offices had the feel of patronage. The lieutenant governor did occasionally select the lowest vote getter for sheriff if he was thought to be better able to serve the proprietorship's interest, and the lieutenant governor could withhold payment for services if he disagreed with the way the sheriff performed.[38]

It would be a mistake to diminish the centrality of these proprietary officials to creating the bonds upon which a governing contract was based. Rather, these local officeholders played a crucial role in connecting local communities to the sometimes distant colonial government. These proprietary appointees lived in the towns and counties they served and had to interact with their neighbors and peers frequently in both official and unofficial capacities. In areas in which the Assembly's role was weak, local administrators served as what one historian described as the "transmitters" and "translators" of local concerns to proprietary officials back east much as representatives were to do in the Assembly. These local proprietary representatives were thus the conduit through which colonists in newly established communities could negotiate with their government. Indeed, as the colony dealt with expanding its legal and political jurisdiction in the years that followed the Frame's drafting, the retained administrative and policing powers of the proprietor grew in significance and served as the most powerful institutions in new settlers' political lives.[39]

If most of these county, land, and legal offices were part of the proprietary institution and thus under the control of the proprietor, the Assembly served as the other major institution of the colonial government because it operated largely free from proprietary influence because all of its members were elected by and served to protect the interest of their constituents. The legislature had a variety of powers at its disposal to check the proprietor and to shape official policy. It could pass laws and taxes, regulate commerce and colonial behavior and distribute public funds on special projects.

In theory, these two institutions formed the foundation for the colonial government. In theory, at least, they would work together to advance the colony's interests, with the Assembly passing initiatives that the governor could execute through his control of the administrative powers of government. But they were also independent institutions that could be at odds with what direction the colonial project should take. Moreover, their decidedly separate spheres of influence meant that institutional rivalries could develop, as the first decades of the colony showed. In the decades to come, as Pennsylvania grew and the proprietor exercised these retained powers, the rivalry between Assembly and proprietor would become acute once again. In time, in many areas of recent settlement, proprietary power would supersede that of the legislature, much to the Assembly members' dismay.

Indeed, the rush to write a frame in 1701 also caused another oversight that only made the inherent tension between these two institutions worse. In every previous frame in which Penn or his representatives participated, the document outlined a plan for how the representative institutions of the colony would change over time because Penn anticipated growth. The Frame in no way addressed what Penn saw as an inevitable political development: political expansion and population growth. This ambiguity created uncertainty between both institutions and among colonists that, in time, destabilized the government as people fought for the political power to fill this hole. While Penn had reservations about the document, he accepted it with the hopes that it could be changed if he held onto the proprietorship.[40]

Before Penn left, he decided to take one final, controversial step to try to preserve his colony from a Crown takeover. The Crown was facing another war with France. While Penn remained a dogged pacifist in his personal beliefs, he proved less doctrinaire in his governmental policy once he realized that the Crown might revoke his charter if his colony proved recalcitrant in defending imperial frontiers. In 1701, as Penn prepared to return to England to protect his colony, he aligned his stance on frontiers to fit imperial prerogatives.[41]

Penn made his case for raiding defense monies to the Assembly before he left for England. He had received a personal request from the Crown to raise funds to support New York's frontiers, which Penn thought might make for a strong inducement for the legislature to act. In a speech to the Assembly, he described New York "as a frontier government" because its vulnerability left it "exposed to a much greater expence in proportion to the other colonies" due to potential invasion by Indian and French enemies. Penn asked the legislature to offer financial support to this "frontier government," which he argued would serve the interests of the empire without contravening Quaker principles of peace. Aid to a neighboring colony was not the same as active support of war, he contended. The Assembly, meanwhile, remained unyielding: New York would go without Pennsylvania help.[42]

From the colony's founding, then, government support for and policy toward frontiers, competition with neighbors over land, proprietary oversight of Indian diplomacy, and tensions between the Assembly and proprietor defined the colony's politics. After Penn departed in 1701 and succeeded in defending himself in England, the colony settled into a period of relative peace and harmony. No one seemed to notice that the much-vaunted Frame of 1701 contained the seeds for the colony's demise. Indeed, the founding's fatal flaw—the failure of the Frame of 1701 to create an explicit means for the government to handle expansion and to manage zones that could become frontiers—remained submerged until the colony experienced the growth Penn so desired.

CHAPTER 2

Growth Arrives

After departing in 1701, William Penn would never again see his colony, though the management of it consumed his mind, his time, and his health. The confrontational politics in Philadelphia continued on the same course, English politics always threatened Penn's position, and Penn's finances grew worse. He even considered selling the colony to cover his debts before suffering a stroke in 1712 that left him crippled until his death in 1718. His widow, Hannah, assumed oversight of the colony until her death six years later. Aided by a trust composed of advisers in Pennsylvania, she managed to keep the colony afloat. Then Penn's three sons, Richard, Thomas, and John, inherited the proprietorship. They, more than their father, would have to deal with managing the expansion of a colony that lacked the means to do so.[1]

While Penn suffered, his colony thrived in his absence. Tens of thousands of colonists from Germanic principalities and the British Isles arrived in Pennsylvania beginning in the 1710s, at around the time of Penn's stroke, and immigration further increased in the 1720s. In 1728 alone, between three thousand and six thousand people arrived from Ireland, while an annual average of one thousand migrants arrived from Germany between 1727 and 1740.[2]

These numbers may appear small to modern readers, but placing these migration figures in their historical context shows how astounding the population growth was—and how dramatically such arrivals were changing colonial society. By 1740, recent non-English arrivals composed nearly half the population. Penn had expected, even hoped for, such growth. But "such numbers of strangers," as the government referred to them, threatened to upend Pennsylvania's dominant Quaker society and exposed the challenge of governing an expanding colony. In the 1720s, government officials

Figure 4. Pennsylvania's early western settlements, 1715–1730. Many new arrivals to Pennsylvania headed toward the Susquehanna River. These new settlements provided opportunity, but government control was far weaker and violence and disorder were more frequent. In 1727, Indians murdered a colonist outside of Snaketown during a trade deal gone bad. The incident revealed a number of governing challenges to those in Philadelphia who were tasked with managing the colony's peaceful expansion.

responded to this dilemma by creating new administrative layers and laws to strengthen the colonial government in the east and protect the Quaker majority. In the west, however, governing officials faced different issues. Here the colonial government was just trying to establish its authority, and colonists took advantage of its weakness. Laws were ignored, and magistrates often lacked, often in violation of Penn's diplomatic agreements, sufficient support to enforce policies. Colonists squatted near Indian lands. Indians and traders conducted deals; many did not adhere to colonial regulations. Some went smoothly, others less so.[3]

No person took better advantage of this situation than Indian trader John Burt, perhaps the most dangerous man in the colony. Indeed, Burt's business dealings at a short-lived trading town called Snaketown led to a murder in 1727 that forced Philadelphia officials to reassess the government's role in regulating areas of new settlement. Government officials knew that they had to address the troubles that arose because of men like Burt. The need to create policies aimed at better ordering the colony's expansion also provided eastern-based policymakers an opportunity to further protect the Quaker and largely pacifist core of the colony. Through the distribution of land and the arrangement of new settlements, proprietary officials were able to redirect new colonists, many of whom were well versed in the violent warfare of Europe and had few qualms with the use of firearms, away from the predominantly Quaker regions and place them in areas that could become defensive frontiers in the event of war. This approach, on the one hand, helped address the problem of governing frontiers in a Quaker-led colony. But the distribution of new settlers also placed these colonists further from the strongest arms of the colonial government.

"A Frontier in Case of Disturbance"

On a late November day in 1724, Henry Hawkins sat in the Chester County jail, alone in the world, penniless, bruised, and battered. He waited for John Mitchell, one of the justices of the peace for the county, to arrive so he could plead his case. When he did arrive, Hawkins told him a story of his travels and travails through "the woods" of Pennsylvania that left many who heard it appalled. For us, Hawkins's story provides a glimpse into the uncertainty that marked the lives of those who would in time become, in their own words, "frontier inhabitants."[4]

Hawkins arrived in Pennsylvania hoping for a new start in the new world. His prospects looked bright at first. Hawkins agreed to a five-year indenture to John Burt, an Indian trader who also claimed to be a gunsmith. Burt promised to train Hawkins in the gun trade, a skill in high demand, in exchange for five years of Hawkins's life. From Hawkins's perspective, in five short years he would be free to strike out on his own. Armed with his new skill and maybe some capital and social currency, Hawkins would have secured the foundation for a profitable and independent business, an opportunity unlike any that the old world offered. Hawkins probably felt like it was more of an apprenticeship than servitude, an investment for his future rather than the forfeiture of his personal freedom. Or so he thought.[5]

Burt, it turned out, cared more about trading than making or repairing guns. Rather than learning the art of the firearm, Hawkins said he was "forced to go along with the said Burt Indian trading." Worse still, when they returned from their journey into the woods, Burt still refused to train him. Instead, he sent Hawkins on another trading adventure, this time to Philadelphia to acquire "more goods to go trading again." Burt placed his servant under the care of Jonas Davenport, a well-connected trader who had secured a tract of land in a Scots-Irish settlement called Donegal near Burt's home. Davenport disliked Hawkins, who likely complained mightily that this was not the work he had signed up for. "Sorely beat and abused by said Jonas Davenport," Hawkins refused to return to his master and instead stayed in Philadelphia.[6]

Hawkins's recalcitrance, however justifiable, nonetheless made things worse. Burt decided that Hawkins was too much trouble to bear and sold him to a local plantation. Hawkins now found himself a farmhand, laboring away in fields and learning little that would help him in the future. That job did not work out either, and he soon found himself again in the hands of Davenport, who then sold him to "an Indian." The Indian, named Chickoekenoke, took Hawkins "back into the woods several hundred miles."[7]

Hawkins's stay there was short too. Chickoekenoke grew frustrated with his servant, just as all his other masters had, and brought Hawkins back to Davenport seeking a refund. At Davenport's place in Donegal, Hawkins saw an opportunity to escape and ran to seek a justice of the peace, hoping the law could provide some protection. An angry Davenport intercepted him, bound his hands, tied him to the tail of a horse, and "ha[u]ld [Hawkins] on the ground a considerable way through a thick muddy swamp." The brutality of the public beating—which shocked a group of women onlookers—drew the attention of the law. Davenport, facing charges of abusing his servant, turned Hawkins over to the authorities, "sorely beat and bruised on the body and one eye almost beat out and like to have broken both arms." Sitting in the jail, "destitute of friends," Hawkins told John Mitchell his tale of woe and hoped the court could intercede in his case, to give him the freedom he so desperately wished he had never given up.[8]

Hawkins proved a poor commodity because he possessed a strong spirit, and because of that, we have his story today. However unusual Hawkins's tale may be, his travels are emblematic. Hawkins witnessed the Indian trade, once the economic foundation for those who lived in the western areas of Pennsylvania; worked on a farm, a new and bountiful industry that had recently begun to lay a new economic foundation for these western areas; traveled through the woods and saw Indian society, a culture whose history predated William Penn's arrival; stayed in a small trading enclave with Burt; and spent time in Donegal, a burgeoning and bustling Scots-Irish community formed in 1720 of recent immigrants like himself. It was a rough-and-tumble world where the only certainty was imminent danger. It was also a fluid society in which Indians and colonists interacted easily and regularly; Hawkins, for instance, was sold as an indentured servant to an Indian, a transaction that would be considered unusual in a few decades. And, as Hawkins's story ends with him racing to find the protection of a justice of peace, it was a world in which the law was a presence but hard to reach, a figment of what it should be. Government officials, from high proprietary officials stationed in Philadelphia like James Logan who expressed dismay and surprise at Davenport's actions, to the local justice of the peace John Mitchell, who indicted Davenport for his abuse of Hawkins, knew that this world on the fringes of Pennsylvania existed. They hoped to put an end to it, for the disorder, violence, and uncertainty it bred threatened their hopes for peace.[9]

Hawkins, meanwhile, was encountering a western Pennsylvania that was fast changing. Once composed of a small, interwoven society of traders and roughnecks, the west was bustling with new arrivals who carried different dreams. The Scots-Irish, of which Henry Hawkins was likely one, were the first to arrive in substantial numbers. This group's cultural lineage came from Scotland, but they passed through Ulster in Northern Ireland, where they provided a toehold for Protestantism, before coming to Pennsylvania, a path that has earned them their name Scots-Irish. Predominantly Presbyterians, they came not to escape religious persecution but economic stagnation. Irish landlords had raised rents on their Scots-Irish tenants in the early eighteenth century, making the Pennsylvania countryside an attractive alternative. Little did these immigrants know that this region would prove to be more than just adequate. The lands in the Susquehanna Valley turned out to be among the most fertile in all of colonial America. The Scots-Irish came to Pennsylvania in large numbers first in 1717. James Logan placed their settlements, such as Donegal and Paxton, near the banks of the Susquehanna, far beyond the Quaker-dominated cultural and political center. By 1729, there were at least six Scots-Irish settlements along the river.[10]

The "Pennsylvania Dutch," a nickname likely rooted in the pronunciation of *Deutsch*, meaning *German*, arrived in fits and starts, and their composition changed over time. Religious refugees seeking asylum were the first group to come to Pennsylvania. These early German colonists often migrated in large, organized groups and sought isolation. Government officials placed them beyond Philadelphia, either west, near the Susquehanna River, or to the northeast, along the Delaware River. According to demographers of colonial Pennsylvania, 1727 marked the first of three massive immigrations from the Rhineland to Pennsylvania. That year alone saw over a thousand Germans arrive at the port of Philadelphia, surpassing the entirety of German immigration in the first thirty-five years of colonial settlement. Most new arrivals traveled in family groups and came to Pennsylvania because of connections to those already settled in the colony. Unlike the previous immigrants, however, these Germans were not small sects that sought seclusion but more mainstream Protestant groups, like Lutherans, who expected to participate in society.[11]

The immigration of Scots-Irish and Germans did more than increase population numbers and expand the geographic reach of the colony. These new arrivals changed the face and faith of the colony, turning a once Quaker-dominated society into perhaps the most diverse in North America. While William Penn had once dreamed of such change, the Quaker elite who ran the colony in the 1720s was unsure about it. As one historian aptly summarized, the original Quaker colonists and their heirs "assumed that Pennsylvania would remain predominantly a *Quaker* colony in which 'weighty Quakers' would always shape public policy." Quakers had, so far at least, created an ordered and peaceful colony, one that had begun to prosper without encountering many of the problems with Native Americans that other colonies had experienced when they began to flourish. The Scots-Irish and German populations, pushing the bounds of the colony and changing its cultural makeup, posed no small threat to this carefully established harmony.[12]

Government officials adopted a number of policies to ease their fears of and solidify their authority over this new population. In 1727, the first year of sustained immigration from the German Palatinate, Pennsylvania instituted a new policy that required all captains carrying German immigrants to register those over sixteen years of age. Also in 1727, Governor Patrick Gordon decided to enforce a long dormant naturalization law that required all arrivals to make a statement at a local courthouse affirming their allegiance to the proprietor, their loyalty to the British Crown, and their support for the legitimacy of George II's ascension. A public declaration of allegiance was an important political act that carried great legal weight in the eighteenth century. The significance of such a declaration was all the more powerful for German settlers, many of whom had lived under seigniorial law in which their liberty was owned by their lords. In effect, the Pennsylvania statement was a renunciation of their previous feudal allegiances and an affirmation of their new ones to a British king and proprietor.[13]

The Scots-Irish, meanwhile, carried a reputation for bad behavior that worried officials as much, if not more, than the Germans' loyalty. Many of the original settlers in Pennsylvania depicted the Scots-Irish as poor, violent, and backward, a marked contrast to the educated, sensible, and prospering culture the Quakers had sought to cultivate in the colony. To deal with this threat, officials created settlements and manors in western areas to house the Scots-Irish, far away from the Quaker core around Philadelphia.[14]

The author of this plan was James Logan, who was William Penn's protégé and closest adviser. Logan came from meager means in Ulster, but, when Penn noticed the young Quaker's brilliance, he enticed him to come to Pennsylvania in 1699. Logan served in a variety of high offices and had his own interests tied up in land speculation and the Indian trade. From the vantage point of his multiple positions, Logan understood the colony's internal politics and its geopolitics better than anyone. He thus knew how to ensure that Scots-Irish migration and settlement patterns maintained Quaker power in the east, while also helping fill proprietary coffers. By 1726, extant tax lists from Chester County, then the county that stretched to the Susquehanna, suggest that 2,300 settlers took up residence in the far western areas of that county. In addition to the official settlements near the Susquehanna River, Logan estimated that in 1726 new settlers cleared and occupied over a hundred thousand acres of previously undeveloped land without license. The changes in the cultural landscape of the colony thus had real physical effects on its countryside.[15]

There was more to Logan's thinking than maintaining stability among and preserving the power of the "weighty Quakers," however. Logan had an intimate understanding of the Scots-Irish, for he, an Ulsterman, was one of them. Instead of sharing the Quakers' dour assessment of the Scots-Irish, he viewed these immigrants and their new western settlements as a benefit. The Scots-Irish at Donegal, a new settlement on the banks of the Susquehanna, were a "good, sober people," Logan wrote to William Steel, a friend and fellow official. Best of all, they were of the stock that "had so bravely defended Londonderry and Inniskillen," a reference to a 105-day-long siege of Ulster in 1689 in which Catholics loyal to James II tried to oust Protestants supportive of William and Mary's ascension. "Those people," he continued, "if kindly used, will I believe, be orderly, as they have hitherto been, and easily dealt with."[16]

Logan realized that these Scots-Irish settlers could help solve one problem frontiers posed to a colony that rejected militarization: they could serve as the first defenders against invasion, just as they had in Ireland. Logan made this rationale explicit in 1729 when he wrote that he decided "to plant" the Scots-Irish settlements near the Susquehanna so they could serve "as a frontier, in case of disturbance" with "Northern Indians," a reference to unallied Indian groups in neighboring French Canada and the Ohio Valley. In that way, colonial officials created an ad hoc means to facilitate expansion that also served the geopolitical interests of the colony. Logan's actions represented an unspoken part of the political settlement forged in 1701. Proprietary officials had the dual tasks of developing western land and providing colonists with legal and defensive protection in these new areas of settlement. The Quaker-dominated Assembly, focused as it was on the concerns of the eastern counties, was happy to outsource such responsibilities in 1701.[17]

But as these new settlers populated areas near Indian settlements, their interactions with their Native neighbors began to affect Indian relations with the colony, often pushing them in directions colonial officials did not want. We cannot know exactly what these settlers thought of Native Americans when they left Europe, but it is more than likely they carried across the Atlantic fear and trepidation about their soon-to-be neighbors, baggage that weighed heavily on their actions with Indians once they arrived. Reports of vicious Indian wars in other colonies and ideas of Native savagery circulated widely in Europe, affecting settlers' perceptions and playing heavily on their imaginations before they set out. The idea of Indians as peaceful allies, although cultivated by Penn and others, was counterintuitive to settlers who heard little of such things. The insecurity and violence that people like Henry Hawkins experienced only added to their worries. Indeed, while Logan hoped they might become "a frontier *in case* of a disturbance" with Indians, John Burt, Henry Hawkins's former master, proved that colonists could be the *cause* of a disturbance.[18]

"The Said Burt Is the Principal Occasion of It"

We know almost nothing about Thomas Wright except that he died on the night of September 11, 1727. His death, however, was the first in a chain of events that pushed Pennsylvania toward the brink of war and revealed the precariousness of the peace that existed in Penn's woods.[19]

Things started out well for Wright on the evening of his demise. His friend and fellow trader John Burt had invited him to a trading party with some Indians who had goods to sell. The group gathered around a campfire near Burt's home in a place called Snaketown, a short-lived trading community that never appeared on a map. Although we may not know Snaketown's exact location, we do know that it sat on the eastern banks of the Susquehanna River about forty miles north of Conestoga. Desolate and small, Snaketown was nonetheless an important part of Pennsylvania because it connected Indian Country to the European markets in the east. Wright knew of the huge demand for such goods, and he figured that if he and Burt acquired the Indians' wares, then they could resell them for an easy profit.[20]

The Indians and the colonists seemed quick friends that night. Burt brought some rum to help lubricate the transfer of goods. After a few drinks, the Indians began to dance around the fire. Wright, feeling playful, stood and joined them, singing and dancing "after their manner." As often happens, the boozy play turned violent when "some dispute arose" between an Indian and Wright. Perhaps the Indian viewed Wright's dance as a mocking gesture; perhaps it was. In any case, tempers flared. As the confrontation heated up, Burt egged Wright on, telling him to "knock down the Indian." Wright grabbed one of the Indians and appeared ready to strike, but he thought better of it. Burt was not satisfied. Instead, he unleashed a volley of unexpected blows on the Indian. Burt and Wright then surveyed the wreckage, saw that they were dangerously outnumbered, and retreated to Burt's home.[21]

The Indians, angry at the insult, pursued and crashed through the door. Wright tried to calm down the drunken melee. While he tried to mediate, Burt only grew more enraged. Burt threatened to kill the Indians and sought his gun. Instead of grabbing his weapon, he grabbed the chamber pot and threw, in the words of the colonial records, "dung" on the Indians. Things seemed ready to explode. Wright grew terrified and fled the scene. The Indians followed. The next morning Burt found Wright's body in his henhouse, his head bashed in.[22]

It fell to John Wright, the local justice of the peace and of no apparent relation to Thomas Wright, to sort through this mess. Wright was an active Quaker who took his public service seriously, sometimes to his personal detriment. Though born into the middle class in England in 1667, his personal finances took a turn for the worse when he was in his forties because he spent more time paying attention to the Friends' concerns than his own. Seeking a new opportunity, he left for Pennsylvania in 1714, embarking for the colonies at the unusually late age of forty-seven and settling in Chester County. He gained instant respect and served in the Assembly, but when he was sixty years old, his economic fortunes took a turn for the worse for the second time. Once again, he headed west in search of more opportunity, purchasing a large tract of land on the banks of the Susquehanna a few miles south of Snaketown. As more people settled in the area, the governor appointed the well-connected and respected Wright as an early justice of the peace. His new position required him to establish government authority and maintain good order as the colony expanded to areas that lacked both.[23]

When Wright learned of the murder at John Burt's, he organized a grand jury to investigate. The jury had no question of guilt. Depositions stated that when Thomas Wright fled, "the Indians pursued him." "It's very certain the Indians killed Thomas Wright," the grand jury declared.

But the jurors did not think the colonists wholly blameless, adding "that the said Burt is the principal occasion of it." Jonas Davenport, likely the same man who had beat Henry Hawkins, served on the grand jury, showing just how small and intimate governing these new communities could be. Davenport held little regard for Burt, later saying that had Burt not "provoked and abused" the Indians, then the initial dispute would have been resolved "amicably."[24]

With the grand jury's inquest complete, John Wright had to take the next unpleasant step in this already sordid affair. Since the fallout from an Indian murdering a settler could lead to more violence, Wright had to notify his superiors in Philadelphia so they could take the appropriate steps to deescalate tensions. Wright sent Jonas Davenport to Philadelphia to bring official news of the murder to the government. On the night of September 26, Davenport reached the Philadelphia home of James Logan, then the secretary of the Provincial Council, and told him of the proceedings in Snaketown. Known as a man with a ferocious intelligence and as a man ferociously loyal to the proprietor's interests, Logan quickly realized how dangerous the events in the west could be to the colony's stability.[25]

The next day Logan gathered the members of the Provincial Council together in a private room at the Philadelphia County Courthouse to address the issues the murder raised. The council was a central, if often overlooked, body in the governance of the colony. Although it wielded little direct power, the council helped governors make all decisions, small and large. Most of the members of the Provincial Council served for many years and provided governors, whose tenures could be short, with the type of wisdom that came with continuity. There is even evidence that the governor needed a quorum of his council present before making a decision.[26]

At the head of the council sat the governor, Patrick Gordon, who had arrived in the colony only a year earlier with his wife and five children. Sixty-two years old, Gordon had a distinguished military career, a cool temperament, and a retiring personality. But having served in Europe and spent most of his adult life in England, the problems of colonial governance struck him as wholly unfamiliar. As he confessed in his inaugural address to the Assembly, he was unschooled in the art of "refined politicks," which, he added, "often serve to perplex mankind." A man as experienced as Gordon knew that he had to rely on the advice of his council to chart a safe course in this still strange land. One of his first acts was to reinstate the powerful James Logan, who had been removed from the position because of disagreements with the previous governor.[27]

Dealing with the fallout of the Wright murder forced Gordon to become familiar with the many roles the colonial governor had to play. Officially, the proprietor was the governor of the colony, while his appointed deputy who served in the colony was the lieutenant governor, but most people called the lieutenant governor "Governor" because he exercised all the day-to-day powers that such officials held. All matters of law enforcement rested with the proprietor, who conveyed them to his governor in residence. The governor in residence was also the chief diplomat for the colony. In that capacity, he had to maintain good relations with Indian allies and manage the geopolitical interests of the British Empire in the region. Finally, the governor was the captain-general, meaning commander in chief, during times of war. In this case, Gordon hoped that the successful deployment of his two other responsibilities would prevent his use of the latter.

Gordon and his council recognized that Wright's murder was an important test of the colony's authority in the newly settled regions. Indeed, the meeting began with a discussion of the murder's significance to the colony's history. "This was," they observed, "the first accident of the kind they had ever heard of in this province since its first settlement." They knew that they would have to respond with care. As they noted, the Indians had "received very high provocations," but in their estimation that still did not justify murder. Moreover, since "a subject had lost his life," the government was duty bound "to take notice of and move in it."[28]

The council then debated how the government should react. The councilors recognized that if they let a murder against a colonist go unpunished, then colonists might question the proprietor's authority, since his promise of protection served as the basis for colonists' loyalty to the colony. At the same time, because the violence was between Indians and colonists, it was necessary that the government's response did not upset the alliances the colony had with Native groups in the region. After weighing their options, the group concluded that since Wright's murder happened in an area in which the colony exercised legal authority and because Wright was a "subject," then the governor needed to publicly condemn the murder and demand the guilty be brought to justice to reassure the colonists he promised to protect. Privately, however, they believed that it would be impossible to identify the guilty Indians and foolish to try. Instead, they told the governor to deal with the murder through diplomatic channels.[29]

The colony had pursued this course of action before. Although Wright's murder was the first in which Indians had slain an Englishman (or at least the first the council knew of), the colony had a history of mediating cross-cultural violence. They had learned that English-style retribution—arrests, trials, and hangings—was an ineffective way to punish violence that occurred between colonists and Indians. Most recently, in 1722, a powerful trader, Edmund Cartlidge, had brutally murdered an Indian in a deal gone bad. The Cartlidge case happened west of the Susquehanna, an area that Pennsylvania had not officially settled and therefore exercised no legal control over. Traders and others often called such areas of legal and political ambiguity "the woods." Dealing with problems of violence in the woods meant that the colonial government could pursue nontraditional justice. In this earlier case, the colony provided reparations for the crime through Indian means: a formal treaty at which the colony offered gifts of condolence and sincere apologies. Faced with the Wright murder in 1727, the council again decided that official diplomacy was the best way "to make the Indians in general sensible of the outrageousness of the action and to oblige them to make such satisfaction as the nature of the case will admit of," even as they publicly called for more traditional punishment to assuage colonists' desires for justice.[30]

But admonishing Indians was not the primary focus of discussion at the Provincial Council's emergency meeting. After settling on the proper course of action, the council shifted topics and used the murder as an opportunity to examine the state of Indian relations in the colony. They offered a dour assessment. From the time of Penn's founding until about 1722, the colony had what the council called "a good understanding and an uninterrupted friendship" with Indian groups in the colony. The problem, all agreed, was that the previous governor was too inattentive to Indian affairs, leaving Indians feeling "slighted."[31]

The council went even further. Citing Burt, the Indian trader, as the root cause of this trouble, the council began to examine their regulations concerning trade and internal policing. Since the colony's founding, government officials had viewed trade as a beneficent means of tying Indians and colonists together and ushering in an era of prosperity, but they realized the promise of trade also carried with it potential pitfalls. William Penn had realized the perils and opportunities of trade when he called for government-regulated trading towns, heavy fines for duplicitous traders, and juries composed of equal numbers of Indians and colonists to mediate disputes.[32]

While the government never put this last policy into practice, it had followed Penn's other proposals by regularly passing regulations meant to ensure trading happened on equal and just terms. By 1727, laws limited all trade for profit to specific market towns and Indian villages, under the assumption that those locations would allow the government to enforce its policies. Indians complained that colonists had often used alcohol to swindle them, so the Assembly banned its use during exchanges. The government also required all traders to receive a license from the governor. In order to qualify for a license, they needed to have a letter of recommendation from their local justice of the peace. Fines for breaking fair trading practices had grown only heavier over time. The point of these regulations was not to limit trade but to ensure that the market was as free from coercion and deception as possible. It was part and parcel of Penn's founding belief that the government needed to play an active role in maintaining peaceful relations with Indians in order to prevent frontiers from forming.[33]

Before the Wright murder, government officials and most civically minded Pennsylvanians took pride in their successful track record. When the Assembly renewed a law entitled "For the Continuing Friendly Correspondence with the Indians" in 1715, it sent a letter to the Board of Trade stating its rationale for doing so. "The whole intent of this act," they wrote, "is to prevent the Indians being imposed upon or abused in trade or otherwise by ill-minded persons, which experience hath shown is impossible to prevent if all manner of persons, without some restrictions and regulations, should be suffered to live among the Indians." Like William Penn, assemblymen saw such laws as setting Pennsylvania apart from other colonies. They observed that their "English neighbouring Collonies, have felt, in the late warrs, with those savages . . . the loss of great numbers of Christians killed, and their houses, plantations, goods, and cattle burnt, destroyed, or carried away, by those heathen." Pennsylvania had not, they pointed out, "lost the life of any one Englishman, by their means, from the settlement of the Collony, to this day, that we know, or have heard of." They told the board that they had accomplished this "peace and tranquility" by "treating and dealing with the Indians honestly," and implied that the empire should advise other colonies to follow their model.[34]

The council expressed similar sentiments in 1727 as it reflected upon the Wright murder, noting "that this government had been formerly happy above most of our neighbours, in preserving a good understanding and an uninterrupted friendship with all our Indians." Gordon shared a common vision for the colony, noting in his inaugural address that his goals were: "to discountenance parties, divisions, and factions in government, to maintain right and justice, to promote vertue, to suppress vice, immorality and prophaness, to assist and protect the magistrates in discharge of their duty herein, to encourage legal trade, and to use the Indians well." The Wright murder threatened the Pennsylvania model of harmony through justice.[35]

During its investigation, the council found that the government's recent performance had failed to live up to the promise of its laws. The situation leading to Wright's murder illustrated all the ways they had failed. The council observed that "it was scarce possible to find a man in the whole government more unfit" for trading than Burt, and yet Burt had received a license to trade on recommendation from the Chester County Court. Burt's license, the council went on, "clearly shews the necessity of having that trade, and qualifications of the persons admitted to it more narrowly inspected, than is at present provided." They also pointed out that laws had long barred the use of alcohol during trading, and yet it flowed freely that night in the woods. The very promise of security that the colonial state was supposed to offer to its members seemed at stake. "Unless some more effectual provision is made," they concluded, then "the publick tranquility," the hallmark of early Pennsylvania life, "will ever be in danger."[36]

Gordon agreed with his council that the government needed to change its ways and become more proactive in regulating trade and managing its alliances with Indian groups. Gordon ordered the chief justice of the colony to issue warrants for Burt's arrest. He also agreed that he needed to craft a treaty with Indians to repair any damage inflicted by these events and renew bonds of friendship. The only problem was that the calendar and custom of the Indians made such a treaty unlikely in the short term. Most of the Indian diplomats "were abroad on hunting" until the spring. The council thus resolved to begin planning for a major treaty after the spring thaw. In the meantime, they hoped that the precarious peace would hold.[37]

CHAPTER 3

The First Frontier Crisis

The spring thaw did not come quickly enough. Soon after Thomas Wright's murder, rumors of Indian war began circulating. Animosity between Indians and colonists turned deadly in the spring of 1728 when a confluence of events made war appear imminent. As officials tried to avoid the colony's first conflict, they had to either confront the issue of expansion that the founders of the government had ignored—or face the potentially deadly consequences.

The most dangerous threat to stability during the crisis was the belief held by some colonists that Pennsylvania had "frontiers," a new development on the geopolitical landscape of the colony. These "frontier inhabitants," as they called themselves, petitioned their government for the support they believed they deserved. At the height of this uncertainty, groups of colonists who feared an imminent invasion formed unofficial militias to provide protection and launch raids on Indian groups. The ad hoc mobilizations eventually resulted in several clashes between Indians and colonists and caused the death of several Indians. The government, primarily through proprietary offices, adapted and averted war by using the levers of the state that the Frame of 1701 left to the proprietor to reestablish order on these "frontiers."

After the crisis passed, proprietary officials realized that they needed a stronger presence in regions of new colonial settlement. They thus devised a means to solve the problems they encountered in 1728: new counties. Through this legal entity, they could maintain order while also providing a renewed sense of security to colonists living far from the colonial capital. Justices of the peace, sheriffs, and courts could be used to implement state policy and prevent such crises from happening again. The frontier crisis of

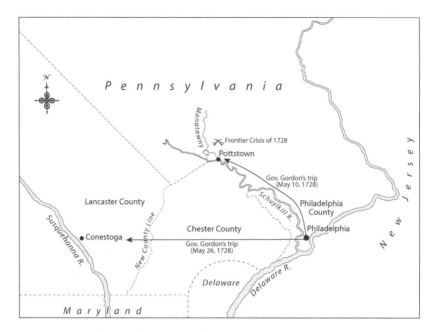

Figure 5. Sites of Pennsylvania's first frontier crisis, 1728. In May 1728, a group of colonists calling themselves "frontier inhabitants" because they feared an Indian invasion clashed with a group of Native American warriors near modern-day Pottstown. The violence created a crisis that obliged the governor to travel there to assert his authority over the organizers. He then traveled to Conestoga to reassure Native Americans and colonists in the region that the colony remained committed to peace. The government also took a step to address the problems western areas posed to stability: they created a new county, Lancaster, which could help the government maintain order in new settlements near the Susquehanna.

1728 thus exposed the problems of the Frame of 1701, and proprietary officials solved the problem through an ad hoc means of colony building that would guide expansion until the American Revolution.

"The Frontier Inhabitants of Pennsylvania"

The frontier crisis began on April 18, 1728, when James LeTort, a Frenchman who renounced his national allegiance to become one of Pennsylvania's most prominent traders, arrived in Philadelphia carrying dire news.

According to LeTort's sources, Pennsylvania was about to suffer an invasion on a scale unknown in British North America. His story was convoluted. It involved the French-allied Miamis residing near Lake Erie combining with the Delawares and Five Nations living in Pennsylvania and New York to launch a joint invasion of Pennsylvania and New York. If he was right, Pennsylvania was about to develop frontiers for the first time in its history.[1]

LeTort's information was so explosive that he soon found himself testifying before the Provincial Council. The council responded coolly to LeTort's concern. They too had sources of information, and none indicated trouble. But LeTort's report did remind the council that a treaty between the government and allied Indians was long overdue. "In the mean time," the council advised the governor, "the present circumstances of our affairs with the Indians rendered it necessary, that these people should be taken notice of and visited by the Governor." The governor agreed and promised that he would "undertake the journey, whenever he can be informed . . . that the Indians were returned from hunting, for he understood there was scarce any Indians at present at or about Conestogoe." Lest anyone accuse him of delaying, he made clear to the council that "nothing should be wanting on his part to establish and confirm the good understanding that had hitherto subsisted between this government and these people."[2]

Meanwhile, on May 3, a couple of weeks after LeTort's visit, John Wright, the same justice of the peace who handled the Thomas Wright murder the previous fall, sent the governor more troubling news. War between the Conestogas and Shawnees, two Native American groups allied with the colony, was imminent. A few days before, two Shawnees had murdered a Conestoga man and woman. The enraged Conestogas demanded the Shawnees turn over the accused. The Shawnees acceded, but the prisoners managed to escape. The Conestogas responded by organizing a party of young men "painted for warr, all armed." Wright ended his report with a plea: "The Governor's pressence pritty speedily is absolutely necessary at Constogo to settle affares amongst the Indians."[3]

Soon colonists living near these warring Indians banded together, fearing that the Indians were preparing an assault on their homes. These colonists also reconsidered their position within the polity and saw something new appear on their landscape: a "frontier." In a desperate plea sent to the governor on April 29, a petition bearing the signature of over eighty men whose English and German last names reflected the growing diversity of the colony declared that they were "the frontier inhabitants of Pennsylvania." "Alarmed by a nois of the Indians," they wrote, "women in childbed" were fleeing their homes, and "several families have left their plantations with what effects they could possibly carry." The few remaining men who chose to stay asked Gordon to act so that they "may be freed from these alarms, for yet we are informed that the Indians are consulting measures against us." As the "frontier inhabitants" stated, they felt crushing "fears" and imminent "danger." They believed their homes now formed a frontier because Indians were planning an invasion, and, as "frontier inhabitants," they expected their government to put them at ease—to "be freed from these alarms." As their words indicated, this crisis struck at the fundamental obligation a government owed to its loyal subjects.[4]

The appearance of a frontier in Pennsylvania threatened to bring the colony's experiment with peace to an end. In official records up to 1728, Pennsylvanian officials most often spoke of "frontiers" to describe other British colonies, such as New York, that faced potential invasions from France or Native Americans. The only document comparable to the 1728 petition was an earlier 1701 petition from the Lower Counties (today Delaware) to the proprietor when settlers there feared a seaborne invasion by the French during Queen Anne's War. The 1701 petitioners drew upon the language of *frontier* prevalent in the Atlantic world by describing their position as the "weak and naked . . . frontiers . . . and dayly threatened with an approaching war." Their fears proved unfounded, and no other petitions from frontier inhabitants were tendered until twenty-seven years later. In 1728, the petition submitted to the governor showed that the conception of a frontier as a zone of invasion remained, as did the language of vulnerability and desperation. But in marked contrast to the 1701 petitioners, the 1728 petitioners feared an Indian invasion from the west at a time when neither the colony nor the empire was at war.[5]

As the 1728 petition made clear and as the future would later bear out, frontiers caused colonists who lived in such regions to feel a series of emotions: fear, a desire for the government's protection, and an expectation that leading individuals—often a general, governor, or prominent community member—would serve as their guardian. But acting like a "frontier government," as Penn had dubbed New York in 1701, posed a problem for Gordon and other officials in 1728. The petition Gordon received that spring meant that the government had to do something, but it was unclear what. Governments had a duty to defend frontier areas because security was a government's responsibility to its members. In Pennsylvania, this obligation fell to the proprietorship. To ignore the plea of these colonists might weaken proprietary authority in the minds of the "frontier inhabitants" who looked to him for the support he promised. Worse, the government's failure to act might force these colonists to take matters into their own hands. Gordon's task was to calm the fears without escalating tensions and possibly leading the colony into a war of its own making.

Taken together, Gordon and his council realized that the letter from Wright and the petition from the frontier inhabitants meant something serious was afoot in the western areas of the province. They reacted to the growing uncertainty by speeding up the schedule for a long overdue treaty with the Indian groups on the Susquehanna. The council remained confident that the governor could use the meeting to reconcile the Conestogas and Shawnees.

Events, however, interceded and forced Gordon to act sooner than planned. On the morning of May 10, just a few days after receiving Wright's missive and the petition, Gordon received an emergency express from Mahanatawny, a small town in western Philadelphia County that housed one of the colony's early iron works. The contents of the message changed everything. "A party of foreign Indians were fallen in amongst our Inhabitants in these parts," it said. A group of about twenty colonists had responded by forming a militia to defend the settlement. A skirmish ensued. One Pennsylvanian was dead; the colonists may have killed the Indian captain, "a Spanish Indian" they called him; the colonists expected more violence soon; they needed the governor.[6]

Gordon raced to the site to investigate and prevent further hostilities. When he arrived later that afternoon, he knew that he had entered a frontier zone. "The country," he reported, "[was] in very great disorder." A new group of petitioners greeted him, this one from Colebrookdale. "We have suffered and is like to suffer by the ingians," the seventy-eight signers told Gordon. Evoking the language of the previous petition, they said they were "your poor afflicted people" with "poor wives and children" who daily felt the threat of invasion. Gordon talked to many others who were "under great apprehensions" that "numbers of Indians [were] coming to attack them." He discovered a group of German settlers who had turned a mill in New Hanover into a makeshift fort, while others congregated at homes "in order to defend themselves." Some were, Gordon later recounted, "so incensed, that they seemed determined to kill any Indian they could find." This was a war zone in which people expected an attack any moment, and they looked to their governor to protect them from it.[7]

Gordon remained above the fray. He looked into the causes of the skirmish by conducting a series of interviews to separate fact from fiction. His investigation revealed that the attack was not as violent nor as large as first reported. The supposedly large group of Indians marauding about the settlements turned out to number only eleven. The colonists, uncertain of what the Indians were up to, created a militia to approach these strangers. As the colonial delegation neared the Indians, someone opened fire. The colonists told Gordon the Indians shot first; he had his suspicions. In any case, both sides fired. The Indians fled. The "Spanish Indian" reportedly killed in action likely survived unscathed. Gordon found that the colonist who was supposedly killed instead "appeared only to be slightly wounded in the belly." Privately, Gordon admitted that "he could not help thinking that our people had given some provocation."[8]

Gordon's hunch was right. In time, it would become apparent that the invading Indians were Shawnees, a group allied with the colony. Conflict always seemed to follow the Shawnees. At the moment, they were at odds with both the Conestogas and another group called the Flatheads who were from the Ohio River Valley. Prepared to do battle with one or the other, the Shawnees were indeed dressed for war when they encountered the ad hoc Pennsylvania militia. But their intended targets were other Natives, not the European newcomers.[9]

Such nuance was lost amid the fear of self-described "frontier inhabitants," however. As new arrivals to the new world who were fueled by rumors and stories about Indians who lived beyond in "the woods," they tended to think of all Native Americans as the same—as "Ingians," as the Colebrookdale petition put it. They viewed the warlike maneuvers of the Shawnees in the darkest possible light and grew certain that this initial foray portended future invasions.[10]

Gordon found himself in a quandary. The frontier settlers were no idle threat to his government. By taking on war-making powers, they challenged his fundamental powers as captain-general and undermined the authority of government. Gordon had to assert governmental control by quelling such independent military actions. Failure to do so would mean the colony lacked a monopoly on the legitimate use of violence, the fundamental claim to legitimacy upon which all governments rest. Conversely, he also had to quell the fears of these "frontier inhabitants" who looked to him for aid.

Gordon's quandary was made all the more difficult because he oversaw a colony that had virtually no military history or culture. Gordon recognized the easy combustibility of the situation and used his authority to "quiet the country." He told settlers to cool their anti-Indian sentiment by warning them that "any rash act might be attended with fatal consequences." The governor's very presence likely calmed concerns too, but the promise of powder and lead in the event of an attack probably had the greatest effect.[11]

By the evening of May 11, Gordon felt satisfied that he had successfully defused the situation. But as he began to pack to return to Philadelphia, another express arrived, this one from Samuel Nutt, a local justice of the peace, that forced Gordon to cancel his journey.[12]

"Arms and Ammunition . . . in Order to Defend Our Fronteers"

As the governor was making his rounds in Mahanatawny, Walter Winter, a Welsh farmer living in the small village of Cucussea in Chester County, was making his own rounds. Along the way, he ran into a German settler who was abuzz with news. He told Winter that Indians had just killed "sundry Dutchmen." Winter, fearful for his and his family's safety, raced through his neighborhood spreading the news and calling for people to collect at his house "to defend themselves against the Indians." As he "was making fast the windows, in case any attempt should be made upon them," the son of his neighbor John Roberts approached with more desperate news. An Indian "with a bow and a great number of arrows" was stationed outside his father's house, poised to attack. The boy asked Winter for help. Winter grabbed his gun, loaded it with a bullet and swan shot, and enlisted his brother John and father-in-law, Morgan Herbert.[13]

As the crew ran over a small bridge that led to Roberts's house, they "saw an Indian man, some women, and some girls sitting on a wood pile." They also saw John Roberts standing in his doorway with a rifle cocked on his shoulder. As Walter, who was leading the charge, came within twenty-five yards, the Indian man stood and, Winter later swore, put an arrow "to the string of the bow." Winter raised his rifle and pulled the trigger, releasing the bullet and swan shot. The shot sprayed the man's chest, throwing him on his back. Walter then commanded the others to shoot.[14]

Chaos ensued. Following Walter's lead, John Winter fired, hitting one of the women. The two young girls bolted, seeking safety in the woods. Walter and John ran to the woodpile. While John, in the words of his brother, "knocked another of the Indian woman's brains out" with the butt of his gun, Walter grabbed the bow and arrow and pursued the children. He shot at one and, although the record is not clear, appears to have struck and injured her. John pursued the girls too and caught the other one, beat her with his gun, and left her for dead in the woods. As Walter returned to Roberts's house with his captive in tow, he saw the Indian man "staggering" into a nearby swamp. The other Indian woman, who had apparently survived the initial assault, now had an axe wound in her head, a deathblow dealt by John Roberts.[15]

The next day the Winter brothers, Morgan Herbert, and "sundry others" ventured to the Indians' cabin nearby, a sign that these settlers were familiar with, perhaps even knew, their victims. There they found the girl John had left in the woods. She was alone in her family's home, frightened, and "much hurt about the head and face." They sent her to Walter Winter's house to join her sister. The crew then returned to the scene of the carnage. After burying the two dead women in a shallow grave, they brought their two young prisoners to George Boone, a mill owner and the local justice of the peace. They expected he would applaud their actions. They even hoped that the justice of the peace would reward them for their war prizes. Shocked at what he heard and saw, Boone took custody of the girls for their protection. He apparently let the Winters go, however, likely because he did not have the proper warrants to arrest them. He did rush out dispatches to the other justices of the peace to warn them that there could be retaliatory attacks. One of these justices, Samuel Nutt, sent an express to Patrick Gordon that alerted him to the murders and asked him to delay his return to Philadelphia.[16]

Fear turned into outright panic as word of the murder spread throughout the communities. Most expected "the Indians will fall down upon us very suddenly," causing all but twenty men to flee the area around Boone's district. Boone stayed, however, and with the twenty remaining turned his mill into a fort. Stocked with a thousand bushels of wheat and flour, they "resolved to defend ourselves to the last extremity." Boone, writing to Gordon the day after the murders, promised that they would "not quit our habitation if we can have any succor from you." He asked the governor to send "arms and ammunition . . . in order to defend our fronteers" and, perhaps more important, "send some messengers to the Indians" in a last-ditch effort to prevent the expected invasion. Boone believed the situation desperate. Failure to defend these "fronteers," these zones now vulnerable to a feared invasion, Boone added, would leave the colony "desolate and destroyed."[17]

Boone's reference to this territory becoming a "fronteer" revealed once again the significance of the word to colonists. Boone and others who lived on perceived "fronteers" began to imagine their place in the polity in a new way and, as a result, began to expect their government, especially the governor who was the captain-general of the colony, to provide them with "succor." These demands only became stronger and more desperate as the perception of being on a frontier solidified.

Moreover, in 1728, these imagined frontiers had a profound effect on unifying settlers in this crisis zone out of a shared sense of danger. Many historians have treated the ethnically diverse population of Pennsylvania as segregated, divided along lines of ethnicity, religion, and custom. Certainly, there were ethnic and other antagonisms within Pennsylvania, but these enmities fueled few, if any, acts of violence. The shared fear of invasion that these "frontier inhabitants" felt, however, brought them together. The spark that sent the Welshman Walter Winter on his murderous rampage came when he heard from a German man that Indians had killed "sundry Dutchmen." Gordon had witnessed this unity upon his arrival. The petition for help he received from the people of Colebrookdale had signatures of men from many different ethnicities, with none other than John Roberts's name at the top. In times of crisis, the all-encompassing "Indians" formed a coherent enemy that helped mute whatever ethnic tensions may have existed in times of peace. Indeed, the ease with which information flowed throughout the settlements and the shared support that followed shows how colonists regularly forged crosscultural ties. The foundation of fear that cemented their bond also escalated tensions between colonists and Indians during the frontier crisis of 1728, ultimately ending with a small but powerful group of "frontier inhabitants" killing a group of Indians indiscriminately.[18]

"Might Lawfully Kill Any Indian Whom They Could Find"

Before the Winters' attack, many worried the colony was on the brink of full-scale war. Now some believed war inevitable. It fell to Patrick Gordon to change that. Gordon, as the proprietor's representative and the captain-general charged with military matters and Indian relations, had to hew a fine line. He understood the stakes. Like most others in the region, he feared that "this piece of barbarity might stirr up the Indians to revenge it on our inhabitants in these parts." The solution, he knew, was for the government to play a forceful role in implementing its policies and establishing its authority. Success, Gordon hoped, would keep the peace. In order to do so, he would have to use all of the implied powers the governor had.[19]

First, as the chief magistrate, he issued a hue and cry instructing all sheriffs, coroners, constables, and others to search "with horse and with foot" for the Winter brothers. That same day, word came that the manhunt had already ended in Philadelphia County. Andrew Hamilton and Edward Farmer, both justices of the peace, had apprehended the Winter brothers and Morgan Herbert in western Philadelphia County.[20]

Gordon and some justices of the peace interviewed the men, hoping to learn what had led them to murder. The Winters' explanations revealed the dangerous logic used by people who believed they lived on a frontier, especially one formed against Native Americans. When the Winters defended their actions, they evoked the rules of war. They argued that after hearing of Indians murdering "some white men," they felt that they "might lawfully kill any Indian whom they could find." Indeed, they believed that they should have received a reward for their actions, as if they had captured an enemy. Officials showed no sympathy and confined the men. On May 15, Farmer and Hamilton sent the men under heavy guard to Chester County's jail for trial. They also issued an arrest warrant for John Roberts.[21]

Gordon next shifted his role to chief diplomat and performed damage control with the colony's Native allies. He ordered the coroner to dig up the bodies of the murdered Indians and give them "a decent burial." He also provided the relatives of the slain with four valuable cloth blankets, called strouds, to lay upon the graves, in recognition of Indian custom, and gave strouds to the two surviving girls. He also found a resident willing to care for the girls' wounds. These acts, he hoped, would show the respect the colony held for their Indian allies and their customs.[22]

Gordon also took the proactive step of sending messages to leaders of important Native American groups "to acquaint them with this unhappy accident." He explained to them that colonists had heard "some stories . . . that there were many hundreds" of Indians approaching who were intent on invasion. The news "raised an alarm" among settlers as word spread.

"An accident" followed in which "four wicked white men killed a peaceable good Indian Man and two women." Gordon assured them that this singular act of a few bad men did not reflect the sentiments of the colony, for the murders "raised a horror in me and all the good people about me." He promised that those accused of the murder would "suffer in the same manner as if they had killed so many white people, for that we make no difference." Gordon hoped his actions and words would demonstrate the colony's true values to both Native Americans and colonists.[23]

Gordon's actions captured the contrast between the government's policy toward Indians and the more hardened view held by the Winters and their many sympathizers in the west. As Pennsylvania expanded as a colony, as its relations with Indians became more complex, and as its population grew more dispersed and diverse, officials in charge of running the colony increasingly confronted the thorny issue of Native Americans' legal status. They could easily make new immigrants subjects, but Indians were another matter. Since William Penn's landing, colonial officials agreed that Native Americans were not subjects to the Crown nor were they Pennsylvanians, yet they also deserved the protection of government.

Solving this problem was fundamental to governing in colonial North America. Officials tasked with enforcing laws needed to determine who received the government's protections. Pennsylvania had gone to great lengths to create naturalization codes to ensure that non-English immigrants from Europe would be loyal to the proprietor and Crown, in exchange for which they received the full rights and protections afforded British subjects. But Natives posed a different problem. William Penn had once imagined a judicial system with mixed juries in which Indians and colonists served as coequals. That never came to be, but the legislature had enacted codes that clarified the protections Indians could expect through the legal system.[24]

The law for regulating Indian-colonial interactions that was passed in 1715, for instance, provided greater clarity on Indians' legal rights and revealed how Pennsylvania legislators thought of their Native neighbors. Moreover, the beliefs distilled in this law represented the underlying assumptions that drove Gordon's actions. The law left little doubt as to the legal protections afforded allied Indians. Within the bounds of Pennsylvania, they would receive the same rights as any colonist. Presaging the words Gordon used to assuage Native Americans in 1728, the earlier law stated that any personal assault against an Indian by a colonist would be prosecuted by

Pennsylvania "as if the said offense was committed against any natural born subject of Great Britain." Conversely, the governor's council dealt with all cases in which settlers accused Indians of violence. In that way, Pennsylvania's colonial government claimed absolute sovereignty over all Euro-Americans and offered its protection to Natives against these newcomers.[25]

But the act created different means for punishing transgressions. Gone were the hopeful days of William Penn's juries of both Indians and colonists. The Assembly realized that Indians might not have a fair trial if they had to face a jury of European settlers. Therefore, instead of integrating Indians within the traditional legal system of the colony, the law established an alternative legal framework to deal with colonists' accusations against Indians: the Provincial Council would be the judge and jury. Giving the council, a proprietary institution, such power also reinforced its role in conducting diplomacy for the colony, since the trial of a Native person would undoubtedly affect Indian relations.[26]

Historians have used acts such as this one as windows into the broader cultural values of a past society. Often historians treat laws that formalize differences between groups as institutionalizing power relationships in which a dominant group restricts rights and opportunities for the minority group. Sometimes historians see in these distinctions the roots of racism. In 1715, the Pennsylvania Assembly created one system that applied to Euro-Americans who committed violence against Indians and another that applied to Native Americans who committed violence against colonists. But the 1715 Pennsylvania statute was not meant to be restrictive. In fact, its intent was the opposite. Although its authors recognized that colonists were unlikely to be impartial judges of Indians, the Pennsylvania code and others like it hoped to address potential power imbalances by giving Indians certain rights and protecting them against the prejudices that regular colonists might hold against them. Even if this law captured a gloomy reality of everyday Indian–white relations, perhaps even tacitly acknowledging the racial antagonisms of common settlers, it also showed the government's continued attempt to offer Indians the protection of the colonial government.[27]

In the spring of 1728, however, war now seemed possible, if not imminent. Gordon hoped to maintain Pennsylvania's tradition of peace, but he had to prepare for the potential for war as well. Before he left for Philadelphia, he used his powers as the captain-general to create a "commission" that would "gather the inhabitants together and put them in a posture of defence" after the murders in case of retaliation. By creating an official authority to oversee militias and defenses, Gordon hoped to take the power away from unofficial and unregulated volunteer militias that could inadvertently start war—that indeed may have just thrown the colony headlong into its first war—and place official authority in the hands of commissioners he knew and trusted.[28]

"A Strong League and Chain of Friendship"

Gordon returned to Philadelphia on May 15. Upon his return, he decided to make clear the colony's position toward its Indian neighbors and allies. Gordon had seen firsthand the virulence of anti-Indian feelings, and he used the power of proclamation to counter such sentiments and enforce Pennsylvania policy. In a series of decrees that were posted throughout communities and read to and by settlers, he reiterated Pennsylvania's policy of peace with Natives with whom the colony had "a firm alliance and sincere friendship." Gordon identified specific Indian groups as allies and explained Pennsylvania's policy of friendship toward them. Settlers were told to treat "the Delawares, Conestogoes, Ganawese, Shawanese, Mingoes or those of the Five Nations, or any other coming and demeaning themselves peaceably amongst us . . . with the same civil regard they would an English subject."[29]

Proclamations would only go so far. Gordon also had to demonstrate Pennsylvania's intentions to Indians and colonists. He began preparing a grand treaty ceremony—perhaps the largest the colony had held—on the banks of the Susquehanna. He wanted to meet with the Indians who seemed poised for war and to reaffirm Pennsylvania's peaceful intentions, and he wanted to calm settlers whose nerves were on edge.[30]

At that point, the Assembly got involved for the first time. They agreed that war was a real possibility and that a treaty was the most likely way to avoid it. After some minor squabbling, they gave Gordon £100 for diplomatic gifts. At that time, £100 was not a paltry sum: with this money the government was able to buy twenty-five coats, twenty blankets, twenty duffels, twenty-five shirts, one hundred pounds of gunpowder, two hundred pounds of lead, five hundred flints, fifty knives, and foodstuffs. Moreover, the materials the government intended to give the Indians—ammunition and arms—signaled the government's view that these Indians were not threats. This singular act was the only role the Assembly played in the entire affair, evidence of both the small part this institution played in problems dealing with expansion and the prominent role proprietary institutions played in the lives of colonists and Indians alike.[31]

On May 26, the treaty ceremony began. The official records state that fifteen Indian delegates sat around the treaty fire with many more watching. Representatives came from the Conestogas, Delawares, Ganaweses (also Conoys or Piscataways), and Shawnees. The Indians and Pennsylvanians had three interpreters each because of the many different languages spoken. In addition to the large Indian presence, over two hundred settlers, many of whom feared war with these Indian groups, came to witness the treaty. The large attendance reflected the stakes.[32]

All eyes were on Gordon. Recent events were surely on his mind as he spoke, and Gordon's intended audience was as much the multitude of colonists around him as the Indians before him. He began his opening speech by evoking the memory of William Penn as a way to rekindle a common bond. Penn, he recounted, had entered into "a strong league and chain of friendship" that had made the two groups "as one people," a common phrase used in these treaties to denote a close alliance. Gordon, as the governor appointed by Penn's heirs, stood before the Indians at the treaty "in their stead." His charge, he told his counterparts, was "to love all the Indians as their brethren."[33]

He then outlined the principles and protocols that held this alliance together. He recited nine rules, each representing a link in the chain of friendship. Indians and Pennsylvanians were to keep all paths clear and open between Indian territories and Pennsylvania, a literal and metaphoric statement that meant both groups should travel and trade freely and keep clear communication. Another stated that Pennsylvanians and Indians were to welcome one another into their homes and treat them "as their friends," not enemies. Finally, he addressed the dangers rumors posed to this peace. Neither Indians nor colonists should believe rumors, he said. When stories of strife between the two sides spread, he advised that both colonists and Indians should seek out leaders for the truth before acting rashly. Then he apologized for the violence. "There are wicked people in all nations," Gordon said, and he promised to try and execute the Winters for violating the foundation of trust that cemented this alliance.[34]

The Indians reacted with enthusiasm. Tawenna, a Conestoga delegated to respond to Gordon's speech, said that they "greatly rejoyced [in] their hearts that they have had no such speech made to them since the time that the great William Penn was amongst them, all was good and nothing was amiss." Tawenna spoke from experience. He had heard William Penn speak at the 1701 treaty where the Conestoga formalized their alliance with Penn by giving Pennsylvania sole rights to lands on the banks of the Susquehanna in exchange for Pennsylvania's promise to preserve a small plot for the Conestoga and to provide the Conestoga with protection from both European and rival Indian nations. Tawenna's reference to Penn living among them also suggests that he was present when Penn made his celebratory visit to their town.[35]

Since the time of this earlier treaty, Tawenna had seen the colony grow. He had seen the effects of colonists pushing further west and had witnessed the violence between Indians and colonists engendered by this expansion. But he was hopeful that the foundation of peace laid by that earlier treaty was still firm. The two groups were, he said, evoking Penn's principles, truly "one people . . . one body and one heart." He then told Gordon not to "grieve too much" over the Winters' murder of the Delaware because they recognized it as "rash inconsiderate actions" of individuals behaving independent of the colony. Tawenna then addressed the murder of Thomas Wright, the colonist killed by Indians in a drunken melee the previous fall and an issue Gordon had raised in the course of his speech to show that both sides were not without guilt. Tawenna explained that the guilty Indians belonged to "the Menysincks [Delawares], who are of another nation, and therefore they can say nothing to it." In so doing, Tawenna laid out the expectations Indians had for dealing with such intercultural violence. Indian groups expected to be treated as distinct groups, not an amalgamated whole. Gordon recognized this distinction in his response, noting "that since the Indian, who killed the Englishman . . . is not of their nation, he would demand Justice from that Nation to which he belonged."[36]

The discussion of Wright and the Winters exposed the unclear and yet pragmatic legal status of Indians in Pennsylvania. On a practical level, Indians' legal status was never entirely coherent nor was it ever explicitly explained. Indians and colonial officials had come to a mutual understanding through ad hoc mediations and diplomacy. What was clear was that Indians as individuals within Pennsylvania had some legal rights, but Indians were not entitled to the same legal system as colonists because they were not British subjects and there was no naturalization path for them (nor, of course, did they seek such a path). As Gordon noted in his reply to Tawenna, the government recognized that individual Indians belonged to specific groups—in Gordon's word, "nations"—and that while these groups might be held liable for the actions of their members, they should not be expected to police other Indian "nations." Individual Indians were thus clearly not members of the colony, but they were affiliated with it. Indeed, keeping Indians separate from the colony was important for Pennsylvania's expansionist aims. By recognizing Indian groups as separate polities that collectively owned the land, the proprietors could legally secure their title in the eyes of the British Empire.

Perhaps the best way to summarize how Pennsylvania treated Indians as both individuals and groups was that they were in but not of Pennsylvania and the British Empire. Pennsylvania did not claim to exert its authority over Indian-on-Indian violence or relations between Indian groups (though it certainly had an interest in and influence over both). The authority of the colonial government, instead, extended only to violence between colonists and Indians, and especially to violence that happened within areas that were part of the established jurisdiction of the colony and not "the woods"—a term that often meant areas of crosscultural interaction beyond official colonial settlement. Thus, all colonists were squarely under the dominion of their colony no matter where they roamed, but Indians only fell under Pennsylvania's jurisdiction when it came to contact involving colonists. Such a status comported with Indians' views in which they wanted to be independent of Pennsylvania but allied to it, as their preference for diplomacy over legal trials suggested. Indians' status may not have been clear, but its ambiguity during these years was effective in practice nonetheless.[37]

After the governor received the Indians' message, some of his advisers pulled him aside. They noted that many of the colonists who had assembled to watch the proceedings were those who lived closest to Indian groups and most feared an Indian war. They told Gordon to "press the Indians to declare to him if they suffered any grievances or hardship from this government, because several reports had been industriously spread abroad as if they had some just cause of complaints." Gordon followed their advice. The Indians responded: "They had no cause of complaint, that William Penn and his people had still treated them well, and they had no uneasiness." Their direct statement eased the anxiety of the populace by rejecting the rumors that circulated.[38]

The treaty was a smashing success. The colony rejoiced from the banks of the Susquehanna to the shores of the Delaware. Word of the speeches reached Philadelphia before Gordon did, and Philadelphians cheered what they heard. When Gordon approached the city, a large crowd awaited him. The *American Weekly* boasted that the welcoming "cavalcade" was "a far greater number than has ever been known to meet together on such an occasion at any time before in this province." Gordon's reception in Philadelphia shows the public's widespread awareness that the colony's distinctive history of peace was threatened by this frontier crisis. The treaty preserved Pennsylvania's tradition.[39]

The reception in Indian Country mirrored that of colonial society. Leaders of allied Indian groups who were unable to attend the treaty sent messages of support after hearing the speeches. One did add a hint of concern to his otherwise supportive words, noting that he hoped "the back inhabitants may be cautioned not to be so ready to attack the Indians as they were at that time." It was a subtle critique of the government as much as it was of the people. The Indians expected Pennsylvania's government to better enforce its authority within its own populace.[40]

With the crisis averted, proprietary officials resolved to improve their ability to maintain order. The rumors of Indian war showed the power of the spoken word, and officeholders used the institutions at their disposal to combat the uncertainty fueled by loose talk. The lessons of the crisis continued to reverberate at a Court of Quarter Sessions held in Philadelphia a couple of weeks after the murders. The judges took advantage of the opportunity to tell the jurors who had come from all over to disseminate the government's message. Before adjourning, the court noted that "it is true something has happened which raised the notice and concern not only of the government but of every good man; but it is really surprising to hear of the many, idle groundless and lying stories which have been bruited and thrown out to alarm and disturb the people, some of which have risen from ignorance and fear." The jurors were then instructed that as they "dispersed in several parts of the country, you may as occasion offers in all conversations endeavor to quiet the minds of the people." They ended their instruction with a striking observation: "The truth is, that the Indians are more calm and prudent than some of our people."[41]

Proprietary officials did more than just offer proclamations and apologies. They also acted on the colony's promise of justice. If Pennsylvania was to assert its monopoly on the legitimate use of violence, it needed to punish the murderers who challenged this monopoly. The Winters were tried in court in June. The trial was, in effect, a contest between official policy toward Indians and the powerful anti-Indian sentiment of colonists beyond Philadelphia. The jurors in Chester County, likely composed of Quaker settlers who still dominated its eastern parts, found the accused guilty on June 19. On July 3, the brothers were hung (Morgan Herbert was given a reprieve), a clear symbol that Pennsylvania's government still abided by William Penn's promise. The council even set the execution date at a time convenient for Indians so they could witness justice being served. This execution was the first in four years, and another would not happen for three more; it was so significant that two newspapers in Boston reported on it.[42]

As the murderous events of 1728 made clear, expansion posed a threat to peace with friendly Indians and to the colony itself, in large part because interactions between colonists and Indians could quickly turn violent. New towns in western regions turned into "frontiers," and the existence of such frontiers posed challenges to both the colonial government and to the overarching ideological foundation of the colony. The emergence of these frontiers in the geopolitical imagination of western colonists forced government officials to act by strengthening the government's claims of sovereignty and power over its people. All totaled, Gordon's invitation for settlers to witness the treaty, the creation of commissions for defense, the proclamations, the court orders, and the final execution of the Winter brothers represented a colonial government establishing itself by asserting its authority in newly settled and distant regions. Notably, nearly all of these actions came from proprietary officials or through institutions the proprietor controlled.

"Bringing Those Who Too Frequently Fly Thither for Refuge, Under the Same Subjection to the Laws with the Rest of His Majesty's Subjects"

Although officials were able to ease tensions in 1728, colonists continued to push west, beyond the traditional center of Philadelphia and the three original counties. Squatters and runaway servants began crossing the Susquehanna River, raising the ire of Native groups who objected to their presence. Reports of violence and disorder became commonplace.[43]

Officials realized that they needed to adapt further to deal with this new growth. County creation became the logical outcome. As the colony expanded, so too should its government. A county centralized government authority in areas of recent colonial settlement by extending legal institutions to enforce laws and restrain settlers. Officials also hoped the county would have a positive influence on colonial development by creating a series of administrative offices that would better serve the needs of colonists.

The founding of Lancaster County in 1729 established a general protocol for the future. First, colonists in the underserved area sent a request for a new county. In this case, prominent and well-connected settlers James Wright, the justice at the center of the Wright murder in 1727, and Samuel Blunston organized a petition asking for greater government because of their desperate situation. The signers made clear that they expected a new county would help institute what this region so desperately needed: order. To that end, they promised to build a courthouse to enforce the law. Gordon concurred that such a division would "greatly conduce not only . . . the peace, good Order, and Ease of those Inhabitants in particular, but also to the Security of the whole Government, by bringing those who too frequently fly thither for Refuge, under the same Subjection to the Laws with the rest of his Majesty's Subjects."[44]

Lancaster County may have solved the problem settlers in the western region faced, but it also exposed a fundamental problem of the Frame of 1701. The earlier frames of government, especially Penn's first Frame, described a means for political expansion to occur. In the earlier Frame, the Provincial Council, the elected upper house, controlled the development of new land. Representation also shifted in the original Frame as populations changed, a process Penn devised to ensure that no area amassed too much political power. The Frame of 1701, however, left all of these issues unaddressed. In the final version, the Provincial Council as an independent legislative unit was abolished, and representation in the Assembly referred only to the original counties, with each of these receiving the same number regardless of population.

Gordon recognized that the proprietary power implied in the Frame of 1701 made him responsible for managing expansion. In an address to the Assembly, he made clear that the authority to create a county was "wholly vested in the Proprietary" because it had to do with legal institutions. Nonetheless, he sought the approval of the Assembly because the new county would have representatives in that body. In a moment of accord between these two rival institutions, the legislature supported the new county, agreeing that it would provide more order.[45]

But the Assembly faced a dilemma. The Frame of 1701 did not outline a process for expanding its membership. With the addition of a new county in 1729, the Assembly had to determine how many members the new unit would send. Rather than grant them the same eight members that the original and more populous counties sent, the Assembly granted the county half of that. The reasons for this decision are not entirely clear, although there are a number of possible explanations. The Assembly was protective of its authority and membership, and the representatives from Lancaster could upset the status quo. Moreover, Lancaster County was needed because its residents appeared unruly, and so the Assembly may have been concerned that these people's representatives would prove similarly destabilizing. Finally, there were far fewer colonists than in the original counties, which made some sort of proportional allocation sensible.

The success of this expanded arm of the colonial government became apparent soon after its establishment. At about the same time the county was created, Captain Civility, the chief of the Conestogas, alerted the governor to an illegal settlement by Edward Parnel "and several other familys who were settled on the west side of the [Susquehanna] river." Pennsylvania officials with stronger tools at their disposal acted just as decisively in honoring their treaty promises as they had in prosecuting the Winter brothers. Gordon vacated Parnel's group "by Governor's Order" and used the levers of the law to make sure his decree was enforced, sending out officials from Lancaster to torch their buildings. Officials also promised Civility that "no person should settle on that side of the river without our consent." As one nineteenth-century historian remarked with surprise, "It is difficult to believe that as late as 1731 what was called an official map was published fixing the river Susquehanna as the extreme and western boundary of the province of Pennsylvania." The Conestogas were not the only Natives who expressed concern with expanding settlements. The Shawnees also expressed displeasure with the new western settlements. To help allay such discontent, the government moved to "dispossess all persons settled on that side of the [Susquehanna] river" so "that those woods may remain free to the Indians." Gordon used the offices of the new county to implement these orders and, in the process, helped restrain colonial settlement, while also reinforcing the centrality of proprietary authority.[46]

While the county proved effective in curtailing unlawful expansion, in 1730, the institution faced a test reminiscent of the Winters' murders. In the heat of late August 1730, word came to Joshua Lowe, the coroner for Lancaster County, that colonists had discovered three badly decomposed bodies near a small creek. Evidence suggested murder. Lowe went out to inspect. Though the bodies were hard to identify, he could tell that the dead were Indians who had had their skulls crushed. Lowe also knew that if colonists had killed these three people, then the tensions between Native and colonial society created by such an act could easily rekindle the fears of 1728.

Lowe decided to follow the terms of the alliance that Gordon outlined in his treaty speech. He alerted the Conestoga and Conoy Indians, the two groups who lived in the area, to the discovery and asked for help in investigating. They accepted. Lowe then convened a formal inquisition composed of colonists and Indians, a move that harkened back to Penn's original vision of joint juries working together to maintain peace and cultivate mutual understanding. The jury quickly decided death by murder but concluded that the bodies were too far decomposed to say more than that. More important, they all agreed that Pennsylvanians bore no blame for the deaths.[47]

Lowe knew there was more to this story, though he did not let his knowledge interfere with the official inquest. In a private letter to Gordon, he said that the dead Indians were likely a Delaware family and that the murderer was suspected to be the jealous husband of one of the Indian women. Lowe noted that since the crime involved an Indian killing another Indian, the colonial government had no responsibility to act. Lowe's statement shows that the understanding of Indians' legal status in the colony that had developed over time and through precedent had made its way down to the most local of officials. Through actions like Lowe's, officials stationed far away from colonial capitals and even farther from the imperial center in England began to expand and assert colonial authority over new ground. While diplomats and political leaders could negotiate treaties, it was here, in areas of new settlement, that the colony was being created through the actions of local officials like Lowe who were implementing and enforcing policies and, in the process, establishing a functional government.[48]

After the handling of the murders in 1730, Pennsylvania's relations with Indians stood on solid ground. Later that year, Captain Civility hinted at the successful settlement of the 1728 crisis in a letter he sent to Gordon. He noted that the Conestogas had followed the spirit of Gordon's 1728 speech—that "wee should not hurt any of your people"—and he thanked Gordon for doing the same by removing the squatters. But Civility's letter also contained a worrisome subtext. Pennsylvanians—including some of the county officials who had promised Civility that they would stop encroachments—continued to secretly survey lands on the west side of the Susquehanna. New settlers from Maryland also began to appear, claiming that the land was their property and not Pennsylvania's. The reemergence of this colonial rivalry in the wake of the frontier crisis of 1728 posed novel challenges to Pennsylvania's colonial government as it tried to maintain an ordered and peaceful expansion while also trying to fend off an aggressive neighbor.[49]

CHAPTER 4

Pennsylvania's Apogee

In the 1730s, as British colonies in North America continued to grow, the Pennsylvania government faced a new test. Maryland began establishing its own claims to land the Penns expected would one day be their own. The dispute over the proper boundaries of Maryland and Pennsylvania had simmered since William Penn received his charter, but only in the 1730s did the rivalry turn into a war, as settlements pushed colonial boundaries closer together and forced the issue to the fore. From about 1732 to 1738, Maryland and Pennsylvania engaged in a protracted border war marked by low-level strife punctuated by moments of extreme violence. Although the idea of a war between colonies seems odd, perhaps even an overstatement, everyone at the time called it one. When the Conojocular War, as it was called at the time, or Cresap's War, as most recent historians have called it, was over, Pennsylvania had secured its border and vanquished its colonial rival.

The conflict is little studied and underappreciated; yet the episode is essential to understanding the colony's political development and geographic growth. It forced Pennsylvania's government to create an ad hoc means of waging war and to change its policy on expansion, the results of which affected the future of Pennsylvania's relationships with Indian peoples. Indeed, the geographic expansion encouraged Indians dislocated by the war to become closer to New France. When the first war between European empires came to the region with the Seven Years' War in the 1750s, the effects of the earlier war between Pennsylvania and Maryland still lingered, influencing both the location of frontiers in Pennsylvania and the identity of the colony's enemies. The frontiers that developed in the 1750s, then, can only be understood through the dramatic changes wrought by this earlier conflict between two British colonies.

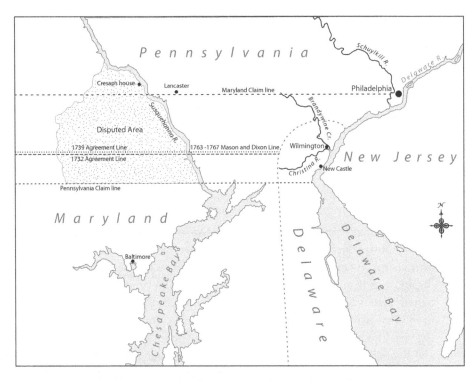

Figure 6. The contested borders between Maryland and Pennsylvania. From 1732 to 1738, Maryland and Pennsylvania clashed over control of the western side of the Susquehanna River. Marylanders staked a claim to the land by establishing a community near Thomas Cresap's house. For six years, Marylanders and Pennsylvanians crossed the river to harass their enemies, culminating in 1736, when a group of Pennsylvanians burned Cresap's house to the ground.

But what is also notable for our purposes is an absence of frontier language that only becomes all the more illustrative when compared with Pennsylvania's later border wars. During the Conojocular War, Pennsylvanians still did not speak of "frontiers" or of being a "frontier people" who inhabited "frontier counties." That such talk did not develop during this colonial conflict helps define the meaning and use of *frontier* in early America. The war with Maryland did not create "frontiers" because the battle was fought against a fellow British colony over expansion and control of western land within the empire rather than against a clear external enemy. The lack of such zones during the war shows that frontiers in the geopolitical imagination of colonists appeared only when Native groups or European rivals invaded—or threatened to invade—a British colony.

When compared to later border wars, the lack of frontiers in the 1730s helped Pennsylvania secure victory over its rival. In this earlier case, as colonists with malleable loyalties compared the two proprietary colonies, they expressed their preference for Pennsylvania's model with its promise of peace and prosperity, giving Pennsylvania the backing it needed to displace Maryland and secure its future expansion west. But in the 1770s, in the conflicts that Pennsylvania lost to Virginia and Connecticut, colonists possessed a far different geopolitical imagination. After the Seven Years' War, a large portion of the colonial population in the contested regions believed they inhabited "a frontier" against Indians. Instead of embracing Pennsylvania's promise of tranquility with Native neighbors, those once again caught in the middle blamed the colony for their inadequate defense of frontier people. To make sense of this later collapse of Pennsylvania, it is important to understand the colony at its apogee, when it was able to defend itself against a colonial competitor and win the allegiance of settlers who had the power to choose the government they preferred.

Before moving to the action, however, the name of the conflict should be discussed. People have labeled it various things over time: Cresap's War for the leader of the Maryland cause, the Conojocular War for the Indian name of the contested region, or occasionally the Maryland War by Pennsylvanians who fought in it. The Conojocular War may be the most accurate and was the term most people used at the time (often spelled various phonetic ways). The name also better reflects the nature of the conflict. The war was fought over territory called the Conegehally. It was not a war of Cresap's making, since Pennsylvanians were often the instigators, nor was it Maryland's War, since from the Marylanders' perspective, Pennsylvania was the one invading their land.[1]

"One Crissop, Particularly, Is Very Abusive"

The conflict between colonies began almost as soon as Lancaster County was created. One of the first hints of trouble came on an otherwise inconspicuous late September afternoon in 1731 when a group of men gathered at a cleared lot in Lancaster, the seat of the new county with the same name, to erect a courthouse on the town square. The new court symbolized the expansion of the colonial government and all that its creators hoped to accomplish with it. In this building, legal disputes could be mediated, offices filled, and punishments meted out. Within a year, however, these county offices and the powers they held would be used for an unexpected purpose: war.[2]

Samuel Blunston stood at the head of the operations that fall day. Blunston held the titles of justice of the peace, recorder of the deeds, and county prothonotary—a central position in county government that had important powers of oversight. Blunston had the perfect pedigree for the job. His roots in Pennsylvania went back to the colony's founding. His father followed William Penn's call and eventually rose to the highest levels of government, serving in various local offices and in both the Assembly and Provincial Council. Samuel, now forty-two years old, was following in his father's footsteps. Blunston arrived on the banks of the Susquehanna in 1728 after purchasing a three-hundred-acre farm.[3]

By 1731, after only three short years in the area, Blunston had become more than a leading figure in the new county. Blunston's many roles meant that he *was* the new government. His task was no small one. It fell to him to establish the colony's authority in a region populated by, in his words, the "idle and dissolute persons who resorted hither to keep out of the hands of justice." A functioning courthouse was going to be essential to his success. He would administer its daily operations, ranging from marriage licenses to road maintenance; enforce its laws; and oversee its expansion through a land office. The courthouse may have been the symbol of the expanding colonial government, but it was Blunston who would give it real force.[4]

As Blunston helped the other men from Lancaster raise the walls of this courthouse, Captain Civility, the Conestogas' chief representative to Pennsylvania, approached him with an interpreter in tow. Civility, worried that the burst of colonial settlement would fray the good relations Gordon had recently cemented, came to express his concerns. He began by presenting a "string of wampum" before Blunston that carried the following urgent message for the governor:

> That the Conestogoe Indians have always lived in good friendship with the Christian inhabitants of Pensilvania, and have behaved themselves agreeable to their treatys with them. That William Penn had promis'd them they should not be disturbed by any settlers on the west side of Sasquehannah, but now, contrary thereto, several

Marylanders are settled by the river, on that side, at Conejohela; and one Crissop, particularly, is very abusive to them when they pass that way, and has beat and wounded one of their women who went to get apples from their own trees. . . . And further says, that, as they shal always take care their people do us no hurt, so they also expect we shall protect them.[5]

Civility's message came as no surprise. The border controversy that Penn first confronted in 1682 still simmered. For most of the intervening fifty years, the dispute was a minor squabble between proprietors based in England. Occasionally, testy neighbors in the disputed southern region would use their loyalty to one lord as a way to exacerbate a personal feud that they had with someone loyal to the other. More recently, however, Maryland began to assert its rights by instigating jurisdictional clashes in an attempt to regain territory Pennsylvania occupied. Most of these disputes occurred on the Delmarva Peninsula in which Delaware and Maryland jurisdictions collided. Early in 1731, as Captain Civility was then discovering, Maryland moved to gain control of the western side of the Susquehanna. By settling the territory, Maryland forced an issue that had only been considered in the abstract until that time: both colonies needed to agree to a border between them if the empire was to function properly. Civility felt the pressure of this uncertainty, and he looked to his allies in Pennsylvania for protection from Maryland.[6]

Maryland, however, had a strong case in the west. The charters of Pennsylvania and Maryland both contained vague wording about the fortieth parallel of latitude forming the extent of each colony. When the charters were first written, no one was sure of the precise location of the line. In fact, most of the Greater Philadelphia region fell under the parallel; a literal reading of the charters employing what eventually became the fixed fortieth parallel line meant that the capital of Pennsylvania belonged to Maryland. While Baltimore demanded compensation for his loss, the Penns argued that Baltimore had it all wrong. They pointed to an early map that gave Penn control of territory well south of the fortieth parallel, evidence they said of the true intent of the Crown. Still, the wording of the charters gave Baltimore the ground, and the competing interpretation created an opportunity for the current Lord Baltimore to reassert his claims.[7]

There was another significant difference in the dispute over the west— the man named "Crissop." Thomas Cresap arrived in Maryland from

England sometime in the 1720s. His early years in North America remain unclear. There is evidence that after finding little initial success in Maryland, he traveled to Virginia and rented land from the Washington family. In any case, by the 1730s, he had developed a reputation as a wily and pugnacious individual. Having no particular loyalties to Maryland or its Catholic founding—though rumors circulated that he harbored sympathies for Rome—Cresap's sole purpose in the colonies was to better himself. Rather than follow the staid, conformist path of the Blunstons, Cresap seized opportunity, if necessary, by force. He was perfect for Maryland's plans. In time, Cresap showed a devotion to Maryland and Lord Baltimore as strong as Blunston's was to Pennsylvania. He also possessed an audacity that made his gambit nearly successful.[8]

Evidence suggests that in 1730 or early 1731, Cresap received a patent from Lord Baltimore for land on the western side of the Susquehanna River. He made quite a show of it too. He built a sturdy homestead near the burned remnants of squatter Edward Parnel's place, a clear sign to his Pennsylvanian neighbors that he would not be so easily cowed. Friends and family members joined him—people "of loose morals and turbulent spirits," according to Blunston. Soon, Maryland had a bustling and tight-knit community on the contested western bank, situated just south of Lancaster.[9]

Cresap's thriving community left Pennsylvania officials flummoxed. Cresap was no squatter, like Edward Parnel, who Pennsylvania's government could evict through force. The Marylanders all possessed a legal claim from a neighboring colony, a partner in the British Empire who shared a common sovereign. Pennsylvania might dispute the validity of the Maryland land deeds, but it could not displace the residents without undermining the authority of its fellow British colony. Worse still for the Pennsylvanians, Maryland appeared willing to actively support the rights of these settlers. As James Logan remarked, because their opponent was another British colony, he did not "know . . . how to make war with them."[10]

"Lands . . . Are More Valuable Now, Then They Were Before Any Form of Government Was Settled, Any Plantation Made, or Any Markets Found"

Fights between Maryland settlers and Pennsylvania officials over property rights and jurisdiction marked the first phase of the war as each side tried to accomplish their goal of establishing an undisturbed claim to the western side of the river. For Pennsylvanians, their challenge was to preserve that side of the river as undisturbed land still in Indian hands to honor the implied rights conveyed to the Conestoga at the Treaty of 1701. The way to do that was to remove the irritant, which meant they needed to target Cresap. For Marylanders, who were not party to the same treaty, their strategy was to persist by attracting settlers and to prevent Pennsylvania from establishing its authority over the region. The situation thus called for Pennsylvania to take offensive actions, though Pennsylvanians clearly saw the Marylanders who had built homes on the western side as the original offenders.

Civility's message that October day provided Pennsylvania officials with the opportunity to seize Cresap. Before the meeting, James Logan had confided to Blunston that "he should be glad if Crissop could be taken." The problem was the government lacked the legal pretext to do so, at least until Civility showed up. When Blunston relayed Civility's concerns to higher officials, he also noted that Cresap harbored Samuel Chance, a runaway servant of Edmund Cartlidge, a prominent Pennsylvanian trader. Cresap, Blunston reported, "threatens to shoot any person who shal offer to take away said servant." Blunston saw in Cresap's seizure of Pennsylvania property a cause to act, writing "if you think it will be of service to the government to have him taken, I believe it may be done."[11]

Though there are no records of the government's response, a few weeks later Edmund Cartlidge orchestrated a ruse meant to capture Cresap. On October 31, Cresap heard three shots from the eastern side of the river, which was the usual call for his ferry. On crossing the river with Chance, the servant in question, he met Edward Beddock, Rice Morgan, and "a Negroe man belonging . . . to Edward Cartlidge." Beddock and Morgan both asked to cross the river. After Cresap had rowed them seventy yards from shore, the two men drew guns and yelled, "Damn you, Cresap, turn to shore or you are a dead man." Cresap immediately tried to pull in his oar. Rice Morgan, believing Cresap was preparing to strike his assailants, "knocked him down . . . with his gun, and one or both of them threw . . . Chance over board."[12]

Cresap recovered and tried to subdue his captors with his oar. The long pole proved too unwieldy for the task, so he took to his fists. Morgan managed to get the better of Cresap. Morgan and Beddock then grabbed Cresap and threw him into the river. Cresap held onto the side of the barge "for the safety of his life" while both men "endeavoured to force [him] to quit" his grip and vowed to murder him. As both sides struggled, the current carried the boat south until Cresap could feel ground under his feet. As soon as he could stand, he let go of the boat and worked his way to an island where an Indian rescued him and brought him back to his house. He did not see his boat for three weeks, and when he finally did, "it was much damnified."[13]

After drying off, Cresap sought Andrew Cornish, the sheriff of Lancaster County, to lodge a complaint with Pennsylvania justices of the peace against Cartlidge and his agents, who were duly—if weakly—punished with a fine. Cresap also brought the matter to Samuel Ogle, the Maryland governor, who wrote angry missives to Patrick Gordon about the unjust treatment of the Marylanders. Gordon took the opportunity to point out that by appealing to Pennsylvania officials for justice, Cresap had implied that his home was under Pennsylvania jurisdiction. Thus, the attempt to capture Cresap, even though it failed, had strengthened Pennsylvania's case. The turn of events taught Cresap a valuable lesson in the way the competing legal systems on contested borders could work to bolster or undermine one side or the other. He would not make the same mistake again. Ogle also seemed to recognize the error and decided to appoint Cresap a justice of the peace, thereby extending Maryland's legal jurisdiction to offer protection to its residents in the region. With both sides exerting competing claims to the land, legal confrontations continued, and the ensuing low-level violence defined life on the banks of the Susquehanna.[14]

With Pennsylvanians vowing to fight Marylanders "to . . . the knees in blood" and Marylanders promising to "repel force by force," Gordon soon worried that the situation could escalate into something worse: civil war. He therefore tried to appeal to the goodwill of Maryland's governor, Samuel Ogle, by evoking the one thing they were supposed to share: an interest in advancing the Crown's aims in North America. Gordon wanted them to work together, lest their civil war create an opening for the French to gain ground in the west. Gordon thus argued that Pennsylvania's model of ordered expansion and peaceful relations with Native peoples was the best means to secure broader imperial interests.[15]

He began his plea by outlining the uncertain nature of imperial North American geopolitics and playing upon the fears of a French invasion to unite the colonies, writing that "the French . . . possessed . . . Canada and that vast country they call Louisiana" and thus "enclose all of these British colonies." Gordon worried that unrestrained expansion on the part of British colonies only played into French hands by sending wavering Native groups closer to New France's imperial orbit. Of particular concern were the Shawnees. Gordon received reports suggesting the Shawnees had "given some offence" to the Six Nations Iroquois and had "retired to a branch of the Mississippi called Ohio" away from their enemies (and by default the British sphere of influence). Gordon heard that once in the Ohio region, "some French spies" had convinced the Shawnees to swear allegiance to Canada. Gordon sought to secure the Shawnee alliance by surveying "10 or 15,000 acres of land round the principal town where [the Shawnees] were last seated." The willingness to grant such a sizable tract demonstrated how seriously Pennsylvania officials took the Shawnees' potential to upset the precarious balance of imperial rivalries. Gordon essentially had carved out an area of Indian autonomy and independence as a way to ingratiate Pennsylvania with much-needed allies, while also providing the colony with a buffer against the French, similar to the one Logan had hoped the Scots-Irish would provide if a frontier against Indians formed.[16]

Of course, Gordon also complained to Ogle of "that rude fellow Cresap's behavior." Cresap, Gordon argued, could upset Native American relations in the empire because "those Indians consider us all as subjects of the same great Empire and their resentments against one part will unavoidably be attended with further unhappy consequences to others." Likewise, Gordon concluded that complaints about Cresap's actions should "concern Maryland as well as Pennsylvania, and as the British Interest may be affected by them, undoubtedly every good subject is concerned."[17]

Gordon's call for comity fell on deaf ears. Imperial interests seemed far removed from the banks of the Susquehanna in the 1730s, especially since no one had any imminent fear of invasion. In other words, because no one believed frontiers existed in the region, colonies could pursue their own self-interest rather than worry about a common external enemy like France. Another part of the problem that only exacerbated matters was that Gordon and Ogle were not the usual type of governors. They were executives of proprietary colonies, and they had to worry about their proprietors' interests as much as, if not more than, the often vague and ill-defined interests of the empire.

Meanwhile, half a world away, the three Penn brothers, who had inherited the colony when their mother died, and Charles Calvert, the Fifth Lord

Baltimore, stood around a large map of the region trying to find a permanent settlement for the dispute. The proprietors carried an air of formal
diplomacy throughout the negotiations, as if they were kings of independent nations. They had good reason to act that way. Proprietary colonies
were, in some respects, feudalistic fiefdoms in which the proprietors, as
lords of the manor, could negotiate with other political entities over jurisdictional and diplomatic matters. In theory, proprietors were subordinated
to the monarch, but in an empire in which communication was slow and
control weak, proprietors could operate with only minimal oversight from
the Crown. Left to their own devices, the two proprietary families agreed
to mediate the dispute themselves rather than depend on the whims of the
empire, an entity neither family fully trusted because it had no clear means
of solving these disputes.[18]

Early on in the meeting, the Penns had agreed to let Baltimore commission a map that would serve as the basis for their negotiations. Baltimore
decided on a map drawn by his agents in Maryland, which he sent to an
English engraver to have further refined. Once Baltimore's map had been
done to his liking, the two proprietary families began divvying up the Middle Colonies. The negotiations lasted throughout the spring of 1732. Finally,
on May 10, 1732, the two proprietary groups signed an agreement at Baltimore's palatial home.[19]

There was a problem for Lord Baltimore, however, one that he would
realize only after it was too late. The map used to draw the lines was deeply
flawed. Somehow a "false cape" existed on the map that led Baltimore to
agree to give away far more land than he intended. Evidence suggests that
the Penns knew of the error, but they said nothing. Baltimore's eventual
discovery of the mistake (he would say deceit) after it was too late would
doom the agreement and signal the escalation of hostilities.[20]

But for the moment at least, optimism reigned. Since everyone knew
that the boundaries sketched neatly on the map would be tougher to draw
in reality, in the summer Baltimore and the youngest Penn, Thomas,
departed for the region to oversee the official surveying. Thomas was a
smart choice. Aged thirty-one, he was the youngest of the three Penn sons
born to William's second wife, Hannah. Thomas, like his brothers, had
lived through his father's shaky finances. Indeed, Thomas had felt their
father's financial straits more than the others. As the youngest brother, he
had been apprenticed to a merchant in London because the family expected
he would have to find his own way in the world. When Thomas and his

brothers inherited Pennsylvania, they knew their future depended upon realizing what their father could not: the vast wealth a proprietary colony was supposed to offer its owners. The older brothers thus turned to the youngest brother, whose business acumen left him well-equipped to lead a proprietary colony.[21]

They all recognized that the Agreement of 1732 was an important step toward solvency. Land grants and the collection of quitrents in the contested region had virtually stopped in both colonies because new settlers refused to pay for land with uncertain titles. The slowing of revenues left the Penns in a precarious financial position, but they expected the new agreement would change that. The proprietors realized that the recent expansion of the colonial government—its legal institutions, markets, and order—had made these lands all the more valuable. Richard Penn, for instance, speculated that the quitrents on new grants could be higher than ever before because the "lands . . . are more valuable now, then they were before any form of government was settled, any plantation made, or any markets found."[22]

As Charles Calvert, the Fifth Lord Baltimore, crossed the Atlantic, he harbored similar dreams. While Baltimore was only two years older than Thomas, he had had a far different upbringing, and he had developed a different character. Baltimore grew up the privileged oldest son of a wealthy baron. His father died when he was sixteen, leaving him a fortune, including the rights to Maryland. By 1732, Baltimore had controlled his colony for more than half of his life. As he matured, he became enmeshed in imperial politics by holding various court appointments and several ministerial posts. His personality mixed with his background left him far more brash, assertive, and abrasive. He was prepared, like his grandfather before him, to confront the Penn family if necessary.[23]

Baltimore and the Penns did have one thing in common. The patriarchs of both families secured their charters in spite of their contentious religious beliefs. By the early eighteenth century, their heirs abandoned the faiths of their fathers and joined the Church of England, a move meant to ingratiate them with the Crown. Baltimore's father renounced his Catholic faith and joined the Anglican confession in 1713. The conversion allowed him to regain control over Maryland's government, something the family had lost with the ascension of William and Mary. The Penns, meanwhile, knew that Quakerism created political problems at a time when they could ill afford such hassle, and so they distanced themselves from the meetings. Thomas would make the split complete with his marriage in an Anglican Church in 1751. Unlike Baltimore's move to conformity, Penn's conversion only distanced him from the Quaker governing elite in Pennsylvania, even as it drew him closer to imperial circles. It also allowed him to embrace the military means necessary to defend his colony from a rival.

After arriving in their respective colonies in the fall, the proprietors and their commissioners met to implement the agreement on October 6, 1732, in Newtown, Delaware. The conference began with a bang—Thomas Penn spent over £100 treating the Marylanders to drinking and displays of gunfire—but ended with a thud. For almost a year, commissioners met sporadically to discuss the articles but were never able to agree on the proper boundaries. The diplomatic charade went on until November 1733, when the warring commissions finally agreed to disagree and wrote an official report about their failure. Indeed, once Baltimore saw the land in person, he was sure that the map used in 1732 was not only inaccurate but somehow the work of the Penns to defraud him. Incensed, Baltimore left for England in May 1733, effectively declaring the agreement dead. At the time, James Logan, who had once wondered how two colonies could go to war with one another, concluded "tis now all over . . . the dye is cast and nothing but war remains."[24]

"He Would Defend Him from the Proprietor of Pensilvania"

By the time Baltimore left, he and his agents had designed a new strategy for Maryland to win the disputed land. First, Samuel Ogle had to establish Maryland's firm control over the land west of the Susquehanna by convincing settlers to become loyal tenants of Baltimore. Second, Ogle had to establish Maryland's legal jurisdiction through the appointment of justices of the peace and other offices. Samuel Blunston described these tactics as an effort "to alienate the minds of the inhabitants of this province and draw them from obedience to their party." In England, meanwhile, Baltimore prepared to press his case in court using the loyalty of the settlers, the establishment of legal offices, and the taxes paid to him as evidence supporting the validity of his claim. In short, Baltimore hoped that a functioning legal jurisdiction would equal political possession.[25]

Ogle knew that the implementation of such a plan would require muscle, and he looked to Thomas Cresap to supply it. When Baltimore made

Cresap a justice of the peace sometime in 1732, he expected that Cresap's ardor would serve his purposes well. The terms of Cresap's commission reinforced the often personal relationship between proprietors and their tenants. Proprietors felt duty-bound to protect those loyal to them, and settlers would only give their fealty to a government that proved it could provide security. As one of the Marylanders stated, because Baltimore "had recd money for that land on which . . . Cressop lived, he would defend him from the proprietor of Pensilvania." Cresap soon enlisted others to support him, formed militias to protect Marylanders, and empowered constables, all of which built a bulwark to fend off Pennsylvanian attacks at the same time that it established Maryland's legal jurisdiction.[26]

Cresap also initiated a policy of accepting a variety of people seeking refuge, such as runaway servants from Pennsylvania and new immigrants, and he invited a number of relatives to join him. Moreover, sometime around 1732, a German community, which had settled near the Codorus Creek on the west side of the Susquehanna River before the conflict between the colonies began, decided to pay taxes to Maryland in exchange for formal recognition of their land ownership. The community was considered a large settlement for the time, with at least fifty heads of household. Their allegiance to Baltimore was crucial because he could use their fidelity as evidence that those who already lived in the region recognized his claims as legitimate.[27]

With Baltimore in England and Cresap operating with a commission on the western side of the Susquehanna opposite Lancaster County, Thomas Penn began to orchestrate Pennsylvania's counterstrategy through Samuel Blunston. Penn once again aimed his institutional powers at Cresap, the representative of Maryland's claim to absolute legal authority over the area. By the winter of 1733, Thomas Penn approved an arrest warrant for Cresap, and rumors that were probably true circulated that there was a £50 reward for his capture. Around that time, Andrew Hamilton, the Penns' main legal adviser, met with Blunston and gave him specific orders for arresting Cresap. Although no record exists of his instructions, correspondence between Penn and Blunston suggests that Hamilton advised the latter to arrest Cresap at any point when he was not at his house. This was likely done for technical reasons. Cresap possessed a grant for his home, which meant Pennsylvania would violate Maryland's sovereignty by raiding it. The area outside of Cresap's home, however, was, in Pennsylvania's view, under its jurisdiction.[28]

During the winter of 1734, Blunston plotted with his aides to snatch Cresap. As a pacifist Quaker, Blunston delegated the violence to the Scots-Irish settlers from Donegal and the Scots-Irish sheriff of Lancaster County, a pattern that would come to define this war and the ones that would follow. The situation escalated on January 29, when Lancaster County sheriff Robert Buchanan received intelligence that Cresap planned to leave his yard to help his workmen cut logs for a new home and a ferry. It was the exact legal opening they had sought. Buchanan rounded up a crew and headed across the river. Cresap, having received advance word of the Pennsylvanians' plan, stayed back and sent his wife to the field to watch for the impending attack. The Pennsylvanians, meanwhile, seized eight of Cresap's men for various complaints, carted them off to Blunston's house (which served as Lancaster's jail), and left the rest. Cresap's wife, meanwhile, escaped and raced back to their home to warn Thomas of the assault.[29]

Some of the disappointed Pennsylvanians decided to head to Cresap's home to capture their prize, contravening the instructions of Hamilton. This smaller group arrived at Cresap's at about seven o'clock in the evening. At first, they asked for nighttime lodging, a ploy to get into the house, but Cresap refused and bolted the door. A standoff ensued with both sides shouting threats through cracks in the logs. Eventually, Cresap opened the door to fire a warning shot. The Pennsylvanians seized the opportunity and began to push in the front door. Cresap and his tenants, frightened by the action, released the door and ran into the back room. The Pennsylvanians tumbled into the house. Two Pennsylvanians rushed after Cresap, but Cresap's assistants beat them back while Cresap nailed the inside door shut.[30]

Outside, the Pennsylvanians realized that Cresap's warning shot had hit Knowles Daunt, one of Emerson's servants. Daunt's leg was crushed above the left knee with fragments of bone protruding. The Pennsylvanians, upon realizing the severity of the injury, retreated from the house and asked Cresap's wife for a candle to aid Daunt. She refused, shouting through the walls that "she wold gladly wash her hands in said Daunt's heart's blood." The Pennsylvanians, shocked and confused at the deadly turn, headed back across the river, abandoning the immobilized Daunt. A fellow servant, Michael Dooling, eventually rescued him. Daunt lasted a few days in Lancaster but ultimately succumbed to his injuries. Cresap remained secure on the western side, but Daunt's murder would eventually catch up to him.[31]

Such deadly violence surprised Penn. The thing that concerned him most was that his colonists had operated outside of the law, which he worried could upset his standing if imperial administrators tried to intervene. Up until this point, most of the conflict had occurred through legal channels. This violence, however, resembled war, and he worried that to an impartial judge Pennsylvania could appear the instigator. Because of the bloodshed, Penn, after consulting with Andrew Hamilton, instructed Blunston, who as a justice of the peace presided over the county court, to "calmly" deal with the eight prisoners grabbed in the initial action. Penn, however, did "not mean that they should not be told how much we shal resent any such incroachments and that all persons must expect to be punished who will be guilt[y] of such irregular practices." Blunston appears to have released them on bail. Necessity likely also drove the leniency, since, as he reported at the time, there were "more prisoners then guards."[32]

Cresap, for his part, left for Maryland to report on what happened. When his superiors heard of the skirmish, they decided to launch a counterattack that was meant to assert Maryland's sole control of the western territory. Cresap returned with twenty militiamen in tow, the undersheriff of Baltimore County, and a resupply of "guns . . . swords, cutlasses and clubs." Their aim was to capture the strongest symbols of Pennsylvania's authority on the western side. They hoped that by doing so, they could show the strength of Maryland's government and better establish their legitimacy.[33]

As the band approached the contested region, the group split into two. One group surrounded Pennsylvania loyalist John Hendricks's house while the other blocked the river to stop an escape. After seizing Hendricks, the group then moved on to Joshua Minshall's house, a Quaker loyal to Penn, and took him. They carted the two men to a jail in Annapolis. The arrest warrants for both Minshall and Hendricks rested on depositions that accused them of aiding the assault on Cresap's house and, in the case of Hendricks, stirring up the Indians to attack Marylanders and giving "menacing speeches" to Marylanders that "they should not hold such lands . . . unless they would become tenants to the [proprietor] of Pennsylvania or acknowledge him as their land lord." Hendricks's words, the deposition stated, had created a "great terror" in Marylanders' minds. As the protector of Baltimore's tenants, Ogle arrested them in order to secure his tenants from their "great terror."[34]

The seizure of Penn's tenants escalated the cycle of violence in which both sides were competing to accomplish the same thing: securing absolute legal control of new ground. A key part of what drove the violence was each government's desire to show that they could provide protection for their residents and that the other government lacked the ability to provide the security colonists expected. The wives of the imprisoned Pennsylvania men knew of the proprietor's responsibility to them and they pleaded with Penn directly that "proper care . . . be taken for their husbands defence." Penn understood his responsibility and sent money to the prisoners and their families, as well as securing a strong legal defense for them in court. It was a smart choice. Hendricks and Minshall, stuck in a "stinking louses hole" and surrounded by those they called their "enemys," promised Penn "to stand and maintain" his rights. They refused to sign anything that Maryland could use to strengthen their legal case because they knew Penn upheld his side of the bargain.[35]

Sparks flew throughout 1734 and 1735 as both sides continued to try to bully their rival into submission. The leaders of both sides added regular colonists who were vocal partisans to their list of targets, hoping that intimidation could sway their allegiance and those still caught in the middle. Marylanders seized one of John Emerson's servants stationed in the contested zone, leaving the man's nursing wife "to fend for herself." Emerson tried to retaliate by seizing Cresap, but he failed to find him. Instead, he arrested William Cannon, Cresap's brother-in-law. Ogle responded to Cannon's imprisonment with a proclamation calling for the arrest of Robert Buchanan, the sheriff of Lancaster, and John Emerson. In the winter of 1735, Buchanan and "thirty men several of whom were armed with hangers and pistols" seized seven Germans working on Cresap's plantation; their crime, a captive would later testify, was "for working for the said Cressop on his land."[36]

Cresap, understandably, grew more paranoid. He worried that Pennsylvanians plotted to "kill and destroy" him and "burn" his house. In such a state of constant fear, Cresap was often seen standing in his doorway "armed with pistols in his belt, a Gun in his hand, and Long Sword by his side Like Robinson Crusoe." Other Marylanders lived in fear of arrest, complaining that Samuel Blunston and the Pennsylvanians used trumped-up warrants to arrest "a great many people over the river for some debt and some quarreling." As these patterns of legal intimidation grew stronger, nearly everyone in the region became affected by the conflict; one historian has estimated that over two hundred households took up active arms for one side or the other. As on Pennsylvanian noted, "the people" did "not seem well pleased with this state of war."[37]

"Surveying Lands to the Inhabitants over Sasquehannah Is What Should Not Be an Hour Neglected"

Amid all of these legal entanglements and bloody assaults, Penn realized that he needed a new strategy if he was going to secure victory. He had to maintain the allegiance of Pennsylvanians already in the region, win new converts, and actively assert his claim to the land, all of which meant that to combat Maryland, he would have to appeal to the needs of settlers. He thus began to learn the political art of colonial competition in which colonists' choice mattered more than proprietary dictate.

This competition for settler loyalty was at the heart of the conflict and was the defining feature of this border war. In the 1730s, Penn knew that land was the common demand made by colonists anxious to own a piece of fertile ground. Penn responded by opening up a period of unmitigated growth. In April 1734, Penn told Blunston that "surveying lands to the inhabitants over Sasquehannah is what should not be an hour neglected." Penn wanted these grants to be as legal as possible so they would have strong standing in a court. He thus dispatched a surveyor as "the only sure means of a regular settlem[en]t." As the race between colonies to settle land heated up in the months that followed, formalities such as surveying became easy to overlook. By May 1735, Penn had dispensed more than 150 additional warrants. In one case, Penn gave Blunston "one hundred blank warrants signed and sealed which are designed for any persons that have an inclination to settle over Sasquehannah without regard to the distance westward." Once, the Penns and their subordinates had tried to restrain settlement to honor their treaties with Natives as well as to facilitate an ordered expansion west. Now, colonial competition forced Pennsylvania officials to abandon this long-standing policy. Instead, they encouraged an unrestricted push west.[38]

Penn's actions also revealed the unspoken assumption that undergirded officials' thinking: land not yet purchased would, nonetheless, be part of Pennsylvania. The steps Penn took would protect this future. They would, conversely, sow discord with Indian groups who claimed the territory and looked upon the new settlements as incursions on their lands. Penn, by changing his policy on expansion so dramatically, did what he had to do to defeat his colonial neighbor but, at the same time, encouraged the future formation of the one thing his colony had tried to avoid: frontiers.

The competition between polities also created new economic and political opportunities for would-be settlers. Normally, the proprietor established land prices and terms. In the case of Pennsylvania, a land office with an agent in charge of setting prices granted lands with the proprietary seal. The proprietor also appointed a number of surveyors to mark and value tracts. Although neighboring colonies' prices might ostensibly influence Pennsylvania's land practices, in most cases there was little room for negotiation on the part of the colonist. With such fierce competition for settler allegiance, however, neither colony could dictate costs or the terms of expansion.

Nowhere was this more apparent than in the "shifting" of tenants. The practice of renouncing one proprietor for another—what we might think of as the power of choice—was the greatest threat to proprietary governments. To allow such behavior would undermine the authority of proprietary institutions. Indeed, in a rare moment of unity, both Maryland and Pennsylvania explicitly rejected the practice when settlers tried to do it in the Lower Counties in the 1720s. The competition for the area west of the Susquehanna, however, changed the rules of the game. Settlers could play one proprietor off the other for better terms. In July 1734, for instance, a Maryland commissioner came to the western side of the Susquehanna and promised to lay out lands for settlers—squatters, really—who had not received official grants from Pennsylvania, although these settlers were sympathetic to Penn. Blunston believed the situation was dire: "Either save them to us or let them know they may shift for themselves." Penn agreed and granted them good terms. In the months that followed, Penn embraced other Marylanders who desired to switch their allegiances. When some new arrivals petitioned Penn to "take licence under" him, they explained that they always "incline[d] to be Pennsylvanians," but they had "been imposed on by the Marylanders" when they first settled.[39]

For new arrivals who happened upon the conflict, Old World backgrounds played little to no role in determining their choice of New World political allegiance. Maryland had both German and Scots-Irish supporters, as did Pennsylvania. Among those most loyal to Cresap were Michael Risner and Bernard Woimer, both recent German arrivals. Penn enlisted settlers in the Scots-Irish settlement of Donegal to form militias to support fellow Pennsylvanians who happened to be German. In one case, a Scots-Irish settler loyal to Pennsylvania tried to convince a boyhood friend in the employ of Cresap to renounce his allegiances and join Pennsylvania. In another case, a German man who lived near Cresap rejected Pennsylvania's entreaties to join their colony. For his intransigence, he was beaten and arrested in front of his wife. What these stories suggest is that personal choice, rather than ethnicity, drove political decisions.[40]

Colonists quickly learned that they could use this situation to get what they wanted out of a government. Indeed, the courting of settlers was so personal that many negotiated directly with the proprietor, and their choice often reflected the type of government that appealed to them. Settlers in Donegal showed an inclination toward Pennsylvania because of past treatment, but in a personal meeting with Penn, their representatives made it clear to him that they refused to be "made tenants in the common sense of the word, this being what [they] can never, with any pleasure, think of subjecting again [their] necks unto." They thus understood the proprietary nature of the colony in terms similar to but decidedly different from the manor life they knew in Ireland. They expected Pennsylvania to offer them greater liberty than the place they had left, where they were subject to the caprice of uncaring landlords. Their speech was meant to let Penn know they would pay him for his protection, as they had done for their British landlords, but they expected him to maintain a different type of government in his woods. Penn had so far proven himself willing to do so.[41]

Memories of this rare moment of opportunity persisted long after the dispute had ended. Samuel Smith surely told his story to many people, and there are records of Cresap sharing his side with people well into the early republic. Memories of it cropped up in more official ways that evoked the personal and often flexible relationship between colonists and the proprietor forged in the midst of the conflict. In 1766, for instance, almost thirty years after the close of the Conojocular War, Thomas Penn received a petition from Jacob and Frederick Fleegar in York County, the very area in which many of the expansionary grants were made in 1734. Their father, they claimed, was one of those arrested who spent time in an abhorrent Maryland jail, but, like the other loyal Pennsylvanians, he never bowed to pressure to renounce his Pennsylvania allegiance. He suffered so much at the hands of the Marylanders that he became "sick and remained in a languishing condition a long time" before perishing, perhaps, they implied, the last casualty from this intercolonial battle for the west. The Fleegars now worried that their father's title was not as clear as it could have been. Thirty-two years later, remembering the good service their father had offered Penn and fearing "land jobbers" would use nefarious legal tactics to steal the land he had duly received, they asked Thomas Penn "to grant them rights for their settlements on the same terms as the other sufferers by the Maryland War."[42]

The battle for supporters also opened opportunities for women to enter the political sphere. Many took an active part in the affair and, in so doing, broke out of social norms to further their individual, familial, and communal interests. A number of Pennsylvania women served as emissaries and provided intelligence to Blunston—among them Esther Harris, whose husband, John, owned a ferry on the Susquehanna, was well-connected among both settlers and Indians, and whose home served as a major trading center. Jenny Wright, wife of John Wright, one of the leading Pennsylvanians in the region, played a similar role.[43]

Maryland proved even more welcoming to women's involvement. Mary Emerson used the competition between colonies to challenge the limited legal rights afforded widows and women in Pennsylvania. Her husband, John, had been a loyal supporter of Pennsylvania, having participated in the failed attempts to arrest Cresap. Penn rewarded him for his service with a ferry license on the Susquehanna. When he died, Penn took Emerson's land and his license from his widow and gave them to John Ross, a resident of Donegal who had also served Pennsylvania's interest well. Mary received some remuneration for the improvement on the land, but she wanted to keep the house and the ferry. By May 1736, a frustrated Mary aligned herself with the Marylanders. She now deemed Cresap, her deceased husband's sworn enemy, "the best friend she ha[d] in the world." In 1737, she threatened to "burn to ashes [the] house" that was once hers. At one point, Ross heard that she and Cresap's wife had hatched a plan in which Mary Emerson would distract Ross with a game of cards, allowing Cresap and his forces to seize him. James Steel, a member of Penn's inner circle, expressed dismay "that the laws of the province and the magistrates of Lancaster County" could not "bridle the insolence of a turbulent woman."[44]

Protection of property drove many of the Maryland women to act. Betty Low was among the most active participants for the Maryland side. Pennsylvania had seized and imprisoned some of her family members, including her husband. In their absence, she led a company of the Maryland militia to ensure that her family's claims would not become threatened because of the absence of strong men at home. Her prominence frustrated Blunston, who called her "one of the worst of them." Blunston, unsure of how to handle a woman acting in such a way, sought the proprietor's approval to seize her. In another case, Blunston sold some property he had acquired on the western side of the river when the male lessee of the tract died. The man's widow, children, and father-in-law, however, refused to vacate. Instead, they switched their allegiances and gave "intelligence and succor" to the Marylanders, hoping that "if the Marylanders could get the better they should keep the place."[45]

"Are Mighty Desirous to Live Under This Governmt, and Some of Them Wil Rather Quit Their Possessions Then Return to Their Former Slavery"

Colonists in these contested areas far removed from the Quaker center thus began to form a distinctive type of politics. When colonies competed for land on contested borders, as they often did in these western regions, common folk gained political power by using their pliable loyalties to bend proprietary wills to meet their desires. Officials for both sides understood this political culture. Representatives canvassed the territory, making arguments for their own side and against their rival. Ultimately, it was this power of choice that transformed what by 1736 had become a tense stalemate into what Samuel Smith would describe to Charles Mason in 1765 as an "open war." The escalation came in August 1736, when the German community members long allied with Maryland exercised their power to choose the government they preferred by publicly renouncing their former allegiance to Maryland and declaring their new fidelity to Pennsylvania. Their loss changed Maryland's strategy and emboldened Pennsylvania.[46]

The German settlers, Pennsylvania officials reported, explained their decision by criticizing Maryland's style of government and affirming Pennsylvania's. The German community specifically complained of the "oppression and ill usage we have met with from the government of Maryland, or at least from such persons who have been empowered thereby," as the reason for their turn. Impertinent Maryland officials like Cresap were just one of the reasons they abandoned the colony. They spoke warmly of the "mildness of Pennsylvania's government," which they believed promised them a measure of peace and security that Maryland did not offer. Pennsylvania's government appealed to them because of what it stood for and because of the proprietor's actions toward his settlers. In a statement to Penn, the German settlers noted that under Maryland, they "received a

treatment . . . very different from that which the tenants of your government have generally met with." In a contest between two colonies vying for
settler allegiance, these German settlers used the opportunity to select the
model of governance they preferred, and, in this case, it was Pennsylvania's
stable and prosperous government that they wanted. They came to see Penn
much as the Donegal colonists had, as a lord who provided his tenants
more liberty than they were used to in Europe, while they saw Maryland as
an Old World government in which a powerful and arbitrary lordlike figure
such as Cresap could prove too mettlesome in their lives.[47]

The shift of the German community altered the course of the conflict.
The Germans, as the first and largest group of settlers on the western side
of the Susquehanna, held significant legal precedent. Maryland planned to
use their allegiance as evidence of that colony's long-standing settlement of
the region. Now Pennsylvania could argue that they had the upper hand.
The Germans' defection so weakened Maryland's position that it threatened
to destroy the colony's entire strategy.

Word of the Germans' disaffection caused Ogle to undertake a new
campaign to persuade the group to reconsider their decision. Ogle's
adopted tactic was a show of force meant to coerce the Germans back into
Maryland's fold. On September 5, over three hundred militiamen from Baltimore County, including the county's sheriff, traveled to the western side
of the river. There, they joined Cresap's militia, which had grown into a
professional force in which members were reportedly paid £12 per year for
service. The large Maryland contingent forced many of the Germans to flee
their homes and take refuge across the river with John Wright. The Maryland militia mustered for nine days and traveled throughout the settlement
with "beat of drum and sound of trumpet to awe those poor people into
complyance." They hoped their show of force would compel insecure colonists to return to the Maryland fold by proving that Pennsylvania was incapable of marshaling a sufficient defense.[48]

Pennsylvanians on the eastern side of the river watched these maneuvers
with alarm. Soon, a rumor spread among those loyal to Pennsylvania that
Maryland's three-hundred-man militia planned to assault Lancaster. In
response, Blunston organized one hundred Pennsylvanians from Donegal
and Lancaster to launch a preemptive strike. Blunston deputized the sheriff
as their commander and provided the men with arms. The troops then
boarded two barges and prepared to do battle. The Marylanders, who were
eating dinner in an open field, fled at the sight of the Pennsylvania flotilla.

Only Cresap stood his ground, blunderbuss in hand, ready to take on his adversaries. Eventually, reason interceded, and he too fled.[49]

The Marylanders regrouped, and in the days that followed, they made numerous unsuccessful attempts to win back the Germans. Once it became clear that the menacing militia was unable to awe the Germans into compliance, the Marylanders adopted more coercive methods—raiding German homes and seizing "Linnen Cloth for Public Dues." Since taxes were a measure of one's allegiance, Maryland militiamen took the linen so they could claim these settlers were still Marylanders. The seizure of goods forced Michael Tanner, one of the German leaders, to meet with the Maryland sheriff, where he explained that the Germans had "reason" to "revolt" because of "Cresaps ill behaviour."[50]

Rebuffed by the Germans, the sheriff of Baltimore County began to play the politics of competition. He expressed sympathy for the Germans and "spoke him very fair and endevoured to perswade him [Tanner]" to discuss matters with Maryland's governor. He also vowed to treat the Germans better in the future and was even willing to defer their taxes "until they were better able to pay." As an added gesture of goodwill, the sheriff returned all the seized goods. If the Germans refused to acknowledge Maryland's authority, however, the sheriff promised to come back "with a much greater force," eject them, and repopulate their land with "lusty young men." The Marylanders' past behavior, however, was too much for most German settlers to forgive. They had become so aligned with Penn and the idea of Pennsylvania that Blunston reported that most "are mighty desirous to live under this governmt, and some of them wil rather quit their possessions then return to their former slavery."[51]

When colonists, many of whom were tenants in Ireland or German principalities, made such a choice, they understood the significance of their political act. Whether it was the Germans who decided that they would rather give up their land than become a Marylander or the Scots-Irish settlers in Donegal who negotiated specific terms with Penn, these colonists were strengthening the hand of this distinctive type of New World lord. But they were also doing something more. In their direct negotiations with Penn, they also articulated an idea of Pennsylvania's government and what it meant. They were negotiating a contract upon which the government rested. This process also helped establish a political allegiance that created a sense of what it meant to be a Pennsylvanian. In this case, Pennsylvania was known for its mildness and opportunity. The border war thus created distinctions between colonies that hardened identities while also helping draw political boundaries.[52]

The stridency of the German settlers' loyalty to Pennsylvania forced Marylanders to recalibrate their strategy for victory. Having lost the battle on the ground for loyalties, they shifted their focus from winning colonists to Native American groups, who could provide Maryland with strong footing if an imperial body was to intercede in the dispute. In particular, Ogle focused on securing a title from the Six Nations Iroquois. British officials had a high opinion of the Iroquois's status in North America, with many in London seeing in this Native group a rising empire much like Great Britain. To the imperial administrators in Great Britain, the Iroquois's domains, which they claimed stretched from Canada to Virginia and included many subservient tribes, matched the scale of their own worldview and strategic thinking. Ogle, aware of the Iroquois claims to the Susquehanna, hoped an alliance with this group could help bolster Maryland's claim in the imperial system. Ogle thus approached the Six Nations Iroquois in 1736, hoping to formally purchase the western side of the Susquehanna from them.[53]

The Maryland entreaties forced Thomas Penn to reconsider his colony's own diplomatic position toward its Indian neighbors. Official Pennsylvania policy had long recognized the Conestogas' right to the land and rejected the Iroquois's claims. Just a few years earlier, colonial officials had even gone so far as to forcefully remove Pennsylvania squatters to uphold their promises to the Conestogas. If Maryland received a deed from the Six Nations and Pennsylvania held one from the Conestogas, however, the Crown would likely have to determine which Indian group was the rightful owner. In such a situation, Pennsylvania officials worried that imperial officials would choose the Iroquoian claim over that of the Conestogas.[54]

In the face of such uncertainty, Thomas Penn decided to do what was necessary to bolster his position in a British court of law. In October 1736, he held a treaty with the Iroquois in which he recognized the Six Nations' claims to supremacy over other Native groups in Pennsylvania in exchange for the conveyance of the land west of the Susquehanna to Pennsylvania. The treaty marked yet another major shift in Pennsylvania's policy. William Penn had, as historian Francis Jennings pointed out, previously "ignored" the Iroquois assertions of dominance over the Conestogas. Jennings also showed that Iroquois claims were largely "fabricated," but in 1736, Pennsylvania, in his words, "gang[ed] up with the Six Nations" to make it "real." From this point forward, Pennsylvania policy recognized the Conestogas as a friendly people lacking any real political power. Similarly, the Shawnees, earlier offered a tract of land by Pennsylvania in the western region to secure their affections, were not consulted in 1736, and the treaty made their land claims and political status subordinate to the Iroquois. Viewed in light of the ongoing Maryland conflict and the contest for power among Native American groups, the treaty was mutually beneficial for Pennsylvania and the Six Nations, as each gained an edge over its respective competitors. For those excluded, the shift in Pennsylvania policy created grievances that would fester.[55]

Such compromises between idealism and pragmatism anticipated the Walking Purchase of 1737, a land grab that historians have interpreted as signaling a larger, more general change in proprietary views toward western expansion, Indian relations, and land acquisition. The Walking Purchase involved the acquisition of a massive tract of land in northern Bucks County along the Delaware River. The means by which this occurred are infamous. The treaty's vague language said that Pennsylvania could acquire land that a man could walk in one day. Betraying the intent of this statement, Pennsylvania dispatched three of their heartiest men to run for a full twenty-four hours and, in the process, seize far more land than the Delawares had intended.

Although the site of the transaction was far from the battlefields of the Susquehanna, viewed alongside the 1736 Lancaster Treaty and the ongoing and costly conflict with Maryland, the Walking Purchase appears less anomalous. Instead, the decisions made by Penn in the western conflict precipitated the change in Pennsylvania's expansionist policies that historians often see signified in the Walking Purchase. Indeed, one of the underappreciated reasons for the Walking Purchase was Pennsylvania's concern that Dutch settlers from New York had begun to stake a claim over the land acquired by it. After having waged a costly five-year campaign against Maryland, proprietary officials took the actions necessary to head off a potential conflict with New York. Little did they know that the Walking Purchase, much like the western grants made by Blunston and the recognition of the Iroquoian claims to land, would influence the decision of Indian groups to side with the French and launch raids on the settlements in the 1750s, creating the frontiers Pennsylvania had previously and proudly avoided.[56]

In fact, there is a direct, though never before noted, connection between the Conojocular War and the Walking Purchase. Solomon Jennings, one of

the Pennsylvanians who participated in the twenty-four-hour run associated with the Walking Purchase, had previously served Pennsylvania's cause
during the Conojocular War, providing further evidence of just how small
and personal politics could be in the early stages of this proprietary colony's
development. Jennings was apparently a remarkable human specimen,
capable of running great distances and fighting off aggressive Marylanders.
When Logan sent him to the Susquehanna in 1735, he introduced him to
Blunston by writing his "courage and conduct are to be relied on, and on
that consideration he has been sent for from a great distance nor will he I
believe disappoint any reasonable expectations that have been conceived of
him." Logan's recommendation proved true. Jennings's scattered appearances throughout the record confirm that he was a loyal enforcer while
stationed on the Susquehanna. After he was dispatched from the scene,
Blunston longed for "such a man as Solomon Jennings [who] would do
wel if he was here." Jennings's experience typified the government's micro-
management of the combat and their muscular use of men to secure borders and provide protection to their loyal members.[57]

"Damn It, Aston, This Is One of
the Prettyest Towns in Maryland"

Backed by settler allegiance and possessing a title from the Six Nations,
Pennsylvania took decisive action to rid the region of Cresap and his fol-
lowers in late 1736. On November 25, Lancaster County sheriff Samuel
Smith led nearly forty people, mostly Scots-Irish from Donegal, to Cresap's
house. They came armed with a warrant to arrest Cresap for the murder of
Knowles Daunt (the Pennsylvanian killed in a raid two years before) and
carried rum and other victuals to sustain them through a prolonged siege.
Stationed outside the house, the two sides offered a few volleys of shot, but
they had little effect. Then, Cresap's very pregnant wife went into labor.
Suddenly, amid the chaos, the house erupted in flames. At the behest of his
wife and children, Cresap and his men fled. The Pennsylvanians fired at the
fleeing flock. Cresap was hit repeatedly. Although none of Cresap's injuries
proved fatal, one of his men received a mortal wound. The Pennsylvanians
rounded up as many of the surviving Marylanders as they could and sent
them to the jail in Lancaster.[58]

Cresap, on the other hand, found himself carted to a Philadelphia jail because Blunston feared the Lancaster jail was too weak to hold him. As the imprisoned Cresap approached the Pennsylvania capital, throngs of Philadelphians crowded into the streets to catch a glimpse of their war prize. They hurled taunts at Cresap as he passed. Cresap, bound and chained, refused to be cowed. He turned to his jailer, George Aston, and shouted "Damn it, Aston, this is one of the prettyest towns in Maryland."[59]

A few weeks later, as Cresap sat in chains, Thomas Penn sent Samuel Blunston a shipment of fresh oysters, a reward for a job well done. Blunston had a small celebration with his lieutenants. He had removed Cresap, and he felt hopeful that the troubles were now in the past. He thanked Penn for the oysters and shared with him his exuberance, writing that "with united voice we return thanks for the oysters etc and find that a chearful glass properly taken warms the blood and lessans any apprehensions. . . . I hope the same [measures] will have the like good effect on you if occasion be and that by this time the burning a log cabbin in which a man had no rightful possession is not so dreadful as it first appeared."[60]

Blunston's respite proved short-lived. His spies on the west side of the river reported that Marylanders still occupied seven plantations and had every intention of staying. Some Marylanders constructed a new fort to replace Cresap's house, while others built a redoubt to protect against an assault from Pennsylvania. Worse, on Christmas Eve, Marylander Charles Higgenbotham arrived at the Low homestead with reinforcements and a captain's commission to replace Cresap. Higgenbotham came armed with cash, too, and lots of it, which he planned to use to convince people of Maryland's dedication to the area. Blunston, aware that he had to strengthen his operations in the face of Maryland's persistence, sent a group of men to protect the all-important German contingent while he prepared for more battle, including securing a cannon.[61]

Away from the battleground, meanwhile, the conflagration at Cresap's house had forced the two colonial governments to make conciliatory gestures. James Logan, in a letter to prominent Marylanders, explained that Pennsylvania "never would encourage" such action "but the case was extremely singular" because "a most inhuman scheme was laid in Maryland . . . to throw out of their dwellings . . . about three score innocent familys," meaning the Germans. Pennsylvania was simply acting to protect their colonists, Logan implied, nothing more. Meanwhile, both sides evoked their shared loyalty to the Crown and their interests in the preservation of the empire as a reason to find "amity between the two governments."[62]

The pacifying rhetoric never made its way to those living within the war zone. Instead, the conflict between these two proprietary governments seemed like a matter of life and death for men like Blunston, and whatever inkling of bonds of British subjecthood that may have once connected these neighbors had vanished. Instead, talk of civil war proliferated. Blunston heard that a band of those loyal to Cresap had formed in Chester County. Blunston, the Quaker who now found himself in command of a professional army, feared that this military body might foment an internal rebellion, recalling that "Rome fell by her own legions and those who now are our defence by an unhappy turn of affairs of indiscreet management may endanger the whole government."[63]

Such constant anxiety and insecurity led Blunston to give up on waiting for imperial bodies to intercede. Instead of waiting for "the grand affair [to be] settled at home [meaning London]," he offered his own solution that seems prescient, given the procedures that would arise in the wake of the American Revolution. Blunston wanted the "the governours of neighbouring provinces" to act as neutral intermediaries between the two warring colonies and "prepos[e] an accommodation." Maryland loyalists offered an alternative scenario, also based on the involvement of other British colonies. Instead of the neighboring provinces adjudicating the dispute, Higgenbotham spread news that Virginia had allied with Maryland and "a large number of forces" were coming to join the Marylanders to wage war. That Pennsylvanians took Higgenbotham's claims seriously suggests just how undefined the institutions of the empire were for those living on the margins.[64]

Violence continued, of course, though it now turned into an all-out conflict with no regard for the law. External constraints were no longer put on local leaders by their distant superiors. Likewise, there were no arrest warrants that served as façades for offensive actions. Almost every night the Marylanders came across "in cannoes" to harass the Pennsylvanians. Blunston made sure "a watch" was kept nightly because those on the eastern side were, he said, "always in danger." John Ross and John Wright spent their nights at Blunston's house, believed to be the most secure. Blunston, for his part, did not "dare . . . stir from home." Once, when Logan's imperial concerns still guided actions, raids with warrants had been the pretext for such maneuvers and such harassment always occurred on the contested western side of the river. Now, both sides regularly crossed the river without any cause, armed and ready to seize rivals under no legal guise.[65]

The Germans who stayed loyal to Pennsylvania were the main targets of this ongoing strife. On December 28, 1736, four days after Higgenbotham's arrival, the wives of the Marylanders imprisoned in Lancaster heard about the death of one of the Pennsylvanian's children. They alerted Higgenbotham, who saw an opportunity to reassert Maryland's commitment. The crew of loyal Pennsylvanians who went to dig the grave brought others to keep "watch while others worked," but even with the watch, "Higenbotham and his company . . . surprised and took them."[66]

Penn, aware of his duty to protect his tenants, took pains to aid the newly imprisoned and their families, knowing that this was the means by which the colonial government forged connections with its members in areas of newest settlement. As Penn noted in a particularly revealing private letter to Blunston, "what advantage the attaining of the Dutch Inhabitants over Sasquehannah is to the private Interest of our Family they have been accepted again as Inhabitants of this Government consequently as our Tenants and undoubtedly the government is concerned in honour to protect them as far as it is possible and tho the Expence is an[d] will undoubtedly be very great I shal provide for all Expences which may arise on such a defence of our Inhabitants as may be judged safe and proper."[67] Penn provided comforts for the imprisoned German men. Phillip Syng, for instance, traveled to Annapolis and brought rum, spoons, candles, and combs, among other items to the prisoners. Later, Caspar Wistar made a similar trip. In doing so, Penn sought to assure these settlers that he was committed to providing the benevolent protection proprietors pledged to their tenants.[68]

Penn upheld his proprietary duties for another reason. He knew that his actions would show imperial officials who might settle the dispute that he considered the Germans his tenants and that these settlers considered Penn the rightful proprietor of the land. Penn made this rationale for supporting the Germans explicit in a letter to his attorney in London. He wrote that had he not recognized the German settlers, "it would have amounted to an acknowledgement that we did not believe they were within our province and consequently the place where I now write [Philadelphia] is within the Bounds of Maryland." Indeed, an awareness of the larger imperial structure pervaded the strategies adopted by many of the political leaders in Pennsylvania. James Logan, for instance, reminded a local leader to "always remember that this is no war between declared enemies but arises from the abuses of subjects agst subjects all under the same head and who are all equally answerable to the same superior authority." Colonists who lived within this contested zone, however, felt little if any imperial presence. For them, an imperial system—this "superior authority" of which they should always be aware—was too much of an abstraction. Instead, their lives descended into near anarchy as Pennsylvanians and Marylanders launched a series of daring raids and counterraids in which no law seemed to exist.[69]

"That All Prisoners . . . Be Forthwith Released"

Eventually, imperial authorities did intervene and put an end to open hostilities. While the situation remained volatile on the banks of the Susquehanna throughout 1737, news of the raid on Cresap's home in December 1736 worked its way through elite circles in London. Once administrators learned of the magnitude of the violence, they finally began to act. King George II, after hearing of the battle, delivered a series of edicts declaring a moratorium on all warlike actions. He required "that all Prisoners . . . be forthwith released," that each colony recognized the rights of settlers in the contested region, and that each proprietor halt all violence. It was, in effect, a return to the pre-1732 status quo, though most people considered it a victory for Baltimore because it acknowledged that he might have a right to the land.[70]

The Crown backpedaled in 1738 after receiving a formal complaint by Penn. The new decree formalized a border for Pennsylvania much further south than Baltimore believed it should be. The Crown considered the line temporary, however, and forced the case to proceed in the Court of Chancery, allowing the British legal system to determine where the official boundaries between the colonies fell. The case began in 1750 and did not officially conclude until 1760. The court decided in Penn's favor and asked that surveyors draw a formal boundary line between the two colonies. Charles Mason and Jeremiah Dixon arrived in 1763 to draw the line that now bears their surnames.

The Conojocular War may have ended easily with a simple edict from the Crown and, anticlimactically, with a drawn-out legal case in London, but this conclusion should not obscure its significance. Indeed, the process of constructing colonial borders and establishing a colonial government in the British Empire reconfigured the geopolitical landscape of the empire.

For six years, the governments of Pennsylvania and Maryland encouraged near constant strife. Although Pennsylvania tried to avoid a conflict, once it began, officials adopted new expansionist policies in order to compete against their rival. In the process, they expanded the British Empire's formal domains and profoundly altered the way colonial and imperial officials imagined the region and its peoples.[71]

Indeed, the expansionist legacy of the war left an indelible mark on the landscape in the decades that followed. Colonists who were granted lands in the midst of the conflict began laying out their tracts, while displaced Natives grew frustrated. Emboldened by their victory, Pennsylvania officials tried to allay Native concerns by exerting greater state power over colonists in these areas, much as they had after the 1728 crisis. In 1750, Pennsylvania created Cumberland County to oversee western expansion and to provide a means to rein in illegal squatters, much as it had for Lancaster County. Almost as soon as the county was formed, proprietary commissioners and a newly appointed justice of the peace tried to burn down all illegal homes. They razed dozens of homes, and they often made sure Indians witnessed their acts, hoping that the destruction would reassure them that the colony intended to return to the earlier policies that had rested on ordered expansion negotiated with Native approval.[72]

Still, such firm assertions of government authority could only go so far where the vestiges of colonial competition persisted. Two large settlements escaped the commission's torch. Little Cove and Great Cove were located in a fertile valley in the Allegheny Mountains near the Pennsylvania-Maryland boundary. As the commissioners reported, the colony had been aware of these settlements since at least 1741, and there is some evidence that they dated to the grants from the 1730s. The governor, however, "did not think it proper to take any other notice" of them because "the two governments were not then on very good terms." The commissioners were also aware that Maryland officials were traveling through Little Cove and Great Cove trying to convince the inhabitants to swear allegiance to Maryland and possibly reignite the boundary dispute in these western areas. Confronted by its rival again, the Pennsylvania government allowed the settlements to continue. Meanwhile, Native groups displaced by the politics of the Conojocular War continued to complain about what they saw as illegal settlements festering in their territory.[73]

And just as Patrick Gordon had warned, the war between British colonies strengthened French ties to the Native groups who were upset with the new settlements and with Pennsylvania's altered stance toward its closest Native neighbors. In time, as the effects of the Conojocular War lingered, Pennsylvania officials discovered that their actions caused frontiers to form once again on the colony's geopolitical landscape as imperial rivalries over the region grew hotter in the 1740s. This new frontier crisis would fracture the government and upend the colony.

CHAPTER 5

Becoming a Frontier Country

As colonial settlement pushed farther west throughout the 1740s, more colonists feared that the western regions of the Middle Colonies were becoming frontier zones as their communities abutted a growing French presence in the Ohio River Valley. Beginning in the 1740s, the French staked a claim to the Ohio River by laying down plaques meant to establish their sovereignty and erecting forts in areas of what is today western Pennsylvania. The situation heated up in the 1750s when Great Britain decided to assert their rights to this same land. The rivalry finally turned violent in 1754, when a young Virginian named George Washington went out to confront these French forces and clashed with them at the Battles of Jumonville Glen and Great Meadows. The concatenation of events in the west created the cause for a war that everyone knew was coming. Known in European history as the Seven Years' War, which officially began in 1756 and ended in 1763, its opening salvos around the three rivers in the Ohio Valley in 1754 began the American phase of the war, also known as the French and Indian War, a misnomer that served to distinguish the American theater from those in Europe, West Africa, and elsewhere.

Though neither Britain nor France officially declared war until 1756, open warfare engulfed the Middle Colonies after 1754. That the Ohio was ground zero for this global conflict came as no surprise. The territory held strategic importance of immense proportions. Control of the Ohio River provided access to the Mississippi. It also meant, in all likelihood, greater trade with Native groups in the interior. The British also knew that if France controlled the interior, their North American colonies would be confined to the coast.

The arrival of war transformed Pennsylvania into what one government official described as "a frontier country." Becoming a frontier country was

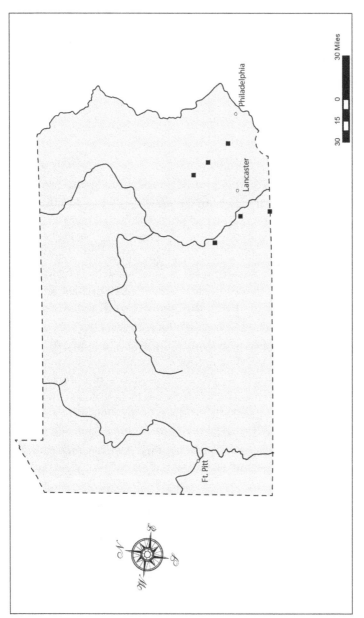

Figure 7. Map showing the number of times a "frontier" was referenced by a colonist or government official in the *Pennsylvania Archives* before the Seven Years' War. Note the virtual absence of the word, signifying that few government officials envisioned frontiers existing on Pennsylvania's geopolitical landscape.

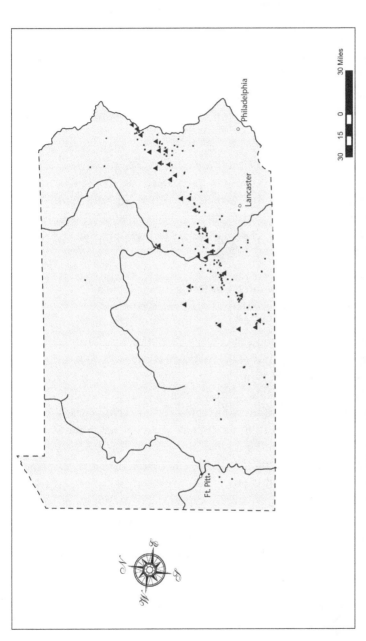

Figure 8. Map that plots the use of "frontier" or "frontiers" to describe areas of Pennsylvania during the Seven Years' War, 1754–1758. The creation of forts paralleled the development of frontiers, and their placement in areas described as frontiers was the manifestation of the government's policy that it should form a defensive position against an invasion. The explosion in the use of the word by both colonists and government officials, and the subsequent development of policies meant to respond to the demands of "frontier people," demonstrate the transformation of Pennsylvania into a "frontier country." Sources: *Pennsylvania Archives* and *Minutes of the Provincial Council*.

an experience that meant different things to different people. For officials and administrators, frontiers were abstract geopolitical zones that they needed to manage during war but that could disappear with peace. For colonists who lived in these regions, becoming a frontier was a deeply personal process through which these civilians turned into combatants in a ferocious war. They became, in their own words, a "frontier people." For Indian leaders, frontiers were contingent zones that they could create through war and that they could erase through peace, much as their colonial counterparts envisioned. But Indian warriors, the young men Indian leaders tasked with invading Pennsylvania and creating frontiers, knew frontiers on a personal level similarly to their targets, regular colonists living in colonial communities. The various perceptions of frontiers shaped each of these groups' behavior during the war. Their experiences with frontiers would linger in the years that followed the terms of peace in 1758.

"The British Colonies, Bordering on the French, Are Properly Frontiers of the British Empire"

Frontiers appeared as a geopolitical concern for officials on June 24, 1744, when Governor George Thomas of Pennsylvania convened a large treaty of Indians and colonial executives in Lancaster. Once the site of war between colonies, it had transformed into neutral ground intended to bring people together. In the weeks and months that preceded the conference, the Six Nations Iroquois had sent word to the colonial governments in the Middle Colonies that the Covenant Chain—the diplomatic alliance between the Iroquois and the British Empire—appeared so brittle that it was on the verge of breaking. They asked Pennsylvania, the colony with the best relations with Indians, to help mediate this dispute. The possibility of losing these Native allies in the midst of King George's War (1744–1748) so alarmed the governors of Pennsylvania, Maryland, and Virginia that they put aside their differences and organized a treaty conference to repair the damage to the chain.[1]

Thomas was asked to open the conference. The stakes were high for everyone, but Thomas surely felt the pressure more than most. He, unlike Gordon before him, entered into this predicament with some training. Gordon had died in 1736, having ceded most of his responsibilities to Thomas Penn while he was present in the colony. Penn appointed Thomas, a planter from Antigua, as his deputy in 1737. While Penn remained in the colony until 1741, Thomas was able to find his footing. At first, Thomas showed a cocksure attitude toward the Assembly, especially when it came to funding a militia, something he believed necessary for the safety of the colony. The Assembly, however, proved unwilling. Rebuffed, he retreated from his demands and instead focused on other ways to accomplish his goals, primarily through diplomacy and the creation of extralegal, voluntary militias similar to those Gordon established in 1728. In 1744, as war seemed imminent, Thomas knew that peace with Indians was very much in his political interest.[2]

"These Indians by their situation," Thomas declared, "are a frontier" to the British Empire, and "if friends, are capable of defending their [colonial] settlements; if enemies, of making cruel ravages upon them; if neuters, they may deny the French a passage through their country." For these reasons, Thomas concluded that "peace and friendship [must be] established between [Virginia and Maryland] and the Indians of the Six Nations." He advised them to follow the model of peace through trade that Pennsylvania adopted, something he noted "will not put you to so much expence . . . as the carrying on a war against them."[3]

By using "frontier" to describe the Iroquois, Thomas wanted to convey to his peers a specific understanding of the geopolitical landscape of the empire. As allies, the Six Nations and other peoples would serve as a barrier to a French invasion: they would be, as the 1776 dictionary definition states, the people "the enemy finds in the front when they are about to enter." But if the Six Nations ceased to be allies, British frontiers would contract, and British rather than Indian settlements would face the "cruel ravages" of a French (and allied Indian) onslaught. Rather than have the empire defend the frontiers, Thomas saw the Iroquois as the most expedient means to protect the colonies from invasion, much as Logan had viewed the Scots-Irish in the 1720s.[4]

Thomas, driven by a conviction that the Iroquois as a frontier were essential to Great Britain's grand strategy in North America, took his analysis a step further. The Iroquois, whose claim of dominion stretched from Canada to Carolina, played such an important role as "a frontier" against the French that he warned Maryland and Virginian officials against waging war on the Iroquois, not because the colonies would lose but because a victory over the Iroquois would only *weaken* Britain's imperial interests by making colonial settlements the new frontiers. "Every advantage you gain over them in war," he cautioned, "will be a weakening of the barrier of those colonies, and consequently will be in effect victories over yourselves and your fellow subjects."[5]

Thomas's integrative sentiments represented a growing consensus among executives in the colonies whose task was to manage their "frontiers." As the expanding British colonies sped toward war with their French rival, officials recognized that this war was likely going to be larger than any previous one, and its outcome was likely going to determine which imperial force controlled North America. The Iroquois as British allies—or even as determined neutrals—could prove crucial to Britain's war strategy because of the layer of protection they provided the colonies. The Iroquois's geographic expanse, in particular, provided British interests with protection that no other Indian nation seemed to match. Indeed, New York's governor expressed an opinion nearly identical to Thomas's in the wake of a 1742 skirmish between Virginians and Iroquois warriors. In a stern letter to Virginia's governor William Gooch, he advised that "we are to consider [the Iroquois] as they are or may be usefull or prejudicial to us, and if you look upon them in that light, they will appear to be the best barrier, against Canada, to all the Provinces, wherefore I think we ought to preserve their friendship by all means we can. If we lose them and the French gain them what will become of all the provinces is but too obvious to every one." Failure to secure Indians as a frontier for the British, as Gooch implied, could doom the colonies.[6]

This understanding of the geopolitical landscape found adherents among the Iroquois as well. Canassatego, an Iroquois diplomat, described his nation as "a frontier country between you and your enemy" in a 1749 meeting with Pennsylvania officials in Philadelphia. Of course, we cannot know for sure that Canassatego used the word *frontier* in his speech. It was likely mediated by an interpreter, as was usual in such meetings. Nonetheless, with all of this discussion of Iroquoia as a frontier, certainly Canassatego understood his nation's importance to the British. In any event, all this commonality of language shows that an important circle of individuals who helped formulate colonial, Iroquoian, and imperial strategy shared an understanding of the empire's frontiers and of Indians', especially the Six Nations', place on this landscape. British and Indian officials alike used *frontier* to describe zones of potential invasion as they planned for a potential conflict against the French. Officials in the Middle Colonies very much wanted Indians rather than their own people to serve as a frontier.[7]

The language of frontiers also helps reveal the subtleties of British strategists' thinking. When British officials spoke of colonial frontiers, they described them in relation to a French enemy, and their tactics focused on how best to defend against a possible French invasion. Indians, in these imperial administrators' thinking, were not their rivals or enemies. The Penn brothers made this view explicit in a petition they sent to the king asking for his support in establishing "a settlement at the back part of the said province . . . to make, in time, a frontier against the French as also to carry on trade with the Indians." The distinction between a "frontier against the French" and a place to "carry on trade with the Indians" was not loose language. Anyone writing to the king considered his or her words very carefully, and this official correspondence showed that *frontier* carried a very specific meaning that, when analyzed by historians, can reveal how historical actors imagined their geopolitical terrain. The Penns, like many others tasked with managing North America's frontiers, saw the French, not Indians, as their primary threat. Indeed, the Penns wanted to trade with Indians to strengthen their diplomatic ties with them and hedge against French maneuvering. *Frontier*, as understood by people at the time, can thus elucidate the way policy makers imagined North America and the people who inhabited it.[8]

The coalescing of this view in the colonial halls of power strengthened the diplomatic power of all Indian groups who lived between British settlements and French claims, not just the Six Nations. Days after the Lancaster Treaty concluded, Thomas met with his council to analyze the colony's own frontiers, which they treated as distinct from imperial frontiers. They realized that Pennsylvania possessed an unusually large area of potential invasion. Moreover, numerous Indian groups other than the Iroquois lived in this zone. While the size and strength of the Six Nations' Iroquois suited the interests of imperial frontiers, Thomas recognized that the colony's frontiers required him to cultivate alliances with other Native groups specific to his colony so he could provide the same protection for Pennsylvania that the Covenant Chain did for the empire's frontiers more generally.[9]

The council singled out the Shawnees in particular because they "lie upon one part of our frontiers." Realizing that the Shawnees' position on the "frontiers" of Pennsylvania meant that they could either provide protection from or support to a French invasion, Thomas "wish[ed] any method could be fallen upon to secure them effectually to the British interest." Years earlier, in the wake of the 1728 crisis, Governor Gordon tried to accomplish the same thing by offering them their own tract of land. Now, with another frontier crisis brewing, the Shawnees once again became a prize in the eyes of Pennsylvania's grand strategists. A strong alliance with them could provide the colony with a much-needed buffer zone.[10]

King George's War, however, never directly affected western Pennsylvania. The fears of a western invasion still remained, though, and only grew stronger as their French rivals took a more assertive—and to British eyes, ominous—position in the west in the early 1750s. Many strategists worried that the French occupied a position from which to launch a devastating assault on the British that could push them back across the Atlantic, or at a minimum hem them close to the seaboard, destroying their dreams of an expansive empire and starving them of the land riches they had imagined.[11]

As tensions between France and Great Britain rivals in North America grew more acute, many leading colonists began to share the imperial perspective on North America's frontiers that their governing officials and counterparts in Great Britain held. Rather than treat each colony as a separate entity, they believed that Great Britain's nearly contiguous frontiers from northern New England to the Carolinas called for a more centralized approach to North American defenses and indeed to colonial governance. In fact, some faulted the contentious character of British colonies as a weakness that only played into France's hands. A passage from the 1754 *Pennsylvania Gazette*, likely authored by Benjamin Franklin, captures the concern about intercolonial combativeness that spurred a move to consolidation: "The confidence of the French in this undertaking seems well grounded on the present disunited state of the British Colonies, and the extreme difficulty of bringing so many different governments and assemblies to agree to any speedy and effectual measures for our common defence and security; while our enemies have the very great advantage of being under one direction, with one council, and one purse."[12]

Franklin's call for union almost came to fruition because of the continued deterioration of the British alliance with the ever important Iroquois. At about the same time Franklin was worrying about the strengths of a united French colony and the flaws of the autonomous British colonies, Hendrick, an Iroquois leader, saw an opportunity to capitalize on the situation. He declared the Covenant Chain, an alliance first forged in 1670s with New York, broken. The news sent shock through the colonies. It would, in effect, bring about the situation that Thomas warned against in 1744. It would mean that the colonies, stripped of their Iroquoian buffer, would become frontiers. In the summer of 1754, seven colonies sent large delegations to Albany, near the home of the Mohawk branch of the Six Nations Iroquois, to try to repair the Chain. The delegates succeeded, though the best concession they could get from the Mohawks when it came to military alliances was neutrality.[13]

But there was a second outcome at Albany, one that has a larger place in our collective memory, even though its immediate influence on historical events was negligible. Franklin spearheaded what we now call the Albany Plan of Union, which would have established a continental governing structure for the North American colonies. Franklin's proposal included a legislative body called the Grand Council, which would consist of forty-eight representatives from all of the colonies, except for Delaware and Georgia, apportioned based upon colonial population, and a "President-General" appointed by the Crown to oversee this body, much as a royal governor oversaw colonial assemblies. The legislative body would possess few powers, but the ones that it did have were of vital strategic and imperial importance. The continental legislature rather than the various individual colonial assemblies would manage Indian relations to ensure the common and fair treatment of all allied groups, mediate intercolonial disputes to prevent things like Cresap's War from happening, and provide for a common defense for the increasingly connected and costly frontiers. To accomplish this oversight, the proposed legislature could collect revenue from the colonies to fund operations. In a letter written to William Shirley a few months after the meeting, Franklin recounted the reason he tried to organize such a structure: "The British Colonies, bordering on the French, are properly frontiers of the British Empire; and . . . the frontiers of an Empire are properly defended at the joint expence of the body of people in such empire."[14]

Franklin's visualization of these extensive and contiguous frontiers in 1754 thus drove his attempt at government building. The rationale for greater governmental control over these frontier regions was driven by the same reasons that caused Pennsylvania officials to create Lancaster County after the frontier crisis of 1728. In both cases, the existence of frontiers necessitated a greater assertion of government. The difference was that Franklin's vision was on a scale that matched the circumstance in 1754. The colonies collectively formed "the frontiers of an Empire," as Franklin wrote, and thus needed a government to match that scope. And Franklin was not alone. The representatives at Albany debated Franklin's proposal at length. Ultimately, the Albany Plan received universal approval.[15]

Only when the delegates presented the plan to their legislatures did they learn of the futility of their efforts. Colonial legislatures universally feared that such an organization might threaten their autonomy. Competition—or the worry that this new apparatus might benefit some colonies at the expense of others—and the desire to control expansion proved to be insurmountable problems. British imperial officials, meanwhile, feared that such a colonial institution might subvert imperial policy or pose a threat to British institutions, such as the Board of Trade. It instead fell to individual colonial leaders to manage their own frontiers as war with France erupted. In Pennsylvania, the failure of the colonial union meant that the colonial government had to confront a war that required militarization on a scale previously unknown. Pennsylvanians, for their part, had their homes and personhoods transformed into frontiers against this unprecedented invasion.[16]

"I Am Now a Frontier"

The outlines of the Seven Years' War are less important for our story than other conflicts but deserve a retelling in order to put the experience of Pennsylvanians in the proper context. After George Washington's retreat from the forks of the Ohio River, the region settled into a tense standoff with the French possessing the ground and the British vowing to reclaim it. Great Britain, meanwhile, had been preparing for this war, and they dispatched a force to Virginia almost as soon as they heard of Washington's defeat. In 1755, General Edward Braddock arrived in Virginia with a plan that he hoped would end the war quickly and decisively. His strategy was to march his two thousand men to the Ohio and destroy the French. Trained in European methods of warfare, Braddock was unable to adapt to the realities of North American life and its terrain, and his offensive strike failed miserably in what remains one of the most devastating losses in British history. His defeat only emboldened raids on British settlements and helped push wavering Indian leaders who lived in the contested region into the French fold. The British also suffered a series of other setbacks in New York, losing ground around Lake George and Niagara.[17]

The conflict turned global after formal declarations of war in 1756, and the British used their financial might to fund operations around the globe, including a series of offensive assaults in North America in 1758. In that year, John Forbes was able to secure Fort Pitt. John Bradstreet secured western New York, and Jeffrey Amherst captured Louisburg. In the next year, the British seized Ticonderoga on Lake Champlain in modern-day upstate New York. Finally, in 1760, Amherst captured Montreal, a complete victory that would force France to renounce its claims to North America at the peace treaty ending the war in 1763.[18]

For our purposes, Pennsylvanians formed the frontline for the first two years of a war that had yet to be officially declared, turning Penn's peaceful kingdom into a battle zone that created frontiers throughout the colony. The colony continued to be an active site of warfare until 1758, when John Forbes was able to take control of the Ohio River and establish Fort Pitt. If there was one defining feature of the war in the region, it was the overwhelming Indian on white violence. Such an experience was different from other places in North America. In the northern theater around New York and Canada, the French and British armies fought traditional battles aimed at strategic posts and cities, with Indian allies joining them. But in the Ohio, the French, who were pressed for men, relied on Indians to wage their offensive, and colonial communities filled with civilians became their chief target. Thus, for many colonists in Pennsylvania, this war was an invasive Indian war as much as it was a battle between European sovereigns for control of the interior.[19]

The war proved devastating for civilians who became combatants. The first attacks came shortly after Braddock's defeat. By 1755, the Pennsylvania countryside from its most northeastern extreme in Northampton County to its western edges in Cumberland was ablaze with raids. The ferocity of the raids scarred a once peaceful landscape, leaving behind burned-down homes, fallow fields, and desolate towns. The course of the war began to change in 1756, however, as the colony made a more forceful defense of its territory. Most notably, in 1756, a colonial militia led by John Armstrong gave Pennsylvanians a symbolic victory at Kittanning. There, he was able to surround and kill Captain Jacobs, one of the most feared Indian warriors, in a fiery assault that left many other Indians dead. While some historians have questioned the tactical significance of Jacobs's defeat for the war, it was a morale booster that gave Pennsylvanians renewed hope that they could repel Indians, who until then they seemed incapable of defeating.[20]

Experiencing war firsthand was a transformative experience for a large segment of the colonial population. The total number of those directly affected by this war—those who witnessed the violence, took part in it, or lost a loved one—is hard to fix. While the exact tally of colonists who lived in these regions is hard to ascertain because we have only scattered tax records and those sources usually count only men who owned property, it is likely that at least 33 percent and perhaps as much as 43 percent of the total colonial population lived in this war zone. Moreover, the war itself exacted a heavy toll. Approximately 1 percent of the colonial population was captured, and the per-capita death toll in the colony mirrored that of Pennsylvanians killed in the American Civil War.[21]

Becoming a frontier and the accompanying tangible encounter with war, while widespread, still depended on one's region. Virtually every part of the colony outside the three original counties was at one point considered a frontier, as seen in Figure 8, just as James Logan had planned when he established new western communities in the 1720s. The divergence between those who lived on a frontier at one point during the war and those who had escaped such an experience would further divide the colony after peace as easterners who had not felt this change tried to mend the wounds of war with their former enemies.

For those colonists who lived in fear of invasion, a frontier was more than a geopolitical abstraction that drove policy decisions. It was a personal experience that shaped their actions and beliefs. Time and again, they described the traumatic process of *becoming* a frontier, a clear sign of the specificity and contingency the word conveyed in the eighteenth century. A petition from Northampton County, which sat to the north of Philadelphia and close to the eastern branch of the warring Delawares, provides one of the clearest expressions of the desperation frontier inhabitants felt. Describing the geopolitical situation of Lehigh and Allentown, the petitioners reported that the two towns had "become the frontier [because] . . . the inhabitants beyond them . . . deserted their several plantations," leaving these two towns the next likely targets.

Such descriptions of the activation of frontiers occurred throughout the war as invasions reshaped the colony's geopolitics. At virtually the same time as the Northampton petition, a correspondent from Lancaster alerted officials that an Indian offensive had pushed settlement east, meaning that "Marsh Creek [a small tributary of the Susquehanna River in York County] . . . is become a frontier." Later, the Moravians at Bethlehem came to similar conclusions about their own place, writing in 1757 that "in these times of trouble and danger," the town had "become the frontier." As a result, townspeople had "established military watches" and had parties "range from place to place and be a guard to their people . . . where they might otherwise be exposed to the incursions of the enemy." Throughout 1754 and 1755, then, something dramatic occurred in Pennsylvania: it transformed into a frontier colony. Frontiers formed—people and places *became* a frontier—when people felt a specific type of fear: invasion. Most frightful in these early years of the war was the sense that these invasions were successful and that frontiers were rolling east, transforming more colonists into "frontier people." People throughout Pennsylvania were thus always calibrating and recalibrating the location of frontiers and who lived upon them during the war.[22]

Just as frontiers had done before, the process of becoming a frontier in the 1750s triggered a set of emotions and associations in people who believed that their homes and personhood had transformed from the countryside into a frontier. Frontier people were desperate and valiant, helpless and steadfast all at once. The logic of frontiers meant that their service was crucial to their community and to the colony as a whole, for without a guarded frontier, enemies could pass easily to the heart and doom the polity. With hundreds of families fleeing east for safety, some people—often male heads of households—decided to persist and, in so doing, form a frontier. But these defenders also expected support from their government. A desperate petition from the "few remaining inhabitants of Lower Smithfield Township in Northampton County" captured this sense when they warned the governor that without further supplies they would be "massacrey'd," fating the "next frontiers" with "fatal consequences." In August 1756, forty leaders in Cumberland County made a similar plea, begging the governor for more aid so they could "continue a frontier," or else they would abandon their posts and turn points east into a new frontier.[23]

For the few remaining on frontiers, the experience was so desperate and isolating that they felt as if their own personhood formed a frontier. Adam Reed, a justice of the peace in Berks County, conveyed these feelings when he warned officials that areas previously settled to his west had turned into a "waist land" and that he and his compatriots now formed a frontier. He stood strong and ready to defend against an attack. But he also pleaded for aid to stop the invasions, writing "you may depend on it that without assistance we in a few days will be on the wrong side of you, for I am now a frontier." To be a frontier was to know valiant desperation, and this sense of heroic dread influenced the political culture of the people who experienced it. For all their bravery, frontier people also felt vulnerable and in need of government aid for strength. This mixture of individual bravery and strength in the face of warfare combined with a sense of communal dependency on government for support shaped the way such "frontier people" viewed Pennsylvania's government and its responsibilities to them.[24]

As more people and places became frontiers in Pennsylvania, regular colonists and officials developed a common vision of Pennsylvania's geopolitical terrain in which frontiers assumed their central attention. An adviser to Pennsylvania's governor similarly described how "the first inroad ever made by the Indians upon the province" in 1755 created a "frontier country" within Pennsylvania that he could visualize as "extend[ing] from the river Potowmac to the river Delaware 150 miles in length and between 20 and 30 in breadth." This official thus linked the creation of a "frontier country" with "the first inroads" (invasion) ever made in the colony.[25]

Colonists in the west envisioned the same map. James Smith, a teenaged resident of Cumberland County who fought in the Seven Years' War, depicted the frontier zone with similar specificity, showing how widely colonists shared this geopolitical understanding of the polity's landscape. Writing a memoir later in life, Smith recounted that after Edward Braddock's defeat in 1755, "the frontiers were laid waste, for above three hundred miles long, and generally thirty broad." The opening of frontiers thus helped colonists at all levels of society better imagine their colony, especially the extent of its reach. But it did not establish a border, or a fixed line between polities, since frontiers were always shifting based upon the location of an enemy or the results of military actions. Nonetheless, the nature of defending against an invasion forced the colony to create a series of forts meant to ward off a French-Indian offensive. Thus, as governments reacted to the appearance of these frontier zones, they transformed the physical landscape as they remade the mental one.[26]

The trauma of living on a frontier in Pennsylvania, a colony once defined by its peace, is hard to grasp. Those who survived suffered lasting psychological scars. Rhoda Barber, in an unpublished memoir about life in Lancaster, Pennsylvania, captured the emotional wounds those living upon frontiers suffered:

In the fall of the year 1755 the inhabitant[s] of this place was alarmd for their situation on account of the indian[s.] Braddocks army had been defeated and dispers'd the preceding summer, the soldiers had gone to winter quarters and the whole frontier lay open, it was reported that the indians were preparing a large number of bark canoes at head of the susquehanna and were coming in a great body to destroy all before them, I heard my mother describe the dreadfull way they were in, alarm'd at the slightest noise in the night expecting every hour to see the canoes coming down upon them.[27]

Frontier people shared this sense of fear, leading them to extend a hand to neighboring communities in 1755 as they had in 1728. In October 1755, people from the Scots-Irish settlement of Paxton rallied together and joined people from Heidelberg to launch a counterattack on their enemy. After a couple of unsuccessful days of scouting, the German contingent led by Conrad Weiser broke up so they could "take care of our own townships," but the impulse toward crosscultural bridge building was clear. The heavily Scots-Irish township of Derry in Lancaster County recognized "the dangerous condition of our frontiers" and because of this "maintained guards in Hannover Township," a community with a large German population, for eighteen months. In 1757, unable to sustain this protection, Derry petitioned the government for aid on Hanover's behalf because they recognized "it is impossible to the frontier people alone to make a stand."[28]

The constant fear of attacks altered regular patterns of life for those who called themselves a "frontier people." Nowhere was this change more apparent than in farming, especially harvesting, a regular and essential activity. Fields brimming with crops became danger zones for settlers on a frontier. John Armstrong, a leading figure in Cumberland County, recounted that "frontier people" developed a way to harvest while at war. These "frontier people" would "convene in pretty large bodies" and have "a prudent distribution of soldiers among them" with "centinels around their working partys by day, and [at] their places of rest by night." Daily life thus became militarized and homes garrisoned.[29]

As support and mutual assistance became a regular part of frontier life, new bonds of community were forged between colonists. What drove colonists together on this frontier was their fear of a common enemy. The identity of this "common enemy" was rarely stated, but it was clear to nearly everyone in the colony from the frontiers to the capital: Indians. Examples of this conflation of the Indian and the enemy are so rampant as to be overwhelming. James Read, writing to his friend in Philadelphia, noted with alarm that one of their mutual friends was "in great danger" simply because "an Indian was seen the very day he left us." In a telling

passage, Conrad Weiser wrote to Richard Peters about how one of the victims of an attack on a homestead in Berks County "begged of the enemy
to shoot him through his heart, which the Indian answered." The "enemy"
and the "Indian" had become synonymous for those like Adam Reed who
had become a frontier and lived in desperate fear of attack.[30]

"In Great Hopes That They Would Drive
All the Virginians Across the Lake"

Indian warriors embraced their status as a dreaded enemy. Their war aim
was to push settlement as far back as possible. They wanted to invade Pennsylvania. They wanted to create fear and open frontiers. They succeeded.[31]

The attacks in Pennsylvania bear this out. After Braddock's defeat near
the forks of the Ohio River in 1755, the French played only a small role in
the raids that turned the Pennsylvania countryside into a frontier. Instead,
Indian warriors took the lead. The successful and successive Indian attacks
pushed the colony's bounds closer to Philadelphia; Indians forced colonists
to retreat southward and eastward. Pennsylvania had settlements hundreds
of miles from Philadelphia before the war, but raids drove settlements back
as far as Reading, about forty miles from Philadelphia, making areas long
thought safe become dangerous frontiers.[32]

Even settlements to the east of the Susquehanna River became vulnerable. Indians successfully attacked Lebanon, well east of the Susquehanna.
Rumors of even greater attacks circulated and could be just as mentally
devastating as the real thing. In 1756, news spread that 1,500 French and
Indian warriors burned Lancaster to the ground and massacred its inhabitants. The false report was so widely believed that over 1,000 Marylanders
mustered and prepared to take back the town. Stories of devastation proliferated among military men as well. At Fort Halifax, "a traveling man"
reported "that the indeans has killed and captivated a great many people,
on the eastern frontears."[33]

While it is difficult to gain clear evidentiary proof of the Indians' motivations because we often have to rely on secondhand accounts infused with
eighteenth-century biases, the accounts we do have reveal common patterns
of beliefs that are confirmed by their actions. James Smith, a Pennsylvanian
captured and adopted by Indians in 1755, provides perhaps the most

detailed and compelling account of the motivations of Indian peoples fighting against the Pennsylvanians. Smith spent several formative years traveling throughout Indian Country in the midst of the war. He kept a journal and then in 1799 published a narrative of his time in captivity.[34]

Smith had some remarkable experiences as an adopted Canawagha Mohawk, a band of the Six Nations Iroquois whose Catholic-leanings meant that they had strong ties to the French. Smith hunted bear, traveled through the Great Lakes, and studied animals most colonists had only heard about. His travels and those of other captives such as Charles Stuart show that during the war, the Ohio Country was a peaceful and polyglot region filled with all sorts of Indian groups. Smith recounted meeting and socializing with Wyandots, Miamis, Delawares, Shawnees, and Ottowas, among others. The groups interacted peacefully with one another, often living together, intermarrying, and traveling freely throughout the area. Nowhere in Indian Country was there the overriding fear that defined life for those in the colony he left. Indian Country, at the moment, was not an area of invasion or vulnerable to attack; Pennsylvania was.[35]

The words Smith heard as a captive may provide some of the best evidence of Indians' motivations and goals. In 1756, James Smith was somewhere in the Ohio Country when he witnessed a war party prepare to launch a raid into Virginia "in great hopes that they would drive all the Virginians across the lake [Atlantic Ocean]." Two of the elders told Smith they hoped the "Indians and French would subdue all America, except for New England, which they said they had tried in old times." The elders expressed confidence because "the white people appeared to them like fools; they could neither guard against surprize, run or fight." When Smith argued that they could never send "the whites" across the ocean, the elders conceded that they did not think they could entirely "conquer America," but "they were willing to propagate the idea, in order to encourage the young men to go to war."[36]

Warriors driven by a desire to push British colonists across the Atlantic used fear as a tactic to send them running, the success of which came through in the desperation settlers expressed in their petitions. As historian Peter Silver has shown, Indian methods seemed "terroristic" and "depended on the multiplication of panic" throughout the populace. Joseph Shippen, for instance, recorded the discovery of a man on the road with "his scalp taken off, skull split open, several other lashes in his head and one of the provincial tomahawks sticking in his private parts." Indians hoped to strike fear in their enemy and to send a message to survivors, as the tomahawk emasculating the provincial soldier suggested. Moreover, unlike European modes of war that focused on armies fighting pitched battles away from noncombatants, Indian warfare considered all settlers and settlements open to attack. These means of waging war made homes and roads part of the frontier by making settlers targets. Such methods dispersed the fear of attack to civilian colonists as well as military men.[37]

And just as colonists looked to leading men, like the governor, to protect them, specific Indian warriors known for their ferocity struck particular fright in the minds of colonists. Captain Jacobs, a Delaware whose enormous physicality haunted panicked colonists' minds, became a hero for Indians who evoked his memory long after his death as a way to rekindle fear in colonists. Shingas, too, was so feared that colonists pleaded for bounties to encourage his death.

The language the elders used and their understanding of the past suggests that Indian warriors fighting against Pennsylvania began to form a nascent pan-Indian solidarity, much as frontier people in colonial society transcended ethnic lines. James Smith, for instance, was captured by a three-person party composed of a Shawnee, a Delaware, and, he claimed, a Conestoga, but he was adopted by a Mohawk family. Many of these groups shared a common experience in which British colonization pushed them from their traditional homes westward into the Ohio, and their shared anger at displacement helped them forge a shared history. The elders even told Smith that their current experience was like those of Indians in New England, connecting the experience of Indians in the Ohio in the eighteenth century with these other groups in the seventeenth century. In other words, as colonists on Pennsylvania's frontiers transcended ethnic divisions and created a coherent sense of community by sharing an opposition to Indians, many young Indian warriors were coalescing against a British imperial project composed of "whites" that had continually displaced Native settlements. The creation of and experience with frontiers thus helped harden a cultural border for many who fought.[38]

"The Land . . . to Be Secured for the Indians"

While some warrior Indians and frontier people shared a common understanding of who composed the frontier and its enemies, elite leaders in both colonial and Indian societies developed a far more nuanced and flexible view of each other and the war. Most British government officials, from officers to assemblymen to proprietary officials, believed that their main enemy was France. That is not to say that imperial and colonial officials were blind to Indians as enemies, but from the imperial perspective, the war was primarily fought over competing western land claims between European powers. Many expected that a French defeat would translate to the quick and easy subjugation of their Indian allies and a return to the status quo antebellum. Often living far from the frontlines and focused on defeating the French power, these officials thus experienced frontiers in a way far different from those who lived upon them. For officials, frontiers remained a more abstract, strategic space that demanded protection but that ultimately should be closed with the end of hostilities.

Their vision of a world in which frontiers could disappear allowed them to end the fighting in 1758. To make peace, they knew they needed to ameliorate the causes of the war. Removing the French was a part of that strategy. The easy explanation cast about for Indian alliances with the French was that the French had "seduced" Native people through power and promises, with some officials even theorizing that Jesuit priests exerted a strange hold over Indians' minds. Even the Pennsylvania Assembly, an institution that was particularly sympathetic to Indian complaints about bad land deals, tentatively endorsed the conclusion that "probably the instigations, present situation and power of the French, might have been sufficient nevertheless to have engaged those Indians in the war against us."[39]

Others, especially powerful Quakers within the colony, believed there was more to the Indians' choice to fight. They suspected that while the French made it easy for them to find an ally, the underlying cause of their aggressiveness stemmed from their recent treatment by Pennsylvania, especially by the colony's proprietary officials. This interpretation meant that warring Indians had their own reasons for fighting independent of the French. Proponents of this view believed that righting these wrongs, such as athe Walking Purchase, could bring these enemy Indians back into the British fold.[40]

Driven by a desire to end the fighting and a belief that Pennsylvania deserved some blame for the war, a group of prominent Quakers in Pennsylvania formed an extralegal association meant to address Indian complaints about Pennsylvania's land dealings and to win over the Shawnees and Delawares. The Friendly Association for Regaining and Preserving Peace with the Indians by Pacific Measures, the name of their organization, was incredibly controversial because it claimed to act on behalf of the colony and empire. Its mission was as clear as its name, and it reflected one strand of William Penn's idealized view of Pennsylvania. Just as official governing officials viewed frontiers as contingent upon warfare, so too did this colonial organization. Those running the Friendly Association wanted Native Americans to be part of the polity as allies and friends; they wanted to erase frontiers from the colony's geopolitical landscape.

As well intentioned as the Friendly Association was, it found few friends within colonial society. Frontier inhabitants who formed their own militias viewed this competing voluntary association as a potentially traitorous group that helped Indians slaughter frontiersmen by giving them aid and succor. The Friendly Association found other detractors. Both proprietary and British officials shared a common goal with the association, but they viewed its self-appointed mandate as a threat to their powers to negotiate war and peace with Indians. By claiming to negotiate war and peace—something akin to the Winters brothers, though with an inverse end in mind—officials disliked the group and its perceived threat to their own authority to manage the war.[41]

Just as perspectives on the war differed depending on one's position in colonial society, so too did the war look different depending upon one's position in Native groups. Many Native leaders who managed diplomatic relations often viewed the choices they made in light of their personal experiences negotiating the imperial realities of North America. Another captivity narrative provides insight into the way the Delawares' treatment by the British affected one Indian leader's decision to side with the French. Charles Stuart, like Smith, was a captured Pennsylvanian who spent two years as an adoptee, traveling throughout the Ohio River Valley and Canada. Upon his return, Stuart recounted an exchange he had with Shingas, a leader of the western branch of Delawares, in which the feared Indian warrior talked about his decision to side with the French. Shingas had been open to a British alliance, until Edward Braddock insulted him. He had initially hoped an alliance with Great Britain could secure land and prominence for Delawares in the west, but Braddock told Shingas that "no savage should inherit the land" and that he "had no doubt of drieving the French and their Indians away" without any Indian partners.[42]

Still, even in the midst of a war between the Delawares and Pennsylvania, Shingas told Stuart about his vision of the future in which Indians and Pennsylvanians could realize William Penn's peaceful vision of cohabitation. He also had a solution to the problems that had recently plagued the relationship. To combat the spread of colonists on Indian lands, he wanted to carve out a quasi-Indian state in which British emissaries would teach Native allies how to produce their own metal, powder, and clothing instead of relying on British and French trade. The western Delawares' attempts to negotiate for their own land and Shingas's dream of a separate Indian state reflected their desire to assert their independence from both the Iroquois and the British, while at the same time conceding Pennsylvania's right to exist. In other words, land policy alone did not alienate these allies of Pennsylvania. Larger issues of diminishing political and economic power within the British imperial world had led these disillusioned groups to fight to secure their own autonomy.[43]

The Friendly Association helped bring about an end to the Indian war in Pennsylvania by helping organize peace treaties in the summer of 1757 and in October 1758 between Pennsylvania and the representatives of the warring Indian groups. In the first treaty, the leader of the eastern Delawares, Teedyuscung, had expressed his willingness to return to an alliance with Pennsylvania if the Walking Purchase was nullified and the Delawares were given a permanent parcel of land on which they could live. Perhaps not coincidentally, Teedyuscung's separate, secured Indian territory mirrored Shingas's imagined peaceful solution to colonization. Pennsylvania made many concessions, including a promise to investigate the validity of the Walking Purchase, but they refused to reserve land for the Delawares.[44]

Many more Indian groups came to the second treaty. Some came interested in peace, but most came from the Six Nations, wanting to assert their political dominance by helping to broker peace and to check any growing Delaware influence in imperial politics. British imperial officers, including the newly appointed General John Forbes, pressured Pennsylvania to find agreement with the Indian groups, which they believed would help secure a British victory on the Ohio. After much negotiation, the two sides reached an agreement in which the Indians present would end their alliance with the French in exchange for the promise that Pennsylvania would prohibit colonial settlement west of the Allegheny Mountains.[45]

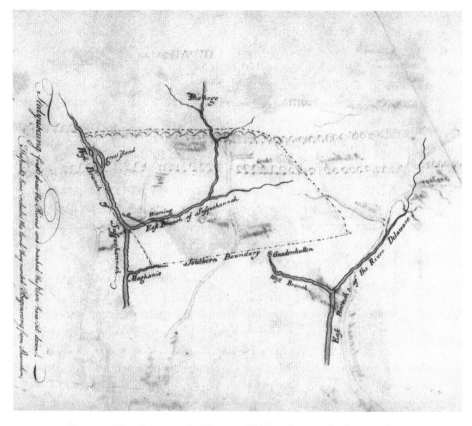

Figure 9. Map drawn at the Treaty of Easton that marks the area that
Teedyuscung of the Delaware requested that Pennsylvania reserve as Indian
lands. Teedyuscung believed that Indians needed the area to maintain
Pennsylvania's promise of peace and cohabitation. The image above comes from a
manuscript that describes it as a copy of the map Teedyuscung drew in chalk on
the top of a large table during the treaty. It was reproduced in Charles Thomson's
An Enquiry into the Causes of the Alienation of the Delaware and Shawnese Indians.
Courtesy of the American Philosophical Society.

The treaty at Easton was a partial victory for many of the Indians,
although ultimately a loss for the eastern Delawares, who received neither
land nor a nullification of the Walking Purchase. Nonetheless, the treaty
granted land back to the Indians and established a clear line of demarcation
between Pennsylvania and Indian Country. The boundary was not meant

to serve as a barrier between enemies, but instead a means through which these groups could build a foundation of peace. Indeed, at both treaties, the parties made hopeful vows to coexist by returning to the ideals of William Penn.[46]

Charles Thomson tried to visually depict this diplomatic attempt to reestablish harmony by publishing a map that marked the negotiated borders between Indian and colonial territory. The well-circulated map included many details that were meant to convey the effect of the war on reducing the jurisdiction of the colony. First, it showed the massive expansion of Pennsylvania's borders after the purchase in 1754. The Easton Treaty ceded about half of that purchase back to the Indians (the Allegheny Mountains are depicted by the strong line that forms a curving arch in the middle of the map). It also marked the land Teedyuscung asked to be reserved for the Delawares (Figure 9). Notably, Pennsylvania was willing to cede land back to the Indians to the west but not to the north, suggesting that officials always viewed these lines as transitory, even as Indians viewed them as permanent.

The 1758 Treaty of Easton was followed in November by British General John Forbes's victory over the French and their remaining Indian allies stationed at the forks of the Ohio at Fort Duquesne, a conquest made possible in large part by the peace agreed upon at Easton. To representatives of Pennsylvania and to Indian groups, these events signaled the closing of frontiers in Pennsylvania. Pennsylvania began shuttering forts, leaving only Fort Augusta on the Susquehanna River, which, by 1763, was seen as a trading post as much as a military one. But there were no treaties signed between those who experienced the frontier firsthand. There was no treaty between the "frontier people" who had spent three years in near constant fear of a seemingly omnipotent and omnipresent Indian threat or the young Indian warriors who fought for their independence. To close the frontier for them, their own authorities would have to enforce peace from within, something both Pennsylvania and Indian groups had managed to do in the past. Never before, however, had the psychological effects of "becoming a frontier" been quite so profound for colonists. To make matters worse for colonial authorities, the experience of living on a frontier fueled a new political culture among self-described "frontier people," one that would animate colonial politics until the American Revolution and make a return to peace difficult.[47]

CHAPTER 6

_____

Frontier Politics

As more Pennsylvanians became "frontier people" during the Seven Years' War, they placed new political demands on their government. Indeed, they wanted their government to become something it had never been before; they wanted it to become what William Penn had called a "frontier government." Frontier people expected their government to man forts, supply forces, and create militias, all of which were meant to provide an adequate defense of the colony's new frontier zones. The attempts by the Assembly and governor to respond to this new pressure fractured the government along institutional lines. Contrary to popular belief, the issue that poisoned the political atmosphere in Philadelphia in the 1750s had little to do with Quaker pacifism. Instead, the controversy between the governor and the Assembly exposed a more fundamental problem of governing frontiers in the colony. Legislators, most of whom represented eastern counties located safely away from the fighting, harbored a deep-seated distrust of proprietary power, the very thing frontier people wanted more of. Assemblymen worried that if the colony became a frontier government, then the proprietary branch would use their newfound military power to ruin what had made the colony great. The governor, meanwhile, stymied and frustrated in Philadelphia, headed to the frontiers to try to rally support for his cause, thus driving a wedge between frontier people and the legislature.

This division in the governing elite caused frontier inhabitants to become more politicized than they ever had been before. They organized their own defenses, creating a new ring of political leadership locally, and used the ballot box to express their displeasure with what they saw as Quaker intransigence. The political controversy surrounding the colony's defense left settlers on the frontier disillusioned with the Assembly, and especially what they considered a Quaker elite that cared little for them,

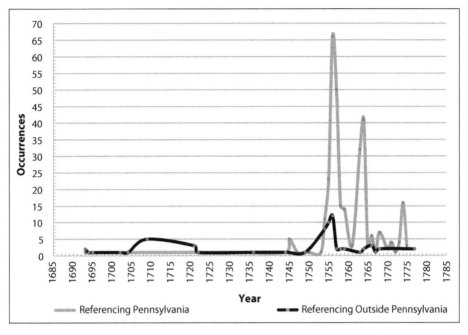

Figure 10. The frequency with which the governor and his council discussed or read about frontiers in other colonies compared with their use of the word to describe regions of Pennsylvania. As the graph shows, for government officials who debated and formed policy, a "frontier" in Pennsylvania did not exist for much of the time before the Seven Years' War. Source: *Provincial Council Minutes.* For dataset, visit mappingfrontiers.com or patrickspero.com.

leading them to enter into an awkward and often overlooked alliance with proprietary officials and the institutions they controlled. The political culture forged on the frontiers in the midst of the Seven Years' War would last until the American Revolution and shape its course.

"Our Present Constitution [Will Be] Transformed into a Government the Most Despotic and Arbitrary"

William West brought frontiers to Pennsylvania politics. West is a person obscured by time, but he was a leading figure in Pennsylvania during the war. West was born in Sligo, Ireland, in 1724. At some point, he crossed the

Atlantic and came to Pennsylvania. By his twenties, he was rising through Philadelphia's ranks, a mobility that reflected the opportunity many immigrants found in the city. His brother, Francis, traveled further west, to Cumberland County, where he became an active citizen, including serving as justice of the peace. William, meanwhile, established a dry-goods company that began to thrive, aided in part by his strong connections to Cumberland County and backcountry traders.[1]

As overt competition on the Ohio River increased, West took a leading role in representing Pennsylvania's interest. In 1752, West traveled to the region to trade with Indians and to scout for intelligence on Virginian and French maneuvers. Later, in 1753, the governor asked West to serve on a commission to carry messages of peace from the colony to Indians living near the Ohio River.[2]

West and others who ventured to the Ohio returned with shocking news. He, along with his trading partners, had kept a detailed journal, which they planned to use to create accurate maps of the region for the government. When they plotted their results on a map and compared them with others, West and his compatriots were convinced that Virginia and France were occupying Pennsylvania territory. When James Hamilton, the governor at the time, saw the evidence, he too was convinced. He quickly called the Assembly to order to prepare the colony for war.[3]

The Assembly's response seems to have shocked Hamilton more than the news itself. After hearing of the report, the Assembly sent the matter to two committees to investigate further. Both committees expressed doubts about the information. One questioned West's memory, while the other questioned the accuracy of the maps presented to the legislature. The Assembly, after reading these committees' reports, concluded that the evidence of a French invasion was too weak to act. Moreover, the Assembly also suggested that based on what they now knew, the territory in question was quite possibly Virginia's, a huge concession of valuable land.[4]

The competing views of Pennsylvania's frontiers—indeed, the debate over whether the colony even possessed a zone of invasion—was a result of the colony's institutional development. The Frame of Government established patterns of responsibilities that gave the legislature and the proprietor different, and sometimes completely separate and oppositional, interests. Indeed, the eastern bias of the Assembly had become even more noticeable as the colony expanded. By 1752, the booming frontier county of Lancaster, for instance, sent only four members, even though extant lists of taxables suggest that Lancaster (3,977) had more residents than Bucks (3,262 in 1751) or Chester Counties (3,951 in 1752), both of which sent eight representatives. But these western counties had little influence in an institution dominated by the twenty-six men representing the eastern counties— counties that were not just heavily Quaker but, by the 1750s, also in less immediate danger. The Assembly, so focused, viewed its historical role as a protector of individual liberty against a proprietary branch that might serve private rather than public interests. Elected representatives also lacked the impulse to act militarily because their constituents felt greater security than those on frontiers who faced warfare.[5]

Meanwhile, the proprietary institution remained invested in western lands and the continued political expansion of the colony through offices controlled and overseen by the governor. This divide between the legislature and governor was rare in British North America, as the Assembly was quick to point out when it tried to compel the proprietors to use their own money for Indian diplomacy. After years of publicly funding treaties, the Assembly feared that the funds provided for diplomacy were often supporting the proprietors' private interest in land acquisition—an interest that might be, from the legislatures' perspective, at odds with the interests of the province and empire. In a speech to the governor, the speaker of the house reminded the proprietors that because they were "lords of the soil, as well as governors in chief of this province," they were "more nearly interested in the prosperity of this colony, than any other governors in America." These "interests" became "so constantly intermixt with those of the province in all treaties with our Indian allies, that we apprehend the surest way to prevent dissatisfactions on all sides, will be to request the proprietaries . . . to agree upon a proportionable part of all such charges on account of Indian treaties."[6]

The Assembly's concerns reflected a sense of powerlessness to control the one aspect of Pennsylvania governance that appeared the most likely to bring on war and upset the founding tenets of the Quaker colony. Richard Jackson, an ally of the Quaker political party that dominated the colonial legislature, expressed the Assembly's view on Indian diplomacy and proprietary land purchases in a widely read critique of proprietary governments. "It appeared," Jackson recounted, "as in course of time was unavoidable, that a treaty and a Purchase went on together; that the former was a shoeing horn for the latter." The proprietors, Jackson insinuated, did not really cultivate good Indian relations with treaties, but instead simply used treaties and the public funds that supported them as a means to increase their own largesse. This proprietors' pursuit of their own interest, the argument went, drove former Indian allies into French hands.[7]

The appearance of frontiers on the colony's geopolitical landscape in the 1750s exacerbated this power struggle. As the disastrous news of Washington's expedition trickled into Philadelphia, assemblymen could no longer avoid creating a frontier policy, and proprietary officials were under heavy pressure to raise defenses. Previously, the proprietary alone was able to manage such affairs because the scale of the conflict was small enough that its resources sufficed. This war, however, necessitated public, namely Assembly, funds to provide for such expansive and distant frontiers, thus making frontiers a pressing political issue in the capital.

By the late summer of 1754, the legislature began to debate a bill to protect the frontiers against the expected invasion. The Assembly also wanted the law to protect the liberty of colonists from a potential proprietary power grab. The task was thus to create an entirely new institution of government, while also ensuring this new organization preserved the principles of their much-beloved Frame of 1701. Though Quakers in general held pacifistic tenets, the political beliefs of Pennsylvania assemblymen had gone through the same transformation William Penn had in 1701. Most of those serving supported the formation of an official colonial militia, while those whose conscience prohibited them from supporting a militia law resigned. Indeed, the debates between the governor and Assembly over funding show that pacifism was never really a wedge issue. It was instead a debate over institutional power.[8]

The Assembly tried to impose three checks on the proprietors in its militia law. First, they tried to levy a tax on previously exempted proprietary estates. The proposed tax would give the legislature an incredible new financial power, one that would provide it with additional leverage over the proprietor. Next, the Assembly wanted to make the officers in the militia elective rather than appointive, thereby taking the power of patronage away from the governor. Finally, it wanted to make service voluntary rather than compulsory as a way to protect the liberty of conscience, while also limiting the coercive powers of the proprietor. If passed, these procedures would give the Assembly much greater oversight of the militia, an institution that they knew could all too easily become an instrument of proprietary power. The proprietors, meanwhile, saw the Assembly's proposals as threats to the independence of the executive part of government, particularly the attempt to tax proprietary lands, which, they worried, would amount to the subjugation of the executive branch to the legislative. Moreover, they worried that these restrictions would hamper his ability to function as captain-general.[9]

The Assembly's understanding of the colony's distinctive history influenced its approach to the militia bill. Assembly members believed that the descendants of William Penn had squandered their father's true gift of liberty, a legacy that only an independent legislature could preserve. In 1757, when the colony considered creating a more permanent militia, elected representatives outlined in explicit terms the danger they saw in a militia, especially one in which officers were appointed rather than elected. "The militia will vote for members of Assembly, and being dependent upon their officers, would probably be influenced by them, and the officers being recommended by the proprietary creatures and commissioned by their deputy, would be directed by them, and thus our proprietaries would be vested with the appointment of both branches of the legislature," they stated. They concluded that "the balance of power between the governor and the people, so wisely established by the Royal and proprietary charters and laws of the province, will be totally subverted, and our present constitution transformed into a government the most despotic and arbitrary." This sentiment gave rise to the now famous passage that the Pennsylvania Assembly delivered to the governor in 1755: "Those who would give up essential liberty to purchase a little temporary safety deserve neither liberty nor safety." In this equation, the proprietor and a militia were the gravest threats to liberty the colony then faced.[10]

For almost two years, the Assembly and the Pennsylvania governor jostled over these issues. The debates were long, heated, and unproductive. Finally, in late November 1755, Thomas Penn broke the logjam by making a one-time cash donation of £5,000, more than the Assembly's proposed tax would have levied on him. His donation allowed for the passage of the bill, but it also ensured that the Assembly failed to create a precedent of taxing the proprietary interest. The impasse officially ended in January 1756 when Robert Hunter Morris, James Hamilton's replacement, signed the bill into law. The liberty of conscience was preserved in the final bill. Morris acquiesced in part because after two years of ad hoc militias operating, it was clear that there was a strong volunteer force in the colony. The appointment of officers, meanwhile, was based on the principle of elective-appointive. Rather than give the governor patronage power, local militias elected their officers, with the governor approving them as he did county sheriffs and coroners. But that was no real concession since it had already become the de facto policy. After the passage of this first act, subsequent money bills became regularized. In the ensuing three years, the Assembly passed four different bills raising £490,000 in total.[11]

With a militia law in hand, the Assembly recalibrated their approach to the politics of frontiers. Rather than demand political concessions from the governor, legislators embraced the plight of those who inhabited frontiers to attack the capability of the proprietary to wage war. As they said to the governor, "We have granted a sufficient number of men to protect the province and the supplies to support them . . . The rest was the duty of the governor." Since the war was not going well, they continued, "It will readily appear who it is that neglected the protection of the province, or has failed on their parts to put it into a posture of defence." The Assembly thus changed their agenda from a contest fought against proprietary power to a contest over which institution most cared for, in the words of Isaac Norris, the speaker of the house, "the bleeding circumstances of our frontiers." The Assembly even chastised the governor, arguing that annual elections served as referendums on their performance. Reelection, they argued, would validate their policies. The frontier people's choice surprised them.[12]

"A Sufficient Sum of Money to Maintain Such a Number of Regular Troops as May Be Thought Necessary to Defend Our Frontiers"

No one knew the politics of frontiers better than Nathaniel Grubb. Grubb was a powerful assemblyman from Chester County. He was also a Quaker who supported the militia bill. Indeed, he helped write the bills the Assembly passed; so it came as some surprise to him that his name was one of the most reviled among frontier inhabitants. The trouble began when a prominent proprietary official claimed that Grubb responded to a report of an Indian attack by saying the murdered were "some Scotch-Irish . . . who could well enough be spared." Such sentiments deeply affected the opinions of those who believed they composed frontiers—those who could "be spared." We do not know if Grubb made that statement. He denied it vigorously. But the truth of his words is less important than whether people at the time believed them. Perception in politics is more important than reality, and the reality was that those on the frontiers believed Grubb uttered those words. In fact, they believed those words encapsulated the general view of all those who inhabited the Assembly.[13]

For frontier inhabitants, the government's early inaction fueled a deep suspicion that the colony was incapable of providing the protection it was supposed to offer. Petitions from frontier towns and counties streamed into the colonial capital begging for aid, all evoking the same type of despair the petitions from 1728 did. The new ones made it clear that only the government could free them from their fears. As early as 1754, shortly after Washington's defeat at the Battle of Great Meadows, the governor received petitions from Lancaster and Cumberland Counties, and the towns of Hanover, Donegal, Derry, and Paxton. They demanded something the colony had never before had: "a militia law or . . . a sufficient sum of money to maintain such a number of regular troops as may be thought necessary to defend our frontiers." Frontier inhabitants were thus driven by the belief that Benjamin Franklin himself articulated, that government's fundamental duty was to provide protection to "frontier people" in exchange for their "obedience."[14]

The failure of the government to respond to their cries led to a desperation that mobilized settlers to become far more politically active than ever before. Before the war, it is unclear if those in the backcountry engaged much with colonial politics. There is reason to suspect that they had little interest in the Assembly, if for no other reason than its general lethargy. Pennsylvania's Assembly averaged one of the lowest number of bills passed per year in all the colonies. Such inactivity created the liberty that Pennsylvanians were proud of, but it could also foster apathy in politics.[15]

The politics of frontiers, however, made settlers who inhabited such zones more politically astute and energized. John Elder, a prominent clergyman in Lancaster, summarized the dread he felt when he wrote that the "frontiers" sent "petition time after time, yet to no purpose; so that we may seem to be given up into the hands of a merciless enemy." Elder went on to blame the political paralysis on the "unreasonable debates of the two parts of our legislature instead of uniting in some probable scheme for the protection of the province and the preservation of its inhabitants." Elder, as a minister with a large following, likely conveyed more than his personal frustrations in the letter. Frontier people saw a government stymied by arcane debates and legalese while they sought the most essential of all things: security.[16]

When their petitions failed, some frontier settlers used radical action to spur the government to act. During the debates between the Assembly and governor, rumors circulated that "2000 inhabitants" were "preparing to come to Philadelphia from Chester County" to pressure the governor and Assembly "to pass laws to defend the country and oppose the common enemy." Although this march did not happen, others did. And where someone like John Elder disparaged both the legislature and the governor for the impasse, as time wore on, frontier inhabitants aimed most of their animus at the Assembly, which they associated with an intractable Quaker elite. The most radical action occurred in November 1755 when the Quakers held their yearly meeting in Philadelphia. In an attempt to force the Assembly to act, a group of frontiersmen brought a wagonload of frozen corpses to the city. They carted them throughout the town, "cursing the Indians, and also the Quakers" everywhere they went. They ended their protest by laying the bodies in the "state-house yard" as a means to appeal to the legislature. They hoped the shock of mutilated bodies lying exposed for all to see would convey the fear and desperation frontier inhabitants felt. Their desperate act was meant to make those sitting secure in the heart of the polity understand the suffering state of the polity's limbs.[17]

Their tactics worked. The slaughtered corpses brought fear to the capital and forced people living in the cities to confront the politics of frontiers. Many in the colony's heart expressed sympathy with the plight of their western brethren, who they recognized as protecting the east. According to an oral history of the November march, many Philadelphians joined the "frontier inhabitants" in solidarity as they marched through the town. Afterward, some Philadelphians with the support of the governor helped raise an unprecedented £700 bounty through voluntary subscription for the scalps of the prominent and much-feared Indian leaders Shingas and Captain Jacobs. At about the same time, 150 Philadelphians banded together to pen their own petition to the Assembly. Organized by the mayor and his council, most of whom were proprietary men, these urbanites evoked the language of frontier petitions when they complained that even those in Philadelphia were "deprived of that most essential right and great first privilege, which God and Nature gave us, of defending our lives and protecting our families." As this and the other petitions made clear, providing for frontiers was the most fundamental duty of government ("that most essential right and great first privilege"), and Pennsylvania's Assembly appeared to fail that test.[18]

The two-year delay in passing a bill—during which frontier settlers had to create their own defenses and petition the government for support— were formative for self-described "frontier inhabitants" in solidifying their political perceptions. Even after the passage of the militia bills, frontier settlers continued to harp on the Assembly and its supposed pacifism. Edward Biddle, a colonial officer from a prominent Pennsylvania family, reported to his family in Philadelphia that "the people" in Reading "exclaim against the Quakers and some are scarce restrained from burning the houses of those few who are in town." Nathaniel Grubb's alleged quip about the expendability of frontier lives gained traction and was still circulating years later. In February 22, 1757, when the house was preparing another act for £100,000, a soldier in Derry believed that "the Assembly will never give any sum or sums for the King's use until Mr. Franklin returns to England." The legislature passed a bill a month later. But for frontier inhabitants, their perception of the Assembly drove their beliefs and they had missed, or dismissed, the Assembly's claim that they held the mantle of the "distressed" frontiers.[19]

The frontier settlers' opinion of the legislature came about, oddly enough, because these colonists shared a political goal with the Assembly members. The settlers, like the legislators, wanted more political power so they could shape their material lives. With war, however, frontiersmen recognized the effect malapportioned representation had on their power (or lack thereof) within the legislature. In that way, frontier settlers embraced popular rights much like easterners who were critical of the proprietor, but on the frontiers, colonists saw the Quaker Party and the institution they controlled as obstructing the very thing the party proclaimed to embrace. In the view of the frontier people, the Assembly failed to represent the people because it denied its own people the security it was supposed to provide.

Instead of finding an ally in the Assembly, frontier settlers entered into a hasty, awkward, and yet real partnership with the governor. The electoral politics during the war provide a window into this alliance. Self-described frontier counties often elected proprietary officials to the Assembly, many of whom were not even residents of the counties they represented. Frontier counties did so because they wanted their best men—what one person called "the chiefs of the frontiers"—to stay local to lead the fight. To accomplish this, they identified Philadelphians who would represent their interests. The story of William Allen, who was in 1756 the chief justice, one of the most important proprietary officials, is emblematic. Both Northampton and Cumberland Counties elected him to the Assembly in 1756, even though Allen was not a resident of either county. Allen chose to sit for Cumberland County. The frontier people in Northampton decided to elect William Plumstead, the mayor of Philadelphia who helped organize the petition for a militia law and a well-known proprietary supporter, in Allen's stead. Berks County, meanwhile, sent Thomas Yorke in 1756, another resident of Philadelphia known to support war measures. Though Yorke proved less of a stalwart proprietary servant in the Assembly, after the war ended, Governor William Denny appointed him a justice of the Court of Common Pleas in Philadelphia.[20]

Cumberland County's other representative was William West, the prominent Philadelphia trader who had earlier ventured to Fort Pitt on government business and whose brother was a justice of the peace in the county. West's ties to Cumberland County remained strong throughout the war, so much so that when a crisis struck Cumberland in February 1756, Governor Morris again turned to West for help. The frontiers were then experiencing the height of war, and their frustration led some frontier settlers to threaten to once again march to Philadelphia to "make certain demands of the legislature." Pennsylvania's governor thought the march could prove disastrous. It would upset the delicate balance recently struck between governor and Assembly. Moreover, it would weaken the already degraded frontier defenses.[21]

Morris, knowing of West's connection to the county, asked him to go to the scene and dissuade the marchers. West discovered a desperate situation when he arrived in the frontier counties. Cumberland County residents had fled to York County, where there was a standing guard of about one hundred men. The frontier settlers that West met all complained of the Assembly's inaction. They were particularly angry at the Assembly's decision to adjourn in the midst of war. They begged him to "lay before the Legislature their grievances and distresses and demand the protection and relief they had a right to expect." They told him that if the house would not reconvene on its own, then the governor should recall the members. West relayed all of this to Morris, who did call the Assembly back to session.[22]

That October, Cumberland County residents elected West to the Assembly, a sign that they, like the other frontier counties, trusted this Philadelphian with proprietary ties to provide them with "the protection and relief they had a right to expect." A year later, voters in Cumberland County sent an even clearer and far more dramatic message to the Assembly. They elected John Stanwix, a colonel in the British Army who was soon to be a brigadier general, as one of their representatives. He had arrived in Carlisle in 1757 and in time oversaw five companies of British troops who provided protection for the frontiers. Stanwix never ran, never sat, and may never have even known of his election. But getting Stanwix to sit was not the residents' real aim. They knew that the frontier counties lacked the representation to change the fundamental makeup of the Assembly. They offered Stanwix as a protest vote. The frontier people wanted strong military men like Stanwix to run the government, not the supposedly pacifist and militarily feeble Quaker Party that then controlled the legislature. But even if Stanwix's election was merely symbolic, it showed that residents on frontiers had become so politically engaged that they could organize the election of a British Army officer to their legislature.[23]

"The People Will Be Thereby Taught to Depend upon an Assembly for What They Should Only Receive from Government"

By 1756, Pennsylvania's governor, Robert Hunter Morris, had learned to accept the acrimonious politics of Pennsylvania and the partnership between frontier settlers and the proprietors it encouraged. When Morris arrived in Philadelphia with his commission in 1754, he knew that his primary task was to oversee the creation and maintenance of the colony's frontier defenses. As he said in his inaugural address to the Assembly, "The particular matter I have at present to recommend to your consideration is the state of the frontiers." The Assembly responded with similar pleasantries, but soon the debate over the "state of the frontiers" turned their relationship sour. At one point, the Assembly accused Morris of utter incompetence. Morris never seemed to grasp the Quaker Party's hostile view of the proprietorship. When the Assembly accused him of trying to destroy liberty within the colony, Morris pleaded, "Whose liberty have I taken away, or whose property have I invaded?"[24]

Morris's duty to defense, and his apparent inability to provide it, caused him great frustration. Indeed, it struck at the core of his authority and undermined the fundamental bond between colonists and the proprietor.

Eventually, he learned to use his impotence to his advantage. He knew from the petitions and meetings with frontier representatives that living upon frontiers brought a desire for government to act. The governor, by echoing the rhetoric of frontier petitions, tried to instill the same fear in the Assembly, or at least in the city, that the frontier people possessed. In November 1755, he announced that frontier settlers were "quitting their Habitations, and crowding into the more settled Parts of the province, which in their turn will become the frontier if some stop is not speedily put to the cruel Ravages of these bloody Invaders." By warning that those in "the more settled Parts of the province" could "become the frontier,' Morris wanted those in the capital, the heart of the colony that should be secure, to feel as if they too were threatened. To do so, he appropriated the rhetoric he heard from those on the frontiers.[25]

The paralytic politics in the capital threatened the power of the proprietary branch both in the empire and in the colony. The proprietor and his representatives thus waged their own political campaigns in imperial circles and with the larger populace of the colony. Morris, as the Crown's representative of the colony, received directives from imperial officials and military commanders and requests for aid from neighboring colonies. The Penns, aware that their father lost the charter during wartime, worried that inaction could jeopardize their proprietorship. Thomas Penn's conversion to Anglicanism and stronger connections within the British government provided them with greater confidence that their charter was secure. But they also had an easy target of blame: an intractable Assembly that was too democratic. As Morris's replacement Robert Denny complained to imperial administrators frustrated with Pennsylvania's inaction, "The powers of government are almost all taken out of the hands of the governor, and lodged in the Assembly; and as to what little remains, scarce a bill comes up without an attempt to lessen them."[26]

The Penns found a sympathetic ear in imperial circles. Rather than revoking the Penns' charter, Crown officials instead debated placing new requirements on colonial assemblies that would have restricted Quakers from serving. And after the Pennsylvania legislature did pass a militia law, the Crown nullified it as soon as its text arrived in England, noting numerous deficiencies with the law and even declaring that the voluntary service and the election of officers was "defective and mischievous." In its written rationale, the Crown rebuked the Pennsylvania Assembly, advising it to show greater respect for the executive powers of government. In so doing,

it showed that its ideology was more attuned to Thomas Penn's desire for
an independent executive than the Pennsylvania Assembly's emphasis on
popular politics. The Crown had good reason to worry about a strengthened legislature. The governors in the colonies were the ones to receive,
follow, and implement Crown orders, some of which might be unpopular
locally but essential for the imperial project the governors served. Imperial
officials had learned to distrust colonial legislatures whose loyalties were
often to their electorate. They preferred to rely on an individual whose
appointment depended upon obedience to the Crown.[27]

Morris, as the representative of the proprietor whose duty was to provide protection, felt the weight of this controversy throughout the war,
while elected assemblymen in the east could rest easy that their constituents
supported them and that their principles guided their actions. Frontier settlers reminded proprietary men like Morris of their duty. One of the first
petitions the government received signaled their dependence on the governor. After "the late defeat of the Virginia forces," Cumberland County, the
newest to be created, came "under your honour's protection [meaning
the governor's]" and "beg[ged] your immediate notice—we living upon
the frontiers of the province and our enemies so close upon us." Although
no attacks had yet come, these petitioners understood their new geopolitical
position within the imperial world. They were a frontier because they occupied the area most vulnerable to a potential attack, and they expected their
governor to be their closest ally and protector. Similar petitions flooded
into Philadelphia, all echoing these same sentiments.[28]

Morris recognized that the political stakes in his face-off with the
Assembly could undermine his credibility. He also worried that the Assembly was actively trying to sow these seeds of doubt. If they could not weaken
the proprietor through law, he worried, then they would try other means.
When he learned that Benjamin Franklin, as speaker of the Assembly, had
sent arms to local militias on the frontiers, he was convinced that their
ultimate aim was to undercut the proprietary branch and undermine him.
"This I esteem a very extraordinary measure," he advised Thomas Penn,
"as the people will be thereby taught to depend upon an Assembly for what
they should only receive from government, and if it is not criminal I am
sure it ought to be so." When Morris spoke of "government," he meant
the military and coercive arms of a state, and he was the person who possessed those powers as captain-general. Franklin's provisioning of arms,
from Morris' point of view, undercut the executive powers of the colonial

government. If the Assembly acted on military matters instead of him, then the authority of the proprietor and his governor would collapse. And if the Assembly succeeded in subverting the military powers of the executive, then the governor might lose his most logical political allies: frontier people desperate for military aid.[29]

Morris, lacking the financial and legal means to give the frontier settlers what they wanted, had to find some other way to respond to the petitions that flowed into the capital. He decided that the best solution was the same one Gordon had used in the crisis of 1728 and that Penn used in the war with Maryland in the 1730s. He would bring the governor to the people, to win allies, to show that he supported frontier settlers' cause, and to campaign against those he believed were threatening his power to provide protection. He regularly toured the frontier, supervising technically extralegal defense measures and granting commissions to officers that had symbolic power but very little meaning because the militias lacked public funds. He sent other agents, like William West, to do the same. His travels and those of his representatives also made him even more aware of frontier sentiments, and through these meetings, bonds of trust were forged. Morris would tell frontier inhabitants that "his heart bled for them," but, without a militia law or funds, all he could do as captain-general was to commission officers.[30]

Morris's travels helped cement the bond between proprietor and frontier inhabitant. By moving the proprietary branch to frontier areas, its new locus of power, Morris showed his sympathy with its inhabitants. He also learned that he could use his popularity on the frontiers to pressure the Assembly to act. In November 1755, as tensions between the governor and Assembly reached a new peak, he threatened to remove the Assembly to Lancaster, believing that such a location would pressure the Assembly to provide greater defensive aid. Finally, on November 8, 1755, Morris left Philadelphia in "dispair" and "set off for the back counties; and if they have not all the assistance their present distresses make necessary, it will not be for want of inclination in me but power." He brought with him "a Quorum of the Council" so he could pass any bills sent to him. It may be more than coincidence that a few weeks after Morris traveled through the frontier regions, frontier inhabitants brought the dead corpses to Philadelphia to pressure the Assembly to act. It is certainly possible that Morris's campaign through the frontiers, in which he berated the legislature for its delays, inspired frontier inhabitants to act.[31]

But while Morris's tours strengthened the link between governor and frontier inhabitants, it did not strengthen the colonial government. Instead, the bitter rivalry between Assembly and proprietor empowered frontier inhabitants in ways that Patrick Gordon had tried to avoid in the 1728 crisis. Because there was no militia bill, frontier settlers formed their own ad hoc militias and could select their own officers. Morris's willingness "to appoint for officers all such as should be recommended by the respective bodies of people who desired to be formed into companies" gave local settlers an enormous amount of autonomy, which fostered a deep belief among settlers that they could rely only on themselves, not the colonial government, for their security.[32]

Frontier inhabitants thus seized new authority from their colonial government and placed this new power in local leaders, the "chiefs of the frontiers" as they once said. The growth of this new political leadership, one that replaced traditional leaders who provided protection like the governor, revealed something else: the inability of the government to react to the problems of expansion as it had in the past. The politicization of frontier people and the acrimonious politics of the east brought about by war would prove a powerful and profound challenge to the government's ability to maintain peace after the Treaty of Easton.[33]

"So Many Cruelties Have Been Practiced upon the Whites by the Indians, That the Innocent Are Not Secure from Their Revenge"

Hints at the problem between official policy and colonial sentiment became apparent as soon as the two polities tried to enact peace. In July 1758, the governor of Pennsylvania asked Christian Frederick Post, one of the colony's Indian emissaries, to travel to Indian communities in the west to reestablish diplomatic relations with the colonial government. As Post traveled, he saw "many plantations deserted and laid waste," leading him to "reflect on the distress, the poor owners must be drove to, who once lived in plenty." Along the roads, Post observed red poles, markers, he believed, of Indian execution sites. But he could not let these reminders of war color his mission, which was to end divisions between the Indians and the British. In private meetings with Ohio Indians, he let them know that "the English were at war with the French, but not with those Indians, who withdrew from the French, and would be at peace with the English." Post succeeded, and a few months later, after attending the second Treaty of Easton, Post was again sent on a peace mission to the Ohio.[34]

As he marched west this second time, joined by the colony's new Indian allies, he soon learned that the vision of peace between Indians and the British was going to be hard to enforce among the people whose homes he had seen "deserted and laid to waste" on his earlier trip. While Post maintained very friendly relationships with his fellow travelers, his trip was punctuated by several tense moments when these Indian warriors clashed with their former British adversaries in a war of words that recounted the battles fought between both sides. In language that echoed what Smith heard elders say to Indian warriors, Post's charges declared that the British fighters were "fools" who Indians easily defeated and could do so again. As he passed a fort standing near Big Cove and Little Cove, "Some of the Irish people, knowing some of the Indians, in a rash manner exclaimed against them." Later, however, as he firmed up commitments of peace with Indian leaders on the Ohio, these Indian representatives ignored the simmering tensions that Post had seen on the journey and declared "there shall be an everlasting peace with all the Indians, established as sure as the mountains, between the English nation and the Indians, all over, from the sun rising to the sun setting." Post's travels suggested that peace between former combatants was something leaders could accept as a matter of policy, but on a social level among colonists, the process of becoming a frontier was a hard one to undo.[35]

Doctor John, a Delaware man who lived with his family of four in a group of cabins on Conodoguinet Creek in Cumberland County, was one of the unfortunate victims of this change in society after the Treaty at Easton. Doctor John, who had been at war with Pennsylvania just a couple of years earlier, had returned to the area with his family and was now described by county officials as "a friend to the whites." On January 15, 1760, Doctor John was at the home-turned-tavern of Peter Title in Carlisle, a booming frontier town that served as an important waypoint for supplies and men. On that winter night, a number of people gathered at Title's unlicensed tippling house to escape the winter doldrums through some swill and idle chatter. Doctor John made his way there too. Doctor John's return and visit to Title's house suggest that on a superficial level, at least, people who had lived on frontiers tried to return to normal.[36]

But a terse exchange between John and Title revealed how difficult closing this frontier could be for people who had fought during the war. A
dispute seemed to begin with a discussion of Captain Jacobs, the Delaware
warrior whose bravery during the war was legendary. Jacobs was killed at
the battle of Kittanning in 1756, and in the tavern that night, his legacy
seemed to be the topic of discussion. It is unclear who brought up Captain
Jacobs in the bar, but something got John to say "that the white people had
killed his Captain Jacobs, but that he had one twice as big, and that they
[whites] were fools, for when he caught a white prisoner he would lie down
on the ground till he would kill and scalp him." John bragged that he had
killed "sixty whites" during the war and vowed to do the same with just
two or three other Indians if war broke out again. Such an exchange suggests that Title and the Pennsylvanians had goaded Doctor John by rubbing
the murder of a respected Indian leader in his face, and John had responded
in kind by evoking the memory of a frontier where colonists lived in fear
of Indian attacks.[37]

Such heated talk meant that many settlers and Indians were still waging
a war with words and memories. It also suggested that the memory of the
war for settlers and Indians was far different from the ebullient views of
officials who welcomed peace as a sign of victory. John's talk of killing sixty
whites, his claim that he would easily do so again, and his mocking of
settlers' behaviors in the face of death all suggested that he knew which
buttons to push to play upon settlers' emotions. He knew that for many
colonists who had lived on a frontier, the war was not a victory. Indians had
returned, Pennsylvania settlement had been pushed back, and unknown
numbers of Europeans had been killed and captured. Settlers had won only
a few pyrrhic victories over Indians, and after the war, colonists tended to
commemorate losses rather than triumphs. Braddock's Field, for instance,
became an undisturbed memorial that drew somber visitors for decades
following his disastrous defeat. The geography also reflected loss. Residents
would tell travelers decades later how Bloody Run, a creek near the Cono-
cocheague, got its name from an Indian attack that had killed a family
living on it. Even today, residents tell visitors how the creek's water ran red
with blood from warfare with Indians.[38]

In early February, almost three weeks after the exchange of words in
Carlisle, news of the confrontation at Title's had spread throughout the
settler population, and angry colonists took deadly action. A group of settlers entered Doctor John's cabin in the middle of the night and murdered

him, his wife, and their two children. The bodies of his wife and one of the children were never found. The murderers took the scalps of Doctor John and his son, which symbolized legitimate wartime behavior.[39]

Such an act was a serious test of Pennsylvania's renewed policy of peace with Delawares. One early history of the murders recognized their importance by calling the incident "the first case of murder, by the whites, of friendly Indians." We know that they had their history wrong, but the recollection of the incident in the nineteenth century and the sentiment of the interpretation reflect the significance of this act at the time. In fact, the murders in 1760 were reminiscent of the Winters brothers' killings of 1728, in which settlers motivated by rumors of Indian attacks killed Indians as though they were wartime enemies, even though official policy said otherwise. Unlike in 1728, however, the murder of Doctor John and his family appeared to have been particularly targeted at an Indian who claimed the mantle of the Delawares' cause and threatened and demeaned his colonial neighbors. As the reports to the governor suggested, his crime was that he "behaved insolently." He had spoken freely and used his words to resurrect the memory of life on a frontier for colonists. Soon, that memory turned into a violent reality when some colonists decided to seek retribution for the fear his words instilled in them.[40]

Officials of the colonial government took swift action. Francis West, William's brother, was the justice in Cumberland tasked with dealing with the murder. He immediately repudiated the murders, conducted an investigation, and held a grand jury inquest that confirmed murder as the cause of death. West also vowed to "afford protections to every peaceable and friendly Indian that shall sojourn in this county," and the Assembly offered a £100 reward. The proprietor sent immediate messages to the Delawares offering the colony's condolences with the promise that "no pains should be spared to discover and punish the authors, and not to omit any ceremonies it were proper and usual on this occasion." Within days, the governor's proclamations calling for information reached Fort Pitt, setting the colony atwitter with talk of the crime and its potentially devastating repercussions. A few weeks later, John Loughry of York County felt compelled to come forward with information. He implicated James Foster, John Mason, William George, and the sons of Arthur Foster in the murder. The men came from various parts of what had been the frontier during the Seven Years' War; one came from Paxton in Lancaster County and the rest lived in Cumberland County. The crew, Loughry told authorities, had planned

the murder in advance, tried to enlist his support beforehand, and confessed to him afterward.[41]

While much of the action officials took is reminiscent of the colony's
reaction to the 1728 murders, there were also important differences that
reveal the ways war had transformed Indians' status within the colony itself.
The governor's proclamation against the murders instructed Pennsylvanians "to avoid all quarrels and contentions with any Indians who either
do reside or are passing thro' this province," but, instead of requiring Pennsylvanians to treat Indians, as they did in 1728, "with the same civil regard
they would an English subject," the government "earnestly recommended"
settlers "to treat all the Indians with civility and brotherly kindness." This
statement, along with others like the local justices' promise to protect Indians that "shall *sojourn*" in the area, suggest a subtle but significant change
in their expectations of Indians' place in the polity. Indians were not neighbors who received the same protections as colonists but travelers to be
treated by colonists with "civility and brotherly tenderness" for strategic
reasons, "as a measure highly conducive to the safety and peace" of the
colony. War had caused this transformation, as Francis West expressed in a
letter: "So many cruelties have been practiced upon the whites by the Indians, that the innocent (Indians) are not secure from their revenge."[42]

The greatest difference between the 1728 and 1760 murders is that in
1728, Pennsylvania hanged two colonists for the murder of an Indian family.
In 1762, when relatives of Doctor John came to Philadelphia for an update
on the case, Governor James Hamilton dodged a direct response. Instead,
he pointed out that "some white people have been killed by Indians in
Several parts of the province since the peace, as well as a few Indians by
white people," but neither side had exacted justice. While the governor
reassured the family members that the colony promised to find and execute
the guilty, he also excused both the Pennsylvania officials and Indian leaders for their lack of action, stating there was no "fault in those who conduct
publick affairs on either side" for not finding the murderers and argued
that the family should not let Doctor John's murder "interrupt the peace
and friendship that have been so happily restored between the English and
Indians."[43]

The governor's response offered a dubious vision for maintaining peace.
Hamilton essentially outlined a policy of peace between polities and those
"who conduct publick affairs" but not between their constituents who
interacted on a daily basis. It was a world in which neither Pennsylvania

officials nor Indian leaders seemed capable of stopping regular violence between settlers and Indians. Theoretically, structural changes to Pennsylvania's landscape should have made the enforcement of policy easier than ever. Proclamations traveled from Philadelphia to Fort Pitt in record time along a road created during the war, passing through a line of forts that housed British officers and the remnants of Pennsylvania's militia. Pennsylvania had more justices of the peace and counties than ever before. But the policy of peace was hard to enforce because of the very reason that these changes to the landscape had occurred: Pennsylvania's countryside had turned into a frontier country, and many colonists continued to believe frontiers existed.[44]

Many Indians had also changed their perceptions of Pennsylvania and its inhabitants. Warriors had mobilized behind a shared belief in removing the British Empire and its colonists from North America. For these Indians, white settlement was very much the "front" that they wanted to enter and reclaim. For Indians fighting on this frontier, "whites" were now associated with British colonizers, even more so after the expulsion of the French imperial presence in 1763. Doctor John's language was strikingly reminiscent of the elders who spoke to James Smith mocking "whites" as "fools" and bragging about how easy it was to defeat British settlers and their officers. Just as Pennsylvanians were creating ideas of Indians as "merciless, savage," as Burd described them in his letter from Fort Augusta in 1758, Indians were creating a competing idea of those on the other side of the frontier as fools and cowards.

These characterizations suggest that colonial and Indian warriors on this frontier created a conception of their enemy rooted in culturally defined ideas of bravery and masculinity. For both Indians and Euro-American settlers mobilizing for war, the terms upon which they defined the other struck at the core of their ideas of cultural superiority. Euro-Americans condemned Indians for not fighting by the codes of European warfare, and Indians mocked Euro-Americans' inability to fight with the same bravery and cunning they did. These conceptions helped bolster warriors for either side, while also creating a strong cultural antipathy of the other. Only the bravest of colonial warriors could defend against a "savage" enemy who defied the laws of war, and their losses had to do not with cultural inferiority but with the illegitimate tactics of their attackers. Indian warriors, for their part, found validation in their culture by so easily defeating foolish enemies who learned little and showed nothing but cowardice. The competing memories of former combatants, then, would be hard to surmount, even if political leaders called for a return to peace. Indeed, when war and frontiers returned to the region in 1763, the perceptions forged in the Seven Years' War returned and only deepened Pennsylvania's governing crisis.

CHAPTER 7

The Permanent Frontier

On December 28, 1756, James Burd penned a long letter to a friend relating the events of the past several years. Burd served as an integral part of the colony's defense. He organized a militia, served as its colonel, created roads, and constructed forts. In fact, he wrote the letter while stationed at Fort Augusta on the Susquehanna River. Unlike past forts on the river that protected Pennsylvanians from neighboring colonies, this one was built to ward off an attack from French or Indian enemies. Sitting secure in his fort for a moment, he reminisced about Pennsylvania's past. The colony he remembered had been "the most pleasant, peaceable, country in the world." War would forever change that. This place of peace had "become a land of murders and rapine."[1]

After the war ended, the government wanted to make Pennsylvania "the most pleasant, peaceable, country in the world" once again. The years that followed proved that it would not be easy. The fear and hatred colonists knew during the war lingered in homes and haunted memories. Soon, colonists on former frontiers who interacted with their former enemies who were also their neighbors showed that such animosities could quickly turn into violence that resembled wartime behavior. Pennsylvania officials thus faced a dilemma reminiscent of the frontier crisis of 1728. They had to convince a large swath of their population that frontiers no longer existed, while also providing these colonists who were fearful of their Native neighbors with a sense of security.

At the same time, Indian resentment toward the British began to rise as colonial settlement began to spread further onto Indian lands and British military officers treated Indian groups as conquered subordinates. In 1763, Indians unhappy with the postwar settlement waged another battle meant

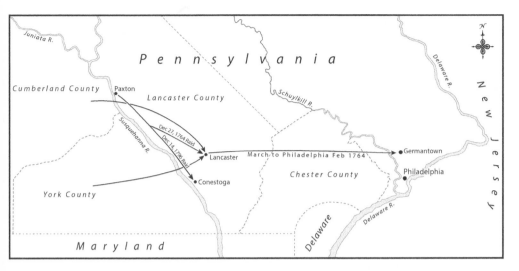

Figure 11. The sites of the Paxton Boys' assaults on the Conestoga Indians and the path of their subsequent march to Philadelphia, 1763–1764. In 1763, Pennsylvania was caught in the midst of another Indian War. In December, a group of self-described "frontier inhabitants" raided Conestoga and killed a group of Indians who had proclaimed their neutrality in the war. The government brought the remaining Indians to a workhouse in Lancaster, Pennsylvania, for their safety. A raid on the workhouse by frontier inhabitants a couple of weeks later killed these survivors. In February, a large group of frontier inhabitants, unhappy with the government's frontier policy and treatment of Native Americans, marched to Philadelphia in protest. The Paxton Boys' Rebellion established the political foundations for a frontier crisis that challenged colonial and imperial governance and would remain unresolved until the American Revolution.

to send the British Empire into retreat. Known as Pontiac's War, the fighting reopened frontiers on Pennsylvania's landscape, and frontier inhabitants acted as they had before, forming volunteer militias and providing for their own defense. As Pennsylvania returned to "a land of murder" once again, frontier people found that their government was slow to react because of the contentious politics in the east. The politics of this war cemented frontier people's perceptions of their colonial government's inadequacies.

In the midst of this war and political strife, an event happened that transformed the colony. In December 1763, the Paxton Boys massacred the Conestoga Indians, who had lived on a manor William Penn laid out for them in 1701. The Paxton Boys' actions revealed that something new had formed on Pennsylvania's landscape: a racial frontier. Through their words and actions, frontier people who supported the Paxton Boys made it clear that they believed Native peoples formed a single, coherent group that was an inherent enemy. Indians, according to the logic of a racial frontier, were to receive no benefits of colonial government because they were a perpetual threat. The hardening of this perception mobilized frontier people to challenge their colonial government and established a political culture that would eventually upend the foundations of the colony.

"The Frontier Counties of Pennsylvania . . . Will . . . Associate Themselves for Their Mutual Defense"

The transition from war to peace was a key moment for the empire. In order to ensure stability, imperial officials wanted to close the frontiers that had opened during the war. The problem they faced was twofold. First, the British Crown had assumed a massive amount of debt in the Seven Years' War, and Parliamentarians in England looked to America for cuts in their expenses. They quickly found an area that seemed ripe for cuts: money used to support Indian treaties and gift exchanges. Indians, however, expected an increase in such activities after the war as a sign of Great Britain's commitment to peace. The new curbs made Indians, especially those in western Pennsylvania, feel a renewed sense of marginalization and mistreatment. Conversely, frontier inhabitants worried that reductions in military forces in western areas might embolden Indians to invade their homes. No one in North America, it seemed, was happy with the empire's immediate postwar policies.[2]

Rather than increase British coffers, the cost cuts and other shifts in policy led to a pan-Indian movement in 1763 that culminated in Pontiac's War, during which Indians from Detroit to western Pennsylvania launched an offensive against British settlements. The war is named for Pontiac, a prominent Ottawa who helped organize a pan-Indian alliance intended to push the British out of the Ohio. The war began in the summer of 1763 with a siege of Fort Detroit. Soon, other Native peoples, predominantly Shawnees and Delawares, aimed their offensive at western Pennsylvania, re-creating zones of invasion within the colony. As John Penn, lieutenant governor of Pennsylvania, reported, "They say themselves are determind never to lay down the hatchet 'till they have driven the English into the sea." The Indian alliance was extraordinarily successful at first, destroying the chain of forts the British Army had built to connect the eastern seaboard with their new western holdings. With only Fort Pitt still standing in western Pennsylvania, one Delaware boasted that "all the country was theirs; they had been cheated out of it, and . . . they would carry on the war till they had burnt Philadelphia."[3]

Pontiac's War also reopened the old wounds of the Seven Years' War— between Indians and colonists living on a war-torn frontier, and between Pennsylvanians on the frontier who demanded greater military aid and those in government they perceived as obstructionist. After a summer of what one historian describes as a series of "dazzling Indian victories," settlers in Carlisle declared themselves once again a "naked and much expos'd frontier" that needed assistance. By October, General Henry Bouquet, stationed in Carlisle, estimated Indians had killed six hundred settlers. Survivors lived in constant fear of Delaware and Shawnee assaults, and the early victories showed that united Native nations could launch a successful offensive war into Pennsylvania without a European ally. Attacks in Pennsylvania continued until Bouquet negotiated a peace settlement with Shawnees in the late fall of 1764 that was later confirmed in a formal peace treaty. The war resulted in a draw, if not a slight Indian victory. Native peoples failed to regain any land, but they secured the promise of greater diplomatic and political power from British officials weary of waging costly wars in North America.[4]

The reformation of frontiers during the war led to a situation strikingly similar to the Seven Years' War. The governor received "petitions every day from the frontier inhabitants requesting assistance against the Indians who still continue their ravages in the most cruel manner." Just as in the Seven Years' War, the legislative and proprietary branches clashed over supplying troops—what newly installed governor John Penn called "the old dispute." Penn had hoped that after the Seven Years' War, the colony would be able to react to war more nimbly. Instead, he found himself bogged down in protracted debates about funding a militia and the various limitations the Assembly could place on military matters. Eventually, Pennsylvania provided for militiamen but restricted their actions to the defense of harvesting parties. After increased pressure from British officials (and after the march of the Paxton Boys), the Assembly in the spring of 1764 agreed to support the British Army stationed in western Pennsylvania, then poised to launch an offensive in Indian Country.[5]

The speed and ease with which volunteer militias re-formed in 1763 speaks to the militarized culture that frontiers had fostered in the Seven Years' War. Officials recognized these cultural patterns and began to involve them in their strategies for defense. While the Assembly and proprietor were locked in argument, General Thomas Gage observed that it was "probable that the frontier counties of Pennsylvania, being left exposed to the incursions of the savages, and no provision made by the legislature for their defence and protection, will of their own accord associate themselves for their mutual defense." Residents of the "frontier counties" proved his prediction correct. John Armstrong, a former officer in the provincial corps living in Cumberland County, formed a three-hundred-man militia and launched raids on Delaware Indians on the western branch of the Susquehanna. Even after attacks had stopped in the summer of 1764, frontier people still maintained their defensive positions. Colonists in Armstrong's Cumberland County, for instance, had "by private subscription hir'd men to patrole . . . whereby a slight cover is thrown over thirty-five miles of the eastern part of the county."[6]

There were, however, important changes to this mobilization. Frontier settlers were quick to assume Indians, no matter their location or allegiance, were enemies. Frontier settlers had also grown more politically astute since the Seven Years' War, and they had learned that well-planned and dramatic acts, like carting corpses through Philadelphia, could elicit a quick response from a government they considered sluggish. The Conestoga Indians served as the unfortunate recipients of this new frontier political culture on December 14, 1763.

On that cold and snowy Wednesday morning, a group of militiamen from Paxton, a town north of Lancaster, met on the banks of the Susquehanna. They mounted their horses and headed toward the Conestoga Manor. For sixty years, the Conestogas had lived there, proud of the treaty they had signed with William Penn in 1701. The government had continued to support them through gifts, and they traded with colonists. As more colonists settled near the Conestogas, they adapted to their surroundings. Their children often carried English names and played with their Pennsylvanian neighbors. While many adopted English names and other European habits, they, nonetheless, remained Conestoga, a distinct people who fervently protected their rights to a separate land.[7]

Then the Paxton Rangers arrived. They entered the Conestogas' homes and killed every Indian they found, six total. The dead were women, children, and an elderly man, Sheehays, who had met William Penn and whose home held the cherished treaty the Conestogas had signed with Penn. The remaining Conestogas, numbering about fourteen, appear to have been out trading.

Once John Penn heard of the murders, he took swift action to protect the surviving Conestogas. John was the nephew of Thomas Penn, who became the sole proprietor after both of his older brothers died. Thomas had no issue, making John and his younger brother, Richard, heirs to the colony. John was a good choice for governing. Born in 1729, he was a profligate youth who buckled down in his twenties and took seriously his responsibility to the proprietorship. By 1763, Thomas was confident that his thirty-four-year-old nephew was ready to take the helm of the colony. John had a heady task before him. He was entering the governorship in the midst of a war and in the beginning years of the British Empire's attempt to reorganize their North American holdings. He was to become the central proprietary figure in the years before independence, serving as governor throughout the imperial crisis with only a brief pause when his obstreperous brother, Richard, took the reins. John arrived in Philadelphia November 1763, and the massacre of the Conestogas was the first of many crises he faced. It was a fitting introduction to the colony.[8]

News of the attack was soon followed by rumors that the Paxton Boys intended to finish the deed begun on December 14; so Penn and his deputies directed the surviving Conestogas to head to Lancaster's workhouse for protection. The workhouse served as the jail and was thought to be the strongest building in the area. Perhaps it was the strongest in terms of keeping people from escaping it. Unfortunately, it proved too permeable for those wishing to enter it. On the afternoon of December 27, a large group, probably the original Paxton Rangers and some new recruits, stormed the jail and turned the workhouse into a slaughterhouse. They killed the remaining fourteen Conestogas, including infants. The murder was brutal and public. A crowd assembled in the town square to watch and did nothing to stop them.[9]

The Paxton Rangers' twin raids came after a particularly brutal and successful Indian attack on colonial settlements in Northampton. Reports circulated that the Conestogas were complicit in this raid and were simply using their neutrality as a façade. Rumors also said that a particular Conestoga named Will Sock had taken up the hatchet against colonists. The allegations gave the Paxton Rangers the immediate cause for their assault. Its deeper cause, however, rested in their experience of living on frontiers during the Seven Years' War. The Paxton Rangers, like many other frontier inhabitants, had come to view all Indians as suspect, and they castigated their government's support for the Conestogas as evidence of a dangerous, perhaps even willful, naïveté within the Assembly. To them, an attack on the Conestogas was a raid on an enemy, a view that cut against the official policy of Pennsylvania, which treated Indian groups as separate entities, some of whom received the government's protection.[10]

The Paxton Boys committed these vicious acts as a way to speak to their government, just as they had when they carted corpses through the streets of Philadelphia. They wanted to show the government the way they envisioned their neighbors. Unlike the scuffles from 1728, which were unplanned and spontaneous, the Paxton Rangers planned these attacks and intended them for public consumption. And the very open nature of the massacres meant that they challenged the policies of the government to which they belonged. For the Paxton Boys, Indians existed outside of the protections of Pennsylvania, and since the Paxton men were members of the colony, they believed that the government should respect their demands. They, in essence, sought to clarify what officials had left undefined for pragmatic reasons in previous eras: the legal status of Indians within the polity. Where vagueness had allowed colonial officials to maintain peace, the Paxton Boys could use the undetermined standing of Indians to assert that such groups were outside of the government's protection.

The Paxton Boys' acts, if unpunished, would set a precedent that would transform the legitimate use of violence within the colony by making the murder of Indians permissible. The government recognized this threat and soon began taking action to assert the promise of protection it offered certain allied Indian groups. In particular, Penn worried that the Paxton Boys had their eyes set on a Christianized group in Bethlehem. Penn, now realizing that no building on the frontiers was strong enough to stop a set of determined men who seemed to have the support of their communities, brought these Indians to Philadelphia, eventually placing them on Province Island in the Delaware River, believed to be the most secure place in Philadelphia.[11]

In January, inhabitants in the frontier counties began meeting and talking about the Bethlehem Indians. Soon, the frontier people began organizing. Then, in early February of 1764, they began marching. Several hundred people left Lancaster and headed east to Philadelphia, a ninety-mile trek in the depth of winter. Just as the Seven Years' War helped build crosscultural bonds within colonial society, the band of men consisted of a motley mixture of "Englishmen, Irish-men and Germans," all of whom had shared a common experience on Pennsylvania's frontiers and now shared a common cause as they marched east in protest of government.[12]

The marchers met with strong support everywhere as they headed east. As John Harris, a wealthy trader near Paxton, boasted to a friend, "The inhabitants of this province on all roads from Paxton to Philad[elphi]a used the volunteers well" during their trek. But as they approached Philadelphia, the protesters found the Schuylkill River ferries destroyed, making direct access to Philadelphia impossible. Undeterred, they headed further north, to Swedesboro, where they found a crossing and then headed south toward Germantown. As they approached that small village near Philadelphia, they met a frantic German preacher, Reverend Paul Brycelius, who had left Philadelphia that morning to meet them. After speaking with him about the situation within the city, they decided to camp at a tavern in Germantown until the next day.[13]

Meanwhile, the city was scrambling. Word could travel fast in Pennsylvania, and almost as soon as marchers left their homes, Philadelphia officials began preparing for their arrival. On February 1, John Penn called a public meeting in the State House Yard. He invoked the riot act, called upon Philadelphians to muster, and ordered British troops to prepare for an assault and to "defend [the Moravian Indians] with fire." Penn was taking the steps necessary to uphold Pennsylvania's promise of protection against violence, while also protecting the city and government he controlled.[14]

The city soon buzzed with speculation about the expected attack. Quakers were particularly instrumental in organizing the defense. Henry Muhlenberg, the most prominent German preacher in Pennsylvania, recorded their activity in his journal: "Friends . . . ran furiously back and forth to the barracks," and "there was a great to-do over constructing several small fortresses or ramparts near the barracks." Militias mustered in the large yard by the Quaker meetinghouse, and volunteer militias marched through the streets.[15]

The governor, however, was concerned about the lack of support he found in the rest of the public. In private correspondence, he wrote, "The people of this town are as inveterate against the Indians as the frontier inhabitants" and speculated that "were it not for a few of the King's troops who are here to protect them, that the whole power of government would not be able to prevent them being murdered." John Ewing, a Presbyterian preacher in Philadelphia, likewise confided to a friend in London that "ninety-nine in a hundred of the Province are firmly persuaded, that they [the friendly Indians] are maintaining our enemies." Muhlenberg believed that few of the Germans about town felt any sympathy for the Indians in Philadelphia. Indeed, according to Muhlenberg, they seemed to agree with the marchers' claim that some of those protected "had secretly killed several settlers" and that the Quakers, out of their own "self-interest," had abetted these murders. Penn expressed a similar belief, writing that some of the Indians under the colony's care had been "concerned in committing murders among the back settlers." But, he noted, that was not the immediate concern of government policy. Pennsylvania had promised protection to these Indians, and it respected its treaties with them.[16]

Penn reached out to Muhlenberg for aid by chastising the German residents of Philadelphia for their apathy and suggested to Muhlenberg that they "might be making common cause with the malcontents." Whatever his personal feelings, Muhlenberg acted accordingly when Penn asked him to support the government. He organized a German militia that "made several tours in and around the city." Their service proved both dangerous and farcical. At one point, a Philadelphia constable unfamiliar with these Germans mistook them for the marchers entering the city and almost opened fire upon them.[17]

Muhlenberg also dispatched one of his trusted preachers, Pastor Brycelius, to Germantown to warn the German congregations outside Philadelphia against joining the marchers and to dissuade any Germans already among them from traveling further. Brycelius left early on the morning of February 6 to carry out his mission. He found no evidence of the marchers in Germantown, where, remarkably, no one he encountered had heard of the march or the potential assault on Philadelphia. Brycelius continued north, "over Chestnut Hill, up to the point where dwellings stop," where he "suddenly and unexpectedly . . . ran into the vanguard of these people."[18]

Brycelius soon became the unwitting emissary between the marchers and the government. The frontier people told Brycelius why they came: "to demand the custody of the Bethlehem Indians, not to kill them, but only to conduct them out of the province" and to present a list of grievances to the government. Brycelius told them of the alarms in Philadelphia and advised them that going further would result in a "blood-bath." The marchers took his advice and halted at Coleman's Tavern in Germantown while Brycelius returned to Philadelphia on their behalf. After hearing Brycelius's report, Penn gathered seven of the most prominent Philadelphians and left at five the next morning to meet with the marchers.[19]

The ambassadors for the Pennsylvania government found about 250 men at Coleman's Tavern, many of whom carried muskets and had spent the night in makeshift camps outside. Reliable reports circulated that four hundred more were arriving that afternoon, and the pressure was on the government's representatives to ease the situation before it escalated further. When the Pennsylvania representatives arrived, the rebels escorted them to an upstairs room where they met Colonel John Armstrong, a justice of the peace for Cumberland County, surveyor for the proprietor, and a frontier hero of the Seven Years' War for the killing of Captain Jacobs at Kittanning. According to Muhlenberg, Armstrong seemed to be "the chief agent of the frontier inhabitants," but the meeting could not begin until the spokesman for the "militant frontiersmen" arrived. Although Armstrong was a prominent symbol of the marchers' wide support, he was not their leader. Shortly thereafter, Matthew Smith, the spokesman for the "militant frontiersmen," arrived with two assistants, John Gibson and William Brown. Smith was late because he had apparently entered Philadelphia secretly that morning to survey the scene for himself and had even talked with some of the government's emissaries before they left the city for Germantown.[20]

At the meeting, the marchers made clear their intent. Just as they had in the Seven Years' War when they marched through the streets of Philadelphia with mutilated bodies, frontier inhabitants wanted to compel their government to act by creating the same sense of fear in Philadelphians as they themselves felt on the frontiers. The chief difference was that the Paxton Boys were a more politically coherent and unified group whose actions were meant to display their strength to Philadelphians through a show of martial force, while the protesters in 1755 demonstrated their helplessness by carting slain bodies through town. The ferocity of their murders and the size of their march were meant to show that a unified frontier people were more powerful than government institutions, like the jail in Lancaster they invaded. They thus hoped that their prowess would force legislators to meet frontier demands and force the Assembly to meet the terms of its contract with frontier people in which the government provided them with protection in exchange for their loyalty.[21]

The representatives of the Paxton Boys used the meeting to air their grievances, all of which had to do with government policy, especially their impression of the Assembly as unsympathetic. Their chief complaint was that the malapportioned representation did a disservice to the political body because the legislature failed to empathize with those on the outer limbs of the political body. Their radical actions, they said, were driven by their political impotence. Their exclusion from government drove them to such violent and forceful acts in order to prod their government to act as they believed it should. Evoking the purported words of Nathaniel Grubb, they accused the Assembly of having dismissed them as "nothing but a mixed crowd of Scotch-Irishmen and Germans; it did not matter whether they lived or died" and for showing, in their estimation, greater preference for supporting Indians than frontiersmen. They also clarified what they hoped to accomplish with the march. They assured the governor that they were loyal to the Crown and province, using their service in war as testament to their allegiance. Instead, their only goal was to "to take the Indians out of the barracks, and to conduct them out of the province," an act they believed essential to establishing their vision of a colony in which Indians had no place among its members. The marchers then worked with Benjamin Franklin and Philadelphia Mayor Thomas Willing, both part of the government's envoy, to help put what they said into print. By the next day, February 8, the marchers had departed.[22]

"They Were as Much Enemies as Any Other Tribe of Indians on the Continent"

What the Paxton Boys said before leaving crystallized the political debate that would rile the colony for the next decade. The marchers' *Declaration and Remonstrance*, written before they left Germantown, was the opening salvo in a war of words that soon engulfed the colony. By the Assembly election in October 1764, Philadelphia printers had churned out more than sixty pamphlets and prints that engaged with the issues raised by the massacre and march. Most historians have focused on the print war as a unified whole, as if all the prints should be reflective of the colony. Such a perspective obscures the politics of frontier inhabitants. Known frontier settlers only authored a few pamphlets. Focusing on these specific pamphlets rather than the pamphlet war as a whole can help elucidate their reasons for rebellion.[23]

The *Declaration*, the first of these prints, established the fundamental position of the frontier people who marched. They described Pennsylvania as a colony that was at perpetual war against a singular Indian enemy. According to the Paxton Boys and their supporters, only European settlers could be members of the colony who received its government's protection, while all Indians—including those that appeared to be allies—were enemies who were prone to disguise their true allegiance under a "cloak of friendship." As the *Declaration and Remonstrance* stated, "We . . . conceive that it is contrary to the maxims of good policy . . . to suffer any Indians of what tribe soever, to live within the inhabited parts of this province, while we are engaged in an Indian War; as experience has taught us they are all perfidious."[24]

The Paxton Boys' argument thus exposed the nasty logic of eighteenth-century frontier life. The perception of being on a frontier, as defined by its eighteenth-century meaning and as expressed by the actions of the Paxton Boys and the words of their supporters, created a unified conception of Indians as perpetual and inherent enemies. Extreme fear had turned into a hatred so profound that a racial paradigm formed in the minds of frontier people. Other racial categories in colonial America were not framed by wartime values, but with Native peoples, warfare went hand in hand with their racialization. As a result, the creation of a racial other was inseparable from the belief that this race had to be defeated, removed, or decimated, all ideas articulated by the Paxton Boys. By holding a singular view of all Indians as enemies who belonged to a separate polity, settlers saw a frontier anywhere Indians were. This logic meant that Pennsylvania had a frontier so long as Indians inhabited the landscape, regardless of what official treaties said. While phenotype, the typical marker of race, was less apparent in the words of the frontier settlers, the logic of the argument—the lumping together of separate groups into a unified whole who deserved no rights—is hard to describe as anything other than racial. As the author of the "Apology," another Paxton apologetic, said of the Conestogas, "they were as much enemies as any other tribe of Indians on the continent."[25]

Such a development was not confined to Pennsylvania or to this era. Similar language and rationales seemed to appear wherever frontiers against Native Americans existed. In the seventeenth century, Virginia passed laws regulating its frontiers premised on the belief that the colony was in a "continuall" war with Indians. In 1707, Cotton Mather's *Frontiers Well-Defended* used animalizing metaphors for all Indians, casting them as subhuman "beasts of prey," "wolves," and "tawny serpents" who threatened colonists. The experience of warfare in these other colonies confirmed in the minds of "frontier inhabitants" ideas of Native American savagery and barbarism that had long circulated throughout society but had not become a normative assumption. This rationale, occurring at different times in different places, led to a new conception of what good frontier policy meant. Advocates who held this view of Indians as perpetual enemies argued that the government should take a permanent hostile posture toward them. Their perception of Indians forged through war made them believe that offensive actions were necessary for defensive needs.[26]

The racial frontier seen by those like the Paxton Boys conflicted with the views of those who governed the colony. Where the Paxton Boys wanted removal of Indians as a matter of good policy, their opponents proposed a very different approach, which revealed a far different understanding of the colony's geopolitical landscape and Indians' place within the polity. The stark differences within colonial society became clear when rivals to the Paxton Boys described the Conestogas' location in the polity. As the governor declared in an official proclamation denouncing the Paxton Boys, the Conestogas were a group who had lived "peaceably and inoffensively" and "in the heart of the province." Benjamin Franklin, a foe of Penn's, nonetheless expressed a similar belief, writing that while "the inhabitants of the frontiers" may be justified in attacking their enemies in the "woods," nothing could "justify turning in to the heart of the country, to murder their friends." Franklin and others thought that having the Conestogas in the "heart" of the colony was a good thing, a testament to Pennsylvania's legacy of peace and evidence of the group's innocence. For them, Lancaster was no longer a frontier. It was protected, a part of the colony's heart. Instead, points west were frontiers.[27]

The Paxton Boys, meanwhile, used a similar language of the body politic to critique the eastern interpretation of the colony's frontiers. They expressed great "distress" with Pennsylvania's government "supporting, in the very heart of the provinces . . . between one and two hundred savages." The body metaphor reflected their understanding of a frontier that should guard the "heart" of a state, a conception rooted in a long tradition of frontier rhetoric. To the Paxton Boys, the presence of Indians in such areas as Bethlehem and Lancaster—and now, of all places, Philadelphia, "the very heart of the province"—turned these supposed safe locales into frontiers, exposed and vulnerable zones defined by fear of attack.[28]

These competing conceptions of the colony's geopolitics revealed a profound dispute within colonial society, one that would animate politics in the region for decades. The Paxton Boys intended the massacre to prove their loyalty and service to the colony's frontiers by treating Indians as perpetual enemies, while those opposed to the Paxton Boys accepted—even celebrated—the Conestogas' presence in the colony's "heart" as evidence of Pennsylvania's benevolence. The debate over the Paxton massacre reveals that colonists and officials shared a common language of frontiers and even largely agreed on the political *meaning* of frontiers. Frontiers were zones vulnerable to attack that required active militarization and fortification. The disagreement was over the *existence* of frontiers in a given place and against whom they formed. When Franklin used the heart metaphor to describe the Conestogas' position in the polity, he was arguing that their place proved that they were not a threat. Indians, in Franklin's estimation, had a place in Pennsylvania. The Paxton Boys disagreed with Franklin's fundamental logic. Their actions showed how dangerous, deadly, and destabilizing such a divide over frontiers could be within a polity.[29]

The exclusion of frontier counties from the Assembly, the Paxton Boys argued, caused this divide to develop. A line in the *Declaration* attacking the Quaker hold on the Assembly powerfully captures this sentiment: "Such is our unhappy situation, under the villainy, infatuation and influence of a certain faction that have got the political reigns in their hand and tamely tyrannize over other good subjects of the province!" Thomas Barton, a frontier preacher from Lancaster, was far more explicit, declaring in his pamphlet that the "frontier-people . . . would have been safe in any part of the known world except in the neighbourhood of the RELENTLESS and OBSTINATE QUAKERS of PENNSYLVANIA." According to eighteenth-century political beliefs, actions like tyrannizing over one's subjects legitimated violent actions on the part of the tyrannized. As Barton also said, quoting a British lord as evidence, "The people . . . seldom or never assemble in any riotous or tumultuous manner, unless when they are oppressed, or at least imagine they are oppressed." For Barton, the cause of this "distemper" was the "caprice and obstinacy of a destructive faction," meaning Quakers, that "have treacherously held a correspondence with our avowed enemies" and failed to support the frontier as a government should.[30]

Such disaffection with their legislature led frontier pamphleteers to craft a defense of political power that privileged local authority over colonial or imperial authority. They thus took to defending the strongest institution of the government they could control and manipulate: the legal system. Matthew Smith and James Gibson, the putative authors of the *Declaration and Remonstrance*, took particular issue with the prominent rumor that the Paxton Boys were going to be tried in Philadelphia if caught, an action that would "deprive British subjects of their known privileges." They emphasized the British tradition of trial by a jury of the accused's "equals in the neighbourhood," who could best know "the circumstances of the fact." The "circumstances of fact" in the case of the Paxton Boys included their friends and neighbors views of Native peoples' position within the polity, which were predicated on the idea that Lancaster County was a frontier. The question at the heart of the Paxton Boys' protests was not one of guilt or innocence, but of whether Native peoples had the protection of the state or not. Smith and Gibson recognized that a jury in Philadelphia very well might seat colonists who did not share the Paxton Boys' view of Indians, and thus punish the Paxton rangers for their murders. A trial outside of their neighborhood, they noted, would be "putting their lives in the hands of strangers, who may as justly be suspected of partiality to, as the frontier counties can be of prejudices against Indians." The only way to handle this difference was to allow communities to regulate themselves.[31]

Frontier settlers also wanted to restrict commerce with all Indians, believing exchanging goods with friendly Indians was the same as trade with an enemy because these "falsly pretended friends" were likely to carry on a "secret correspondence and trade" with declared enemies. Of course, this demand went against what the government and Indians wanted. Trade for both was essential to maintaining harmony and stability. Trade for frontier inhabitants, however, meant the opposite. They believed trade simply provided Indians with the means to continue to fight. And when it came to trade, the Paxton Boys aimed their vehemence at Quakers and the Friendly Association in particular. They argued that the Friendly Association infringed on the governor's power as captain-general to wage war and establish peace for the colony. Israel Pemberton, the leader of the association and a prominent Indian trader, acted, they said, "as if he had been our governor or authorized by the King to treat with his enemies." The Paxton Boys believed that this extralegal association "taught" the Indians "to despise us as weak and disunited" and gave them a narrative that justified their disaffection from the colony based upon allegedly illegal land purchases. The Friendly Association had, in the words of the *Declaration*, "given them a rod to scourge the white people that were settled on the purchased lands."[32]

Underlying all of these complaints was something else: a logic of politics that would, eventually, connect the frontier inhabitants with their eastern brethren. Historians of the American Revolution have used Radical Whig rhetoric, which is often associated with republican political theory, to help explain the coming of the American Revolution. For these historians, the rhetoric of opposition leaders in Great Britain provided colonists with a means to explain the power dynamics of their political world in which they increasingly saw governors and imperial officials as their oppressors after the Seven Years' War. The frontier settlers use of this same language of political tyranny in this dispute against the Pennsylvania Assembly showed how far-reaching such rhetoric was in the British Atlantic world, especially on the eve of the imperial crisis.[33]

But the adoption of Radical Whig rhetoric also revealed the malleability of such ideas. Colonists in urban seaports opposed to imperial policies used such language in the 1760s to challenge royal governors and imperial policies that they believed intervened too much in colonial affairs. Theirs was an argument against government authority that they viewed as too coercive—against a too-powerful and arbitrary Parliament. Those who wrote in defense of the Paxton Boys used a similar language but did so for far different reasons. Like those in the seaports protesting against Parliament and taxes, frontier settlers accused Quakers of maintaining an arbitrary government to serve their ends rather than the interests of the colony. They did not accuse Quakers of undue interference, however. Rather, Quaker passivity and Assembly inaction were the signs of tyranny and oppression.

Indeed, where many colonists in seaports used such rhetoric to attack royal governors who were seen as implementing the illegitimate prerogatives of imperial officers, one Paxton pamphleteer argued that the "executive part of the government, at least, deserves . . . esteem and affection" because it had frequently tried to meet frontier demands. Smith and Gibson in the *Declaration* also offered a defense of the proprietor when they argued that the Friendly Association—an evil "faction"—conspired to invent and encourage Indian complaints against the proprietor to serve its own political ends. In other words, the Paxton Boys did not argue against government; they wanted more of it. As colonists living on frontiers, they felt, as Barton wrote, "they have a right to demand and receive protection" from their government. When these frontier sentiments merged with eastern complaints in a decade, they would combine to transform governing in America.[34]

"What Nation Under the Sun Ever Dealt with Individuals of Another Nation at War with Them and Not with the Whole Body or Nation?"

The division within Pennsylvania over the status of Indians presented officials with fundamental questions about the nature of their colony. Who were its members and who were not? Who deserved protection and who did not? And what did protection mean? Determining answers to these questions was the founding principle of the contract colonists entered into with their government. While it is surprising that eighty years into a colonial endeavor such questions remained unclear, government officials had embraced that ambiguity precisely because it allowed them to maintain peace—or, in their view, to provide security and protection to colonists. Colonial officials often argued that by providing Indians with goods or by addressing legal violations through diplomatic rather than legal channels, they were winning allies that would bring peace to frontiers.

Ultimately, the Paxton Boys and their supporters rejected such a policy. Instead, they wanted their government to create a clear separation—both physical and political—between colonist and Indian. It was a proposal strikingly similar to the ones Shingas and Teedyuscung offered in the Seven Years' War, though their aims were far different. Shingas and Teedyuscung imagined separate Indian polities within or near Pennsylvania as a solution to the growing animosities between both groups and to fend off encroachments of empire; frontier settlers, meanwhile, demanded that all Indians be removed from the British Empire and placed in separate areas. Indeed, the Paxton Boys and Indian leaders seemed to share an odd agreement about the status of Indians. Where leaders of various Indian groups asserted a strong sense of independence and autonomy, the Paxton Boys agreed and gave it to them. Of course, the fundamental difference was that Indian leaders hoped this division would foster exchange and peaceful relations, while colonists viewed removal as essential because they considered Indians as perpetual enemies. As one pro-Paxton sympathizer noted in the "Apology of the Paxton Boys," "The Indians that lived as independent Commonwealths among us or near our borders were our most dangerous enemies . . . altho' they still pretended to be our friends."[35]

The author of this essay also elaborated a new frontier theory of the colonial government that justified the Paxton Boys' actions by offering a legal argument for Indians' exclusion from its protection. He said that a sovereign state (meaning Pennsylvania) cannot have a separate legal jurisdiction (meaning Indian groups) operating within it, something that officials of the colony had permitted as a means to maintain peace since Pennsylvania's founding. Using the concept of the "state" explicitly as its point of analysis, the pamphlet argues that "no nation could be safe especially in a time of war, if another state or part of a state be allowed to live among them, free and independent, claiming and exercising within themselves all of the powers of government, the powers of making war and peace." The author repeatedly referred to Indians as belonging to independent states or "commonwealths." The Conestogas, he argued, were "an independent commonwealth in the heart of the province" that "retained their claim to freedom and independency and exercised all the powers of a free state, the power of making war and peace, of exercising criminal jurisdiction, etc."[36]

By casting Indians as "independent commonwealths," the author at once excluded Indians from Pennsylvania and the British Empire while also granting Indian groups a political coherence similar to European nation-states. This depiction, on the one hand, imbued Indians with greater political agency than British imperial officials actually tended to give them but, on the other, offered them less protection from violence. Such an independent polity, as the author notes, could not exist within another, larger state because it would threaten the very security the larger state was supposed to provide its members. As the author concluded, "What nation under the sun ever dealt with individuals of another nation at war with them and not with the whole body or nation?" Such an understanding of the state, its members, its legal protections, and its enemies justified the Paxton Boys, according to the "Apology." Its logic would reemerge in the years to come.[37]

John Penn wanted desperately to bring the Paxton Boys to justice to show that their view was wrong. He received additional pressure from Natives, imperial officials, and the Assembly. The murders were a test of his office as well as the authority of Pennsylvania's government more generally. Penn was "convinced the murderers deserve to be hanged," yet he ran into opposition when he tried to find the murderers. In a letter to his uncle Thomas, John recounted his frustration with the code of silence frontier inhabitants adopted: "There is not a man in the County of Cumberland, but is of the rioters party, if we had ten thousand of the king's troops, I don't believe it would be possible to secure one of these people tho' I took all the pains I could, even to get their names I could not succeed, for indeed nobody would make the discovery, tho ever so well acquainted with them, & there is not a Magistrate in the County would have touch'd one of them."[38]

Months later, Penn explained why he stopped trying to bring anyone to justice: "Much the greater part of the inhabitants are pleas'd to hear of the death of an Indian at any rate, and are still persuaded those very Indians were concern'd in committing murders upon the frontiers, so that we may give up any further thoughts of bringing any of those rioters to justice." Years later, when Rhoda Barber recounted how "strange" it seemed that the murderers, known to all, "were suffer'd to go unpunished," she realized that the historical context of the frontier explained the mystery: "It can be accounted for by persons who understand the state of the colony at that time." Indeed, far from inspiring revulsion, the Paxton Boys spurred one of the largest political mobilizations in colonial American history.[39]

The Assembly viewed the inability of the colony's legal institutions to punish—or even identify—the murderers of the Conestogas as a sign of proprietary weakness and sought to bolster their power through a radical change to the colony's charter. They wanted to transform the colonial government from a proprietary colony to a royal one. In *Cool Thoughts*, Benjamin Franklin argued that the proprietary nature of the colony was the root cause of the colony's "wretched situation." The government "has scarce authority enough to keep the common peace," he complained. He also responded with sarcasm to Barton's claim that from a technical standpoint the Paxton Boys did not commit murder, carefully noting how "mobs assemble and kill (we scarce dare say *murder*) numbers of innocent people in cold blood, who were under the protection of the government." Moreover, in contrast to the Paxton Boys' claims that the Assembly had failed to provide them with protection, Franklin accused the Paxton Boys of causing great numbers to have "no confidence in the publick protection."[40]

Franklin saw the root of the problem as a conflict "between the proprie-taries and the people." The history of other proprietary governments in British North America led him to conclude that there was "but one remedy for our evils, a remedy approved by experience, and which has been tried with success by other provinces; I mean that of an immediate royal govern-ment, without the intervention of proprietary powers, which, like unneces-sary springs and movements in a machine, are so apt to produce disorder." For Franklin and his supporters, the cause of the disorder within the colony was the exact opposite of the reason proposed by the Paxton Boys and their supporters. Franklin blamed the proprietor and the proprietary nature of the government for the controversies, while the Paxton Boys saw the Assembly's apportionment and the Quakers who seemed to control govern-ment as the problem. Where the Paxton Boys demanded a change to the legislature, Franklin and his party determined that it was the executive branch that needed reform and proposed that a complete new government was needed that rested on royal authority.[41]

After the Paxton Boys returned, the Assembly circulated a petition for a change of government, believing that most Pennsylvanians shared their view. Their attempt to start such a movement could not have been more ill-timed or ill-conceived. At about the same moment the Assembly began advancing this petition, Parliament had just passed the American Duties Act and rumors of the Stamp Act proliferated. The idea of royal govern-ment was anathema to many colonists who were growing concerned with imperial intrusions in their local affairs. But even if the measure might have found adherents at a different time, its arguments rang false among those who inhabited the colony's frontiers, where many viewed the petition as an attempt to bolster the Quakers' power.[42]

One of the chief ways the proprietary branch and frontier inhabitants maintained their alliance in this postwar world was through the appoint-ment of locally prominent people as justices of the peace. These individuals could, on the one hand, enforce law and collect taxes for the proprietor, but, on the other hand, they could be sympathetic to frontier views of Indians. Penn adopted this strategy at the height of political discord between the proprietor and the Assembly when he declined appointing a Quaker prothonotary because such an official would not be "of any use in promoting the interest of our family in the county but on the contrary must from his principles oppose it." Instead, he suggested a stop to the appointment of Quakers to offices in favor of the appointment of local allies, as "we might gain a good deal of interest in the country by a judicious disposal of offices."[43]

Still, the alliance between the proprietary and frontier people was weak and founded upon independent, and unrelated, interests. The proprietor needed frontier support to check the Assembly's attempt to take the government away from him. He also needed to address their concerns in order to have a better chance of collecting quitrents. In a way, Franklin was right that the proprietary nature of the colony enabled problems like the Paxton Boys to develop, but not for the reasons Franklin or the Assembly believed. It was not because the proprietor was too strong an institution—a tool for the enslavement of Pennsylvanians—but because the proprietorship was too dependent on frontier settlers' loyalty for their power. The proprietary branch may have been inherently undemocratic, but that did not mean settlers were without ways to negotiate with it and reshape its policies. Indeed, in frontier counties largely excluded from the legislature, frontier people had learned to shape undemocratic state institutions through colonial competition in Pennsylvania's war with Maryland and political mobilizations like the Paxton Boys rather than the more recognizable politicking practiced in the east.

The divisive politics in the east between the legislature and proprietor thus helped frontier people implement and enforce their view that Indians as individuals and groups fell outside the protections of the colony, even as Penn renounced such views. John Armstrong, the justice of the peace who joined the Paxton Boys, was an example of this policy in practice. Armstrong, after fighting in the Seven Years' War, wrote that he could "forgive everybody except the Assembly and the enemy Indians," a sentiment that came through clearly in the Paxton march (of which Armstrong was a part) and the pamphlets that followed, a fact made all the more apparent by the silence of the justices of the peace, many of whom knew who the Paxton Boys were but did nothing to bring them to justice. Instead, their inaction, and Armstrong's march to Philadelphia, made the Paxton Boys' attacks appear legal.[44]

In October 1764, the annual election for the Assembly made clear the sentiments of the colony. The Assembly-led proposal for a change of government proved deeply unpopular. No one quite understood how profoundly unpopular it was until election tallies were totaled. The two most powerful members of the Assembly, Benjamin Franklin and Joseph

Galloway, lost. Franklin, out of work, soon found himself representing the Assembly in London, where he continued to press for a change of government. Galloway won reelection in the next year. But as things returned to normal in the east, the problems that the Paxton Boys exposed continued to animate frontier people. In the years that followed, the problem of governing frontiers only grew deeper.[45]

CHAPTER 8

The British Empire's Frontier Crisis

The Paxton Boys' Rebellion posed a greater challenge to the colonial government than to the imperial one. In the wake of the rebellion, however, and with the close of Pontiac's War, the British Empire determined that it needed to take a more assertive role in managing frontiers, lest colonists like the Paxton Boys force the empire into more costly wars. Imperial officers descended on frontiers to enforce new regulations meant to keep the peace that the colonial government seemed incapable of maintaining. Frontier people were just as stridently opposed to these imperial policies as they were to those of their colonial government. Soon, imperial officials had their own governing crisis as more frontier rebellions sprouted up in the 1760s when colonists tried to prevent the empire from enforcing unpopular policies.

The empire's frontier crisis began in 1765, the same year as the better-known Stamp Act crisis that affected ports in the East, when imperial officers tasked with maintaining peace began to try to draw clear boundaries between Indian Country and colonial settlement. To accomplish this, officials sought to create stronger ties to Native groups who lived in the interior of North America. As they saw it, these Native partners would increase trade and serve the larger mercantile purposes of the empire. Colonists disagreed with imperial policy for many reasons, but at the core of their protest was the status of Indians in the empire. To forcefully register their views about government policy, frontier people in Pennsylvania mobilized in two major rebellions. Rather than try to petition their colonial government to reform, through these rebellions they seized power from governing bodies so they could effect on the local level what their colonial and imperial governments refused to do.

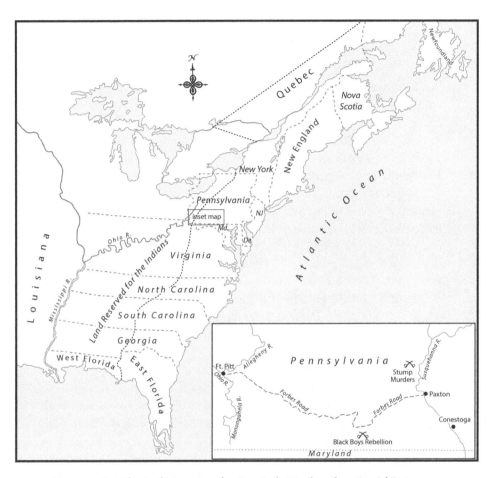

Figure 12. British North America after Pontiac's War based on Daniel Paterson, *Cantonment of His Majesty's Forces in N. America According to the Disposition Now Made, 1766* (1767). Note the designation of "Land Reserved for the Indians," showing an attempt by imperial officials to better establish clear borders between Indian settlements and colonial ones. The inset shows the sites of the Black Boys' Rebellion (1765) and Frederick Stump Affair (1768) in Pennsylvania. These rebellions followed the Paxton Boys' Rebellion and deepened the imperial crisis on the frontiers.

This crisis of empire in the western areas of Pennsylvania from the Susquehanna River to the Ohio River Valley came down to a simple, though deep and profound, disagreement. The British Empire wanted to use Indians as allies and trading partners to serve their own geopolitical and mercantilist ends, while those colonists who identified as "frontier people" after the Seven Years' War had come to a distinctive conception of the empire that excluded Indians. They attempted to implement this view by reshaping political institutions on the frontiers: they drew upon past experiences to create ad hoc militia-like bodies to protest official policy and enact their own, and they influenced institutions of the government to strengthen their authority at the expense of proprietary and imperial power. By 1768, frontier people had inverted political authority on Pennsylvania's frontiers. Where once the proprietary offices created and enforced a coherent Indian policy that offered protection to allied Indians, frontier people superseded this authority with their own, leading many to question whether government even existed in these areas. It did, just on frontier people's terms.

"Protect the Indians in the Enjoyment of Their Country, and to Extend the Trade"

As imperial officials took stock of their North American colonies at the end of Pontiac's War in 1765, they heard of the continuing violence on the frontiers and they knew of contested colonial borders from New Hampshire to the Carolinas. The two problems appeared of the same piece, and both called for a common solution: the creation of clearer borders between polities and their peoples. Officials hoped that stable boundary lines, both of the kind that formally separated colonies in the empire and those that separated areas of British settlement from Indian Country, would usher in an era of order, prosperity, and peace. In the 1760s, officials wanted to contain colonial settlement east of the Appalachian Mountains, which would, in turn, allow them to strengthen government power in colonies to better manage their subjects. To implement this vision, they empowered a new cadre of imperial officials in North America, most notably William Johnson as superintendent of Indian affairs for the Northern District and Thomas Gage as Amherst's replacement as commander in chief of the British Army in the colonies. The Ohio region, with its access to the interior that made it a valuable piece of the mercantile empire, assumed center stage in their strategizing.[1]

One of the chief problems they encountered as they tried to draw these lines was locating the frontiers in the empire's new domains. The crisis was similar to the debate the Paxton Boys carried on with their colonial government, but the issues raised had more to do with imperial policies than with colonial ones. After Pontiac's War concluded in 1765, frontier settlers began to take issue with new imperial initiatives that struck them as too similar to those they associated with the Quaker Party. This divide began to emerge as soon as officials plotted their new holdings. For high officials, the empire's frontier regions were well beyond the fringes of settlement in Pennsylvania, a conception of geopolitics that was far different from the "frontier settlers" who composed the Paxton Boys. As one prominent official stationed in the Great Lakes region wrote in a 1767 report to his superiors, Detroit was the "frontier British post in America that ought to be the barrier."[2]

The distance between Detroit and Lancaster, Pennsylvania captures the depth of the divide between imperial policy makers and self-described "frontier inhabitants." Where colonists as far east as Lancaster thought that they faced a possible Indian war and treated the murder of an Indian as something deserving praise, as if the perpetrator had vanquished a foe, imperial officials saw Detroit as the western "barrier" against unallied Indians. They instead wanted to secure as trading partners and diplomatic allies the very Indians that frontier people were killing. Just as with the Paxton Boys' Rebellion, frontier settlers and imperial officials alike agreed on the geopolitical meaning of frontiers within a polity; they just disagreed over where and against whom they formed.

British policy makers in London, unaware of or unconcerned about this divide, planned to maintain the peace by treating Indians as individuals who received many of the empire's legal and military protections, even if they were not full-fledged imperial subjects. Indians would have their own status as a semi-independent people within the empire in what they and imperial administrators called Indian Country. Creating such a space, however, depended upon drawing a clear line of separation between colonies and this territory. This border within the empire was not to be a frontier line that distinguished a group outside the empire who posed a threat, like the French had been, but a porous one, much as intercolonial borders were intended to be. Indeed, officials talked of an "open road" to Indian Country. They saw a flourishing trade with Native peoples and restrained westward expansion as keys to maintaining peace and stability in a mercantile empire coming to terms with its territorial vastness. As Thomas Penn summarized, "It not being [the king's] intention to make distant settlements, but protect the Indians in the enjoyment of their country, and to extend the trade by having forts and trading houses at convenient places."[3]

The Crown made this policy official with the Royal Proclamation of 1763. The king decreed that a new line, drawn in Pennsylvania along the Appalachian Mountains, was to be the limit of colonial settlement. The territory to the west was to remain in Indian hands. The proclamation was meant to assuage Native concerns about British expansion and recognize the Treaty of Easton's 1758 terms as part of official imperial policy. The decree also contained a number of regulations for traders, all of which were meant to systematize intercultural trade and ensure fair practices. Adopting a policy that had long been part of Pennsylvania law, the proclamation required that all traders receive a license and restricted their trade to designated areas, usually forts where they could be watched.[4]

The idea of the "open road" to Indian Country and a clear boundary thus created an unofficial new polity that was part of the empire but also independent. As historians have noted, many British officials believed the line would continue to shift westward, much as William Penn had assumed his colony would expand over time. Rather than serve as a permanent border, by clearly demarcating colonial and Indian territory in 1763 the British could use the borders as a basis from which they could better negotiate with Indians for land titles in the future. Such an ordered and peaceful process of expansion was meant to reduce conflict and better secure imperial interests and control. Moreover, the separation conferred on Indians some rights and privileges within the British Empire, specifically the promise of protection from harm. As the proclamation declared, Indian nations who "live under our protection, should not be molested or disturbed," a policy declaration that set up a conflict between British colonists who had very different ideas.[5]

The proclamation was ineffective because it suffered from the global nature of the Seven Years' War. Although France had essentially left what became western Pennsylvania when its military evacuated and abandoned Fort Duquesne in 1758, the British Crown could not implement any plans for North America while war still raged on the European continent, on what Colonel John Stanwix, stationed in New York in 1757, called that other "frontier." Only with the European theater of war closed and the Peace of Paris signed did Britain begin to create such policies as the Proclamation to consolidate its North American holdings. Therefore, by the time the Proclamation was issued in 1763, colonists in western Pennsylvania had essentially been living without real restrictions on expansion for five years. Native peoples felt this expansionist pressure acutely, leading in part to Pontiac's War. The combination of expansion and war meant that the Proclamation of 1763, while held up by historians as a glimpse at an empire that might have been, never had a chance of being implemented.[6]

Although Britain considered itself the victor in Pontiac's War, the costly conflict forced imperial officials to rethink their policy toward Native America. They held out hope that a renewed effort at winning Natives' trust would usher in a new era for British North America. Thomas Gage, Amherst's replacement as commander of the British forces in North America, embodied the imperial vision of cautious optimism. Gage corresponded with all of the new forts in British North America, from Florida to Detroit, and oversaw the transfers of power from French to British hands. He also took a more lenient stance toward Native peoples than Amherst had. He reopened trade, sought to build alliances, and tried to restrain colonial settlers from encroaching on Indian lands. By 1765, he believed Indian affairs had taken "a favorable turn, and we might expect a long series of peace with them." But Gage had misunderstood the growing divide between colonists on the empire's frontiers and the policies he was to implement. Just as he believed Indian relations were taking a turn for the better, colonists viewed the alliances the empire promoted as a cause for concern, and they took action to let imperial officials know it.[7]

"The Current Prevailing Opinion of the Frontier People on Both Sides of Susquehannah Runs in Favor of Stopping the Goods"

The empire's push to open trade and strengthen alliances with Indian groups—in effect, to close the imperial frontier and replace it with an open road—collided with frontier people in 1765 in what was one of the largest challenges to imperial authority in North America until minutemen faced off against British troops at Lexington and Concord in 1775. In late February

1765, George Croghan, deputy superintendent for Indian affairs in the Northern Department, an imperial position reporting to William Johnson, prepared to hold a treaty with Shawnees and Delawares at Fort Pitt in which these Native groups would end their participation in Pontiac's War. Croghan understood the complaints of these nations and wanted to reinstitute gift giving and reopen trade as a sign of goodwill. To do this, he ordered one of the largest pack trains of goods ever shipped west for peaceful purposes. Croghan, a man with a strong profiteering streak, had his own interest at heart as well: He owned a significant share of the cargo. He intended to reap a quick profit by flooding the market with goods as soon as he made peace. Croghan's plans proved too ambitious. Instead of opening an era of peace, his acts fueled the growing governing crisis in the region borne of competing visions about the empire's frontiers and against whom they were formed.[8]

It would be a mistake to characterize Croghan's intent as simple self-interest, however. The goods were necessary for the treaty, which Croghan and his superiors hoped would formally end Pontiac's War and establish a new foundation for peaceful Indian relations between the empire and its colonies. Croghan knew that one of the Indians' main complaints was the way the British had treated them and that diplomatic gift giving and the reopening of trade served as a measure of Britain's respect and good intentions. Croghan intended to splurge, hoping that the show of goods would represent Great Britain's sincerity. Imperial officials such as William Johnson concurred, writing to Croghan that the British "must endeavour to prejudice them in our favour by a strict regard to our word." Croghan agreed, noting to Thomas Gage that "a trade must be opened for them or we shall never be able to regain [their] confidence." Diplomacy, trade, and a lasting alliance with former enemies posed a challenge to settlers' view of Indians in which all correspondence was suspect. Trade, as the Paxton Boys and their supporters insisted, served to empower their enemies, not bring peace.[9]

At over eighty horses long, Croghan's enormous wagon train caused quite a stir in frontier communities, with rumors about its cargo flying ahead of its progress. Some speculated that the train was illegal, others that it contained contraband. By the time the goods reached Fort Loudon, the drivers of the train heard rumors too, particularly of "200 men . . . in arms [intending] to stop the goods." Inhabitants near the fort warned the traders to halt. As these emissaries made clear, the primary issue that concerned settlers was the contents, specifically whether any of the barrels contained ammunition. Trading such dangerous materials to enemies had the potential to devastate communities on a frontier. At each stop, locals demanded to search the cargo for ammunition, and they questioned the validity of the drivers' passports.[10]

On the morning of March 6, 1765, a group of men with blackened faces attacked the train at the base of Sideling Hill near modern-day McConnellsburg. The men killed several horses and demanded that the carriers surrender the goods. The drivers complied, abandoned their cargo and fled, leaving the raiders free to destroy nearly all of the goods. When the traders returned to Fort Loudon with their story, the British commander sent out a scouting party to arrest the group. The troops found only two men, who they promptly bound and brought back to the fort, and seized a number of guns.[11]

The capture of men and arms by the military seemed to frontier people to intrude on their rights. They refused to let such actions go unopposed. On March 9, the group, now larger in number and well armed, surrounded Fort Loudon to demand the return of the prisoners and guns. The commander of the fort, Charles Grant, acquiesced and released the prisoners rather than "risque . . . loosing a great many innocent lives." He kept the seized arms, however, and this decision would only further embolden frontier settlers who saw the continued possession of their private property as a violation of their rights.[12]

The raiders and their supporters adopted the name "Black Boys" after their face painting. Their tactics—surprising the cargo train, imitating Indian calls and dress, and hiding in the woods as they fired at the horses—were all meant to copy the successful raids that Indians had conducted on the frontier communities a few years before. The Black Boys, who lived in the area of some of the most devastating raids of the Seven Years' War and Pontiac's War, knew the fear of a frontier and used such tactics as a way to strike the same sense of terror in those carrying the goods. Their leader was James Smith, who had taken up the cause against Indians after he returned from captivity. During his time as a captive, Smith began to form his own ideas on Indian policy, something he explained in his memoir. While he said he respected some individual Indians, he concluded that Indians as a group were a perpetual threat. He believed that his time in captivity had taught him the key to defeating these enemies: colonists needed to stop using European war tactics and adopt Indian modes of fighting. The Black Boys were his attempt to implement these ideas.[13]

The Black Boys' initial uprising ended on March 13, when the men raided William Maxwell's house after hearing that Maxwell had hidden the contraband on his property. Much to the chagrin of Maxwell, the inspectors confirmed their suspicions when they discovered eight kegs of gunpowder hidden in his yard and blew them up. The raiders spoke with German accents, thus showing the continued cross-cultural alliances on frontiers. Indeed, Smith himself showed how language did not serve as much of a barrier. As a youth growing up in Cumberland, he learned German and used it during his captivity to speak with fellow prisoners, and, it appears, afterward.[14]

The Black Boys mobilized other frontier communities behind their cause, turning their initial raid into a regionwide political movement. Smith and his brother-in-law, William Smith, a justice of the peace, also oversaw an ad hoc but coordinated inspection regime that claimed the right to stop and inspect any traveler and issue passes to those who carried only goods the Black Boys approved of. They thus claimed the power to control trade and the movement of individuals within the polity, powers that only the provincial government had previously possessed.[15]

Other groups taking up the Black Boys' mantle aided in preventing the resumption of trade with Indians. Near Fort Loudon, "about twenty men well armed were riding thro' the settlement in the day time and examining all the houses there for goods." At least two British sergeants were stopped and searched by this group. Another group formed near Lancaster. Referred to as the "Paxtonians"—and if not involving the same people as the Paxton Boys, at the very least including proud imitators—they "stop'd three or four waggon loads of goods at Harris's, which was intended for Shamokin." As John Armstrong, a justice of the peace in Carlisle, observed, "Irish, English, Dutch and Welch from Potomack to the Kittatinney hill" all partook in these actions, and "the current prevailing opinion of the frontier people on both sides of Susquehannah runs in favor of stopping the goods." At one point, the Black Boys near Fort Loudon even captured the lieutenant in charge of the fort while he was out "taking the air on horseback" and held him hostage until he signed a bond that stated he would release the colonists' guns he still held. This seizure of a British officer may have been the boldest challenge colonists made up to that point to an individual holding a position of imperial authority in British North America.[16]

The strong support these actions received among frontier people shocked colonial and imperial officials. The destruction of property—even though some items were technically contraband—was an act so extreme that military officers talked of executing the guilty. According to one official who confronted the rebels, the insult to government's authority "by far exceeds the Paxton affair." But for those who believed they lived on a frontier, trade with the enemy was not permissible, and the actions the Black Boys took to destroy these goods was justified as a proper means of defense.[17]

Dealing with the rebellion once again fell to John Penn. The Black Boys tested the limits of military-civil relations and revealed the tensions inherent in the overlapping imperial and colonial jurisdictions on the edges of the British Empire. British officers tried to steer clear of invading civilian legal jurisdiction, which they briefly intruded upon during their initial response to the attack. But after this initial spontaneous foray, they asked Penn to come to their aid to find and try those responsible for the destruction of goods. Penn traveled to Carlisle, the county seat of Cumberland County, in early April to cool tempers and punish the guilty. He was greeted by traders wanting compensation and settlers petitioning him to stop "any goods going out at present, but what is for his majesties presents only."[18]

The petitioners articulated their core beliefs, and in their exposition, they also articulated their worldview. Above all else, trade was to be curtailed, if not halted, with Indians, a view that ran counter to the very policy the empire was enacting. They claimed the convoy contained "warlike stores" that were "destined for the savage, faithless and unrelenting enemy." Where Crown officials saw a brisk trade with Indians as a way to provide colonists with security because it would form the foundation for a lasting peace, the idea of the Crown permitting merchants to trade with Indians in such goods resurrected memories of what Indians had done with such items on the frontiers of Pennsylvania: "horrible images of murdered families, captivated brethren . . . our houses and farms involved in flames and our whole country in one general desolation." Instead, the petitioners begged officials to starve Indians of supplies, to reduce the Indians "to the lowest want and distress," believing that Indians should feel the same desperation that many of them had felt during the war in order to make them humble.[19]

The petitioners took particular aim at the Quakers in Philadelphia who seemed more concerned with profits than they were with the well-being of their fellow subjects on the colony's frontiers. They were, the petitioners accused, "so bent upon enriching themselves by an Indian trade that they will do it at the expence of so much blood and treasure as it must cost the Crown and Colonies." In fact, such action seemed to make Quakers and other traders treasonous, leading the petitioners to wonder "what does it avail us, that the French are removed. . . . If our own fellow subjects . . . are still continuing to supply them with the means of our destruction." The petitioners did not believe Indians were seduced by the French in the Seven Years' War, as many colonial officials did. Rather, the French simply provided Indians with the means to wage war. Now, in these petitioners' view, Quakers proposed to do the same, inevitably involving the frontier "in a third" Indian war that would allow enemy Indians "to repeat all their cruelties upon us for several years." This petition and the "horrible images" they conjured captured the sentiments of a frontier people, a sense of identity that had solidified over the course of the past decade. To these "frontier inhabitants," Indians were and always had been their real enemies. They were the ones who created the deep dread they all shared as frontier people. The Quakers' control of government had only made their fears worse by failing to provide them with the sense of security from government they sought.[20]

The petitioners believed that the governor—their political ally—could be their best advocate back east. They thus asked Penn to give them "protection against the attempts of our fellow subjects who being remote from danger, sit at ease and know not what we feel." To "feel" the "danger" meant that for settlers the frontier they described was a mental and physical experience as much as it was a location. Becoming a frontier person produced a set of emotions in those who felt that way—a mix of desperation, vulnerability, fear, anxiety, and anger—that fueled their demands for a more responsive government. Above all, they expected their government to empathize with their feelings of exposure to danger. A healthy political body would be able to feel weakness and illnesses and hope to fix these ills; an unhealthy one would ignore such suffering. In this case, they accused Quakers who, in their eyes, controlled government and trade. This powerful sect, they said, was "void of compassion for the distressed people of the frontiers." The apparent inability of this "faction" that controlled government to share the frontier people's feelings drove frontier people to take bold actions to force the government to feel as they did. At the same time, they also looked to the governor, the person who had often expressed sympathy for their plight and the captain-general of the colony, to help build connections between east and west.[21]

Penn knew this too. He also knew that with the Assembly trying to take the government away from him, he needed allies to help him protect his family's control of the colony. His troubles in the east thus made him open to frontier people's demands, a pliability that only emboldened frontier settlers to seize more power. This weakness became apparent as soon as Penn arrived in Carlisle to sort out the mess. The governor held an inquest and convened a grand jury. He also summoned William Smith, the justice of the peace for the area in which the initial attack happened, to explain his actions. British officers leveled heavy criticism at Smith for his apparent support for the Black Boys, and these accusations contained some truth.

In a sworn testimony, William Smith at once denied any direct involvement in the attack, while also defending the Black Boys' actions using the logic of someone who believed he lived on a frontier. At first, he couched his justification in imperial policy, explaining that the Black Boys were enforcing their understanding of the law, which prohibited trade with enemies, a view also expressed by the petitioners. He also offered a sympathetic defense of their actions, taking particular issue with the inclusion of ammunition in the trade good. He explained that the Black Boys' goal was to stop "the ammunition," which they believed would have allowed Indians "to continue the war and again kill and murder his Majesty's subjects on the frontiers who had already suffered the most extream misery and distress." John Armstrong privately concurred, describing the goods as "ammunition, calculated to bring fresh distruction on the frontier inhabitants when put into the hands of a people with whom no peace is yet fully made." Armstrong, a fellow justice of the peace, supported an acquittal, worrying that convictions would only embolden more violent actions.[22]

For the Black Boys, having two of the elites in the region sympathize with their cause meant that local law enforcement officials who represented the government were more likely to let the Black Boys act without penalty.

Indeed, with William Smith on their side and John Armstrong favorable to them, frontier settlers saw their local control of the law as the way to reshape the policies of government on frontiers. Through these legal institutions, colonists could implement their own views of frontier policy, which were often at odds with the ones imperial and colonial officials wanted. Penn did little to slow this transfer of government power to the local level. In fact, his actions only strengthened this shift. One of the other things he did in Carlisle was convene a grand jury to indict those suspected of participating in the initial raids. After hearing the testimony against the accused, a jury of the Black Boys' peers found the sworn depositions "not sufficient testimony to convict a single person." Instead, the local jury affirmed the local view of Indians as enemies. Gage knew that the acquittal, a mark of their peers' approval, "rendered [the Black Boys] more bold and audacious." Nor were the jury members unusual; as William Johnson reported, "Many of the back inhabitants . . . judged them doing a meritorious act."[23]

The grand jury's decision gave the Black Boys free rein on the frontiers of the British Empire. In the days that followed, they created a far more formalized system of trade regulation. For months, bands of frontier inhabitants searched all westbound goods for ammunition and other "warlike stores" and even issued their own passports. Aided by William Smith and his legal arguments, the Black Boys used their understanding of the law and the delegation of powers within the empire to justify their actions. His argument embraced the proprietary branch of the colonial government and the unrecognized powers conferred to it in the Frame of 1701. Only proprietary officials, William Smith and the Black Boys held, had the power to regulate traders. Since justices of the peace like William Smith were the local representatives of the proprietary, they had the authority to search trade goods to ensure they carried no illegal trade items for enemies.

Armed with this jurisdictional justification, the Black Boys told British officers who tried to stop their regulation that they "were not under the General's Orders, but that it is their Governor's Orders they are to obey" and that likewise "no goods whatever could be safe in going along the communication, without a pass from a justice of the peace." Their arguments thus asserted local civil authority over the new imperial regime that was embodied in the troops occupying the frontiers. The Black Boys were saying that the empire was to serve their needs, not the other way around.

They were able to do so by using their understanding of the powers delegated to colonies from the empire and bending this conveyance of power to the most local of colonial officials as a way to suit their interests. The Black Boys thus shaped colonial institutions to serve their own ends, and, in the process, empowered frontier communities to remodel the policies of the colonial government and the empire to which it belonged to their liking.[24]

The British officers knew that the Black Boys posed a challenge to the empire and to the order they were trying to create. They also suspected that the Black Boys offered such arguments because they had the upper hand with the governor. Military commanders repeatedly complained to Gage that John Penn seemed if not to approve of the Black Boys' actions, then at least tacitly to allow them to happen. As Grant wrote to Gage, "I fear the Governor may be too apt to listen to their false assertions." Colonel John Reid, Grant's superior, likewise complained that "Governor Penn has issued no Proclamation, nor taken any other steps as yet, agreeable to his promise to me, to quell these insurrections, and as the rioters openly avow his countenancing them, I fear little is to be expected." Gage, for his part, blamed the bitter politics in Philadelphia—partly caused by frontier actions—for giving frontier settlers an opportunity to seize power at the expense of the government, writing "the factions in the government of Pennsylvania, if it can be called a government, seemed to have favored the infamous riots of the banditti upon the borders of the province."[25]

Imperial officials, however, saved their most vitriolic words for the Black Boys. While the Black Boys cast their actions as those of loyal subjects protecting their peers and the empire from external enemies, imperial and colonial officials viewed them as a "lawless" and "seditious" group of "rascally" "traitors" who were in "an actual state of rebellion" and deserved "exemplary punishment." The only way to coerce them to behave to the empire's liking, some argued, was through a show of imperial might. "Have a body of troops quartered upon them till they are brought under proper subjection to the laws," one colonel suggested.[26]

For Penn, things were less clear-cut. While he opposed the actions of the rebels, calling James Smith a "villain" and eventually removing William Smith from office, the wide support given to them put him in a difficult position. If he tried to assert proprietary authority too forcefully, he risked a larger rebellion. At a time when Penn was at odds with his Assembly—the change to a royal government was still much talked about—he needed to maintain an alliance with these frontier settlers more than ever. Penn worried that too forceful an action could backfire and create a violent response from frontier settlers, which would only embolden his political enemies and doom his control over the colony.[27]

Even if Penn did want to exert more force, it is unclear that he could have since he would have to work through justices of the peace to do so. These local representatives of proprietary authority often supported ad hoc actions taken to defend local mores; indeed, they often spearheaded such efforts. William Smith embodied the problem Penn faced with local law enforcement. Smith had served as a justice of the peace since the 1750s and was a well-known and respected figure. But instead of being a loyal enforcer of government policy, he played a central role in the uprising by providing the cover the Black Boys needed to turn lawless actions into legal ones. As a testament to how important William Smith was, the rioters named his house "Fort Smith" and used it as their central meeting point.[28]

Other local officials found themselves caught in a similar bind. Local magistrates, torn between their desire to maintain their authority among their neighbors and their duty to proprietary and imperial officials, often found it easier to avoid confrontation. John Armstrong, a justice of the peace in Cumberland County who was even more prominent and connected than Smith, was aware of this problem. A war hero and former Paxton marcher, he described himself to George Croghan as the person who could "tell . . . what the people say and what motives they avow for this conduct." Although Armstrong disavowed the Black Boys' actions in private letters to imperial officials, his actions—or lack thereof—suggested his sympathies rested with his friends and neighbors. Many of the imperial officials who ran afoul of the Black Boys suspected he provided tacit support. Grant, for instance, described Armstrong as someone who "favours the rioters." Even if Armstrong did not actively support the Black Boys, his awareness of their popularity certainly affected his opinions on the proper government response. The Black Boys thus exposed the strengths and weaknesses of the proprietary power on the frontier. The Black Boys embraced proprietary offices like the justice of the peace that they were able to meld to meet their needs, while simultaneously weakening the power of the proprietor and his governor.[29]

The culmination of the Black Boys' movement came in November when James Smith staged a two-day siege of Fort Loudon, yet another audacious act against a symbol of imperial authority. Smith did so to reclaim the guns that the British military had seized in March. Smith claimed that the military authorities did not have the jurisdiction to arrest, seize, or hold the private property of civilians. Grant, "much fatigued for want of sleep for two nights and two days . . . owing to the . . . firing on the fort," finally gave up the guns. Perhaps there is no greater evidence of the governor's difficult position than how he treated the colonists' seized weapons at Fort Loudon. When Grant returned the guns, he refused to hand them over directly to the Black Boys. Instead, Grant ceded them to a middleman, a neutral justice of the peace that both sides seemed to like, until the governor decided on their status. Penn knew he still needed to tread lightly with his political partners. In a letter written a couple of weeks later to William Smith, Penn described his "pleasure" in returning the arms "forthwith . . . to their respective owners." Indeed, he expressed surprise at the "formality" with which the military treated what appeared to him a straightforward exchange.[30]

The Black Boys' Rebellion confirmed for many people that Pennsylvania's government was far too weak for the task the empire expected of it. Back east, as reports of the Black Boys' actions circulated among the governing elite, many questioned whether the colonial government possessed the coercive powers necessary to support its authority. As a prominent Philadelphian wrote to Benjamin Franklin, then in London lobbying to change Pennsylvania proprietary government into a royal one, "What is lamentably too true, [is] that we have only the form without the powers of government." Thomas Gage, likewise, wondered if "the government of Pennsylvania" can even "be called a government." John Penn admitted as much in private correspondence, writing to the proprietor, his uncle Thomas Penn, that the Pennsylvania government suffered from "extreme weakness" and needed to be strengthened. He put the blame for this weakness on the Assembly, arguing that the members' pacifism and unwillingness to pass a permanent militia law made controlling the west nearly impossible. Penn wrote repeatedly about the need for a militia law and advocated stationing British troops in Carlisle to support the government. Indeed, in his advocacy of a permanent militia as an "aid [to] the civil powers" and "the only natural defence and support of government," he elaborated a modern view of state power that was driven by the exigencies of a frontier crisis that required a stronger central government to control settlers, not protect them.[31]

Many agreed with Penn and argued for an official militia to police colonial society. James Burd, an officer in the provincial militia who saw his colony descend further into the barbarity he had written about in 1758, decided after the Paxton Boys' massacre that without a formal military force, the colony had no way to enforce its monopoly on the legitimate use of violence: "I am heartily concern'd for that murder of the Indians in Lancaster, not so much upon the acct of the Indians, as the thorough contemp[t] shew'd the government, neither can any one forsee where such a vyolent encroachment upon the laws of the land will end; the consequence is extremely dangerous in a country where there is no standing army to inforce its laws and support the government." Franklin also recognized the utility of such an institution after learning of the Black Boys, but as an opponent of proprietary power, he advocated a permanent British rather than colonial military presence on the frontier, which he hoped would offer "security of internal peace among ourselves without the expence or trouble of a militia." In short, many individuals invested in securing peace thought a stronger and more permanent military presence was essential—not to protect those who perceived themselves to be on a frontier in western Pennsylvania, but to implement state policy within these communities. But such a program was also one that was nearly impossible to accomplish with a legislature that viewed any colonial military institution as simply a means to increase proprietary power, and an empire saddled with debts that limited their ability to fund such an expansion of military power on the frontiers of North America.[32]

Imperial officials, meanwhile, wanted to better regulate trade through a stronger administrative presence on the frontiers. In April 1765, a few weeks after the Black Boys' attack, William Johnson admitted that the British struggled to open the Indian trade because they did not have "a sufficient number of inspectors" to regulate exchanges, ironically the very duty the Black Boys were taking on themselves. Instead of integrating frontier people like the Black Boys into the empire and possibly tempering their actions and animosities through a chain of command, however, imperial officials pushed a people teetering on the brink of radicalism further away because they viewed them as lawless mobs. Of course, tensions between civilian and military institutions may have proven insurmountable—by the end of the crisis, James Smith and his supporters did lay siege to a British fort—but there may have been a moment in which imperial officials could have shifted frontier impulses away from hostility toward Indians and toward the service of imperial goals.

Instead, the Black Boys' Rebellion only led to the breakdown of trust between "frontier people" and the governments to which they belonged. In the wake of the Black Boys' Rebellion, imperial officials dismissed frontier inhabitants, while the Black Boys treated traders and diplomats as their political enemies. As trust between frontier people and government eroded, frontier people became even more disillusioned—and assertive.[33]

"No Jury in Any of Our Frontier Counties Will Ever Condemn a Man for Killing an Indian"

The Black Boys and their supporters, like the petitioners to the governor, were united in a shared belief that Indians were enemies. While the Black Boys were not as openly hostile to Indians as the Paxton Boys, they were nonetheless part of a broader movement in which people who believed they lived upon a frontier began to remake their political institutions to match their beliefs. Over the course of the 1760s, this manipulation meant that Indians were placed outside the protection of the colonial government. Meanwhile, officials grew frustrated with their inability to control local legal and extralegal institutions, and the Pennsylvania movement seemed to be reaching across colonial borders. In 1765, amid concern about Indian murders in western Virginia, Governor Fauquier of Virginia complained that "the Paxton Boys of Pennsylvania have sent messages offering their assistance to prevent any one of the criminals being brought to Justice; for they publickly say no man shall suffer for the murder of a savage."[34]

A year later Governor Penn faced yet another challenge to the colony's governing authority when Pennsylvania tried a man for the murder of an Indian in Northampton County. What Penn discovered was troubling. Murderers did not need to rely on vigilantes like the Paxton Boys to shield them. Instead, acquittal by sympathetic locals provided the most effective protection. Writing of the Northampton County jury's failure to convict, Penn stated that "no jury in any of our frontier counties will ever condemn a man for killing an Indian. They do not consider it in the light of murder, but as a meritorious act. This is unfortunate but I know of no remedy."[35]

In the winter of 1768, the frontier people showed how far they would go to protect the autonomy of local legal institutions. In January of that year, Frederick Stump, a Pennsylvanian of German descent, and his indentured servant Hans Eisenhauer, also known as John Ironcutter, entertained

six Indians at Stump's house. Stump was well known to proprietary officials. Two years earlier, Pennsylvania's government had singled him out as
a squatter and threatened him with arrest if he did not vacate Indian land.
Since the end of Pontiac's War, Indians had complained vociferously about
such encroachments, and imperial and colonial entities had worked to
remove squatters. Pennsylvania's Assembly even passed a law that threatened squatters on Indian lands with the extreme penalty of death, and proprietary officials had acted on this law, burning many houses, including one
Stump had built. Such coordinated effort shows that while severe divisions
between institutions existed, they could still work together to enforce agreements made with Indians considered allies and recipients of protection.
Tensions between Indians and the colonial government continued as squat-
ting persisted, however, so much so that rumors of another Indian war
began circulating throughout the colonies in 1768. These concerns—and
certainly other things—spilled over one night at Stump's house. After a
number of drinks, Stump murdered all six Indians because, he claimed, he
began to fear that his guests "intended to do him some mischief."[36]

Fearing that his actions might provoke an Indian war or get him in
trouble, Stump dragged the bodies to the frozen creek behind his house,
chipped a hole in it, and hid the evidence of his crime under the ice. The
next morning, surely waking up with more than a headache on his mind,
he realized that neighboring Indians would notice six people missing, so he
traveled fourteen miles to a small Indian settlement of two cabins, where
he murdered a woman and three children, threw their corpses in a cabin,
and burned it down. He did this "to prevent them carrying intelligence
of the death to the other Indians." Drunken violence was not entirely
unknown in Pennsylvania, although there is no record of such drunken
brawling resulting in mass murder. But Stump went further. He went on
an offensive to kill others who might have carried "intelligence" of his
actions to other Indians, who would in turn retaliate with their own raids.
In other words, Stump's actions were founded upon his assumption that
he inhabited a frontier, that Indians were threats, and that they deserved
no rights. Even though Stump lived near Indians daily, such everyday interactions should not betray the volatile state of the region. Colonists were on
edge because they feared, as the Black Boys put it, a "third Indian war."[37]

Stump's attempt to hide his deed failed. Word of the murders soon
spread everywhere. Penn quickly issued proclamations to arrest Stump and
his servant. Penn described the victims as "Indians, who, for several months

past, have lived near the frontiers of this province in a friendly and quiet manner, and have at all times, since the establishment of the general peace with the Indians in 1764, behaved themselves peaceably and inoffensively to all His Majesty Subjects." The proclamation, on the one hand, expressed the colony's long-standing policy that protection extended to these Indians, but its language and substance also reflected the unofficial change in Indians' status brought about by war. In 1768, officials never implied Indians should be treated the same as colonists, as it had in previous proclamations delivered for similar reasons. By noting how friendly and inoffensively the Indians had lived, it suggested that not all Indians behaved that way and that "unfriendly or offensive" behavior—however subjectively defined those concepts were—was open to unfriendly offensive responses. Indeed, such "insolent" behavior is what cost Delaware Indian Doctor John his life in 1760. Finally, the proclamation spoke of "frontiers of this province," a recognition that during this period of heightened tensions, parts of Pennsylvania were areas of potential Indian assault.[38]

Most imperial and colonial officials became convinced that Stump's actions would spark a conflict akin to Pontiac's War. Frontier people thought so too. Driven by this fear, one person living on the frontiers took the initiative to prevent the expected reprisals. William Patterson enlisted nineteen men—induced, actually, by the promise of money—to find and arrest Stump in the Juniata region of Cumberland County even before Penn's proclamations were distributed. Patterson was a former officer in the provincial militia who was widely known and respected. During his service, he demonstrated the ruthless necessity that such a position required, receiving a £100 bounty for Indian scalps during Pontiac's War.[39]

After the Stump murders, however, Patterson decided he needed to protect Indians in order to preserve the peace. Patterson received word that Stump was holed up in the house of a sympathetic neighbor. When he approached the house, Patterson used his knowledge of frontier inhabitants to his advantage; he "pretended to the People in the House, that he came there to get Stump to go with them and kill the Indians at the Great Island." Only when the house's owners were convinced Patterson was hunting Indians, not Stump, did they bring the accused out from his hiding place. The ad hoc and extralegal police force then arrested Stump and brought him to John Armstrong in the Carlisle, who placed him in the jail.[40]

Word of Stump's arrest raced throughout the frontier counties. Traveling with it was the worrisome rumor that the government planned to ship him to Philadelphia to be tried. There was truth to these rumors. Edward Shippen, for instance, a member of one of the wealthiest and most powerful families in Lancaster County, believed that the Assembly should pass "an especial law . . . or the tryal of Stump, in Philadelphia." Shippen knew that Stump's peers were more likely to consider him a hero than a criminal, and therefore, they needed to bring him to Philadelphia where, as the Paxton Boys had acknowledged, murderers would face a less sympathetic jury.[41]

In fact, frontier people began to turn on their own for the apparent opposition to Stump's actions shown by some. As soon as Stump was jailed, he received the "compassion of many," while Patterson, his captor, received "the indignation of the ruffians to such a degree that it is said a party have sett out to chastise him." Patterson ultimately had to publicly defend his actions, pleading that his "sole views [were] directed to the service of the frontiers." He believed that by capturing Stump he helped protect the frontiers from Indian reprisals. Others, however, believed quite the opposite, that freeing Stump was of more "service to the frontiers." In one indication of how at odds Patterson was with reigning opinion, he had to pay his recruits and defend himself from public scorn, while the Paxton Rangers and Black Boys, which risked far more, were all voluntary.[42]

For Shippen and others, a trial in Philadelphia would serve symbolic as well as legal purposes; it would clearly assert the official position that murdering Indians was illegal. People who perceived themselves to be on a frontier knew this, too. When word got out that the government requested Stump's transfer to Philadelphia, presumably for trial, the news "spread almost beyond credibility, like an electrical shock, over all the county, and into adjacent counties and governments; and, unexpectedly to all here, had occasioned a very general alarm." Soon, a "number of reputable inhabitants of the town [Carlisle], with some from the country, met and remonstrated against it." Those in Cumberland County worried that sending Stump away would be "setting a precedent, that might hereafter be of pernicious consequence." Unable to gain assurance that Stump would not be sent to Philadelphia, an extralegal, ad hoc company of about eighty men, made up primarily of Scots-Irish Presbyterians, stormed the jail and freed Stump and Eisenhauer. Unlike Patterson's company, there is no evidence any of these men sought remuneration. Instead, they acted to prevent the precedent they feared. As a letter writer opined in the *Pennsylvania Gazette*, a trial in Philadelphia "was the grand point" that motivated the rescuers.[43]

After the jailbreak, Stump's rescuers confined him somewhere in the countryside while they negotiated his return with two local pastors. The chief issue continued to be the place of Stump's trial. The preachers eventually struck a deal in principle in which the rescuers "would agree to the prisoners being restored, on condition they were assured they should not be sent to Philadelphia." With this pact in place, John Holmes, the sheriff, along with William Lyon and John Armstrong, rounded up a posse to take Stump back into custody. Once they met the rescue party, however, a confrontation ensued that nearly ended in the "shedding of much blood." Negotiations between government officials and the rescuers continued, until the rescuers finally confessed that they "had unluckily permitted Stump to go to see his family, on his promise of returning in a few days," but he, unsurprisingly, absconded. The rescuers' identities were all known in the community, and twenty-three were indicted in May 1768, but no record of their trial exists, suggesting they went unpunished. Stump's trail also went cold, although rumors persisted that he headed south to another colony.[44]

The freeing of Stump epitomized politics on the Pennsylvania frontier. Justices of the peace seemed to support these extralegal actions or were too weak to stop them. Governing authority thus rested more in the hands of self-described frontier people than it did officials in the east or their local representatives who were meant to implement policy and enforce laws. Penn learned of the rising power of frontier people and their manipulation of local legal offices to serve their ends when a delegation he sent from Philadelphia to investigate Stump's rescue returned with unsettling findings. Many people reported that George Ross, a lawyer from Lancaster and member of the Assembly, had enflamed passions with a stirring defense of local legal authority. William Allen, the proprietary official conducting the investigation, also suspected that John Armstrong might have acted slowly and ineffectively because he too opposed moving Stump to Philadelphia, or at least knew that most of his fellow townsmen did. Allen complained that Armstrong worried too much about being popular with local settlers and not enough about enforcing the law. He confided to Thomas Penn, the proprietor, that because Armstrong had done nothing explicitly wrong, Allen could not "charge him with a design or even a desire to have Stump rescued but his little scheme of pleasing the populace, was attended with that consequence." Elected officials like Ross and justices of the peace like Armstrong depended on the respect of their neighbors. They were thus attuned to the sentiments of "the populace" and made sure their behavior conformed to the popular opinion upon which their authority rested. Frontier inhabitants also had created the means to muscularly enforce these views and pressure such officials. Oral rather than print, their mode of information dissemination was so effective that word could spread "like an electrical shock" and tally groups to raid jails and defend murderers.[45]

To many Pennsylvanians, especially those back east, the murders and the subsequent rescue of Stump evoked memories of the Paxton Boys, suggesting how popular mobilizations against Indians had lasting political ramifications. In an odd coincidence, before word of the Stump murders reached Philadelphia, the Assembly sent a long message to John Penn asking why the Conestoga murderers remained on the loose. The Assembly feared that an Indian war was imminent because of encroachments onto Indian lands and the still festering wound of the Conestoga massacre. Although they did not refer to the Winters' murder in 1728, the Assembly believed the government needed to act as it did then, stating that only the "dread of exemplary punishment, steadily and uniformly inflicted on past delinquents, that alone can deter the wicked from the perpetration of future offence." Instead, they bemoaned the "debility" of a government that allowed such behavior to continue.[46]

The Stump murders once again drove a wedge between governor and Assembly, further weakening the two branches that composed the colonial government. Both now harbored conspiratorial notions of the other. The relationship between the two branches had so soured that Penn now believed the Assembly was actively trying to undermine stability in an attempt to convince the Crown to take the colony away from his family. Penn heard that when the Assembly's message was printed in the newspaper, frontier people linked the Conestoga murders and still popular march with the freeing of Frederick Stump. Intelligence from Lancaster reported that the "murderers of the Conestoga Indians have united themselves to the adherents of Stump, or rather this [the Assembly's] message has done it, for they now consider their's and Stumps['] as one common cause." Penn then grew convinced that the Assembly's speech was simply an attempt to "keep the country in hot water" and thus keep "alive their favorite scheme of a change of government." Indeed, the similar reaction of the proprietary and legislative branches to the Stump murders showed that while both institutions shared a desire to make peace with Indians, their mutual mistrust could undo their ability to achieve this common goal, making governing frontiers an impossible task. Meanwhile, the antipathy frontier settlers held toward the Assembly only grew stronger and helped forge greater solidarity among them.[47]

The Stump affair also caused some on the frontiers to reevaluate their alliance with the governor. Penn led the charge to bring Stump and Eisenhauer to justice. Within weeks, word on the frontiers spread that "Governor Penn has turned against us [the frontier] and takes part with the Indians," a statement that exposed the importance of Indian policy to the political loyalties of these settlers. It also makes explicit the political alliance that had existed between frontier people and the governor.[48]

Throughout the 1760s, frontier groups like those who freed Stump continued to act independent of government to implement their vision of what imperial and colonial policy should be. Specifically, they wanted to separate colonial society from alliances with Indians. Bands of unofficial militias continued to try to regulate trade with Indians and push imperial policy toward a more hostile position against Indians, all of which reflected their view that they lived on a frontier and that Indians were their enemy. In 1768, for instance, George Croghan complained about a reformed Black Boys movement whose aim was to stop all trade with Native peoples. The impetus for this group's formation was a rumor that a huge shipment of goods was again traveling to Fort Pitt. According to Croghan, they wanted to stop the train and disrupt the diplomacy so that "no [negotiation] may be carried with the Indians." John Penn began to recognize a distinct frontier political culture that transcended colonial borders and saw, like Croghan, that their chief aim was to stop the empire from reaching peace with Indians. "The turbulent and ingovernable spirit of the Frontier inhabitants as well in Maryland and Virginia as in this Province," he said, "[would] continually be counteracting the efforts of the government to establish a lasting peace with the Indians."[49]

"I Dread That Any Indians Should Come on the Frontiers, as the Inhabitants Declare They Will Murder All Who Do"

Other western areas of British North America rioted in a manner reminiscent of the Pennsylvania frontier at the same time. In South Carolina, a group of westerners calling themselves Regulators formed to protest the lack of strong law enforcement. In North Carolina, a separate group also calling themselves the Regulators mobilized against the power of large land-owners and an eastern elite. While areas in western Pennsylvania, North Carolina, and South Carolina aimed their protests at changing local governing institutions, the Pennsylvania mobilizations remained distinctive. Pennsylvanians focused their political behavior on security and opposition to Indians. Indeed, issues of defense served to distract from economic and other political problems that were prominent in other British colonies. The difference was that most other colonies had regular and permanent militias and governments that treated Indians with hostility and suspicion. Colonists in these other areas could thus channel their political concerns toward different matters, like taxes and land policy.[50]

On Pennsylvania's frontiers, however, fear of Indians trumped economic concerns, or, rather, the presence of Indians and the inability of the colonial government to meet settlers' demands served to explain the "distressed" situation of those who believed they lived upon a frontier. Moreover, Pennsylvania settlers did not see the proprietor as the cause of their poverty or his institutions as the cause of the colony's problems. Instead, they blamed their legislature and Quaker merchants in Philadelphia for abetting the Indian attacks that had decimated their communities. The foundation for these beliefs coalesced during the Seven Years' War, but they found their fullest expression in the years following it as frontier people began to come to grips with their current circumstances. The frontier people's explanation for the causes of their desperate situation engendered a strong and abiding distrust in the government's ability to provide the security and protection they demanded, which in turn fostered an adamant emphasis on local authorities and their control of legal institutions. For frontier inhabitants disillusioned with government, the only people they could trust were themselves.

To many at the time and many more since, the actions of the Paxton Boys, the Black Boys, and the rescuers of Frederick Stump revealed a society that had descended into anarchy. An understanding of the politics of the frontier people shows that this perception is mistaken. Though often violent and illegal or extralegal, settlers' actions were purposeful and coherent. Indeed, participants in every major political mobilization on the Pennsylvania frontier framed their actions and justifications through their understanding of the law and the government. These mobilizations were thus not a product of a stateless society. They were actions meant to change the mode of governance on the frontier. Such coordinated voluntarism done to support widely shared cultural values served as the foundation for a new civil society—one whose actions were also extraordinarily uncivil.[51]

Meanwhile, the events of the early 1760s offered further proof to imperial officials that a line between frontier settlers and Indians was more important than ever. Now, however, governing officials wanted a border to separate the Indians from regular colonists who they could no longer control or trust. John Penn noted as early as 1765 that "a spirit of revenge" would lead his colonists to murder "any Indians that may come to settle near them." He thus advocated that Indians steer clear of certain lands and, most of all, stay on their side of the imagined border. Thomas McKee, the assistant deputy superintendent of Indian affairs who lived near Paxton, made similar reports during the Black Boys' Rebellion. A friend to Indians, he lived in "dread that any Indians should come on the Frontiers, as the Inhabitants declare they will murder all who do." McKee, as one of the new imperial officials empowered to maintain peace through cordial relations with Indians, also found himself the target of these frontier rebellions. His family, he told his superior, "are in the greatest consternation, being in imminent danger of having our house set on fire, or bodily hurt done us, as I have often been threatened by the rioters." For imperial officials like William Johnson, a boundary was needed to keep these colonists away from Indians to maintain the peace the empire so desperately wanted to preserve.[52]

Colonists and Indians wanted a border too, though for different reasons. Colonists petitioned John Penn "imploring [his] protection," which meant "remov[ing] [and] preventing those savages from settling so near our borders." They wanted a secure border to provide them with a defense against Indian assaults they assumed were in the offing. Native Americans, for their part, wanted a border to provide them with their own security from expansionist and increasingly murderous colonists. The difference between the two views, however, was that Indians shared a vision similar to imperial officials for how this bordered zone would function. By drawing a boundary, both sides could continue to negotiate their diplomatic alliances and economic relationships. This stability, imperial officials hoped, would foster trading partnerships between British merchants and Indians, which would in turn provide colonists with the security they sought. Frontier settlers, for their part, agreed that a boundary was needed, but theirs was a different idea. They wanted a border to separate Indians from their polity because they had designated them enemies. Theirs would be a closed, militarized border used to designate those outside the protections of empire: a frontier.[53]

Johnson accomplished the empire's aim with the Treaty of Fort Stanwix in 1768. Years of settler violence, population increase, and the failed efforts of both colonial and imperial officials to implement the Proclamation of 1763 forced imperial officials and Indians to try to create a new boundary. Johnson negotiated the treaty at a site in northwestern New York with the Six Nations' Iroquois. The Iroquois granted all land west of the Allegheny and east of the Ohio Valley to the Tennessee River to Britain. The treaty established the Ohio River, rather than the Allegheny Mountains, as the new western boundary between Indian Country and the British Empire. He hoped the fixed but open border would reset Indian relations and put the empire on sounder footing.[54]

CHAPTER 9

Independent Frontiers

With the Treaty of Fort Stanwix in 1768, British officials like William Johnson hoped they had solved the problems the west posed to the empire. Instead, they only exacerbated them. The empire still lacked a clear process for the coordinated expansion of the colonies that composed it. The treaty opened new areas for colonial settlement, and colonies anxious to formally establish their claim to this territory rushed into the region and competed with one another over land rights and borders just as they had before the Seven Years' War. The influx of new immigrants, who crossed the Atlantic in droves after a brief respite during the war years, only increased the pressure on colonial and imperial governments to expand. One historian has estimated that by 1771, about 25,000 new colonists inhabited the region around Fort Pitt, composing about a tenth of the entire population of Pennsylvania. With so many colonists living in the area, it was incumbent upon the British Empire to install a governing presence to provide order and regulate colonists' behavior.[1]

By the 1770s, a new idea for solving the problem of expansion began to gain momentum in elite circles: the creation of a new, inland colony around Fort Pitt. Ideas like it had circulated before, but after the Treaty of Fort Stanwix, it became a much more viable option. Even Pennsylvania proprietary officials were cautiously supportive of a new colony in the west—so long as it did not take land granted to their colony. John Penn concluded that a new colony would more clearly establish Pennsylvania's jurisdictional boundaries, which would help his government enforce laws. Even better, he thought that a new colony could fix Pennsylvania's vexed political situation by removing the controversial issue of frontier defense and societal disorder. A colony in the Ohio Valley, he reasoned, would provide a buffer

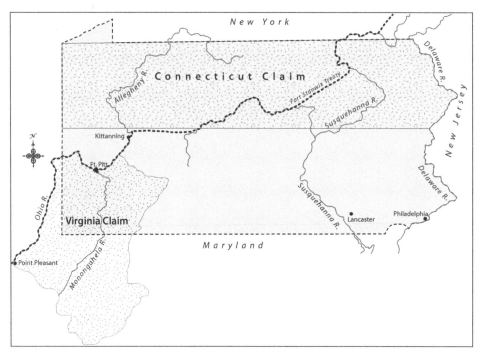

Figure 13. The jurisdictional claims of Virginia and Connecticut during the 1770s. Following the rebellions on Pennsylvania's frontiers, the two colonies began to assert rights to land that clashed with Pennsylvania's own claims. Pennsylvania tried to fend off both colonies, often resorting to violence reminiscent of the Maryland War in the 1730s. In this case, however, Pennsylvania failed to secure its claims and the government retreated. On the eve of the American Revolution, Connecticut settlers had established their own county in the northeastern area of the modern state, and Virginia controlled the area around Fort Pitt.

against potential Indian attacks and, more important, enhance the possibility for peace by providing a safety valve for the "worst of the people" who "will retreat to this new country" leaving "the best who are of most consequence . . . behind" in Pennsylvania. It would do for the empire what Lancaster County had done for the colony after the frontier crisis of 1728.[2]

With proposals abounding, imperial officials in London took a variety of approaches to organizing the new territory. Some had personal interests in speculative land companies; others believed the answer to the problem was to set up new colonies; and still others wanted to continue to restrain settlement even though the land was purchased. Two problems hindered the implementation of any coherent imperial policy, however. First, the bureaucracy moved so slowly and colonists were so quick to take matters into their own hands that by the time approved initiatives got under way, they were already moot. The second problem was the rapid succession of administrations in London, which exacerbated poor relations among all parties—Great Britain, the colonies, and Indians.[3]

In the end, the empire's inaction allowed competing colonies to fill the political vacuum. During these years, Pennsylvania was besieged, fighting two conflicts over its borders, one to the north against Connecticut and one to the west against Virginia. Unlike its earlier war with Maryland, Pennsylvania lost these two conflicts in large part because the victorious colonies of Connecticut and Virginia successfully appealed to the values of frontier people, while Pennsylvania offered a less persuasive vision for expansion, security, and Indian relations. In each case, frontier people chose to back a different government and its model for providing security and expansion. Thus, even as competition and conflict unsettled official forms of authority, frontier people's choices consolidated areas and interests on the verge of the American Revolution. This consolidation came at the expense of the British Empire, whose authority had withered away in the face of intercolonial competition.[4]

"Our Discontented Frontier Inhabitants"

Pennsylvania officials began worrying about Connecticut's claims soon after the Seven Years' War ended, with one official writing in 1761 that "these deluded [Connecticut] people will come over like blackbirds and settle." The official was right. In the 1760s, settlers from Connecticut began arriving en masse on the Susquehanna River about a hundred miles north of Lancaster, laying the foundation for another border war with Pennsylvania. The origins of this dispute, as was the case with most of these border conflicts, rested in different legal readings of the boundaries outlined in the colonial charters of Connecticut and Pennsylvania. Connecticut's 1662 charter extended its western boundary to the Pacific Ocean, but subsequent grants to New York and then Pennsylvania impeded this claim.[5]

For almost a century, Connecticut did not assert any right to what remained noncontiguous land that was still in Indian hands. In the 1750s, however, land became tight in Connecticut, and it began to look westward for new opportunities. During the Albany Conference, as representatives from the various colonies tried to create a union for expansion, Connecticut's representatives quietly met with Iroquois representatives to secure a highly dubious deed for the land around modern-day Wilkes-Barre, Pennsylvania. The group that secured the purchase organized as the Susquehanna Company, which modeled itself on the joint-stock companies that had established such colonies as Virginia. Many of the stockholders were prominent in Connecticut politics, and aside from profit, their ultimate goal was to bring the region under Connecticut's authority. As an eighteenth-century version of a public–private partnership, the company would assume the risk—and possible reward—of settlement, with the colony eventually gaining long-term benefits if the venture proved successful.[6]

The Seven Years' War interrupted the company's plans, but when the war ended, Connecticut's expansion proceeded with gusto. At first, the governor of Pennsylvania wanted to burn their houses and throw them out, but Richard Peters, the head of the Land Office, cautioned that such action might cause more problems. Instead, he hoped to reason with Connecticut's governor to stop his people from settling on the land, much as Pennsylvania had tried to do before Cresap's War. Diplomacy failed and settlement proceeded. More troubling, Pennsylvania's governor soon learned that "many of the [Pennsylvania] people favour them [Connecticut] and many others would be glad to get land on the same terms."[7]

By 1763, dozens of families were settled on the northern branch of the Susquehanna River, much to the chagrin of local Delaware Indians and proprietary and imperial officials, all of whom asked that the settlement cease. Pontiac's War was the only thing that proved effective in stopping Connecticut when devastatingly successful Indian raids forced colonists to return to their home colony. The company and its stockholders, however, continued to claim the ground and plotted their return. With the opening of new territory after the Treaty of Fort Stanwix, Connecticut men marched back into the disputed lands.[8]

While Connecticut treated the opening of these lands as reason to allow unfettered expansion, Pennsylvania's proprietary officials reacted to the Fort Stanwix treaty according to their traditional method of ordered settlement: creating manors, laying out towns, and distributing lands through the Land Office. In 1769, the office decided to offer a lottery to limit the amount of land any one person could own and make the process as open as possible. Rumors proliferated that the proprietor had rigged the system to allow the well-connected to acquire large tracts of land to resell at inflated prices to regular colonists. The proprietor tried to dispel these rumors, but in time, evidence came to light that some individuals had indeed worked in concert to acquire large parcels, although it is unclear if the proprietor was complicit in the scheme. Hugh Williamson, who traveled throughout Lancaster County as the proprietor's emissary to the people, reported that "the inhabitants very generally complaining of the supposed malconduct of the government in the distribution of lands."[9]

Frontier settlers feared the power of such landholders and wanted a more open process and even distribution of lands. It is important to note that their complaints had less to do with land already purchased than with the way the newly opened land was being distributed. Edmund Physick, a member of the Provincial Council who also served in the Land Office, recounted similar conversations he had with frontier settlers: "I was greatly affected with the complaints of the people who remembered an advertisement published a few years since wherein the proprietaries expressed their great abhorrence of monopolies, and made a Regulation that no man should have more land granted him than 300 acres. They allowed the proprietaries had power to grant any quantity they thought proper, but never expected that power could operate in prejudice to their own interest and the publick good."[10]

This statement showed that while tensions existed between frontier settlers and the proprietary, colonists still recognized the proprietor's authority to grant land and had long trusted him to do right. They now intended to point out an error and negotiate a mutually agreeable solution with him by "representing their case by a petition to the governor." Moreover, they shared the same assumption that the proprietor had always had that all land in the charter would eventually be Pennsylvania's. Indeed, they explained to Physick that "these were the lands they wanted for themselves and children, and if they met with a disappointment there would be no spaces left sufficient for a number of families to settle together so as to be able to support even a mill for grinding their wheat."[11]

Physick placed Pennsylvania's predicament in the context of colonial competition, fearing that neighboring colonies would steal disgruntled colonists away through better policies if Pennsylvania hesitated to respond to their pleas. Physick also understood that the experience of the frontier shaped new settlement patterns. Because proprietary colonies were more directly invested in land development and quitrent collection than others, proprietary offices always had to pay attention to settler concerns in the face of what neighboring colonies offered potential settlers. In this case, Indian war had changed the way settlers viewed the colony and their needs within it. As Physick noted, Pennsylvania was no longer the land of peace and prosperity. Instead, based on his travels among settlers, he saw that "the people cannot soon forget the terror of an Indian war and rather than live dispersed in an inhospitable dreary part of the country, they would chuse to leave it [and] have gone to Virginia." In a few years, when Virginia began to intrude on western lands, this shift would become a reality.[12]

Just as Pennsylvanians were growing disillusioned with their colony's ability to provide what they needed, a large contingent of Connecticut settlers established a town under the leadership of Seven Years' War veteran Colonel John Durkee. To counter Connecticut's jurisdictional claim to the area, John Penn began doling out lands as well. He did so using proprietary patronage, granting hundred-acre lots to those who had served his interest and empowering these individuals to make similar grants to anyone else willing to defend the proprietary cause.[13]

In November, a group of Pennsylvanians, under the leadership of Samuel Ogden, launched an offensive and successfully pushed back the Connecticut claimants. After a two-day siege and the loss of one Connecticut life, the New Englanders agreed to meet for a peace treaty. The treaty stipulated that fourteen men from the Connecticut settlement could stay for one year to harvest the crops they had planted, but the rest had to return east. Almost as soon as this treaty was signed, leading Connecticut leaders denounced it, asserting that those who represented Connecticut lacked the authority to negotiate terms of peace. They vowed that Connecticut would return.[14]

Return they did, and armed with new tactics that would put Pennsylvania permanently on the defensive. The Susquehanna Company began marketing itself to those living along the Susquehanna River, especially to those in points south in Lancaster County. The new settlement promised prospective members a role in the government, which was run by a quasi-town committee; a permanent militia; and cheap land—all things the Paxton Boys and subsequent protesters had sought in vain to change within Pennsylvania. Moreover, Connecticut offered a shared experience and reputation for fighting wars against Indians. Since at least the 1750s, those who promoted the movement of Connecticut people to western areas argued that the empire would benefit from such settlers because they have "often had wars with the French and Indians." In short, the Connecticut people and the policies they carried to this new land looked a lot like what the frontier people had tried to effect in Pennsylvania on the local level throughout the 1760s.[15]

This shifting of allegiances, which had been so decisive to the outcome of Pennsylvania's earlier war with Maryland, again proved determinative. This time, however, the trend ran away from Pennsylvania. Penn believed Connecticut's power would "gain strength every day especially as we are in no situation to give them any opposition." He sent emissaries to Lancaster to implore people to remain loyal to Pennsylvania, but it was to no avail. Though Scots-Irish are often identified as the primary adopters of the Connecticut cause, Hugh Williamson reported that young Germans from Hanover in Lancaster County were also prominent among those taking up the Connecticut mantle.[16]

The exodus seemed to be rapid and universal. In January 1770, Penn heard that "half the county of Northampton are friends to them." He complained that the county sheriff failed to find recruits to fight off the Connecticut settlers, even though the sheriff "offered them pay." Another report from Lancaster told Penn that "people are continually going up to Wioming to join the Connecticut people all armed, with drums beating and colors flying." The most prominent group was led by Lazarus Stewart, a former militiaman from Pontiac's War. He named his loyal band the "Paxton Boys," donning the still popular mantle of that murderous political movement.[17]

The only way to solve the problem was to adjust Pennsylvania policies to surpass Connecticut's promises and undo the duplicitous actions of the land lottery. As Physick reported to Penn, "I now know but of one method to disengage our people from them, and that would be for those who have had private grants to sell their lands at a low rate and others to give up their rights who obtained them by pitting several tickets into the lottery for the same piece of land with intent to defraud honest men of the chance."[18]

Such was the policy the Penns enacted in Cresap's War, but things had changed for the proprietorship. John Penn's flexibility was limited by his uncle's ledger books. After Thomas Penn granted lands on the Susquehanna at half their proposed value, his accountant reported that continued support of the cause made no financial sense. Penn agreed and insisted that the Pennsylvania Assembly foot the bill for defense. John Penn seemed to be at his wits' end, describing it as "a most expensive and troublesome affair and has given me more vexation and uneasiness than any thing." By 1771, Pennsylvania's proprietary had essentially ceded the fight and instead planned to take its case to the Crown. Pennsylvania established Northumberland County in 1772, which would help in a legal case to show an explicit claim to jurisdiction, and Pennsylvania's representatives in England began approaching the Board of Trade.[19]

The change of strategy, however, only weakened Pennsylvania's case among the frontier people. As early as 1770, credible rumors of a Pennsylvania retreat provided the impetus for Pennsylvanians to leave the colony and join the Connecticut cause. Many came to believe that "the proprietors of Pennsylvania have given up the contention with the New Englanders and thereby acknowledge their right and as they sell their lands cheap, are determined to settle under them." The proprietor's brand suffered further degradation from those still loyal to the colony when in 1771 Pennsylvania militia retreated from their chief garrison. When quitrents were collected in 1772, many settlers in the area paid only half of their due. They refused to pay the full amount, they claimed, because the proprietor had not proven his ability to protect their property.[20]

John Penn and proprietary officials in Pennsylvania saw the weakening of support as the death knell for the colony. Penn had done many things to rebuff Connecticut's moves. Pennsylvania could match their competitors in militia strength since Connecticut's militias were originally volunteerlike forces. They could also match Connecticut's speed of expansion since, with the Treaty of Fort Stanwix, they had no external constraints limiting their ambitions. Connecticut offered cheap land, and Penn responded with terms comparable to Connecticut. But Pennsylvania still lost because colonists whose allegiance proved negotiable concluded that Connecticut represented a government they could trust to meet frontier demands. Indeed, such considerations spurred the Pennsylvanians under Lazarus Stewart and the self-proclaimed Paxton Boys to provide the Connecticut claim with military backing against Pennsylvania. As Edmund Physick noted, the Connecticut claimants "never could have supported themselves" without the help "of our discontented frontier inhabitants." John Penn agreed, concluding in a letter to his uncle that "the greatest danger is from the Pennsylvanians who have through this whole affair given them every possible encouragement, and many people in this town have bought rights under them, and when they find the government gives not further opposition to these intruders, they will certainly join them in order to get their lands." Just as with Pennsylvania's border war with Maryland a generation earlier, the shifting allegiance of colonists caught in the middle of the battle played a determinative role in the conflict's outcome. Once Penn realized he was losing colonists, he knew his chances of winning were diminished.[21]

The "discontented frontier inhabitants," like the reformed Paxton Boys, embraced their newfound political power to build the government they wanted. They created an air of authority by donning official dress and performance. The members of the militia wore "white cockades," created numerous forts, mustered, and marched throughout the towns, all actions to give the air of official governing authority and martial culture. They were also given real political power in the government. The Susquehanna Company could only grant new lands through a vote of stockholders. But once admitted, each settler became a "proprietor," a landowner with rights within a town committee. In January 1771, for example, the company rewarded Lazarus Stewart for capturing a Pennsylvania fort by voting him a proprietor. They appointed him, along with longtime Connecticut partisans Zebulon Butler and John Durkee, to a four-person committee charged with "order[ing] and direct[ing] affairs relating to the well ordering and governing of the settlers." The company also gave Stewart and "his associates" their own township, called Hanover, in exchange for "special services done the company."[22]

In 1773, the new settlers drew up a more formal charter for a county made up of several towns founded by those loyal to Connecticut's claim. The county operated in a decentralized manner, giving settlers the greatest political freedom possible. Each town had a meeting to decide pertinent issues. The settlers erected six towns, with all but two headed by a militia officer. The residents of each town elected a director to oversee the town and to confer among the other directors about issues that the county as a whole faced. They elected a town "officer," choosing a military rather than civil title to describe the constable. Incorporating the frontier political culture into the charter, they also explicitly said "the law regulating the militia of the colony, shall be particularly attended to."[23]

A year later, Connecticut formally recognized the Susquehanna Company's land as part of its colony by establishing it as Westmoreland County. One historian estimates that the area had grown from a couple of hundred

settlers in 1771 to around two thousand by the time of the county's formation. New settlers flocked from all over, including Vermont and New York,
although most came from land-poor Connecticut. But this opportunity had
been facilitated by the initial large exodus of Pennsylvanians willing to
embrace Connecticut's claims.[24]

Violence between the colonies flared throughout this period. At one
point in 1771, nearly a hundred men, women, and children loyal to Pennsylvania huddled in a blockhouse on the northern banks of the Susquehanna
River for two weeks, weathering a relentless assault. When they finally
capitulated, the Connecticut leaders, according to European customs of
war, welcomed their conquest to dinner, where they drew up formal articles
of capitulation. The culmination of what later became known as the Pennamite Wars came in 1774, when an ad hoc and voluntary group of 700
Pennsylvanians formed an association to defeat their rivals. Many of these
volunteers held Pennsylvania titles to the land, and those who did not,
believed they would get land if they succeeded. The proprietor gave civil
powers to the militia too by deeming it a body under control of and authorized by Northumberland County. The tide seemed about to turn—until the
Pennsylvanians met with a swift and ignoble defeat against a force of only
250 Connecticut militiamen. Pennsylvania had lost the war for one of its
borders.[25]

"The Americans Will Not Submit to the British Parliament, and They May Now Defend Themselves"

At virtually the same time Pennsylvania ceded the northern frontier to an
expanding New England colony, it was losing a similar battle with Virginia
on its western frontiers. The origins of this other conflict began in the mid-
1760s when Thomas Gage began shuttering forts in the west. The forts were
costly, seemed unnecessary in times of peace, and upset Native allies. The
underlying assumption that drove this decision, however, reflected the
imperial position that these lands no longer formed a frontier, or an area
of potential or imminent invasion. In 1772, Gage issued orders to close Fort
Pitt, the last vestige of imperial authority in the area. The fort had served
as a center for trade and diplomacy, but the British now thought Detroit a
more appropriate place to focus their western imperial project. The troops
tore down Fort Pitt, and the property was sold to two traders. The fort had

exercised the strongest political authority in the region. As soon as the British military vacated it, a political vacuum emerged into which colonial competition fused with the politics of frontiers, transforming the region on the eve of the American Revolution.[26]

The various reactions to Fort Pitt's abandonment reflected the nature of the imperial crisis in the west. The fort's symbolism meant very different things to different people. Colonists were dismayed, to say the least, and wanted protection from a colonial government to fill the void left by the removal of imperial authority. "The people have allways looked upon this place as a barrier between them and the Indians," George Croghan explained. Governor John Penn also understood that they "look[ed] upon that fortress as their safeguard against the incursions of the Indians." Colonists possessing an overriding fear of Indian war began petitioning Pennsylvania for military support.[27]

The desertion of the fort also caused some colonists to equate the policy with other unpopular imperial measures then upsetting colonists back east. Rumors circulated that Gage wanted to cow frontier people into obedience by using their fear of Indians as a means of gaining their deference. If the fort was removed, the rumor held, settlers would either have to abide by imperial policies that advocated peace with Indians or face a war with no military support. In late 1773, David McClure, one of many itinerant preachers who traveled through the area during this time, heard that a British official, thought to be George Croghan, had sent Indians a war belt, "informing them, that the English colonists refused to obey the Great King of England; and if he should send an army to chastize them, his allies and friends, the Indians, were invited to join them."[28]

British officers at the fort certainly expressed such sentiments, showing a level of disdain for unruly frontier settlers that reflected a common opinion held throughout the chain of command. When McClure returned to Fort Pitt, he asked one of the soldiers "the reason of their destroying the fort, so necessary to the safety of the frontier." The soldier replied that "the Americans will not submit to the British Parliament, and they may now defend themselves." Thomas Gage made a similar statement about Fort Pitt, suggesting that it would be best to "let them [colonists] feel the Consequences" of their anti-Indian actions, leaving the British Army "out of the scrape." Such talk of letting Indians fight colonists and rumors of the British encouraging Indians to war only confirmed settlers' fear of Indians and their desire for protection from a government other than their imperial one.[29]

Indians, for their part, tended to embrace the position of imperial offi-cials and Pennsylvania's Assembly. Instead of seeing the area as a frontier to be militarized, they saw it as porous boundary through which trade and diplomacy—but not colonists looking to settle land—could flow. As George Croghan noted, "I don't find that the Indians are any way uneasy att [sic] the Troops being removed." McClure, then visiting an Indian com-munity several miles downriver, noted that when word of Fort Pitt's destruction reached Indians on the Muskingum River, they expressed feel-ings of "joy." To them, the fort represented British colonization, expansion, and war. Its closure, they hoped, would bring some modicum of peace and stability.[30]

With such competing sentiments swirling around an area devoid of clear governing authority, leaders of neighboring colonies saw opportunity, much as their predecessors had in Cresap's War. This new round of inter-colonial competition had the same effects it had elsewhere and previously. As colonies vied to control land and win colonists, a new round of sanc-tioned and massive expansion was unleashed, and Indians that the empire had once sought as allies found their concerns displaced as colonies rushed to secure their jurisdiction. Indeed, before Mason and Dixon finished the boundary between Pennsylvania and Maryland in 1767, Pennsylvania offi-cials were already concerned that Virginia posed a new threat to their west-ern claims. In 1766, John Penn had learned that "there are many people settled to the westward upon the unpurchased lands upon grants from the government of Virginia." In 1771, a Pennsylvanian complained of the "intestin broyls" subsisting among Virginians, Pennsylvanians, and settlers without allegiance to any colony. With the closure of Fort Pitt, Pennsylvania tried to establish its authority over the region in 1773 in much the same way that it had incorporated new territory in the past, by creating a new county called Westmoreland, appointing a number of commissioners in charge of establishing all the necessary legal offices, and opening a court of law.[31]

Virginia, meanwhile, responded in kind. Under the leadership of a new governor, John Murray, the Fourth Earl of Dunmore, the colony began to assert its jurisdiction alongside Pennsylvania's, creating a situation nearly identical to Cresap's War a generation before. In fact, Thomas Cresap, elderly but energetic, lived in western Maryland and threw his support behind Virginia. He provided tactical advice, and his son, Michael, served as an enforcer for Virginia. Dunmore, for his part, had grand visions for the west, believing that he could create his own fiefdom.[32]

Dunmore appointed John Connolly in late 1773 as his subordinate to secure the west, much as Baltimore had done with Cresap forty years earlier. Connolly, a physician originally from Lancaster, Pennsylvania, had ties to the elite of the region through blood and marriage. He was a nephew to George Croghan and son-in-law to Samuel Semple, a prominent tavernkeeper in Pittsburgh whose lodgings once hosted George Washington. His prominent connections and intelligence brought Connolly to the attention of Washington and other Virginian speculators, and eventually to Dunmore himself. Seeing greater opportunity in Virginia, with its large landowners and speculators, the Pennsylvania-born Connolly decided to renounce his former allegiances and ally with Virginia. Both Connolly and Dunmore realized that Pennsylvania posed the biggest threat to their plans for Virginia's political expansion. To beat this competitor, they both knew they would have to harness the self-interest and political beliefs of the populace by doing exactly what Pennsylvania would not do: militarize the region in response to settlers' fears of Native Americans and create the means for rapid expansion. In so doing, Dunmore and Connolly allowed frontier people to play a more active role in shaping policy even as they established Virginia's authority in the region.[33]

Connolly arrived in Pittsburgh with his commission in January 1774 and immediately started building a bulwark of loyal Virginians. He distributed militia appointments, recognized land grants, and cajoled settlers into swearing allegiance. When all else failed, he brought casks of rum to entice enlistments. Connolly also wanted to project an air of competence, authority, and order. He therefore regularly mustered, designed official uniforms to designate officers, and recruited new soldiers. Connolly also established the necessary institutions of Virginia's legal authority. He opened a courthouse at Fort Pitt and built a ducking stool in front of the fort for punishing "evilly disposed women." Such symbols of authority—in the case of the ducking stool, patriarchal as well as legal—were clearly meant to convince the populace of Virginia's authority and ability to provide the security they desired.[34]

Meanwhile, Pennsylvania established Westmoreland County's judicial center in Hannastown thirty miles east of Fort Pitt. The hamlet lacked proper shelter, and lawyers complained about having to write on tree stumps and working in the rain. But it did have one thing going for it. The three commissioners who were appointed by the proprietor to establish the legal institutions of the county chose the spot because two of them had land interests around Hannastown and hoped a county seat so located would earn them a nice profit. New settlers, however, did not share the commissioners' enthusiasm for the location and begged for a court of law near Fort Pitt, where most of them lived. Such complaints fell on deaf ears. Thus, Virginians at Fort Pitt not only created the appearance of authority and defense but also provided easier access to a court. For settlers tired of traveling to Pennsylvania's judicial center, siding with Virginia was a matter of convenience as well as principle.[35]

Just as with Cresap's War, each colony took aim at officers representing its opponent's jurisdiction. As soon as Connolly appeared on the scene as a commissioned militia officer and justice of the peace, Arthur St. Clair, Penn's main agent in the area and a justice of the peace, had him arrested. Connolly was released on bail with the promise to return for his court date, but bail did little to slow Connolly. While free, he recruited more men and captured the ruins of Fort Pitt, renaming it Fort Dunmore. A Pennsylvania justice of the peace reported in early April that Connolly "is in actual possession of the fort, with a body guard of militia about him, invested, as we are told, with both civil and military power to put Virginia law in force." When Connolly's Pennsylvania court date arrived, he returned as promised to the Westmoreland County Courthouse, but he arrived with 180 militiamen in tow, "with colours flying, and their captains, etc., had their sword drawn." The confrontation passed, but a few days later, Connolly arrested three of Pennsylvania's justices of the peace for trying to exercise an alien jurisdiction on Virginia territory and sent them to jail in Williamsburg.[36]

Aside from arrests and armed confrontations, Dunmore and his allies also employed rumor to undercut Pennsylvania's authority. Virginians spread reports that Pennsylvania had no right to the land and that any grants made under that government would be void. The uncertainty surrounding the borders made such accounts believable, and few colonists wanted to risk losing lands they had laid out and improved. There were also rumors—maybe even originating from Thomas Cresap—that Maryland was going to reignite its own border dispute and reclaim all the territory south of the fortieth parallel.[37]

More important, leading representatives of each colony tried to use reason to persuade colonists caught in the middle. Virginian and Pennsylvanian officials canvassed the area, campaigning for their respective causes, even squaring off in public to debate the merits of each colony. In late

January 1774, after Connolly had appeared on the scene, St. Clair delivered a speech to a large crowd assembled at Fort Pitt in which he explained the benefits of Pennsylvania over Virginia. So important was his speech that a number of the justices of the peace from Pennsylvania helped St. Clair craft the case, which appealed to reason, economics, and religion to promote Pennsylvania over Virginia. St. Clair argued that Pennsylvania's higher land prices were a sign of good government and its promise of security. St. Clair also defended Pennsylvania's unwillingness to support a militia, arguing that a fort would only increase tensions. He believed that Pennsylvania's policy toward Indians, based on its history of peace through trade and coexistence, had proven to be the best means of securing peace.[38]

According to St. Clair, Pennsylvania's most effective booster was George Wilson, a Virginian by birth who, when given the opportunity, renounced his membership to that colony and joined Pennsylvania. Unlike St. Clair, a British-born former officer, Wilson was of the region, and his intelligence, fused with his uneducated style, appealed to local audiences. According to St. Clair, Wilson in "a very handsome speech of about one hour . . . opened the Constitution of the Province, compared it with that of the neighboring colonies, and pointed out where it excelled them." St. Clair believed that "it was lucky it was spoken so publicly, as many people from the doubtful part of the country were present."[39]

Those loyal to Virginia countered with their own arguments. They often appropriated rhetoric from the urban east that criticized Parliament as arbitrary and applied it to Pennsylvania's government. The *Virginia Gazette* lauded Dunmore's willingness to "penetrate to the seat of our grievances" and, taking aim at Pennsylvania's high land prices, "render himself an eye and ear witness of the indispensable necessity of granting back lands, and by doing this not only to deal justice to his own people, but with the same blow give a check a[n] aspiring encroaching spirit of the princely proprietor."[40]

As these differences between the colonies crystallized, frontier people started to join Virginia in droves. In explaining their decision, they invoked lines of attack against Pennsylvania similar to those propagated in print. A petition filed on behalf of colonists in the region accused Pennsylvania's officers of being "calculated for enriching individuals [rather] than the public good" and prone to "adhere strictly to their masters interest, however contrary to the good of the settlers, his Majesty's subjects." The petition also chastised Pennsylvania for its inadequate support of frontiers, claiming the colony was well known for its "ill provided defence of the country in cases of emergency."[41]

The most powerful point of divergence, however, had to do with Pennsylvania's policies toward Native peoples. When settlers believed they lived on a frontier vulnerable to attack, they sought government support to provide protection. In a petition settlers sent to Virginia asking for aid, 587 signers explained that they considered their "lives and properties in imminent danger, from contiguity to the faithless and barbarous natives, whose treaties, alliance, and sincerity, are never to be relied on." Such sentiments were nearly identical to the ones expressed by the Paxton Boys and the Black Boys in their petitions. Connolly and Dunmore played on these still present and powerful feelings to strengthen their support base and woo unaligned settlers. Indeed shortly after this petition, Virginia declared the Shawnees "enemies" and warned settlers of a "certain imprudent people"—meaning Quakers in Pennsylvania, a group he well knew received the ire of frontier people—who continued to "carry on a correspondence with and supply . . . dangerous commodities" to these enemies, accusations that the Paxton Boys and Black Boys had also levelled. Connolly made clear to those around him that he understood the political demands of frontier inhabitants and intended to meet them. "The people of the frontiers want nothing but the countenance of government to execute every desirable purpose [war]," Connolly advised his rival St. Clair, "and your province appearing backwards at this critical juncture, will most indubitably be highly displeasing to all the western settlers."[42]

St. Clair responded to Connolly by offering the Pennsylvanian vision of the west, one that showed a vastly different strategy toward Indians and frontier defenses. The costs of war to both colonies and settlers would be too high, he argued. Instead, St. Clair suggested that Virginia and Pennsylvania offer Indians "ample reparations . . . for the injuries they have already sustained" and ensure that "an honest open intercourse [be] established in the future." Such an arrangement would be "a more cheap, easy and expeditious manner of re-establishing the peace of the country than any offensive measures." Trade and diplomacy would provide stronger security for colonists, St. Clair held, a view inimical to the very people the policy was meant to protect, but aligned with both colonial and imperial strategies.[43]

Actions taken by each government reinforced the words each side uttered. While Pennsylvania refused to create militias, Virginians increased their open hostility to Indians, especially the Shawnees, whom they viewed as the most powerful Native group in the area and the one that most strenuously defended claims to their land. In the spring of 1774, two separate attacks, one near Pipe Creek and another near Yellow Creek, made war all but inevitable. The Pipe Creek clash happened on the Ohio River west of Fort Pitt on land surveyors were beginning to mark for Virginia. The Yellow Creek assault happened nearer Fort Pitt and was particularly brutal. In a premeditated and unprovoked attack, Virginians under the leadership of Daniel Greathouse killed the entire family of Logan, the son of an important Iroquois headman whom imperial officials considered an ally. After his family was butchered—his pregnant sister's child was reportedly ripped from her womb and "stuck on a pole"—he vowed revenge and allied with the Shawnees and Pluggy, a Mingo who also had strong ties to the Shawnees.[44]

The Virginians premised their entire strategy on acquiring a complete monopoly of state power in the region. Law was an important part of that, but so too was recognition from Native groups that Virginia had the rights to the land and that Virginia would be their sole trading partner. The Virginians' plan became most pronounced as they strategized for war. "All officers going out on parties [were] to make as many prisoners as they can of woman and children," Dunmore instructed his commanders. "Should you be so fortunate as to reduce these savages to sue for peace," he continued, "I would not grant it to them on any terms till they were effectually chastised for their insolence and then on no terms without bringing in six of their heads as hostages for their future good behaviour and these to be relieved annually; and that they trade with us only for anything they may want." Virginia's complete control of the Indian trade, Dunmore knew, would make whatever vestige remained of Pennsylvania's claim to the region vanish. Just as both Ogle and Penn knew in 1736, Indians' recognition of the rightful colonial possessor was just as important as colonists' allegiance. In this case, however, war with Indians was necessary for Virginia to secure colonists' allegiance and ensure the Shawnees recognized Virginia as the legitimate colonial power in the region.[45]

The spark for Dunmore's War thus can only be understood by appreciating the role of colonial competition in spurring Dunmore's offensive. In fact, many people at the time saw it that way. Pennsylvanians suspected that Dunmore's posture toward the Shawnees was simply a ploy to force more settlers into the Virginia camp. As St. Clair wrote those back east, "Indian war was part of the Virginia plan" from the beginning because a war would give the Virginia militia "the appearance of necessity." He worried that the Pennsylvania Assembly would refuse to provide the same support because "the white people [were] the aggressors." Virginians thus understood how to use the politics of frontiers to strengthen their cause. If they created fear of war against Indians, then they could assert their state power and win adherents.[46]

The long-term memory of Dunmore's War in Pennsylvania agreed with St. Clair's early interpretation that this was an offensive war of choice. Years later, James Smith, the leader of the Black Boys who lived near Bedford during the conflict, noted that "this time the white people were the aggressors." An obscure settler in Fort Pitt who left a narrative of his life echoed that sentiment, similarly stating "the whites were the aggressors." Others believed it was a scheme by Dunmore to divide colonies during their struggle against Britain. In any case, from the view of those unallied with Virginia, it was clearly an offensive and unnecessary war.[47]

Virginians, however, held a starkly different interpretation of the war's cause. Years after the conflict, many Virginians described the war as defensive fight brought about by "the commencement of the Indian depredations and hostilities on the western portion of Virginia." Dunmore, ultimately despised for his loyalty to the Crown during the Revolution, still received praise from those filing pensions for their service during this war. One pensioner commented that Dunmore realized that because of "the many out rages [Indians] perpetrated, that an Indian war was not only likely to take place, but inevitable, and wisely made preparations for the same." Such a belief in the inevitability of Indian war reflected the logic of a racial frontier against an Indian threat that made a permanent military presence necessary. Moreover, Dunmore's War revealed how the logic of a racial frontier transformed the meaning of good frontier policy into one in which an offensive war was fought under the guise of defensive need. Frontiers in Dunmore's War thus began to be areas of expansion and offensive action rather than zones of contraction and defensive fortifications.[48]

The difference is even more dramatic when one looks at the awareness of the war in each colony's eastern society. Although all of the violence of Dunmore's War occurred in remote areas, the talk of Indian war spread throughout Virginia, while Pennsylvanians to the east paid little notice to what was happening. The disconnect reflected the difference between a colony that incorporated areas as it expanded and a fragmented one divided over expansion and the inclusion of new settlements. In areas far removed from the events happening around Fort Pitt, Virginia men mobilized out of a martial and masculine duty that they believed frontiers demanded. William Preston lived in Fincastle County in southwestern Virginia where "not a Drop of blood spilled or an Indian seen." Nonetheless, he and his neighbors still "joined . . . to build a little fort for our own Defence" because they feared their town was "now almost a frontier." William Fleming, an officer from Virginia who traveled hundreds of miles west to face the Shawnees in battle, had a similar view on the war. When he explained his reasons for fighting in a letter to his wife, he told her he acted out of honor, duty, and the defense of his family, all because they were "included amongst the frontier settlers": "As much as I love and regard you both I can not allow my self to wish me with you till the expedition is finished knowing that it would [sink me] in your esteem and that you would dispise a wretch that could desert an honourable cause, a cause undertaken for the good of his Country in general and more immediately for the Protection of his Family as included amongst the Frontier settlers." The sentiments of those who considered themselves Virginians showed the extent to which the colony had fostered a martial culture and the incumbent obligations that living upon a frontier impelled.[49]

The Shawnees too recognized the differences each colony represented. St. Clair remarked, "'Tis some satisfaction the Indians seem to discriminate betwixt us and those who attacked them." St. Clair also received messages that the Indians still hoped "to become as one people," a rhetoric of friendship dating to the days of William Penn that still persisted in Pennsylvania. In late July, St. Clair was "still sanguine to hope this province will escape the mischiefs of a war, as all operations of the Indians are evidently aimed at the Virginians." Competition thus gave Indians the ability to empower the colony with whom they preferred to do business. In fact, the Indians' choice may have emboldened Dunmore even more. He needed to defeat both Pennsylvania and the Shawnees in order to secure absolute control of the west, and he knew both were intricately linked.[50]

Perhaps there is no better testament to Virginia's fundamental difference from Pennsylvania than the often overlooked story of the Battle of Point Pleasant in October 1774. As hostilities over the course of 1774 fomented between colonists and Ohio Indians, colonists throughout Virginia rushed to mobilize. The Battle of Point Pleasant pitted Virginia militias from Augusta, Botetourt, Culpepper, and Fincastle Counties against Shawnees in an area that is today on the southwestern border of West Virginia. In other words, settlers near Fort Pitt were not alone in embracing the view of a frontier against Indians; all of Virginia had adopted an offensive posture out of a perceived "defensive" need. Members of the Virginia House of Burgesses, for instance, warned Dunmore to take a less hostile approach to their "sister colony" Pennsylvania but told him they expected he would use all his powers "to repel the hostile and perfidious attempts of those savage and barbarous enemies." Such was the rhetoric of frontiers, embraced by all levels of Virginia government and society and integrated into colonial policy, that allowed Virginia to launch a war of choice deep inland. In Pennsylvania, there is scant evidence of a similar awareness in the halls of power or in eastern society.[51]

To counter the Virginians, St. Clair knew he had to respond in some way to the growing sense of fear among those still loyal to Pennsylvania. By May 1774, he was mimicking Virginia by creating a Pennsylvania militia and constructing a number of forts. In this venture, he collaborated with George Croghan, who had become disillusioned with the Old Dominion because he believed that the war would hurt his financial interests in land and trade. These two power brokers, along with a few other subscribers, funded the militia themselves. The difference between Pennsylvania's and Virginia's mobilizations is a striking reflection of the structural and historical differences between the two colonial governments and their history with militarization. Where Virginia's forces had the full support of their colony and official commissions, Pennsylvanians formed an ad hoc association that paled in comparison. St. Clair and other Pennsylvania officials realized, however, that the colony had to offer some semblance of the same service as Virginia to settlers still clinging to Pennsylvania loyalties. As St. Clair explained to John Penn, he had formed a militia "to afford the people the appearance of some protection" to make sure a "desertion [was] prevented." By June 16, St. Clair reported "forts at different places so as to be more convenient, are now nearly completed, which gives an appearance of security for the women and children."[52]

But St. Clair's attempt to build a façade of a frontier government was for naught. Pennsylvania became so irrelevant in the area that those still loyal to that colony had to desert Fort Pitt and open a new trading post in

Kittanning a few miles northeast of Fort Dunmore. Even this shell of a colony came under attack by the Virginians, illustrating the extent to which Dunmore's War had to do with defeating Pennsylvania. By February 1775, Pennsylvania justice of the peace Devereux Smith reported to John Penn that Virginians had "taken possession of most of the lands here, and say they have rights from the Virginia officers." Court records bear this out. From 1775 until 1779, Virginia established three counties in the area, and the records of their judgments are not just complete but extensive. Thousands of cases appeared before the court, evidence of how well the Virginia state functioned in the area and the extent of settlers' support. Indeed, in the 1780s, lists of Virginia settlers in what eventually became Pennsylvania revealed that over a thousand settlers took up land under Dunmore and their total holdings exceeded five hundred thousand acres, or the majority of what is today southwestern Pennsylvania.[53]

While Dunmore's tactics exposed significant differences between Virginia and Pennsylvania in the 1770s, the outcome of the conflict also revealed changes in the nature of colonial expansion in the British Empire when compared with the earlier clash Pennsylvania had with Maryland in the 1730s. During Cresap's War, proprietor Thomas Penn took an active hand in managing the fight. He frequently visited Lancaster and corresponded nearly daily with his officials. The scale of the contest also meant that Penn could fund the defense of his territorial claim himself. He did so by providing supplies, ammunition, and cash payments and giving land deals to those who served his interest. Finally, Penn adjusted the colony's expansionist policies to allow for a burst of expansion, doling out lands and negotiating new purchases with the Iroquois to offset Baltimore's moves and to win settlers. But these were not the sole reasons Penn won in the 1730s, because Marylanders adopted similar tactics. Instead, the determining issue revolved around which proprietary government colonists in the contested region preferred. Pennsylvania appeared to be the better choice because it offered security, order, and the promise of peace, while Cresap and Maryland promised the opposite.

During Dunmore's War, Lord Dunmore acted as the Penns had in the past. He recognized colonists' claims and forced Indians to cede large expanses of land to Virginia. Penn was unable to take similar actions in 1774 for a variety of reasons. Some had to do with reforms undertaken by the proprietor's office. For instance, Thomas Penn and his nephew John Penn had systematized the Land Office and began taking a far more active hand in managing settlement patterns, all of which was meant to increase their collection of quitrents. Such a change allowed Virginians to cast Pennsylvania as an arbitrary government operating to benefit the private interests of the proprietor.[54]

One of the other causes of the proprietor's weakness in the 1770s was the way the politics in the east hampered the power of the government in the west. While the institutions of Virginia's colonial government supported Dunmore's War, the institutions of Pennsylvania were divided. The proprietorship, responsible for defense and expansion, never acquired the institutional strength to marshal the fiscal and military resources necessary to secure Pennsylvania's territorial claims in a more complex imperial world. While in Cresap's War, a contest between two proprietors, Penn could fund the war personally, in the larger contest with Virginia, one that included an armed conflict with Native Americans, the proprietary institution alone lacked the funds and power to compete. Instead, the proprietor had to rely on the Pennsylvania Assembly for public funds, but that institution distrusted proprietary prerogatives. With such public support lacking, Pennsylvanians in the region relied on ad hoc volunteer militias rather than the more formal militias Virginia created. There was a hint that things may have been changing in the legislature. In an attempt to offset Virginia's tactics and rhetoric, Pennsylvania stopped collecting taxes on all land in Westmoreland County from 1773 to 1776, and in July 1774, well after facts on the ground had shifted in Virginia's favor, Pennsylvania's legislature allotted a sum for a two-hundred-man militia that carried heavy restrictions with hopes that the money would "remove the panic into which the inhabitants . . . had been thrown." But such an action was too little, too late.[55]

In the end, the largest difference between the 1730s and 1770s, and likely the most significant determinant of the outcome in the later border wars, was colonists' perception of a permanent frontier between white and Indian peoples, which helped them decide which government would best serve their needs. This view began to form in the region during the Seven Years' War and crystallized through the political mobilizations of the 1760s. During Cresap's War, Pennsylvania's policy toward Indians had little influence on settlers' choices, even though it did influence Pennsylvania's own strategy. If anything, Pennsylvania's history of peace with their Native neighbors was a positive influence in that earlier conflict. That changed after the Seven Years' War when Pennsylvania became a frontier colony and people began to imagine themselves as "frontier inhabitants." In the 1770s, protection was defined as security from a perceived Indian threat. In the battle for the west, Pennsylvania could not offer its would-be settlers what they sought, just as it could not offer such things to northern settlers in its other conflict with Connecticut. A besieged Pennsylvania was thus forced to retreat because colonists had determined that the colonial government was incapable of governing frontiers.

"That the Savages May Be Encouraged to Attack the Frontiers"

In March 1774, after both Virginia and Connecticut established legal authority over former regions of Pennsylvania, land official James Tilgham wrote a long letter to Thomas Penn detailing the situation on both fronts, concluding with an apology for "these foreign troubles" but expressing confidence Pennsylvania would prevail in imperial circles. On the ground, however, things looked very different. The proprietor could not marshal the support necessary to win colonists or fight battles. The governor tried every method possible to establish the colony's authority, including direct appeals to settlers, adjustments to land policy, and force. But none of that was as strong as the offer of a frontier government.[56]

After all these attempts failed, John Penn took to diplomacy, both directly with the other governors and through the Board of Trade. While the board had worked to Penn's advantage in the past, it was still the uncertain route that was often pursued by the loser as a last recourse. Maryland, for instance, approached the board twice, once in the 1680s and again in the 1730s, after Pennsylvania had established a strong foothold in contested territory. Penn's diplomatic forays had all the pretense and formality of negotiations between foreign states, with Penn outfitting commissioners to meet with fellow governors and detailing points of negotiation. Penn's efforts met with resistance from both Virginia and Connecticut, in large part because these colonies had already succeeded in securing the territory. They had no desire to pursue mediation since imperial arbitrators might decide against them.[57]

But expending diplomatic measures on two fronts could prove tricky; at least once, Virginia used Penn's maneuverings with Connecticut to its own advantage. With Connecticut, Penn argued that the northern border was Pennsylvania's through charter and conquest, claiming that during the

Seven Years' War, Pennsylvania defended the territory and Connecticut did not, an act that established jurisdictional precedent. When Dunmore heard this argument, he told Penn that if that was true, then the territory in dispute toward the west clearly belonged to Virginia, which had established a fort there during the Seven Years' War. As he said in diplomatic correspondence with Penn and his commissioners, "We are strengthened in this opinion by the principles you yourselves adopt . . . in your dispute with Connecticut." Dunmore bolstered his argument with two other points. He argued that the Pennsylvania Assembly stated that it did not believe the territory was Pennsylvania's during the Seven Years' War and that all unpurchased land conquered during the war reverted to royal colonies, which gave Virginia all land not settled after the Seven Years' War. Dunmore also argued that longitudinally, Fort Pitt was beyond Pennsylvania's charter grant. Pennsylvania's almost complete reliance on diplomacy after 1774 reflected a defeated colony and marked a stark contrast with Cresap's War.[58]

Just as with Cresap's War, however, the result of colonial competition was consolidation, although in this case consolidation came at the expense of both Pennsylvania and the empire. After the 1768 Treaty of Fort Stanwix, nearly all imperial and colonial officials realized that the Ohio River Valley needed planning, coordination, and regulation, but they adopted no clear measures to organize it. Instead, their policies led to imperial disintegration as officials removed institutions of power from the region. When the imperial presence on these opened lands dissipated, a new era of renewed colonial competition began. The nature of this competition gave colonists an opportunity to choose and shape government policies that matched their beliefs. In the border wars Pennsylvania fought against Connecticut and Virginia, frontier people selected colonies with reputations for martial culture, local governance, anti-Indian policies, and cheap land. Those living upon these edges of the empire thus played a fundamental role in building the colonial governments to which they belonged and, in so doing, affected the policies and performance of the empire to which these colonies belonged.

The violence between colonies reflected a key part of the underlying imperial crisis along the British Empire's fringes. As colonies from New Hampshire to Virginia fought over borders in the 1760s and 1770s, the empire's inability to mediate these disputes bred uncertainty among settlers in these contested regions and challenged the strength of imperial and colonial governments within the British Empire. Indeed, expansion created a political crisis more fundamental than the one riling eastern seaports. Those eastern debates surrounded Parliamentary authority and the relationship between colonial governments and imperial ones. In western regions, the problem had to do with creating governing authority more generally. The empire's inability to establish a means to fix intercolonial borders on its frontiers emboldened colonial governments to assert their own sovereignty, which often led to clashes with neighbors that only further weakened governing authority. And as competition between colonial polities returned, frontier settlers used their loyalty to shape the policies of the competing colonial governments. In the British Empire's western regions, frontier inhabitants took the reins of government and enacted their vision of an empire with active frontiers against Indian neighbors, a view that was at fundamental odds with the official policies of both the British Empire and Pennsylvania.[59]

In time, the crisis over imperial frontier policy became intertwined with complaints about taxation and mercantile regulations. As the imperial crisis heated up in urban seaports, colonists there were coming to conclusions about the empire that were similar to those of their western brethren, though for different reasons. Until the 1770s, these two crises ran on separate tracks, but the two problems within the empire began to merge when the empire closed forts within zones many colonists considered frontiers. That decision fueled a growing perception among all colonists that the British Empire had failed to serve their interests.

Soon, those in the east began to fuse their complaints with those in the west, creating a common cause. In 1773, Benjamin Franklin, then in London, wrote a widely disseminated essay that expressed the profound disillusionment colonists felt toward the British Empire. After complaining of taxation and other policies that affected more urban areas, he spoke of the imperial crisis in the west. If imperial officials wanted to destroy the empire, he wrote, they should "send armies into their country . . . but instead of garrisoning their forts on their frontiers with those troops to prevent incursions, demolish those forts, and order the troops into the heart of the country, that the savages may be encouraged to attack the frontiers." Such policies, Franklin concluded, will "strengthen an opinion that you are unfit to govern them." Franklin's widely read argument mirrored the feelings of those around Fort Pitt. For colonists, failure to protect frontiers challenged the contract upon which the governed and governing rested. Indeed, the victories of Connecticut and Virginia over Pennsylvania meant that these colonists had declared their own independence before those in the east did in 1776.[60]

The failure of the British Empire to provide for frontiers—indeed, its apparent turn against such zones and their inhabitants—became a central argument for independence. A public letter from the Continental Congress to "the Inhabitants of Great Britain" explaining colonists' grievances criticized the Crown for "let[ting] loose" "a cruel and savage enemy . . . upon the defenseless inhabitants of our frontiers," a complaint that reflected a particularly Virginian understanding of Dunmore's War. Later, in the Declaration of Independence, Thomas Jefferson similarly accused King George III of supporting offensive raids "on the inhabitants of our frontiers." Jefferson's accusation only makes sense in light of the events that transpired in the Middle Colonies during the 1770s. This shared understanding of the colonial frontier, its location, and the empire's failure to provide for it helped east and west forge a bond during the imperial crisis that would soon transform governance in North America.[61]

CHAPTER 10

Creating a Frontier Government

For Pennsylvania and its peoples, the American Revolution was as much a prolonged and profound internal struggle to create the state itself as it was a fight to secure national independence from Great Britain. The outcome of this fight in Pennsylvania also made it one of the most complete revolutions in North America. In most other colonies-turned-independent-states, revolutionary leadership came from existing political bodies, often legislatures, and the structure of government changed little after independence, except for the removal of British and Crown authority. The opposite happened in Pennsylvania, where the political leadership was upended, the government remade, the society transformed, and borders established.[1]

The completeness of this revolution becomes all the more apparent when one looks west. First, the new revolutionary state was able to accomplish the very thing its colonial government had failed to do: secure its borders. It succeeded in part because structural changes to the national government and a newfound sense of union among citizens reduced strife between states. Second, and more important, inhabitants on the state's contested borders, many of whom had sided with one of Pennsylvania's colonial competitors just a few years earlier, were incorporated into Pennsylvania's polity for the first time. This began occurring when eastern revolutionaries embraced their western brethren because these urban leaders realized that frontier people, with their hatred of the old government and willingness to fight, would provide the movement for independence with the muscle necessary to succeed. In turn, these frontier inhabitants made the revolutionary government of Pennsylvania reflect their mores. By 1783, as the war with England wound down, the most revolutionary thing to have happened in Pennsylvania was the creation of the state itself. Pennsylvanians accomplished this transformation by creating the one thing they

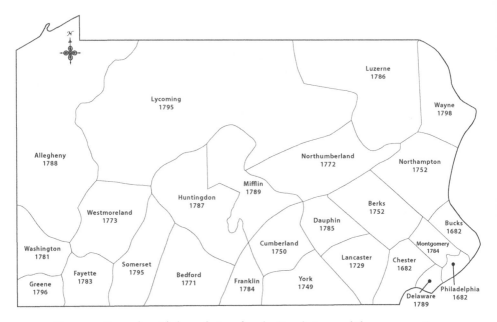

Figure 14. Pennsylvania's boundaries after the Revolution and the new counties created after the war. One of the most revolutionary things to happen to Pennsylvania during the War for American Independence was the establishment of its borders and the strengthening of government authority in western regions.

never could in the colonial era: what William Penn had once called a "frontier government."

"The Very Naked and Defenceless State of This City and Harbor, Now in Its Turn Become the Frontier"

The process of creating a frontier government began in May 1774, as soon as Paul Revere arrived in Philadelphia carrying word of the Coercive Acts. In response to the Boston Tea Party, Parliament sought retribution by sealing Boston off from oceanic trade and replacing a civil governor with a military one. Such a forceful action convinced many colonists that King George III had turned on the colonies. Word of foreign mercenaries employed to implement this policy added fuel to the fire. As the members of Pennsylvania's Provincial Conference, more than half of whom came from frontier counties, would declare in 1776, the king's actions "excluded the inhabitants of this as well as the other American colonies from his protection," thus breaking the "reciprocal [allegiance] between a king and his subjects." Similar sentiments toward the king were expressed in private correspondence as well. Edward Burd, a prominent Pennsylvanian, wrote to Jasper Yeates in Lancaster that "if [the king] not only withdraws his protection but attempts [his subjects'] destruction, I should think it amounted to a discharge of their allegiance which is only due in consideration of the protection afforded."[2]

With the Coercive Acts and occupation of Boston, revolutionaries in Philadelphia who were busy preparing for a potential invasion of the city saw the deficiencies with the colonial Assembly that frontier people had long complained of. Indeed, the removal of the king's protection did something dramatic to Pennsylvania's geopolitics: it had rendered the entire area a frontier, necessitating a new form of government. Revolutionaries in Philadelphia thus began adopting the same language of frontiers to critique the Pennsylvania government as those in the west had used, and they used this rhetoric to argue for the same reforms to the government's military policies. A petition penned by Philadelphians and addressed to their Assembly in 1775 captured this newfound perspective when the authors declared in language reminiscent of western communities in the 1750s that "the very naked and defenceless state of this city and harbour, now in its turn [has] become the frontier."[3]

Further west, the Lancaster County Associators—the official name used to describe the volunteer militias—used a nearly identical argument of defensive necessity to justify their formation. They promised to "learn the art of Military discipline, to enable them to support and defend their just Rights and Privileges, against all arbitrary and dispotic Invasions, by any Person or Persons whatsoever." Such language appeared throughout Pennsylvania's revolutionary ranks, and the fear of invasion served to unite previously unconnected and disparate areas within Pennsylvania into a new and coherent whole that was founded upon a shared need to defend the state from an external enemy. Those who became revolutionaries thus also became a frontier people.

Fear of invasion therefore defined much of the revolutionary mobilization, and this fear shaped the contours of the revolutionary government. As a result, new institutions served to create a new contract between the revolutionary government and its members, especially those who shared a common view of a British enemy. The Committee of Safety was the first and primary means by which the negotiation between government and residents in local communities was performed. The committee's primary purpose was to, as its name implied, provide safety to its members. Its charter, therefore, stated that the institution was formed to provide for the "defence of their lives, liberties, and property," and every officer was commissioned to provide "for the defence of the liberties of America and for repelling every hostile invasion thereof."[4]

In Philadelphia, a central Committee of Safety called on people in each county and township to form similar committees to coordinate their resistance. Soon other, smaller committees dotted the landscape, and correspondence now traveled from Philadelphia out to them and back with greater efficiency. The very existence of so many committees helped unite east and west in a way that had been absent before the Coercive Acts. As Arthur St. Clair, chair of the Westmoreland committee, declared, they promised to "resist and oppose" a British assault and support "any plan that may be formed for the defense of America in general, or Pennsylvania in particular." Volunteer militias meant to aid the committee's work met in the city streets and the countryside, helping more people become directly connected to the revolutionary movement being orchestrated in Philadelphia.[5]

The militias operated under a premise that had defined frontier life during the imperial crisis and was to define revolutionary Pennsylvania and its new government. Unlike the British Army, the officers of these volunteer but official military forces were to be elected, a model that had first been adopted by local Pennsylvania militias that formed during the Seven Years' War and Pontiac's War. As James Burd recounted, a Lancaster County battalion "took it into their heads that every man has a right to vote." The men, according to Burd, "were indulged" with "one private man from each company" charged with collecting "the votes of their respective companys." But the power dynamics were not quite as Burd cast them. These demands were not "indulged" by elite men like Burd out of generosity; enlisted men dictated the terms upon which the militias would function because the very existence of the institution depended upon their willingness to volunteer. The men demanded this privilege as a term of their service and took their responsibility seriously. Similar processes happened elsewhere. The official revolutionary militia, then, resembled the practices those on frontiers had developed in the colonial period.[6]

The martial spirit these militias fostered took on new prominence in Pennsylvania life. Militias mustered in streets, trained in open spaces, and took enlistments at households. As militias organized throughout communities, their public presence reminded those outside of them that Pennsylvania was preparing for war. Rhoda Barber, a resident of Lancaster who wrote a memoir later in life, remembered watching men using broomsticks in place of scarce rifles as they drilled in Lancaster's town square, the site of the Paxton Boys' massacre. The militias also showed a willingness to assert their own political agendas, much as their predecessors the Paxton Boys had. They used their military might to pressure people to join their cause and used their to growing power to assert their authority within the revolutionary government. In June 1775, for instance, after the Committee of Safety and Lancaster Committee of Correspondence allowed conscientious objectors to avoid service through payment of a fee, a militia company in town stormed the square, seized the handbills that announced the policy from a member of the committee, and used the paper for target practice. Demonstrations continued, and the Committee of Correspondence's doors were tarred and feathered.[7]

The rioting in Lancaster forced the Lancaster Committee of Correspondence to confront this new, powerful idea of rule by the people. The tensions that emerged rested in the still unclear relationship between a militia and a civil government that both claimed to be founded upon principles of popular sovereignty. Unlike the Assemblymen in 1763 who remained unmoved by the Paxton Boys, the members of the committee believed the unrest challenged their authority. They therefore resigned and called a special election to reaffirm the committee's legitimacy. The resignations showed a government responsive to such dramatic actions, but by quitting, the committee members signaled to the militiamen that in the end, power ultimately resided with the militia, who now knew that public opposition to civil authorities could lead to new elections. Militiamen, empowered by such a precedent, increasingly argued that they were the arbiters of the popular will and stewards of the public good. The militia, in effect, claimed—and through this confrontation and others like it became—the voice of "the people."[8]

Even with such ardent revolutionaries armed and ready to fight, leaders in Philadelphia still faced a larger issue: the bulk of the voting populace appeared distressingly cool to independence. In a hotly contested Assembly election in May 1776, moderates secured control of the legislature, a shock to those who were a part of the growing network of revolutionary militias and committees that operated alongside the traditional colonial institutions. Nonetheless, those favoring a more aggressive posture toward Great Britain used their nascent and still extralegal frontier government to disempower the Assembly. Many of those who were elected to the Assembly and favored independence refused to sit, denying the body a necessary quorum. More important, the militias also let their voices be heard. Nine hundred men from Northampton County's Second Battalion declared the Assembly "not competent to the exigencies of our affairs," a statement that was meant to accuse the body of being incapable of providing its fundamental duty of protection. Other militia groups from Chester and Lancaster applied similar political pressure. James Allen, a moderate member of the Assembly, lamented in his diary the majority's inability to muster a strong opposition to these forces of revolution: "Moderate men look blank," he complained, "and yet the majority of this city and province are of that stamp; as is evident from the election of new members."[9]

By June 1776, the colonial Assembly, beaten down by external forces like the politicized militias, disintegrated. The same fate awaited the individuals who once led these colonial institutions. Individual Quakers soon found themselves targeted by militias, the government, and new laws. In 1777, for instance, the revolutionary government suspended habeas corpus and sent militias to round up suspect Quakers, including to the home of Israel Pemberton, the Quaker who received the wrath of the Paxton Boys. Eventually, the government sent these prisoners to a farm in Winchester, Virginia, where they remained confined until Washington interceded in 1778. John Penn, meanwhile, fared only marginally better. Never quite as unpopular as the Quaker Party wished, the government put Penn under house arrest. He worked his way back to England during the war. Afterward, he returned to Pennsylvania, where he lived comfortably. The state eventually compensated his family for their loss of land.[10]

With the two chief colonial institutions destroyed and the traditional governing elite removed from positions of power in 1776, radicals filled the political vacuum by calling a new convention to frame a government to meet the needs of the new order. The convention's composition was unlike any colonial political body. Each county sent an equal number of representatives: eight from each of the eleven counties and eight from the city of Philadelphia. Thus, the makeup of this body was heavily weighted toward

formerly underrepresented "frontier counties." Indeed, rather than forming a small minority, as was the case in the colonial era, these counties sent
64 of the 96 members. Among those serving was James Smith of the Black
Boys, elected from Westmoreland County. Those leading the movement for
independence in the east were so inclusive because many believed the frontier regions were more likely to support independence than the eastern
counties. Frontier representation, they realized, was essential to creating the
government they too wanted because it would provide a check against the
moderates and loyalists that they believed inhabited the eastern areas.[11]

From the beginning, the frontier political culture infused the debates
about the new Constitution. The Constitution's preamble enumerated the
reasons for independence as conceived by the representatives at the convention. The words they offered were the same ones frontier inhabitants had
used for over a decade. Paraphrasing the Declaration of Independence, the
preamble cast the struggle for independence as one that the king forced on
the colonists. The revolutionaries were thus mobilizing out of a shared need
for protection, the very thing frontier people had called for. In withdrawing
the foundation of subjects' allegiance to the king—"security and protection
of the community"—the king had "not only withdrawn that protection,
but commenced, and still continues to carry on, with unabated vengeance,
a most cruel and unjust war against [the colonists]." Thus, the foundation
of the revolutionary government was based on providing security, the very
thing frontier people had long asked of their colonial government.[12]

Opposition to the old constitution, which was equated with Quakers'
obstinacy, was one of the other driving principles of the convention. The
representatives at the convention believed that the educated class, meaning
Quakers and other eastern and establishment folks who had previously
dominated the government, had "been productive of all the evils that have
happened in the world." At one point, Thomas Smith, a frontier lawyer
who supported independence but disliked the democratic nature of the new
Constitution, received the ire of his fellow representatives when they
warned him, "You learned fellows who have warped your understandings
by poring over musty old books, will perhaps laugh at us; but, know ye,
that we despise you." The drafters of the Constitution wanted to tear down
the old political guard defined by its eastern elitism and replace it with a
new one. Even a man of the frontier like Smith was subject to harassment
because his legal training smacked of eastern privilege.[13]

The new government overturned this old system. As Thomas Smith described it, the Constitution they wrote was devoted to "popularity." It provided for equal representation in the Assembly, meaning that the western areas of Pennsylvania would dominate the legislature. In time, it would evolve to take into account population, an innovation that would likely help the rapidly growing western regions. Rather than have a disconnected and independent judicial system, judges' salaries were to be paid by the elected Assembly, thus making them, in theory, dependent upon the goodwill of the body of the people. Justices of the peace, holders of one of the most powerful legal offices, were no longer appointed but elected. Infusing local law enforcement with local popular opinion was exactly what the frontier had done in practice during the 1760s. And then there was the entirely new institution of the militia, created by an act in early 1777. Every county now had its own militia, led by a county lieutenant whose districts were subdivided with a sublieutenant for each smaller area reporting to him. Indeed, the new revolutionary government of Pennsylvania looked a lot like what the frontier had long wanted and what Virginia and Connecticut had created in the 1770s. As historian David Freeman Hawke concluded of the new Constitution, "The backcountry delegates no doubt headed home pleased with a job well done." They had created a frontier government in Pennsylvania.[14]

In fact, they had done more than create a frontier government. Through their new alliance with easterners distrustful of the old colonial elite in Philadelphia, they had taken the reins of government from the east and placed them in their own hands. With a majority of the Assembly composed of frontier representatives, including James Smith of the Black Boys and Matthew Smith, the signer of the Paxton Boys' *Declaration and Remonstrance*, self-proclaimed frontier inhabitants had taken over the entire government. Their beliefs, many of which were forged in the frontier crises of the 1760s and 1770s, would be a major driver of policy during the revolution, and their control over policy would help do the thing the colonial government could not: secure Pennsylvania's boundaries.

The revolutionary Assembly's most controversial act, the passage of a Test Act, demonstrated how completely the government had transformed into a frontier government that vigilantly guarded against the threats from within and without the polity. The point of the act was to solidify the authority of the new state by marking in explicit terms its members and those excluded from it. Those who did not swear an oath lost virtually all rights: they could not buy or sell land, vote, be elected, or sit on juries. They were also forced to surrender all arms to the lieutenants and sublieutenants of the militia. The basis for the loss of rights was the idea of a contract between the state and its members in which, as the law itself stated, "allegiance and protection are reciprocal, and those that shall not bear the former are not nor ought to be entitled to the benefits of the latter." This principle is the very one that had driven politics for those who lived upon contested colonial borders and frontiers throughout the colonial era.[15]

The power of the frontier government was also deployed to force those within its own fold to conform to its policies. In a revolutionary moment in which the new state's authority was precarious, no group's compliance mattered more than those who supported the revolution but opposed the new government. Leaders of the new state worried that a vocal group of dissenters from within the revolutionaries' camp would only embolden loyalist arguments and could push those in the middle away from the revolution.

Thomas Smith, the Bedford representative who complained about the Constitution but was otherwise a strong supporter of independence, learned this lesson in the fall of 1777. Smith, who also served as prothonotary of Bedford County, refused to relinquish the country records to Robert Galbraith after the revolutionary state removed him from office. The transfer of this property symbolized the formal transfer of sovereignty from one regime to another, much as the turf and twig ceremony had done for Penn in 1682. Smith, however, denied the new state had the authority that it claimed. He, along with four other members of the county committee of correspondence, wrote to the council explaining that they supported Independence, and while they "exceedingly dislike the present constitution," they still promised "to support it with our lives and fortunes." Smith and company explained the refusal to hand over the books as a legal matter in which they viewed Galbraith's authority as questionable. They promised to hand over the documents once "the sentiments of the people were to be taken for a new Convention, and when that was known if there was a majority he would then immediately give them up." Smith was thus basing his refusal on the concept of popular sovereignty, just as the new government was basing their right to claim the books on the same authority. This confrontation tested the legitimacy of the new government.[16]

Privately, James Cannon, one of the chief architects of the state, recognized that the new state faced a popularity problem within the ranks of supporters for independence. He complained that the hostility toward the Constitution stemmed from the inability of the Provincial Convention to better disseminate its contents to the broader public. It was the messaging, he argued, not the Constitution that sowed dissatisfaction. Leaders in Philadelphia were convinced that "the people" would support the Constitution if they only had the chance to read it. Cannon believed the revolutionaries had failed to adequately sell the benefits of the new Constitution to residents.[17]

The problem Cannon identified resulted from the relatively sealed organization that the new state had built in the years before its seizure of power. The revolutionary committees and militias that formed the initial basis of the government worked in tandem to share and spread information, and while these institutions had a following, they were still a minority of the population. There was much confusion for those outside these networks. Cannon recognized this and complained that "it was a great error not to print and distribute properly 10,000 copies of the Frame of Government, that the people might see and judge for themselves. This and a prudent conduct would settle the matter I believe." The Assembly heeded this advice and sent copies of the new Constitution to Bedford County so residents might better judge the qualities of the new government.[18]

In November, the Council of Safety, the new and official name for the formerly extralegal Committee of Safety, went a step further in trying to establish compliance within the populace. They ordered the public arrest of the still quarrelsome Smith. After his confinement—and eventual transfer of the books—he was released and allowed to resume an active political life. Smith seems to have bowed to the pressure, too. He and his allies all publicly swore allegiance to the new Constitution. Galbraith viewed the switch of these former opponents as central to strengthening the state's claims to legitimacy, much as the loyalty of colonists had done during border wars. Smith's new loyalty was, Galbraith wrote, "not only a sufficient acknowledgement to Bedford County, but the state in general." Thereafter, Galbraith reported, "many who were for some time past backward in taking the oath came into court and took it," creating "a good aspect in Bedford County . . . with regard to the Constitution." By May, he reported "more business done in a week then used to be done formerly under the old Constitution," and, to top it off, "a reconciliation" happened between Galbraith and Smith. Later that year, Smith appeared before the council seeking guidance on frontier defenses, and a few months after that, he provided the surety necessary for a new prothonotary of Bedford County, David Espy, who had once opposed the Constitution with Smith. Smith was soon elected to the Assembly, and in 1781, he began to serve in the Continental Congress.[19]

The contest over the record books demonstrated the ways in which the new frontier government used its coercive force to establish its authority over an uncertain populace. Previously, justices of the peace in such areas tended to be weak and unwilling to upset local settlers, as John Armstrong demonstrated during the Stump affair, but now they were willing to firmly enforce state authority even if a sizable portion of the population was resistant to it. The reason they had this new strength was because they had a militia ready to enforce laws, the police force Franklin and Penn had both deemed necessary for the colony's internal peace during the imperial crisis of the American Revolution. Created in the midst of the revolution, however, this military force was being used to overthrow the very thing Franklin and Penn wanted to preserve. The new strength of the government symbolized the transformation of the colonial government to a more modern state that was built upon the need to provide defense and that could use its force to compel compliance and obedience throughout its population.

"The Best and Perhaps Cheapest Means of Protecting the Frontiers Will Be Found in the Invasion of the Indian Country"

More dramatic than the way the frontier political culture influenced the east is the effect the frontier government had on western communities of the revolutionary state. At the start of the Revolution, residents around Fort Pitt who supported independence agreed to abide by "the laws of Virginia, the civil magistrates of which colony we are fully determined to support in the execution of their officers as the only security for the welfare of the people." The commanding officer at Fort Pitt, John Nevill, a Virginian and Seven Years' War veteran who hailed from Frederick County, Virginia, only reinforced Virginia's authority at Fort Pitt. By the end of the war, however, Pennsylvania controlled the region, a transition facilitated in large part by its new frontier government that was better able to provide "security for the welfare of the people."[20]

The change in the west began as soon as the eastern regions became a frontier. For Nevill, the revolutionary government of Virginia, and the Continental Congress, that theater was the more important one for winning the Revolution. They adopted policies far different than the popular policies advocated by Dunmore and Connolly a few years earlier. During the first year of the Revolutionary War, Congress held official treaties with Indian groups in the Ohio Valley to establish mutual neutrality. In fact, at one point, a delegation from Congress promised Delaware Indians a fourteenth state if they stayed out of the fight.[21]

At Fort Pitt, official policy clashed with regular militiamen who believed that they were very much on the frontlines of a war. On April 1, 1777, Nevill rejected orders to launch a very targeted and limited attack on Pluggy's Town. In a long letter cowritten by Congress's appointed diplomat to the Ohio Indians, George Morgan, the two officials offered an assessment of the region's geopolitical interests at odds with those of the frontier people who feared an Indian war more than they feared the British Army. Nevill and Morgan advised Patrick Henry, the governor of Virginia, that offensive action would likely "deprive us of all our Indian allies and multiply our enemies." Instead, they believed maintaining peace and controlling settlers from spreading onto Indian lands "during the British war" would not only "tend greatly to the happiness of this country, but to the interest of the whole state." In their view, the current war was not between Indians and citizens but between the British and Americans. Indians, in this analysis, were best kept at bay, and Nevill and Morgan advised Virginia "to punish robberies and murders committed on any of our allies [meaning Indians]."[22]

Many frontier inhabitants living around Nevill and Morgan—including their subordinates—disagreed with their commanding officers in much the same way they had disagreed with imperial officials during the 1760s. Nevill and Morgan reported that it "seems the inclination of some" that "all Indians, without distinction, who may be found are to be massacred." Indeed, "parties have been formed to massacre some who have come to visit us in a friendly manner." Such parties included Virginia officials on the frontier. Nevill believed "the spies who have been employed by the County Lieutenants . . . seem to have gone on this plan with a premeditated design to involve [Virginia] in a general Indian war." He advised Henry not to rely on reports from these people, as "many persons among ourselves wish to promote a war with savages, not considering the distresses of our country on the sea coast." Nevill was not arguing that Indian war was to be avoided forever. Instead, he acknowledged that if "God [were] to bless us with Victory to overcome our British Enemies on the Sea Coast, we shall have it in our power to take ample satisfaction of our Indian Enemy."[23]

Even while the commanders on the frontiers tried to maintain the peace, violence between Indians and settlers fighting for American independence increased throughout 1777. Edward Hand, the general for the Continental Army stationed at Fort Pitt, wrote that "the people here are well disposed savage like, to murder a defenceless, unsuspecting Indian," and reports of murder and assaults between settlers and Indians were prominent. At first, the Wyandots were suspected of launching attacks on Americans, and Pluggy, a Munsee, continued to reject American land claims. By the fall, the violence and uncertainty pushed many Shawnees and Delawares, who had tried to maintain neutrality, into the British camp, believing the American nation was unable to control its own residents and that a British victory would offer them greater security.[24]

Settlers who believed their homes formed a frontier against Indians demanded their governments provide for their defense in words that resembled the petitions offered during previous wars in the region. A petition from Bedford County used the language of frontiers to describe their position within the polity as the "fronteers" that were "left weak and defenceless." Because of this situation, the "Indians being well acquainted with such weakness have become the more daring." Things in the west began to resemble the experience of the Seven Years' War and Pontiac's War, in which frontier defense proved weak and frontiers rolled east. If Congress failed to provide more supplies, they wrote, then "Cumberland and even York will soon become a Fronteer." Such language also shows how stable the conception of *frontier* was throughout the colonial period. As a geopolitical term, it still meant an area that was created by the threat of invasion and demanded government support.[25]

The difference between the colonial and revolutionary worlds, however, was the aid frontier inhabitants received from the new frontier government of Pennsylvania. Unlike Virginia officials, Pennsylvania's government answered their call. Responding to a request for arms from Archibald Lochry, lieutenant of Westmoreland, the Council of Safety promised to "send up all the rifled Guns, of which that county is very bare that may be had and to supply ammunition to the Settlers to make some defence of their habitations and at large." The council members echoed the sentiments of their citizens when they petitioned Congress to provide additional aid. Failure to do so, they warned, would mean that "the Allegeny Mountain will soon become the frontier."[26]

Indeed, throughout the war, the Pennsylvania government proved itself particularly concerned with the frontier situation. State officials often called on counties to raise supplies for the Continental Army or Pennsylvania's defenses, but it never sent such requests to Bedford, Westmoreland, or Northumberland because they were thought to be under imminent threat of attack. Instead, these "frontiers" received the aid they had long thought they deserved. Those enlisting, for instance, entered official rolls. They took an oath that they joined "voluntarily" and promised to "serve on such Parts of the Frontier of Bedford County as the Persons deputed in said County by the Commissioners at Fort Pitt shall judge most conducive to the common Safety of the Inhabitants, and also to be [subject] to the Orders of the Continental Officer Commanding the Western Frontiers of Virginia and Pennsylvania." Thus, these chains of command that linked the frontiers to Philadelphia helped integrate these western communities to the new state, while also continuing to engage in local patterns of voluntary military mobilization for "such Parts of the Frontier."[27]

Residents of frontiers who looked to their revolutionary governments for protection soon recognized the clear differences between these two governments. The Virginia legislature, driven by the belief that the British Army was the primary adversary, restricted frontier militias to defensive protection because waging a war on two fronts would prove a costly distraction from their main aim. Patrick Henry likewise took a suspicious, if not combative, view of frontier motivations and actions. In a scathing letter that blamed frontier settlers for the loss of the Shawnees to the British, Henry believed white aggression had forced these one-time allies to take up arms with the British. He thus proved reluctant to provide military aid to the frontier, worrying that it would be used to further war aims that the Virginia government did not condone. "Shall this precedent establish the right of involving Virginia in war whenever any one in the back Country shall please?" Henry asked angrily. Indeed, he used the epithet "Tory" against those who engaged in acts of aggression against allied Indians. He insisted that the war was fought for independence from Britain, not against Indian Country: "Is not this the work of Tories?" he asked, concluding that "no man but an enemy to American Independence will do it, and thus oblige our People to be hunting after Indians in the woods, instead of facing Genl Howe in the fields." As Henry saw it, stirring up an Indian war served to weaken America's cause by forcing "backwoodsmen" to stay home instead of "joining Genl Washington to strike [a dec]isive Stroke for Independency at this critical time."[28]

Henry's reaction to this episode helped clarify the difference in policy between these two revolutionary governments. Instead of supporting these offensive actions, Henry asked that those who murdered Indians be brought to justice. Focusing on that fundamental contract between the governed and governing, he argued that failure to do so would break the contract between citizens and the state in which government provides protection while members respect the laws. Indeed, Henry used the same language Pennsylvania officials deployed to prod reluctant people to recognize the authority of the new state. But instead of demanding allegiance for protection, Henry threatened to revoke Virginia's promise of protection. "If the frontier people will not submit to the laws, but thus set them at defiance," he wrote, "they will not be considered as entitled to the protection of government." Pennsylvania officials, however, empowered militias and supported their attacks, and the state received credit for their policies. As Archibald Lochry wrote, the "bennifit these raingers has been to this destresst fruntier" was immeasurable, and those who volunteered should be "paid by the state" for their services. These additional ranging parties often worked in conjunction with the commandant of Fort Pitt to raise troops and provide him with aid.[29]

To understand just how different Pennsylvania's policy was from Virginia's and how radical a departure it was from the colonial era, consider a letter the Pennsylvania Council of Safety sent to William Irvine, the commandant of Fort Pitt, advising him that the government was then considering whether "the best and perhaps cheapest means of protecting the frontiers, will be found in the invasion of the Indian country." This statement is the exact opposite of what Arthur St. Clair had argued during his conflict with Virginia in the 1770s. Irvine soon recognized that these differences had real effects on the loyalties of citizens mobilizing for war. At a meeting of militia officers in April 1782 he observed that "the Council of Pennsylvania have directed their civil officers to order out agreeable to law such members of militia, from time to time, and may think proper to demand." By contrast, he noted, "the Virginia civil officers on this side of the hill say they have no such instructions." Irvine found that he had not "drawn any [militiamen] from the counties of Virginia even for their own defence." Moreover, the more responsive policies of Pennsylvania had effects on enlistment in the two militias. One of the Virginia officers at the meeting reported that "most of the men in his district [were] now enrolled in Pennsylvania."[30]

As more men joined with Pennsylvania, Irvine learned to rely almost exclusively on Pennsylvania's military presence—or at least volunteers who now claimed allegiance to Pennsylvania—for frontier defense. Like Hand, Irvine hoped to create a joint frontier force composed of Virginia and Pennsylvania militias because "the frontiers of Virginia and Pennsylvania are so connected." He found Virginia's willingness to provide defense for the area wanting, however, and instead worked with Pennsylvania, thus helping further establish the authority of Pennsylvania over the area. Because he "[could not] expect any [help] from Virginia," he began "making such arrangements, as part of the Pennsylvania militia will cover some of Virginia."[31]

Pennsylvania's transformation into a frontier government allowed these local groups to establish the principle that Indians received no protections in the new American polity. In 1782, militiamen seized the freedom provided by the government. In April, Pennsylvania's new county lieutenant wrote Irvine about a Colonel David Williamson who proposed "a voyage down the river" to deliver much-needed flour. But Williamson promised more than just the transfer of supplies. Inspired "from a real love to his country," he also proposed "to carry an expedition against Sanduskies with the militia of his country together with what volunteers might be raised in Westmoreland."[32]

In truth, Williamson's "voyage down the river" seemed aimed more at invading a settlement called Gnadenhutten than conveying flour. A group of Moravian Indians had lived in Gnadenhutten for years, creating a peaceful, religious commune under the auspices of Moravian missionary David Zeisberger. Throughout the revolutionary war, this group of Indians had sought to maintain neutrality and had made every effort to convince both the British and their allied Indians and the Americans that they meant no harm. They were much like the Conestoga Indians. And like the Conestogas, their attempts proved how hard it was to maintain neutrality on a frontier in which battle lines hardened along racial ones. On the one side, "frontier inhabitants" in the United States considered all Indians enemies. On the other side, a pan-Indian alliance with the British pressured wavering

Indians, like the Delawares at Gnadenhutten, to help, even if only surreptitiously, push colonial settlements eastward. In such a world of clear binaries, revolutionaries suspected the community provided covert aid to the British and their Indian allies, while the Indians allied with the British often harassed the settlement in hopes of forcing the group to side with them.[33]

In the spring of 1782, word began to circulate around Fort Pitt that the Moravians had taken an active hand in aiding a Delaware war party by providing them with food and respite. To an independent settlement trying to maintain neutrality, such action would make sense, but it fueled suspicion among Americans that this community was neither peaceful nor neutral. Instead, just as the Paxton Boys had accused the Conestoga, these residents claimed that the Gnadenhutten used their neutrality as a way to provide covert aid to enemy Indians. Thus, influenced by the same suspicions and fears that the Paxton Boys had expressed about independent Indian communities being inherent threats, Williamson and his militia set out. When Williamson's party arrived at Gnadenhutten, the pacifist Indians offered no armed resistance to the Americans. Williamson himself embraced the idea of popular sovereignty that so infused revolutionary Pennsylvania. Rather than acting arbitrarily, he held a vote to see what the militia should do with the Moravian Indians. When the vote came back that they should be killed, the militiamen bound their victims, placed them in a church, set the structure on fire, and watched it burn as the dying Indians sang hymns.[34]

Although Williamson's actions were not officially condoned, the relaxed policies of the Pennsylvania state toward independent militia actions had provided the opportunity for it to occur. Virginia's militia captains had written about settlers' desire to massacre Indians since the beginning of the war. They had tried to tamp down these sentiments through policy and through their own actions. Although violence had occurred, there had been nothing on this scale. Pennsylvania's policies, however, had created volunteer ranging parties authorized by the state and gave them the freedom to act as they wished, a significant change from the colonial policies Pennsylvania had adopted during Dunmore's War.

The massacre at Gnadenhutten thus represented the continuation of patterns long established in areas that considered themselves a frontier against Indians. The difference between this massacre and earlier ones, like that of the Paxton Boys, was not settlers' conception of Indians but the official response. Williamson was not disciplined for his action. Instead, he was promoted. He served as second in command for a failed offensive in the summer, and he would eventually serve as sheriff in Washington County. Unlike the Paxton Boys, whose identities were never known, the identities of the militiamen at Gnadenhutten were well known and acknowledged. The reasons for these differences did not have to do with changes in societal conceptions of Indians but instead in government policies toward Indians. The official response—or lack thereof—showed how much the revolutionary state of Pennsylvania had become a frontier government. Indians as permanent enemies of the state, a position long advocated by people who conceived themselves as "frontier people," became institutionalized within the revolutionary government, in part, because the government of the state now had frontier representatives as an integral part of it.[35]

"The Prospect of Fixing a Permanent Boundary Between Virginia and Pennsylvania Gives the People Much Satisfaction; Next to Chastising the Indians They Desire That May Take Place"

Changes in policies toward Indians were only a part of the way that Pennsylvania secured its political boundaries. The creation of a new national confederacy formed to fight the British helped turned rival colonies into partners fighting a common enemy. The new Continental Congress, which assumed many of the functions of the British Empire and resembled the failed Albany Plan of Union in its purpose, claimed the authority to address boundary disputes. In 1775, for instance, the Congress sent out a circular to Virginia and Pennsylvania stating that property would be protected regardless of which colony's deed a landowner held. The courts of Pennsylvania and Virginia were to function alongside each other as if they were independent counties, with settlers belonging to Virginia using their courts and those allied with Pennsylvania using theirs. Congress ordered this policy of mutual recognition as a way to promote union.[36]

Later in 1775, the Virginia Convention, which met to create a new state Constitution, offered to withdraw Virginia's claims in all existing land disputes as a sign of genuine friendship toward neighboring states. Though this action was not binding, Pennsylvania would later use the proposal to bolster its own claims. Moreover, as early as 1777, Pennsylvania and Virginia officials initiated far more open and honest negotiations to settle the boundary dispute. Unlike colonial negotiations, in which leaders jockeyed to find the argument that would prevail before the Board of Trade or Crown, patriot negotiators simply sought a mutually agreeable solution because the idea of union was pervasive and heartfelt. To top it off, Virginia officials in Williamsburg began to view the area around Fort Pitt as troublesome and potentially costly rather than profitable. Pennsylvania officials, with a new Assembly composed of many frontier representatives, meanwhile, had institutions that more actively asserted their claims to authority over the area.[37]

Belief in union shaped much of the official negotiations over the disputed territory. Thomas Jefferson, fresh off of declaring thirteen colonies free states, turned his attention to making the states work together toward the common cause of national independence. In July 1776, he drafted a letter on behalf of Virginia delegates in the Continental Congress to send to the Pennsylvania Convention in which Virginia proposed a truce between the two warring entities and assured the Pennsylvanians that "the colony of Virginia does not entertain a wish that one inch should be added to theirs from the territory of a sister colony." In November 1776, the Continental Congress appointed Jefferson to try to work out a permanent solution. Jefferson concerned himself with the minutiae in an attempt to ensure a satisfactory outcome for all involved. "If the Monongahela is the line," he speculated, for example, "it will throw 300 Virginia families into Pennsylvania . . . not one-third of that number of Pennsylvanians would be thrown on the Virginia side. If the Laurel hill is the boundary, it will place on the Virginia side all the Virginia settlers and about 200 families of Pennsylvania settlers. A middle line is thought to be just. . . . This would give tolerable satisfaction to Virginia, would throw about 150 Pennsylvanians into Virginia and about 20 or 30 Virginians into Pennsylvania." Pennsylvania agreed with Jefferson that it was essential to the cause of "peace and unity" that they resolve the dispute, but Pennsylvania officials refused to acknowledge a temporary line, "which would cut off so large a part from this state." Indeed, such a line would "instead of being the basis of Union . . . be the occasion of much confusion." Rather than settle on an unsatisfactory temporary line, both governments agreed to address the issue in the future and for the time being respect each other's claims.[38]

For settlers living in the area, the boundary dispute and the Indian war were the two issues foremost in their mind. As Edward Hand observed,

"The prospect of fixing a permanent boundary between Virginia and Pennsylvania gives the people much satisfaction; next to chastising the Indians they desire that may take place." Virginian George Rogers Clark, who ventured to the region to raise recruits in 1778 for an attack deep into the Ohio, found "the whole was divided into violent parties between the Virginians and Pennsylvanians." Henry and others saw that these two issues—defense and jurisdictional uncertainty—worked symbiotically to the detriment of the larger cause against Britain.[39]

In 1779, the two states confronted the issue again when representatives from Pennsylvania and Virginia met in Baltimore. By 1779, the geopolitics of the area had changed as the potential pitfalls of uncertain jurisdictional boundaries moved from abstraction to pressing reality. Two things had happened in the intervening years. First, while Virginians continued to operate in the area as if it was Virginia territory, officials began to back off a vigorous enforcement of Virginia's claims. Patrick Henry wrote the Virginia House of Delegates that "the unsettled state of the boundary line . . . is likely to prove the source of mischief." A committee that formed to address the problem concluded that the competing jurisdictions caused the "civil power . . . of both [states to be] enfeebled, to the injury of the common cause." By 1779, on the other hand, Pennsylvania, which had essentially ceded the territory in the colonial period, had created a number of militias in the area and a state apparatus to react to Indian war in ways more adaptable to settlers' demands. Second, Virginian George Rogers Clark's expedition to Vincennes, located in current day Indiana, in 1778 and 1779 had pushed Virginia's control deep into the Ohio, making Fort Pitt seem less vital to its interests now that the state had acquired a vast tract of land.[40]

Much of the negotiation in Baltimore focused on picayune details and interpretations of colonial charters. In retrospect, the negotiations seem to have been a formality to reach a predetermined outcome. After both states made extreme jurisdictional claims through the exchange of letters, a common tactic in such negotiations that followed colonial precedents, Virginia officials proposed a simple compromise: extend Mason and Dixon's line to Pennsylvania's "western limits" to create a southern border. They also sought to fix the western boundary by drawing a line that ran from the end of the Mason-Dixon Line north to Lake Erie, in effect sealing Pennsylvania off from further expansion. Pennsylvania recognized the compromise, noting that doing so would benefit Virginia's future claims to "lands to the westward of Pennsylvania" because Pennsylvania would renounce any claims to these lands. Therefore, Pennsylvania achieved its southern and western borders—the borders of the modern state—and Virginia still could claim the western land along the Ohio that it had fought for during Dunmore's War.[41]

Both sides felt victorious. Pennsylvania's assembly quickly approved the resolution. Virginia's legislature took almost a year to do the same, in part because the exigencies of war within Virginia slowed regular government business to a crawl. The Virginia legislators showed some unhappiness with the agreement but approved it, citing their "desire to cultivate and maintain the most cordial harmony with their sister state of Pennsylvania" and on condition that the property of all Virginians in the area was to be transferred to Pennsylvania with no punishment. Thus, just as a change of policy in Pennsylvania helped effect a change of loyalties on frontiers, so too did the newfound sense of union between states lead to the agreeable resolution of a border dispute, something that had failed to occur in the colonial era.[42]

"The Towns of Northumberland and Sunbury Will Be the Frontier in Less Than Twenty Four Hours"

In July 1778, the Pennsylvania lieutenant for Northumberland County, the area that had been contested by Connecticut, reported to the Pennsylvania government that "from all appearances the towns of Northumberland and Sunbury will be the frontier in less than twenty four hours." The Pennsylvania Council of Safety agreed with the county lieutenant's assessment of the situation and treated Northumberland as one of the state's "frontier counties." Indeed, during the war, the council designated specific counties "frontier counties," which stretched from the state's northern regions to its most southwestern. These counties received special instructions on defending their frontiers and enjoyed certain benefits, like lower taxes, meant to relieve them from their distresses.[43]

There was essentially an extended frontier ring from the state's northeastern corner to its southwestern terminus that reflected the consolidation of frontier society that had happened in the 1770s. William Moore, one of the councillors of Pennsylvania, connected the western and northern frontiers in a grand offensive strategy. Moore wanted "to carry three expeditions into the Indian Country—one from Fort Pitt—one from Northumberland into the [Genesee] Country and one toward Oswego from such place as the General shall think most practicable." Although the offensive never came to fruition, its outlines demonstrated how officials of the revolutionary state envisioned the frontiers that formed the boundary of their polity. It also showed the belief that offensive raids were the most effective way to provide defensive protection to loyal citizens, the implementation of ideas expressed by the Paxton Boys. And as in the west, the new support for military operations helped secure Pennsylvania's own borders in the northern region once controlled by Connecticut.[44]

But it was the Continental Congress that provided the ultimate impetus for settling the dispute between Connecticut and Pennsylvania. The authors of the Articles of Confederation displayed an intimate awareness of and frustration with a British Empire that showed little real initiative in managing an expanding landed empire. The confederation that they created gave the Continental Congress the power necessary to handle expansion and boundary disputes. The ninth article established a process for Congress to settle border conflicts. Rather than leaving the specifics of mediation vague as the British Empire had, the drafters wanted to clearly establish the parameters and protocols for settling boundary questions by instructing Congress to create a special court composed of five judges from states not involved to adjudicate it.[45]

In 1782, the Articles faced one of its first tests when Pennsylvania petitioned Congress to settle its conflict with Connecticut over the Susquehanna lands, triggering this ninth article. Congress swiftly empowered a special court at Trenton, New Jersey, manned by five judges hailing from Virginia, New Jersey, New Hampshire, and Rhode Island. Meanwhile, Connecticut acknowledged the jurisdiction of the court, an important test of the government and the union it hoped to build. For over a month, lawyers from Connecticut and Pennsylvania presented their cases to the tribunal. At the end of arguments, the court sided unanimously with Pennsylvania.[46]

Some have since speculated that Pennsylvania, Connecticut, and Congress had entered into a secret agreement in which Connecticut would cede its claim to northern Pennsylvania in exchange for a large swath of land in the Ohio called the Western Reserve. The origin of this idea rests in a pronouncement Congress made a month after the court case that acknowledged that "Virginia and Connecticut have . . . made cessions." While this statement is true—Connecticut did accept the decision of the court and lost territory—some have held that because Congress lumped Connecticut and Virginia together, it showed that Connecticut willfully gave up their domains much like Virginia did.[47]

Such an interpretation requires quite a bit of a reading between the lines. Indeed, Connecticut's actions before the court depict something much different. If there was a prearranged agreement, one would think the trial would have not have taken as long as a month. If the case was predetermined, then the lawyers for Connecticut should have put on a lackluster performance. Instead, they went to great lengths to produce numerous copies of Indian deeds of dubious validity that they believed would bolster their cause. Furthermore, the letters of Joseph Reed, one of Pennsylvania's legal representatives, suggest that those arguing for Pennsylvania, while confident in their case, were not colluding with the court.[48]

Whether the speculation for collusion is true or not, the unanimity of the decision at Trenton helped strengthen the national government's authority by making it harder for the losing party to contest the decision. Regardless of the reasons behind the decision, the Trenton court and the subsequent creation of the Western Reserve showed the national government's commitment to addressing issues of growth in a way far different than that of the British Empire. The new national government was composed of and influenced by Americans who had long envisioned landed expansion as part of a national project, and the Articles and the actions of Congress reflected this vision. While some of those once loyal to Connecticut continued to protest the Trenton decision, Connecticut never tried to undermine it, leaving the disgruntled Connecticut settlers turned Pennsylvanians with little recourse. Eventually, the people from Connecticut either recognized the authority of Pennsylvania or, as happened around Fort Pitt with the Virginians, moved on.

By the end of the war in 1783, the state of Pennsylvania itself had undergone its own internal revolution. Pennsylvania went from a colony whose borders were receding to a state that had secured its borders. It also succeeded in incorporating all of its regions into government bodies, and it created new institutions that enforced state policy within the body politic. The establishment of the state thus enabled the solidification of its geography. It was a radical transformation effected in only a short period. It was made possible because the government had become what frontier people had demanded: a frontier government. The consolidation of the state only continued in the wake of the war, as the government created nine new counties, most of which were in former frontiers regions, in order to better incorporate people into the polity. The changes wrought by the revolution and the processes unleashed soon brought about something even more dramatic: the closure of frontiers in Pennsylvania and the transformation of their significance in the new nation.

Frontiers in a New Nation

Daniel Drake experienced the closure of Pennsylvania's frontiers firsthand. Indeed, he wrote about it in a memoir meant for his children. Drake's first memories came from Red Stone Old Fort, a community George Croghan established near Fort Pitt in the 1780s. Drake's parents had struck out from New Jersey for the opportunity western Pennsylvania offered. Their first home was a former sheep pen rented from a farmer. Drake continued to trek west and rose as the nation grew, eventually becoming a successful doctor in Cincinnati, a bustling inland metropolis. He died in 1852 in an enormous home that sits preserved for tourists, a testament to the prosperity many Americans experienced in the years following American independence.[1]

Drake's life is a success story, but the memoirs of his life illuminate something else: the experience of living on a frontier in the early republic. Drake's early life was strikingly similar to Crevecoeur's distressed frontier man James, described in *Letters from an American Farmer*, who lived in Pennsylvania before the Revolution. Drake's very first recollection came from his time in western Pennsylvania, around 1789, when settlers still considered their homes part of a frontier. He described his home—by then, a larger log cabin—as a semifortress and his daily routine as similar to that of a combat zone. Every night, his father would remove the gun from the living room and bring it under his bed "in case the Indians should make an attack." As he was put to bed, his parents would remind him of the war with the Indians, telling him to "lie still and go to sleep, or the Shawnees will catch you." Every morning, the family's "first duty" was to "look out the cracks for Indians, lest they might have planted themselves near the door." Fear of Indians defined everyday life for everyone on this frontier.

Daily conversations seemed to revolve around "Indian wars, midnight butcheries, captivities, and horse-stealing." Drake remembered being surrounded by young men "who delighted in war much more than work." He recounted the "many wonderful tales" these young men returned to tell of their daring exploits.[2]

But there is an important difference between Crevecoeur's James and Drake. Where the constant anxiety of a frontier forced James to flee his farm, Drake could also remember the year when the fear stopped: 1794. Indeed, he could remember the moment: when Anthony Wayne and the U.S. Army defeated the united Western Confederacy at the Battle of Fallen Timbers in Ohio. "Up to the victory of Wayne in 1794," he wrote, "the danger from Indians still continued; that is through a period of six years from the time of our arrival." That victory, at least as he seemed to remember it, meant that he no longer lived with the same fears he once had. He was no longer an inhabitant of a frontier.[3]

"A Poor Distressed Peepel"

The closure of frontiers in Pennsylvania transformed politics in the new state. Citizens on former frontiers no longer looked to their eastern government for military aid. Instead, as they took stock of their situation, they began to focus on other issues, especially their economic livelihood. Westerners realized that even with the fear of Indian invasion removed, they still suffered severe hardships and their governments still seemed to ignore their plight. Throughout the 1780s, they began to mobilize once again, forming militias, blocking roads, and harassing government officials. In 1791, after the federal government passed an excise tax on whiskey, westerners who relied on the distilled spirit's production for economic sustenance began to feel as if their governments had turned on them once again, and their protests escalated even more.[4]

The tactics these disgruntled westerners used called upon the political culture that had developed in frontier regions during the colonial era. Their forms of resistance consisted of local officials, such as justices of the peace, who chose not to implement laws that locals opposed; juries that could reject policies by wielding the power of popular justice; nonviolent and violent protests that made enforcement difficult; and the formation of militias, all of which evoked the Paxton Boys, the Black Boys, the rescuers of Frederick Stump, and the militia mobilizations during the wars. The rhetoric citizens in these areas used to oppose state laws echoed that which was used throughout the colonial period. In the early republic, citizens in the region protested laws that raised taxes on farms, businesses, and other regulations, deeming them "grievous and unequal burthens" on "a poor distressed peepel."[5]

While the language of inequality and a "distressed" people echoed the same cries frontier people made in the colonial period, citizens in the new nation applied this language to new ends: economic rather than military security. This political reorientation signaled an important transformation within the territory: the end of frontiers as a driving political issue for these settlers. Frontiers made people who inhabited them privilege military and defense policies as their primary concern. Now fiscal matters came to the fore as settlers no longer felt the fear that frontiers brought. Instead, economic uncertainties supplanted their concerns about defense.[6]

Things came to a head on August 1, 1794, when over seven thousand militiamen from the four westernmost counties of Pennsylvania congregated at Braddock's Field, still strewn with bones and other detritus from the British Army's defeat in 1755. At the same time, an army of more than twelve thousand marched west under the auspices of the U.S. government to confront them. The symbolism of Braddock's Field was clear. These militiamen prepared to play the part of the French and Indians who defeated the much larger British forces under Edward Braddock. At issue was the federal tax on whiskey distillers. It was, they said, "unequal, oppressive, and particularly distressing."[7]

The tax was sure to affect the livelihood of many, but their objections ran deeper. While the protesters opposed the federal government's authority to levy this form of internal taxation, what really riled them was the belief that the tax was meant to limit westerners' economic potential and benefit wealthy easterners. To these protesters, the whiskey tax was unacceptably akin to the British policies that had encouraged them to revolt in 1776. The disgruntled westerners mimicked the same patterns that colonists had in 1776. They organized committees to coordinate protests and sent numerous petitions to federal authorities. When these appeals failed, they formed militias and seized tax collectors. Matters escalated quickly, and the militiamen who met at Braddock's Field wanted to present a united front that showed their militant opposition to a federal law that they believed was unjust. Just as patriots took up arms to reject British taxation, so too did the Whiskey Rebels in 1794.[8]

Federal officials interpreted the Whiskey Rebels' actions in just such a light. They feared that if this armed protest went unchecked, then these westerners could undermine the new federal authority. The area, to quote a defender of the federal government, was "a center of terrorism" that threatened the republic's survival. Secretary of the Treasury Alexander Hamilton took the lead in trying to enforce the collection of the whiskey tax. Hamilton believed that the protests challenged the foundations upon which a government based on the authority of the people rested. Since this law was duly passed by the legislature, then it was an entirely justified form of taxation. In this view, policy disputes were to be mediated by representatives and electoral results, not through brazen acts that flaunted federal authorities. Thus, Hamilton led twelve thousand militiamen from New Jersey, Pennsylvania, Virginia, and Maryland toward Braddock's Field to demonstrate the strength of a government that truly rested upon the authority of all of the people rather than a disgruntled minority. After brief negotiations, the federal government granted the rebels amnesty in exchange for recognition of the American state's authority. Although there is limited evidence of the tax's enforcement after this compromise, Hamilton had made his point. Westerners would have to find another means to change government policies to suit their needs.[9]

"Their Election of Submitting to the One or the Other . . . as It Comported with Their Interest or Their Caprice"

Westerners soon found the means to affect government policies by harnessing the politics of competition they knew so well and rechanneling it in a new, more legitimate form. One of the reasons for the creation of the federal government was to tamp down state rivalries. Indeed, erasing the vestiges of colonial competition was one of the driving rationales that Alexander Hamilton marshaled in favor of the Constitution in the *Federalist Papers*. Hamilton, like Dickinson before him, was well aware of the uncertainty border disputes bred. After the war, he represented New York's interest in its court cases about the location of its eastern border. He also knew of the strife in the Middle Colonies. Without the power of a strong federal government, his experience led him to conclude that the nation would be marked by constant warfare between states in which "the frontiers of one state [would be] open to another," thereby allowing "the populous States . . . [to] overrun their less populous neighbors" through "conquests." The federal government, however, would prevent such things by creating the powerful, centralized force the British Empire lacked. It would force compliance and union and prevent interstate rivalries from becoming so strong that they would breed disorder and war. It would also transform the forms of political expression new citizens took.[10]

No one understood this change better than William Findley. Findley is known today as the first "Father of the House," a nickname inspired by his long tenure and leadership in the early U.S. Congress, but in the 1790s, he was best known as the leading politician from western Pennsylvania and an ardent Jeffersonian Republican. In 1796, however, he became a historian when he penned *A History of the Insurrection in the Four Western Counties of Pennsylvania*, a treatise meant to defend himself and the Whiskey Rebels, who were also his constituents, from the attacks of easterners claiming they were nothing more than lawless vagabonds. His book also captured the importance of competition between colonies and then states for those who lived on frontiers in the era of the American Revolution.[11]

Findley's own adulthood spanned the very period of the revolution, and he knew the politics of frontiers and border wars as well as anyone. Born in Ulster, Ireland, Findley in his early twenties joined thousands of other Scots-Irish who sought a new life in Penn's Woods. He arrived around 1763 and settled in Carlisle, Pennsylvania. Findley rose quickly in his new home. He served in local militias and eventually became an officer in Cumberland County. After the Revolution, he traveled farther west seeking greater opportunity near Pittsburgh. In Westmoreland County, he held various local offices, became a leading anti-Federalist voice during ratification, and then represented his region as a member of Congress, a position he held for almost a quarter of a century. When the Whiskey Rebellion broke out in 1794, Findley managed to stay out of the melee, instead serving as something of a neutral mediator rather than a participant. Nonetheless, he understood the plight of his constituents better than most. Indeed, many of his political opponents back east accused him of abetting them. Two years later, as people still discussed the Whiskey Rebellion and Findley's possible role in it, he decided it was time to defend the rebels' actions to those unaware of their history and politics.[12]

Findley started his narrative by telling a history of Pennsylvania that focused on competition between colonies (and then states) in the region. This depiction of Pennsylvania's past was very different from the ones being produced at about the same time by Philadelphians seeking to make sense of the American Revolution. Findley's history paid little attention to the Stamp Act or the battles fought in and around Philadelphia. Instead, it recounted stories of border and Indian wars that those on the frontiers knew. He included this backstory in order to illuminate the politics of the region and the cause of the rebellion for those unaware of it. He started with the time when western Pennsylvania had been part of Virginia. "About the year 1774," he wrote, Virginia's royal governor Lord Dunmore had "opened several offices for the sale of land within the bounds of what are now called the four western counties of Pennsylvania." "The purchase price" under Virginia "was trifling," which was "an effectual inducement to apply to Dunmore's agents in preference to the Pennsylvania land office." Dunmore also "commenced an unprovoked war against the Indians" that caused this "frontier" to be "cruelly wasted by perpetual savage depredations."[13]

Findley went on to place this conflict between Virginia and Pennsylvania within Pennsylvania's other experiences with border wars. He related stories of "the bloodshed and violence" during the "Conejaghally War," the conflict fought between Maryland and Pennsylvania in the 1730s for control of westward expansion. He then told of a similar conflict in the Wyoming Valley, an area north of Philadelphia. There, Connecticut settlers had caused "bloodshed and numerous acts of outrageous violence" when they claimed the territory as their own. According to Findley's account, Pennsylvania was in a constant state of war during its colonial era, whether against a fellow British colony, the French, or Native Americans. Findley knew of this peculiar history, which included events like the Conojocular War that preceded his arrival because it continued to resonate with those who lived near still tenuous borders. In such regions, stories of these other border wars circulated in oral traditions rather than printed histories, but they were very much alive and were well known for people living where the political boundaries remained blurred.[14]

For settlers living in these contested regions, the competition had forged a unique political culture. Although Findley was familiar only with the specifics of the Virginia-Pennsylvania case, he said the dispute created "a strange state of society" in which settlers could use such competition to their advantage by playing one side off the other. Representatives from each colony crisscrossed the region trying to convince settlers to swear allegiance to their government. The practice of campaigning for settlers meant that those living in the area were the true arbiters of the dispute. Residents, Findley noted, made "their election of submitting to the one or the other . . . as it comported with their interest or their caprice." Such patterns had defined the politics of border creation since the 1730s. This competition bred bitter rivalries and factions among settlers who ostensibly should have been neighbors and fellow subjects: "party animosity," Findley called it.[15]

By the time of the American Revolution, an ascendant frontier society used this colonial competition to establish the type of government they wanted. In the earliest years of the new nation, these same patterns persisted as settlers continued to use competition to achieve their ends. Those unhappy with laws of specific states often voted with their feet. As Findley noted in A History of the Insurrection, in the 1780s, those that "had strong prejudice against the government of Pennsylvania, sold their plantations, and gave place to others." In such an environment, states were hesitant to pass or enforce unpopular laws. For example, Pennsylvania had passed an excise tax on distilled spirits during the revolutionary war, but its enforcement was spotty, especially "in those counties bordering on other states." As Findley noted, since "neighbouring states" had no excise laws, it became "impracticable and odious" for Pennsylvanians to try to enforce theirs. Competition thus continued to affect states' approaches to governance and their relationships with their citizens.[16]

As the federal government sought to impose its authority over the region through the implementation of a new whiskey tax, citizens versed in the politics of competition refused to acquiesce to this new political world. Instead, they sought ways to replicate what they had lost in the colonial era. Some Whiskey Rebels threatened to secede and form a separate country; others wanted to create new states. Others tried—or threatened to try—to negotiate with foreign powers. Westerners used these tactics to re-create the politics of competition that had defined the political culture of the region before the Revolution. The suppression of the Whiskey Rebellion signaled that in the new nation, those forms of competition were illegitimate.[17]

Nonetheless, these Americans frustrated by the lack of negotiating power ultimately did discover a new means to maintain competition within the federal polity. They rechanneled the "party animosity" Findley described in the colonial era into partisan politics. It was an almost natural transition. Parties embodied competing versions of the new American state, just as the border disputes Pennsylvania had with Virginia, Connecticut, and Maryland revealed the different types of governments these colonies represented. Where Pennsylvanians and Virginians campaigned for supporters in the 1770s, Republicans and Federalists did the same in the 1790s. Republicans advocated a weaker federal government and stronger local governments that supported the growth of small farmers and the landed expansion of the nation. Their vision of local controls of government and a fear of an eastern elite comported with the politics frontier people had embraced during the imperial crisis. Federalists, however, represented a more active and centralized federal government that supported an ordered expansion reminiscent of the imperial vision British officials had promoted.[18]

The western counties' shift toward electoral politics channeled westerners' mistrust of distant representative bodies into the contentious realm of party politics and allowed them to back their particular views of the state within national institutions. After the standoff in 1794 ended, humbled rebels reoriented political behavior away from popular mobilization and toward electioneering, which turned out to be a far more effective weapon. This transition did not begin with the Whiskey Rebellion, nor did the rebellion's suppression serve as the conclusion of a process begun with the Revolution. But as western Pennsylvanians—and later, citizens in Northampton County who took part in a similar tax revolt called Fries' Rebellion—began to adjust their political behaviors to the realities of a strong federal government, they created a strong bloc of Republicans within Pennsylvania whose actions shaped both state and national politics, giving much-needed energy and support to the nascent national party system. It is no coincidence that William Findley, one of the early leaders of the Republican Party, hailed from the former frontiers of Pennsylvania.[19]

"The Best Defense Is Offense"

In time, frontier settlers' engagement in electoral politics transformed the very meaning of frontiers within the polity. During the crisis of empire on the frontiers in the 1760s and 1770s, settlers used colonial competition to create frontier governments within specific regions. No longer satisfied with the defensive posture of frontiers that the British Empire embraced, some citizens demanded a new right, one that called for more than just protection of frontiers. They demanded offensive actions reminiscent of the Paxton Boys and the Gnadenhutten Massacre. In a new political environment, they used party competition to accomplish their aim on a national scale. In time, the success of this new policy would lead to the completely new conception of a frontier itself.

Hugh Henry Brackenridge, a powerful newspaper publisher and lawyer in Pittsburgh, who also happened to be Findley's archnemesis, helped craft this redefinition. In 1792, an essay he wrote about the country's frontier policy appeared on the front page of the Philadelphia-published *National Gazette*. He was aware of the debates in Congress about how the new government should treat its frontier areas. He wanted to provide the perspective of someone who lived on a frontier. He began by noting that there were two different frontier policies that the new nation could adopt. One was to "surround the frontier with a rank and file of men, like the wall of China, and take care that these should never sleep." This was a purely defensive frontier, much as the traditional frontier had been conceived.[20]

This option he found ineffective, however, in large part because of his belief that Indians were inherent and perpetual enemies, a view forged among those living on frontiers. "*They* have been the aggressors," Brackenridge emphasized. A purely defensive posture would, Brackenridge surmised, be "but a help and no effectual defense" because it would amount to nothing more than "watching the beasts of prey who come against our folds." The other option was "penetrating the forests, where they haunt, and extirpating the race." Such an offensive posture, framed by the idea of a permanent Indian enemy constantly threatening invasion, meant that the frontier was to be an expanding and active zone of military operation. The reason, he concluded, is that "the government [is] bound to give *peaceable possession* of the soil" to its inhabitants, and only removal could provide the type of security he believed government owed its citizens. As Brackenridge concluded, "The best defense is offense."[21]

As memories of frontier experiences lingered and the stories told by inhabitants of new frontiers zones circulated, voters who either lived on frontiers or could remember living on one demanded that the new national government respond to these areas in a way that comported with their beliefs, often taking the same position Brackenridge did. As Massachusetts representative Fisher Ames declared in a speech to the House, "Protection is the right of the frontiers; it is our duty to give it." Ames's words were almost identical to Thomas Barton's defense of the Paxton Boys in which he declared "they [frontier people] have a right to demand and receive protection." That such words came from a leading congressman marked a striking contrast to the British Empire's management of this territory and was a product of the political changes wrought by revolution.[22]

From the country's inception, then, officials were aware of frontiers in the nation and considered their management a central priority for the new government. These officials, many of whom depended upon a happy electorate for their positions, tended to embrace the view of self-described "frontier people" in ways the British Empire never had. After the American Revolution, the American government maintained more "frontier forts" than the British Empire had before the war. Positioned as a line that followed the Ohio River south, their presence sent a signal of American sovereignty to the Spanish, British, and Native Americans. These garrisons also served a more immediate and practical purpose by providing a sense of security to area residents who feared an Indian war. Brackenridge's policy proposals came to further fruition in the early nineteenth century as the federal government became dominated by the Republican Party with a voting base that consisted of many frontier people and former frontier people like William Findley.

By the War of 1812, the "war hawks" in the Republican Party demanded the government take a hostile position toward Natives, and argued for war against them much as they sought war with Great Britain. Indeed, the success of the hawks in encouraging a war against Indians in the greater Ohio region, and the eventual success of the army on the battlefield, led to a complete redefinition of the American frontier. During the war, as the American state took active control of a frontier perceived as national in scope, Americans were more likely to read about and refer to a singular, coherent western frontier rather than the fragmented and less coherent "frontiers" discussed in the colonial era. The predominance with which Americans spoke of "the frontier" rather than many different "frontiers" became only stronger after the end of the Black Hawk War of 1832, another significant conflict between an expanding American nation that confronted strong resistance from Native Americans protective of their land. This dramatic shift signals the creation of a "frontier line." This line had within it Brackenridge's new model of "*the* frontier" as an offensive rather than

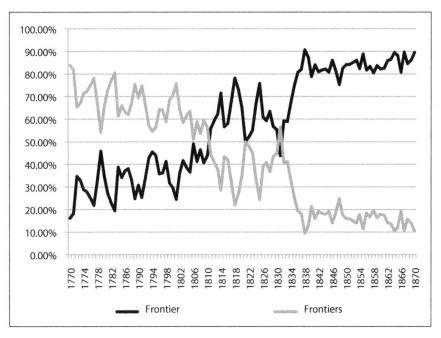

Figure 15. Usage of *frontier* versus *frontiers* in American newspapers, 1770–1870. Before the nineteenth century, most Americans spoke of frontiers in the plural and referred to specific sites vulnerable to invasion, including seacoasts. With the rise of the nation-state, however, Americans began to imagine a single, coherent frontier line in the west. Source: Early American newspapers. Dataset available at mappingfrontiers.com and patrickspero.com.

defensive zone. The frontier had become an expansive and expanding geopolitical zone of conquest that referred almost exclusively to the west (Figure 15).

Such a conception of *the frontier*—a literal frontier line that demarcated the extent of the American nation-state—also served to place Indians squarely outside the American state. This view of the frontier was reflected in developments from the Indian Removal Act of 1830 to the passage of the Fourteenth Amendment, which excluded Indians from citizenship in 1868. As Andrew Jackson noted in advocating for removal in 1830, "By opening the whole territory between Tennessee on the north and Louisiana on the south to the settlement of the whites it will incalculably strengthen the southwestern frontier and render the adjacent States strong enough to repel future invasions." A product of his time and place, the first president born as a frontiersman premised his view of national security and thus his national geopolitical strategy on the idea that Indians as separate nations were inherent and perpetual enemies; there would be, he assumed, "future invasions." In time, the success of this new expansionist policy rendered obsolete old ideas about defensive and contracting frontiers. In other words, the transformation of frontier policy after the American Revolution led to a new conception of the spaces that still bore the same name.[23]

By 1890, when the U.S. Census declared the American frontier closed, the government had altered the official meaning of a frontier. Fear, war, or vulnerability no longer defined a frontier, according to the federal government. Instead, it was an area of open space that contained less than two white inhabitants per square mile. Many believed that this "free land," as it was often described, created a safety valve that relieved urban and eastern areas of the class animosities that seemed to rile European cities, creating a distinctly American culture. So pervasive and powerful was this idea that many leading Americans worried that the closure of frontiers threatened America's stability, showing how antithetical the new definition was to *frontier*'s earlier, eighteenth-century meaning. Even the language used to describe frontiers was radically altered by this redefinition. Open frontiers in the eighteenth century were seen as a threat to a polity because they signified an area exposed to invasion. By the nineteenth century, however, an open frontier was something Americans wanted because it represented a chance for prosperity. Indeed, we still today speak of opening frontiers in science and space as a thing of great opportunity and potential.

The idea that America's open frontiers had closed even shaped Franklin Delano Roosevelt's reasoning for New Deal policies. He claimed that "equality of opportunity as we have known it no longer exists. . . . Our last frontier has been reached, and there is practically no more free land. . . . There is no safety-valve." Roosevelt went on to argue that with the frontier closed, the country needed a safety net to provide the security that the frontier once offered. In the eighteenth century, open frontiers were vulnerable zones that called for greater government involvement. In the Roosevelt's reconceived notion, open frontiers and the prosperity they brought were a reason that the federal government had remained limited before the Great Depression. The closing of frontiers required new government

intervention in order to provide the security that open frontiers had provided a previous generation.[24]

While this modern formulation would have made no sense to an
eighteenth-century ear, its redefinition is inextricably linked to (if also
obscured by) this past. What made the notion of frontiers as areas that
provided stability and opportunity possible in the nineteenth and twentieth
centuries was the way settlers and governments in earlier periods, especially
in the era of the American Revolution, thought of frontiers as war zones
that faced invasion. This defensive zone turned offensive with the creation
of the United States and the greater integration of "frontier settlers" into
institutions of power. In time, with Indian Removal and war, the effects of
this changed geopolitical strategy made the American frontier appear a
place of sparse population, abundant land, and great economic opportunity. It is a troubling history of how fear and desperation can turn into
hope and opportunity.

Frontiers

Meanings, Controversies, and New Evidence

Frontier: few words have inspired American historians to spill more ink. For much of the twentieth century, many historians placed the word at the heart of the American experience. Late in the century, other historians took a decidedly different tack, arguing that "the f-word" be banished. My reanimation of the word, then, would seem to require some explanation.

The origins of the *frontier* controversy date to 1893, when Frederick Jackson Turner delivered his presidential address, "The Significance of the Frontier in American History," to the American Historical Association. One sentence in Turner's essay is frequently used to define the essence of his thesis: "The existence of an area of free land, its continuous recession, and the advance of American settlement westward, explain American development." For Turner, the existence of a frontier region ("an area of free land") provided a safety valve for the social and economic discontent that had plagued Europe. This safety valve gave rise to high levels of property ownership, which in turn spurred the individualism that defined America's political and economic character. Finally, for Turner, "the advance of American settlement" explained the United States' geographic expansion as part of a civilizing mission that transformed a wilderness into a modern nation. This process defined America's national character as frontiersmen and pioneers built local political institutions that were influenced by their circumstances and shaped the politics of the nation more generally. For Turner, the frontier was thus a place in which the process of Americanization occurred.[1]

For several decades, Turner's ideas reigned supreme in a new field of historical inquiry often called "Western History" or "Frontier Studies." Yet Turner never lacked critics, and his death in 1932, Richard Hofstadter noted, "unleashed a veritable avalanche of criticism" that was "precipitated in large degree by the new ideological currents set in motion by the Great Depression." These "debunkers," as Turner's most ardent supporters labeled them, took Turner's thesis at face value, agreeing that there was such a thing as an American frontier, that it played a role in America's political development, and that it shifted over time. They disagreed with the Turnerians, however, by arguing that the frontier played a far less significant role in the country's past. A particular target of the debunker's wrath was the claim that the frontier served as a "safety valve" for urban discontent. A range of economic historians relegated this idea to the realm of popular myth.[2]

Beginning in the 1960s, but picking up speed in the 1980s and 1990s, a new generation of historians, styled as "revisionists," took more fundamental issue with Turner's frontier thesis. These critics focused their energy on two fronts. First, they wanted to address all of the perspectives of American life that Turner's thesis failed to consider. Turnerianism, they argued, was "ethnocentric and nationalistic," made "English-speaking white men . . . the stars of the story," and was crippled by "gender bias and linearity." A second and often overlapping group challenged Turner's argument that the process of settling on a frontier was responsible for America's distinctive character and greatness. Instead they portrayed the frontier as a font of moral shortcomings, a site of imperialism, greed, violence, and deception. The criticism became so considerable that many scholars questioned the usefulness of the term *frontier* in historical analysis altogether. As Patricia Limerick, Turner's most prominent critic, concluded, "The frontier is . . . an unsubtle concept in a subtle world."[3]

By the 1990s, it appeared that the weight of criticism had crushed Turner's concept of the frontier. Some scholars were so disgusted with Turner and his well-known thesis that they sought to erase "the frontier" from historians' lexicon altogether and construct a new vocabulary to describe historical processes involving geographic zones once considered "frontiers." These approaches all aimed to downplay the ethnocentrism prevalent in many previous works and to incorporate the stories of indigenous peoples who struggled against European imperial projects. Casting frontiers as "borderlands," meaning areas of diplomatic contention and complex economic and cultural exchange between groups, stripped the United States' westward expansion of the inevitability and glory implied in Turner's thesis. Instead, borderlands studies emphasized the ways in which different cultures and peoples interacted and negotiated their daily lives in areas of intercultural cohabitation. The concept of borderlands—a term coined in the nineteenth century to describe the geopolitics between two neighboring polities—also allowed historians to discuss with greater sophistication the national and imperial struggles over land and goods that often shaped intercultural relations in these territories. Studies using borderlands as their primary frame of analysis have grown exponentially in the past decade. The new approach has helped historians clarify their interpretations by better establishing the meaning of an analytical term, which in turn allowed them to define better the specific characteristics of areas of expansion and contestation.[4]

But the use of this word to supplant *frontier* creates an anachronism that *frontier* does not have. Unlike *frontier*, which was widely used in the eighteenth century, *borderland* was a word created in the mid-nineteenth century to try to define that world. According to the *Oxford English Dictionary*, its first usage was to describe the boundary between Scotland and England, an area that had once been a frontier but, through the Union of Scotland and England in 1707, had now become a peaceful border. Its continued usage throughout the nineteenth and to the present century coincides with the growth of stronger nation-states with the military might, diplomatic desire, and governmental wherewithal to make and enforce much clearer borders between polities. No one in the eighteenth century, in other words, thought of their home as a borderland, in large part because borders, at least in North America, were often so nebulous and porous.[5]

Try as they might, then, scholars had a hard time banishing *frontier* from the historian's toolkit. The word was too prominent both in the historiography and in the record to ignore, and Turner's thesis, even if it was to be dismissed, was too enticing a target. By the late 1990s, scholars, most of whom were sympathetic to the revisionist critique, began calling for the "f-word" to be reintegrated into the field. The growing consensus was that historians should try to redefine "frontier" to suit the field's changing analytic demands. Fredrika Teute and Andrew Cayton captured this sentiment when they wrote that they approached the frontier with "a revisionist notion" that is "influenced by a renewed appreciation of American pluralism and social difference." Such a usage, they argued, makes "the essence of the frontier . . . kinetic interactions among many peoples, which created new cultural matrices distinctively American." This redefined frontier gained prominence within the field. In the *American Historical Review*, Jeremy Adelman and Stephen Aron noted that "the frontier," reconsidered as a "zone of intercultural penetration," could have "a new historiographic lease on life." Even Patricia Limerick, who had earlier led the charge against *frontier*, expressed reservations about her past stance.[6]

By the twenty-first century, this debate had cooled. Scholars no longer seemed quite as concerned with defining *frontier*. There was a general consensus that while the word itself was more palatable than it was in the 1980s, its use should be, as James Merrell noted in an important review essay in 2012, "stripped of its Turnerian baggage." But therein rests a conundrum. It is unclear what *frontier* means divorced from its own history or "stripped of its Turnerian baggage," as Merrell put it. Turner's earliest acolytes and his debunkers took his thesis, and thus his conception of *frontier*, as *the* definition of the American frontier from which they worked. Even the revisionists who hoped to eschew Turner were, in truth, following in his methodological footsteps. *Frontier* remained for them as it did for Turner an analytical category, what Turner had once called an "elastic" term, that historians could define and redefine to suit their needs. But if historians continue to treat *frontier* as Turner did, then the debate about the frontier's significance will simply continue in this unsatisfactory pattern, changing every generation or so to meet contemporary mores.[7]

Indeed, Merrell's conclusion reveals a more fundamental problem that has plagued this historiographical debate since its inception. For over a century, as scholars held a raucous debate about the proper meaning of *frontier*, a more fundamental question has largely gone unasked. What did *frontier* mean within its historical context? How did this meaning shape the actions and beliefs of those who used the word? And where did such zones exist at given points in time? This book is a step toward answering these questions, while also perhaps opening new ones.[8]

While this book focused on Pennsylvania to answer these questions, evidence from other colonies reveal common patterns that further elucidate the importance of frontiers to colonial governance and American society. Throughout colonial America, colonists and officials defined specific areas as frontiers. Such zones were always contingent on the presence of a clear enemy who threatened invasion. Pennsylvania, with its long history of peace before frontiers appeared on its geopolitical landscape, is a particularly good case study, but the usage of *frontier* in other colonies further clarifies the importance of such zones and, in some cases, adds additional insights.

Searchable databases now allow us unprecedented access to answers to new questions about frontiers that can reveal the way colonists imagined and spoke of their own geopolitics. Figures 16 through 18 track the frequency of the word's use in colonial newspapers. Although there are problems with this data—for instance, increases in the term's use may be a product of more newspapers in circulation—two general trends appear. The first is that in colonial America the word *frontiers* was more widely used than the more common contemporary singular use *frontier* (Figure 16). The plural usage reflects beliefs that a colony possessed many vulnerable areas (often identified as certain "frontier towns") rather than an expanding "frontier line," as Turner cast it. The relatively large amount of data used to create this graph and the clear difference between *frontiers* and *frontier* suggests that this error in not the result of incomplete or bad data.

The second trend is that there is a clear increase in the word's usage during wartime, which indicates that the existence of frontiers was contingent upon the fear of invasion (Figures 17 and 18). Pennsylvania's publications depict this contingent nature particularly well. Before the Seven Years' War, as this book argues elsewhere, Pennsylvanians rarely spoke of their colony having frontier areas. But with that war, colonists began to see areas as frontiers. This change is reflected in print. As noted below, pamphlets, broadsides, and books printed in Pennsylvania all contained more references to frontiers. While the problem of data may diminish the usefulness of this chart, it should be noted just how perfectly spikes coincide with war and other events. For instance, the spike in 1763 is a product of Philadelphia printers producing more prints in the wake of the Paxton Boys' march. The political crisis frontiers created for governments this spurred more printed material because it was such an important matter to governing the colony.

More important, the most popular newspaper, the *Pennsylvania Gazette,* mirrors the general trend in printed materials. Unlike printed publications such as books and pamphlets, the numbers of which may fluctuate annually, the *Gazette* appeared weekly throughout this period, and the spikes reflect the general increase of the term's use in letters, essays, and speeches. The frequency of the term in the *Gazette* reached an apogee in 1756, which coincided with one of the bloodiest years of the war. Pennsylvania restored peace through diplomacy and military victory in 1758, even

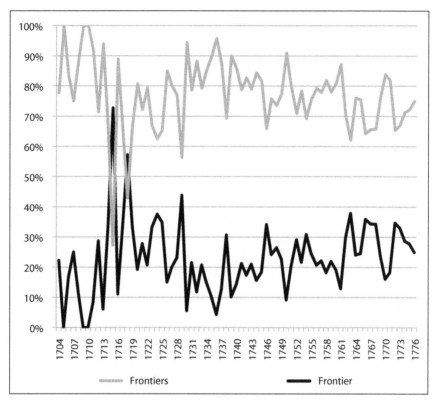

Figure 16. The frequency of *frontiers* versus *frontier* in newspaper articles, 1704–1774. Source: *Early American Newspapers* (published by Readex). For additional data, see mappingfrontiers.com and patrickspero.com.

though war persisted in Europe and elsewhere in North America. The pause in warfare in Pennsylvania is reflected in the term's usage—or lack thereof—as debates about and discussions of the frontier diminished. Notably, the increase in 1768 in the *Pennsylvania Gazette*, which did not register in regular printed materials, reflected an ongoing debate between the Assembly and the lieutenant governor over Indian policy in which both institutions believed war was imminent and the focus on the Stump affair.[9]

Examining such data for other colonies also shifts our historical perspective on the location of frontiers in colonial America. Although *frontier* is often associated with western, interior lands, far from the seacoast, it was not necessarily imagined as such in the eighteenth century. While the

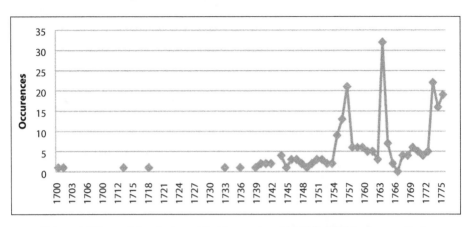

Figure 17. Usage of *frontier* in publications printed in Philadelphia. Source: *Early American Imprints: Series I, Evans, 1639–1800 Online* (published by Readex). Multiple editions and duplicates are not included in totals.

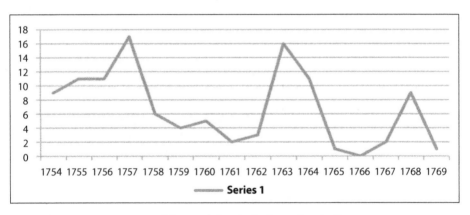

Figure 18. Appearance of the word *frontier* in *Pennsylvania Gazette*, 1754–1769. Source: *Pennsylvania Gazette*, Accessible Archives (Malvern, PA), www.accessible-archives.com.

word's earliest usages do often comport with such a conception, this usage was simply a product of where colonial officials believed their nearest adversary resided. Early settlers in Virginia and Massachusetts all referred to inland towns as frontiers because they feared a conflict with their Native neighbors. As the British colonies became more enmeshed in the Atlantic

World and its rivalries, however, imperial officials began to consider the North American seacoast as a frontier because of its vulnerability to a sea-borne assault from a European adversary. In 1720, for instance, the British Board of Trade began to map out its imperial holdings and referred to Nova Scotia as being one of "the two frontiers of the British Empire" (the other, Carolina, bordered Spanish domains), thereby reflecting imperial officials' primary focus on the potential for European rivals to assault their North American domains via the Atlantic. Later, an Englishman writing about the contours of the empire in 1739 described Great Britain's North American holdings as "sort of frontier provinces: they lie exposed to the attacks of the enemy, most of them by land as well as sea."[10]

Colonial officials and colonists alike held similar views on coastal frontiers, especially as their collective concern focused on the growing power of their European enemies. In 1734, for instance, Massachusetts governor Jonathan Belcher described Boston as the colony's "principal maritime frontier" and asked for additional aid from the legislature to beef up its fortifications. In the 1740s, as the rivalries between the French and British heated up, Massachusetts' House of Representatives, fearing a seaborne as well as a landed assault, began "putting the frontiers both by sea and land . . . into a more proper position of defense." This fear continued throughout the 1740s and 1750s, as legislators continued to provide for ports and inland towns on "eastern and western frontiers." A conception of seaports as frontiers was not confined to New England. In 1740, Georgia officials worried about their "Spanish frontier," meaning Florida, and hoped to establish a naval fleet to protect shallow waters because of their "so large and extended a frontier towards the sea." Such language lingered into the early national period, with James Madison warning in *Federalist 41* that those on "Atlantic frontiers" felt a false sense of security and should embrace a new federal government because of the unprecedented naval protection it offered. Figuring out against whom frontiers faced can thus help historians reconstruct the geopolitical priorities of historical actors. It shows who people considered their primary enemy or enemies at any given moment in time. It can also reveal where disagreements occurred among the various parties over the location of frontiers and against whom they formed, creating political crises like the one that riled the British Empire in the 1760s and 1770s.[11]

Examining the usage of *frontier* in early America also allows us to reconstruct the way colonists imagined the specific spatial politics of their colony and its place in the world. What becomes apparent when tracking references to frontiers is that colonists had a much more global awareness of frontiers before the American Revolution, and their awareness of distant frontiers that existed alongside their local ones helped connect them to their empire through a shared investment in what occurred in such areas. As Figure 19 indicates, colonial newspapers reported on frontiers in Europe just as much as they did the colonies. Colonists read about frontiers in Russia, Turkey, or Europe because they knew events on such tenuous zones in Europe and elsewhere might have repercussions in North America. The presence and fate of frontiers in North America, in other words, were intertwined with Great Britain's interest in foreign frontiers in Europe and elsewhere. Such regular reporting represented a colonist's sense of belonging to the British Empire by connecting them to the imperial machinations that affected the rest of the globe.[12]

Notably, after American independence, reporting on European frontiers diminished as Americans focused more on their new and independent national concerns (Figure 20). This shift continued after the end of war in 1783, signaling Americans' new and general perception that, while still tied to Europe, their own diplomatic affairs were untangled from the intricacies of European alliances that had tied colonial America to foreign events. A frontier in Portugal mattered less in 1790 than it had in 1760 when Portugal was one of the few countries to ally with Great Britain during the Seven Years' War. Tracing what frontiers mattered to Americans over time thus helps trace their own sense of place in the wider geopolitical world.

Additionally, looking at the way colonists described their own colonial frontiers provides a window on their understanding of their colony's geographic growth at given points in time. Indeed, the presence of frontiers forced officials to better define their colony's jurisdictional bounds. In 1676, for instance, as Massachusetts entered into a protracted war with Metacom (also known as King Philip), the General Assembly passed a law titled "For the Preservation of the Frontier Towns" that listed the specific towns that they considered frontiers, moving from Medfield in the southern portion of the colony and ending with Exeter to the north (Figure 21). When these designated locations are mapped, they show the limits of the colony's reach. It is important to note, however, that officials did not speak of a frontier line or of a border, both of which imply greater permanence. Nonetheless, in the midst of war, it was incumbent upon them to clearly define where they believed the polity's reach ended by distinguishing "frontier towns" as

Figure 19. Map showing the general location of newspaper reports on
frontiers in colonial newspapers during the War of Austrian Succession (1740–1748).
Source: *America's Historical Newspapers Online* (published by Readex). For
additional data, see mappingfrontiers.com and patrickspero.com.

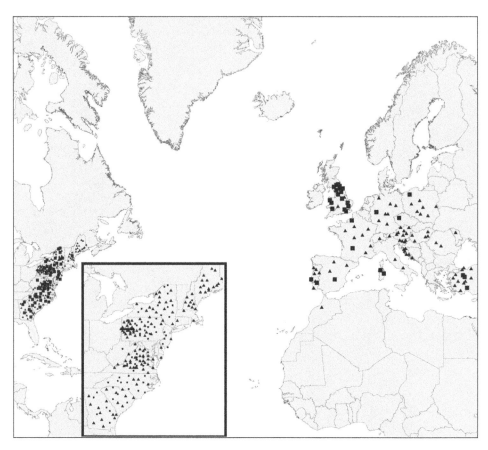

Figure 20. Map showing the use of the word *frontier* in early American
newspapers from 1770 to 1779. Note the squares in Europe before the opening of
the American Revolution and the dramatic shift to North America after war began,
indicated by triangles. For additional data, see mappingfrontiers.com and
patrickspero.com.

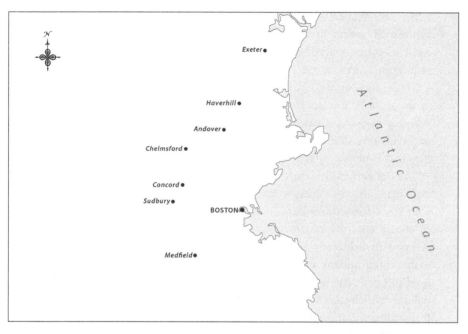

Figure 21. Frontier towns in Massachusetts, 1676. Source: *Several laws & orders made at the General Court, held at Boston for election the 3d. of May 1676* (Cambridge, MA, 1676). For additional data, see mappingfrontiers.com and patrickspero.com.

the furthest areas still in their jurisdiction. When these designations are mapped, as is done in Figure 21 and in the preceding chapters on the Seven Years' War in Pennsylvania, historians can use frontiers to better under-stand the way colonists and governing officials imagined their polity at any given moment.[13]

Other data from this war reveals contemporary descriptions of the colo-ny's geography that sound odd to our modern ears but make sense when *frontier* is placed within its historical context and meaning. As the conflict escalated, Massachusetts continued to pass laws to regulate these frontier towns. Laws required residents of the "frontier towns" to form militias; barred men from leaving such villages during wartime; and required neigh-boring communities, referred to in law as "inland towns," to offer safe houses for women and children. Such a use of *inland* to denote safe zones further east rather than west was not unusual. There are several instances throughout the colonial period in which *inland* or *interior* was used to refer to colonial settlements that sat between the western frontiers and the colonial capital. While today we might think of these terms denoting areas far from the coast, colonists conceptualized such areas in relation to frontiers. In the eighteenth-century imagination, areas called *interior* were safe zones that often bordered a frontier zone or possibly two, with one frontier on the seacoast and another to the west. Petitioners from Pennsylvania writing in the wake of Pontiac's War, for instance, accused Pennsylvania's safe "interior counties" of having no "sympathy with the frontier counties," a clear delineation between frontiers and "interior" spaces.[14]

As the early Massachusetts example suggests, from very early on, officials managing North American colonies needed to craft policies to deal with areas deemed frontiers. In general, most colonies took two approaches to secure colonial control over a potentially vulnerable region of their claimed jurisdiction. First, colonial governments provided security by maintaining militias and forts in frontier areas, and, second, they encouraged colonial settlement as a way to strengthen such zones against a potential enemy. Virginia's legislature, for instance, passed laws for the colony's frontiers since at least 1632, all with an eye toward what one law called the "continuall" threat of "invasions" and "incursions" that the legislature believed Indians posed to the colony. In 1664, Virginia's House of Burgesses passed a law to address the "weaknes of ffronteer plantations" within the colony. The legislators believed that the past weakness "animated the Indians to commit severall horrid murthers" on colonists, so they passed a law to bolster their defenses and continued to pass such laws throughout the colonial period.[15]

Similar concerns over frontiers, which were always cast as areas vulnerable to invasion, figured into the early policies of most other English colonies in North America. The proprietors of Carolina sent a message to their settlers in 1676 instructing them to build "a frontier settlement which if itt be made stronge and as itt ought will be a Security to you from the incurtions of the Indians." By creating and populating these new frontier settlements, the colony would strengthen through sheer numbers the barrier against the "incurtions" from Indians. In 1704, New York governor Lord Cornbury reported that he had just "visit[ed] the northern frontiers" of the colony and "found them in a most miserable condition, in no manner capable of making any manner of defence in case they should be attacked by the French of Canada." He allocated funds to strengthen forts in the area and reached out to neighboring colonies for additional aid because he claimed that New York's northern frontiers, the most likely site of a French invasion (rather than an Indian one, as was the case to the south and often in New England), provided security to the other British colonies.[16]

There was, then, a general consensus among early Americans about what frontiers meant for the governed and governing. Colonists and their governors almost always recognized frontier defense as a fundamental duty that governments provided to their people, something Franklin distilled in his 1760s essay but is also present throughout the sources. In 1720, New York's Governor William Burnett expressed this sentiment when he asked his legislature to provide more funds for the colony's frontiers. "Self-preservation," Burnett noted, is "that first principle of nature." New York's frontiers, he worried, "lie[d] open to the first attempts of the French." To leave these frontiers "open" would be to abrogate the most fundamental responsibility—"that first principle of nature"—governments owed their members: "self-preservation." In short, a successful frontier policy was supposed to make "frontier people" feel secure by providing them with the means for their defense. If the government ignored the pleas of its members on frontiers or failed to protect against an attack, then anxiety could turn into anger so strong that it would break the bonds between the governed and the governing. Contra Frederick Jackson Turner's formulation in which closed frontiers posed a threat to America's stability, in the eighteenth century, the government's first duty was to close the frontiers because the open frontiers Burnett saw (meaning poorly defended sites exposed to likely attack) posed the gravest danger to the polity.[17]

Such sentiments were held in Whitehall too, as imperial administrators grappled with their global empire. Frontiers as specific spaces that demanded the government's attention only became more pressing as the British footprint on North America grew larger over the course of the eighteenth century. Tracing the use of the word by officials and colonists helps capture this shifting and more expansive perspective, especially as distant imperial officials began to craft a grand strategy for the British Empire. When Spanish and French claims to North America began to overlap with British ones in the mid-1700s, colonists and their imperial administrators increasingly grappled with larger frontier zones, leading to attempts at intercolonial cooperation, consolidation, and empire building. The security of Great Britain's southern frontiers, for instance, spurred the creation of Georgia in 1732. In the proclamation announcing the new colony, George II declared that he created this new colony for defensive reasons, out of his "princely regard to the great dangers of the southern frontiers." The king went on to describe how the colony's settlement patterns could protect the empire as a whole from invasion: "As towns are established . . . along the rivers Savanah and Almatabas, they will make such a barrier as will render the southern frontier of the British Colonies on the continent of America, safe from Indian and other Enemies." From colonists to Whitehall, then, the presence and location of frontiers were important policy questions throughout the eighteenth century, and the answers drove actions that shaped events.[18]

There is one final thing to note about the significance of *frontier* in the eighteenth century. It was largely—almost exclusively—a word used by colonists. This finding poses a problem for historians who have paid greater attention to Native American histories in recent years. Some of the most innovative works on early American history have integrated Native peoples seamlessly into their studies to show that Native Americans as individuals and groups were not only present but powerfully affected the course of history. Most recently, historians have begun to explore the everyday life of colonists and Indians living side by side, sometimes constructing a picture of peaceful cohabitation that was destroyed by the interference of forceful colonial and imperial governments that meddled with their daily lives. There is much to be said about all of this work. But for all that historians have added, these perspectives have also shifted the focus away from politics. *Frontier* provides a crucial perspective that adds to our understanding of revolutionary-era America and Indian-white relations during this period.

By placing *frontier* within its historical context, we can see how colonists who believed they inhabited a frontier could affect the politics of their colony and of Indian-white relations more generally. While colonists and Indians interacted throughout this period, once colonists believed they lived upon a frontier against Indians, these daily peaceful interactions could turn violent in a heartbeat. To put it another way, *frontier* was a word used almost exclusively by colonists, and over time it was used by people like the Paxton Boys to denote an area of separation rather than cohabitation with Native Americans. Over the course of the eighteenth century, many colonists came to believe that they formed a frontier—meaning a zone of potential attack—against an Indian enemy. These self-described frontier people manipulated their local political institutions to affect colonial and imperial policies toward Native Americans. Frontier people thus played a central role in shaping the

state to which they belonged. This book is a political narrative of these frontier people and the state they helped build and rebuild in the eighteenth
century. It is a story in which Native Americans' place—quite literally, since
colonists used *frontier* to place Indians outside the state—is essential, even if
colonists assume a larger role in the narrative itself.

   The point of all of these data is not just to call attention to the presence
of frontiers in the historical record or to undertake a mere etymological
exercise. Rather it shows that officials at all levels of government in colonial
America and colonists themselves imagined specific places as frontiers, that
they shared a widely held assumption about what defined such areas, and
that their placement and strategizing about such sites drove government
policies and spurred reforms. While *frontier* remained a relatively stable
term throughout the eighteenth century, its meaning in that period
required government policy that eventually led to a profound change in its
conception. When the new governments created in the wake of the Revolution responded to the demands of frontier people through policies that
encouraged expansion and military aggression, the very idea of *frontier*
changed alongside the success of the new national policy. Studying the
usage and political meaning of *frontier* thus shows how ideas about this
space affected historical events. *Frontier*, in other words, was significant to
historical actors, and taking this significance seriously can help explain the
historical developments they gave shape to.

   Historians engaged in the extensive debate about "the frontier," however, have largely overlooked this point. Instead, they have made themselves
a part of this process of definition and redefinition that has marked *frontier*'s own, very peculiar history. Frederick Jackson Turner may have begun
this trend in the historiography. He inherited the dubious success of the
word's transformation from one of fear, war, or vulnerability in the eighteenth century to one of of hope, economic growth, opportunity, and independence in the late-nineteenth century. The "frontier" as understood by
Turner and his contemporaries in 1893 was thus a concept shaped by historical processes that had redefined the significance of the term. Debunkers
focused their energy on challenging Turner's thesis without realizing that
for many people in early America, the very idea of a frontier as a safety
valve that provided opportunity was anathema to those who lived on frontiers. Instead, frontiers in the eighteenth century were areas of warfare and

contraction from which people fled out of fear. Revisionist historians, meanwhile, who criticized Turner and sought to redefine *frontier* actually followed Turner's lead by treating the term as a purely analytical category that they could redefine (yet again) to reflect current sensibilities, while others believed it should be banished from the early American landscape altogether, relegated to historiographical obscurity and analytical insignificance. They failed to realize that they were following in Turner's own methodological footsteps, allowing *frontier* an elasticity that confused rather than clarified the past.

This book suggests that the better way for historians to understand the true significance of America's many frontiers is to appreciate its importance to the people who used the word. Only then can we recover the way early Americans experienced and explained the world in which they lived.

To see more of the data compiled for this project, including animated GIS maps that buttress the arguments made here, please visit mappingfrontiers .com. Visitors can also download the datasets created, add to them, or manipulate the data to ask their own questions.

NOTES

Introduction

1. Charles Mason, Diary, Jan. 10 and Jan. 17, 1765, MG614, Papers Regarding the Paxton Boys and the Conestoga Massacre, 1764–1766, 1795, LancasterHistory.org, Lancaster, PA.

2. Ibid. On its size, see William Pencak, *Historical Dictionary of Colonial America* (Lanham, MD, 2011), 125, and Thomas Doerflinger, *A Vigorous Spirit of Enterprise: Merchants and Economic Development in Revolutionary Philadelphia* (Chapel Hill, NC, 2001), 76.

3. Mason, Diary, LancasterHistory.org, Lancaster, PA.

4. The Connecticut clash has fascinated scholars, in part because of the extensive records on it, its longevity, the scale of violence, and the audaciousness of Connecticut to claim a noncontiguous region as part of its colony. The other conflicts have received less attention. There is no book and only a smattering of articles on Cresap's War. Works on Dunmore's War are often placed within studies on the Ohio Valley that are not fully integrated into Pennsylvania's history. For work on Cresap's War, see Paul Doutrich, "Cresap's War: Expansion and Conflict in the Susquehanna Valley," *Pennsylvania History* 53 (1986): 89–104; and Charles Dutrizac, "Local Identity and Authority in a Disputed Hinterland: The Pennsylvania-Maryland Border in the 1730s," *Pennsylvania Magazine of History and Biography* 151 (1991): 35–63 [hereafter *PMHB*]. In the same issue of the *PMHB*, Thomas Slaughter examines the border dispute in light of other crowd actions, in "Crowds in Eighteenth-Century America: Reflections and New Directions," 3–34, *PMHB*, 151, (1991). Alan Tully, *William Penn's Legacy: Politics and Social Structure in Provincial Pennsylvania, 1726–1755* (Baltimore, 1977) also discusses the land dispute with Baltimore. For the most recent work on the Pennamite Wars, see Paul Moyer, *Wild Yankees: The Struggle for Independence along Pennsylvania's Revolutionary Frontier* (Ithaca, NY, 2007); for Dunmore's clash with Pennsylvanians, see Albert Volwiller, *George Croghan and the Westward Movement, 1741–1782* (Cleveland, 1926); Patrick Griffin, *American Leviathan: Empire, Nation, and Revolutionary Frontier* (New York, 2008), 97–124; and Richard White, *The Middle Ground: Indians, Empires, and Republics in the Great Lakes Region, 1650–1815* (New York, 1991) 356–65. Daniel P. Barr, "Contested Ground: Competition and Conflict Along the Upper Ohio Frontier, 1744–1784" (PhD diss., Kent State University, 2001), 229–89, offers the most exhaustive analysis of the event. See also Douglas MacGregor's "John Connolly: An American Loyalist" (MA thesis, Indiana University of Pennsylvania, 2000) and "Double Dishonor: Loyalists on the Middle Frontier," in *Pennsylvania's Revolution*, ed. William Pencak (University Park, PA, 2010), 144–67. For another book that examines border creation in the region, see Phillip Schwartz, *Jarring Interests: New York's Boundary Makers, 1664–1776* (Albany, NY, 1979).

5. N. Bailey, *The New Universal Etymological English Dictionary: . . . To which Is Added, a Dictionary of Cant Words* (London, 1776), 229.

6. This definition was used in most previous editions of this dictionary, appearing as early as 1730. See Fulmer Mood, "Notes on the History of the Word Frontier," *Agricultural History* (April 1948): 78–82 also notes the introduction in 1730 of the definition I use here. "Frontier town" can be found in *Encyclopaedia Britannica* (1823) and other editions. The entry also points out that frontiers were formerly called *marches*, although I have found few references to that word in the eighteenth century.

Samuel Johnson's dictionary also included *frontier* as an entry. It was much shorter and less specific than the more popular Bailey *Dictionary*. Johnson identified a frontier as "marches." Although scholars tend to privilege Johnson's definition, American usage of the term comports more with Bailey's definition. Moreover, Bailey's dictionary was far more widely read than Johnson's in the eighteenth century, and Bailey's definition seems to have guided other dictionary makers. See, for instance, "Frontier," in *A Complete Dictionary of Arts and Sciences* (London, 1765). Notably, Noah Webster's 1806 definition of *frontier* incorporates Bailey's eighteenth-century British Atlantic definition almost completely into the American definition, while also adopting some of Samuel Johnson's less specific concept of marches. The definition from the 1828 edition reads, "The marches; the border, confine, or extreme part of a country, bordering on another country; that is, the part furthest advanced, or the part that fronts an enemy, or which an invading enemy meets in front, or which fronts another country." Webster's definition remained unchanged throughout the first part of the nineteenth century and resembled Bailey's definition more than it did Johnson's.

For the quote on frontier provinces, see "From a Book Intitled, the Annals of Europe for the Year, 1739," *Boston Evening-Post*, Oct. 14, 1754. I have examples of numerous other people using the term similarly. For more, please consult my website "Mapping Early American Frontiers" at www.mappingfrontiers.com and patrickspero.com.

For dictionary discussions of the etymology of the word, see "frontier," Dictionary.com. *Online Etymology Dictionary*, Douglas Harper, historian, http://dictionary.reference.com/browse/frontier.

7. Walter Raleigh, *The Cabinet-Council Containing the Cheif [sic] Arts of Empire and Mysteries of State* (London, 1658).

8. Benjamin Franklin, *Great Britain Considered* (Philadelphia, 1760), 21.

9. For Penn, see "Speech of the Governor," *Votes of Assembly, Pennsylvania Archives* (hereafter *PA Archives*), Eighth Series, 1: 282–83. The full quote reads, "I must recommend to your serious thoughts and care, the King's letter to me for assistance of New-York with Three Hundred and Fifty Pounds sterling, as a frontier government, and therefore exposed to a much greater expence in proportion to the other colonies."

10. All citations refer to J. Hector St. John de Crevecoeur, *Letters from an American Farmer*, ed. Albert Stone (New York, 1986), 200–201.

11. Crevecoeur, *Letters*, 200–203.

12. Crevecoeur, *Letters*, 202–3.

13. For representative works on the political history of colonial and revolutionary Pennsylvania, see James Hutson, *Pennsylvania Politics, 1746–1770: The Movement for Royal Government and Its Consequences* (Princeton, NJ, 1972); Alan Tully, *Forming American Politics: Ideals, Interests, and Institutions in Colonial New York and Pennsylvania* (New York, 1994); *William*

Penn's Legacy: Politics and Social Structure in Provincial Pennsylvania, 1726–1755 (Baltimore, 1977); Benjamin Newcomb, *Political Partisanship in the Middle Colonies, 1700–1776* (Baton Rouge, LA, 1995); Gary Nash, *Quakers and Politics: Pennsylvania, 1681–1726* (Boston, 1993); *The Urban Crucible: The Northern Seaports and the Origins of the American Revolution* (Cambridge, MA, 1986); Richard Ryerson, *The Revolution Is Now Begun: The Radical Committees of Philadelphia, 1765–1776* (Boston, 1978); and Steven Rosswurm, *Arms, Country and Class: The Philadelphia Militia and the "Lower Sort" During the American Revolution* (New Brunswick, NJ, 1989). None of these books fully engage with—and many outright ignore—the politics of those who lived beyond Philadelphia.

Scholarship on the Pennsylvania frontier, especially works dealing with Native-white relations, has been growing. See John Frantz and William Pencak, *Beyond Philadelphia: The American Revolution in the Pennsylvania Hinterland* (University Park, PA, 1998); James Merrell, *Into the American Woods: Negotiators on the Pennsylvania Frontier* (New York, 2000); Gregory Knouff, *Soldiers Revolution: Pennsylvanians in Arms and the Forging of Early American Identity* (University Park, PA, 2003); Daniel Richter, *Facing East from Indian Country: A Native History of Early America* (Boston, 2001); Jane Merritt, *At the Crossroads: Indians and Empires at the Mid-Atlantic Frontier, 1700–1763* (Chapel Hill, NC, 2003); William Pencak and Daniel Richter, eds., *Friends and Enemies in Penn's Woods: Colonists, Indians and the Racial Construction of Pennsylvania* (University Park, PA, 2004); Peter Silver, *Our Savage Neighbors: How Indian War Transformed Early America* (New York, 2008); and Griffin, *American Leviathan*. William Pencak, *Pennsylvania's Revolution* (University Park, PA, 2010), has a number of essays that provide even greater insight into the Revolution on the Pennsylvania frontier. David Preston's *Texture of Contact: European and Indian Settlers on the Frontiers of Iroquoia* (Lincoln, NE, 2009) and Kevin Kenny's *Peaceable Kingdom Lost: The Paxton Boys and the Destruction of William Penn's Holy Experiment* (Oxford, 2009) are two notable recent additions. One work that does try to incorporate the frontier into politics is Terry Bouton, *Taming Democracy: "The People," the Founders, and the Troubled Ending of the American Revolution* (Oxford, 2007), but because his focus is on explaining politics in the early republic, he downplays the importance of Indians in the colonial period. Much of this work on the Pennsylvania frontier owes a debt to Francis Jennings, who helped lead the reinterpretation of colonial American history that placed the interaction between colonists and Natives at the forefront of analysis. See, for example, Jennings, *The Invasion of America: Indians, Colonialism, and the Cant of Conquest* (New York, 1976).

14. For more on the borderlands historiography, please see the Coda, "Note on Frontiers," at the end of this book.

Chapter 1. The Hidden Flaw

1. The phrase "most famous" is found in Edward Channing, *A History of the United States: A Century of Colonial History, 1660–1776* (New York, 1908), 2: 322; "radically democratic," in William Murchison, *The Cost of Liberty: The Life of John Dickinson* (Wilmington, DE, 2014); "innovative," in Alan Tully, *Forming American Politics,* 69; "religious liberty," in James Hutson, *Forgotten Features of the Founding: The Recovery of Religious Themes in the Early America Republic* (New York, 2003), 133; "most influential," in Bernard Schwartz, *The Great Rights of Mankind: A History of the American Bill of Rights* (New York, 1992), 46; and "wheel," in Benjamin Wright, "A Government from Reflection and Choice," in *The Constitution of the United States, 1787–1962,* ed. Putnam Jones (Pittsburgh, PA, 1962), 28. Wright's

quote credits Penn's first frame with the initial innovation, but he says it persisted in the final frame as well. Speech of Andrew Hamilton, *Votes of the Assembly, Pennsylvania Archives,* Eighth Series (Harrisburg, 1931), 3: 2505–8.

2. Burton Alva Kinkle, *The Life and Times of Thomas Smith, 1745–1809: A Pennsylvania Member of the Continental Congress* (Philadelphia, 1904), 79.

3. Numerous historians have noted the size of the ship. See, for instance, Joseph Illick's *William Penn: The Politician* (Ithaca, NY, 1965), 45; and David Hackett Fischer, *Albion's Seed: Four British Folkways in America* (New York, 1989), 421. There have been few recent studies of Penn's arrival. The account here is based on the *Papers of William Penn,* ed. Richard and Mary Maples Dunn (Philadelphia, 1982), 1:79–325 (hereafter *PWP*) and histories from the eighteenth and nineteenth centuries.

4. This account is based on earlier histories and a series of letters written by magistrates and Penn that provide details of his arrival and the transition of power. The best writing on Penn's passage comes from older books on Pennsylvania's founding and on William Penn himself. See Jane Budge, *William Penn* (London, 1885) , 30–33; Thomas Clarkson, *Memoirs of the Private and Public Life of William Penn* (Dover, NH, 1827), 125–28; and esp. Albert Bolles, *Pennsylvania: Province and State—A History from 1609 to 1790* (New York, 1890), 1: 120–22. For the primary sources that form the basis of this narrative, see Jean Soderlund, ed., *William Penn and the Founding of Pennsylvania: A Documentary History* (Philadelphia, 1983), 178; and "John Moll's Account of the Surrender of the Three Lower Counties to William Penn," in *PWP,* 2: 304–10, for a firsthand account.

5. Before Penn left England, one of his counselors gave him explicit instructions on how to perform this ritual. John Darnall to William Penn, Sept. 14, 1682, *PWP,* 2: 300–301.

6. For biographies of Penn, see Mary Maples Dunn, *William Penn: Politics and Dissent* (Princeton, 1967), Edwin Bronner, *William Penn's Holy Experiment, The Founding of Pennsylvania, 1681–1701* (New York, 1962) and Joseph Illick's *William Penn, the Politician: His Relations with the English Government* (Ithaca, 1965). For Pennsylvania's grant within this English world, see Gary Nash, "The Framing of Government in Pennsylvania: Ideas in Contact with Reality," *William and Mary Quarterly* 23, no. 2 (1966) and especially Dunn, *William Penn.* Dunn describes Charles' grant as "anachronistic and paradoxical,"81. I used to subscribe to this view, but I now see the granting of a proprietary colony as part of Charles II larger aim to strengthen the English monarchy by creating loyal colonial states that resemble his ideal political world, one based on hierarchy and loyalty to a king, rather than the increasingly liberalizing politics that seemed to surround him in England. On the naming of Pennsylvania, see Augustus Buell, *William Penn the Founder of Two Commonwealths* (New York, 1904), 111.

7. Few historians have written about the use of this old ritual in the New World. For descriptions of the livery of seisin, see Samuel Thorne, *Essays in English Legal History* (London, 1985), chap. 4, and esp. the discussion of the ritual on pp. 42–43. One Pennsylvania historian from the late nineteenth century noted that Pennsylvanians continued to christen new homes with these gifts, a quaint tradition that seems to be dead today. See Rupert Holland, *William Penn* (New York, 1915), 68–69. For an account of a similar ritual in New Jersey, see Brendan McConville, *These Daring Disturbers of the Public Peace: The Struggle for Property and Power in Early New Jersey* (Philadelphia, 2003), 120–21.

8. Charter of Privileges, Avalon Project, Yale Law School, http://www.avalon.yale.edu; Mark Stein, *How the States Got Their Shapes* (New York, 2008), 236–42; Bolles, *Pennsylvania,*

1: 74–75, 110–13. On acreage, see Lorett Treese, *The Storm Gathering: The Penn Family and the American Revolution* (University Park, PA, 1992), 189 and Soderlund, *William Penn and the Founding of Pennsylvania*, 202, fn. 4.

9. Editor's note, *PWP*, 2:127-28, William Penn to the Emperor of Canada, June 21, 1682, *PWP*, 2:261, Bronner, *William Penn*, 60; Soderlund, ed., *William Penn and the Founding of Pennsylvania*, 4 and 71–72.

10. The text of Frame of 1682 can be found at: http://avalon.law.yale.edu/17th_century/pa04.asp.

11. "Conditions or Concessions to the First Purchasers," July 11, 1681, *PWP*, 2: 98–101

12. Penn's peaceful intentions are well established. For examples, see Dunn and Dunn, editors' note, *PWP*, 2: 128; and quotation is from "To the Emperor of Canada," 261. See also Dunn and Dunn, "The Founding," in *Philadelphia: A 300-Year History*, ed. Russell Weigley (Philadelphia, 1982), 5–6. There has been some discussion of when and how Penn came up with this mode of land acquisition. In a letter to the Privy Council, he recounted a conversation he had with Henry Compton, the bishop of London, who advised him to purchase all land directly from Indians. There is also a strong possibility that Penn was influenced by his own experience in New Jersey, where land titles were a mess in large part because various individuals had competing land claims. For New Jersey, see McConville, *Daring Disturbers*, esp. 11–27.

13. Penn most notably acknowledged past bloodshed in his letter "To the Kings of the Indians," *PWP*, 2:127–29.

14. Ibid.

15. For a firsthand account of the ongoing dispute, see *The Breviate in the Boundary Dispute Between Pennsylvania and Maryland*, *PA Archives*, Second Series, (Harrisburg, 1891) Volume 16, and the original *In Chancery. Breviate: John Penn, Thomas Penn, and Richard Penn, Esqrs; plaintiffs. Charles Calvert Esq: Lord Baltimore in the Kingdom of Ireland, defendant* (London, [1742?]).

16. For detailed analyses of the legal negotiations, see Walter Scaife, "The Boundary Dispute Between Maryland and Pennsylvania," *Pennsylvania Magazine of History and Biography* 9, no. 3 (1885): 241–71; William Robert Shepherd, *History of Proprietary Government in Pennsylvania* (New York, 1896), 117–46; Charles Tansill, *The Pennsylvania–Maryland Boundary Controversy* (Washington, DC, 1915); Sydney George Fisher, *The Making of Pennsylvania: An Analysis of the Elements of the Population and Formative Influences That Created One of the Greatest of the American States* (Philadelphia, 1896), 318–46; Nicholas Wainwright, "The Missing Evidence: Penn v. Baltimore," *Pennsylvania Magazine of History and Biography* 80, no. 2 (1959): 227–35, and "Tale of a Runaway Cape: The Penn Baltimore Agreement of 1732," *Pennsylvania Magazine of History and Biography* 87, no. 3 (1963): 251–69; and Tully, *William Penn's Legacy*, 3–17. See also Dunn and Dunn, eds., *PWP*, 2: 379–438, 494–500.

17. "Dead lump" in Soderlund, ed., *William Penn and the Founding of Pennsylvania*, 153; Charter of Maryland, 1632, Avalon Project, Yale Law School, http://avalon.law.yale.edu/17th_century/ma01.asp; Charter for the Province of Pennsylvania, 1681, Avalon Project, Yale Law School, http://avalon.law.yale.edu/17th_century/pa01.asp; Fisher, *Making of Pennsylvania*, 330.

18. William Bronner, *William Penn's "Holy Experiment": The Founding of Pennsylvania, 1681–1701* (New York, 1962), 66; "A Narrative of the Whole Proceeding Betwixt Captain William Markham Deputy Governor Under William Pen, Esq., as also Betwixt the Lord Baltemore, and the Said Pen," *Archives of Maryland: Proceedings of the Council of Maryland, 1667–1687/8* (Baltimore, 1887), 5: 380.

19. *The Breviate in the Boundary Dispute Between Pennsylvania and Maryland*, in *PA Archives*, Second Series, 16, quotation from 398.

20. Dunn and Dunn, eds., *PWP*, 2: 468, 472; and "Purchase of the Mouth of the Susquehanna River," Oct. 18, 1683, *PWP*, 2: 492. Amy Schutt has done the most exhaustive recent analysis of Machaloha and concludes he was likely a Delaware. Schutt, *Peoples of the River Valley: The Odyssey of the Delaware* (Philadelphia, 2007), 66, 209 fn. 11.

21. For discussions of the 1701 treaty, see Kenny, *Peaceable Kingdom Lost*, 11–15.

22. William Penn to John Alloway, Nov. 29, 1683, *PWP*, 2: 502–506; William Penn to the Marquis of Halifax, 12 mo. 9, 1683, *Memoirs of the Historical Society* (Philadelphia, 1826), 1: 421; Bolles, *Pennsylvania*, 136, 143–44.

23. Nicholas Wainwright provides the best overview of the origins of this boundary dispute in two articles: "The Missing Evidence: Penn v. Baltimore," *Pennsylvania Magazine of History and Biography* 80, no. 2 (1959): 227–35; and "Tale of a Runaway Cape: The Penn Baltimore Agreement of 1732," *Pennsylvania Magazine of History and Biography* 87, no. 3 (1963): 251–69.

24. Philip Klein and Ari Hoogenboom, *A History of Pennsylvania* (University Park, PA, 1980), 29.

25. For detailed overviews on Fletcher's short but controversial tenure, see Robert Davidson, *War Comes to Quaker Pennsylvania, 1682–1756* (Harrisburg, PA, 1957), 10–14; Tully, *Forming American Politics*, 34; and Nash, *Quakers and Politics*, 201–205. The Crown's quotation is from Robert Proud, *A History of Pennsylvania in North America* (Philadelphia, 1797), 34–35, and *Proceedings of the Council of Maryland: 1687/8–1693* (Baltimore, 1890), 381.

26. "A Council Held at Philadelphia," June 7, 1694, *Minutes of the Provincial Council*, (Philadelphia, 1852) (hereafter *PCM*), 1: 468; and quotation from Davidson, *War Comes to Quaker Pennsylvania*, 13. For original, see *Calendar of State Papers: Colonial Series, American and West Indies, January, 1693–14 May, 1696* (London, 1908), 14: 115. It should be noted that the Assembly did give Fletcher one grant of money for "the Governor's use," a way to avoid a direct contribution to war. It was given because Fletcher agreed to recognize the Assembly's previous laws in exchange for money. The Assembly did not provide additional funds after that point. The Assembly did reject a militia law, much to Fletcher's consternation, as noted in the above letter to the Board. Bolles, *History of Pennsylvania*, 157–58, and Davidson, *War Comes to Quaker Pennsylvania*, 13–15.

27. Tully, *Forming American Politics*, 32–34; Nash, *Quakers and Politics*, 183–87, 201–205. Population figures are difficult to ascertain with certainty, but by 1700, Richard and Mary Dunn estimate Philadelphia had about two thousand inhabitants, making it one of the three largest settlements in English America. Dunn and Dunn, "Founding," in *Philadelphia*, 10–11, 32. Edwin Bronner puts the number slightly higher at five thousand, in *William Penn's "Holy Experiment,"* 223, 289 fn. 1; Nash, "Framing of Government," 209.

28. Kenny, *Peaceable Kingdom Lost*, 11–14.

29. Ibid. and "Articles of Agreement Between the Susquehannah Kings and William Penn," *Historical Magazine* (New York, 1862), 6: 65. See also Francis Jennings, *The Ambiguous Iroquois Empire: The Covenant Chain Confederation of Indian Tribes with English Colonies from Its Beginnings to the Lancaster Treaty of 1744* (New York, 1984), 236–39. The treaty is also printed as copy in *PCM*, 3: 338–41.

30. William Penn to ?, July 1681, in Shepherd, *History of Proprietary Government in Pennsylvania*, 175. Tully, *Forming American Politics*, 30–38, 68–69; Nash, *Quakers and Politics*, 181, 232; Dunn and Dunn, "The Founding," in *Philadelphia*, 27–32; Richard Beeman, *The Varieties of Political Experience in Colonial America* (Philadelphia, 2004), 204–6.

31. Tully, *Forming American Politics*, 34–36; and esp. Nash, *Quakers and Politics*, 49, 201–205. For Penn toying with the idea of selling the colony, see Nash, "Framing Government," 209. For the "governmentish" quote, see Nash, "Framing of Government" and David Brion Davis and Steven Mints, *The Boisterous Sea of Liberty: A Documentary History of America from Discovery through the Civil War* (New York, 1999), 100.

32. Tully, *Forming American Politics*, 68–69; Nash, *Quakers and Politics*, 232, and "Framing of Government," 209; Bronner, *William Penn's "Holy Experiment*," 206–10.

33. Tully, *Forming American Politics*, 68–85, esp. 69–71; and Nash, *Quakers and Politics*, 27–48, 227–29.

34. Text of the document can be found at Charter of Privileges for the Province of Pennsylvania, 1701, http://www.amphilsoc.org/exhibits/treasures/charter.htm and http://avalon.law.yale.edu/18th_century/pa07.asp.

35. The best account of the proprietary powers is Shepherd, *History of Proprietary Government in Pennsylvania*. For information on the salary being paid by revenue in 1765, see 77. The technical title of the new government was a Charter of Privileges, but for the purposes of maintaining symmetry with the titles of earlier constitutions, I maintain the title Frame of Government here.

36. Wayne Bockelman, "Local Government in Colonial Pennsylvania," in *Town and County: Essays on the Structure of Local Government in the American Colonies*, ed. Bruce C. Daniel (Middletown, CT, 1978), 216–37, quotations on 222. Alan Tully makes the point about the power of county governments in *William Penn's Legacy*.

37. Bockelman, "Local Government in Colonial Pennsylvania." See also George Franz, "Paxton: A Study of Community Structure and Mobility in the Colonial Pennsylvania Backcountry" (Ph.D. diss., Rutgers University, New Brunswick, NJ, 1974), 39–44.

38. Franz, "Paxton: A Study of Community Structure and Mobility," 39; Bockelman, "Local Government in Colonial Pennsylvania," especially 220–22, 224, 226, 229–30, and Shippen quote on 232–33.

39. For transmitters and translators, see Bockelman, "Local Governments in Colonial Pennsylvania," 233.

40. Tully notes the constitution's longevity and innovation in *Forming American Politics*, 69. He represents the consensus view of historians. Edwin Bronner, however, makes the point about the negative aspects of the charter in *William Penn's "Holy Experiment*," 247–49. He does not point out, as I do here, that the document contained no means for political expansion.

41. For Penn's reservations, see Nash, *Quakers and Politics*, 232; Tully, *Forming American Politics*, 68–69; Nash, "Framing of Government."

42. The Governor's Speech to the Assembly, *PCM*, 1: 31; and *Votes of the Assembly*, 1: 283. In an otherwise fine study, *War Comes to Quaker Pennsylvania*, Davidson suggests that the Assembly provided the funds. Every other source I have read has said the opposite, including *Votes of the Assembly*, 1: 289–90, which he cites. Indeed, it appears the Assembly unanimously

voted against considering the request to provide funds. See also the *PWP* 3:448 for a discussion of the Assembly's history of funding wartime efforts in this period.

Chapter 2. Growth Arrives

1. Tully, *William Penn's Legacy*, 3–5.

2. The preeminent expert on German migration is Marianne Wokeck. See her article "Promoters and Passengers," in *World of William Penn*, ed. Richard and Mary Maples Dunn (Philadelphia, 1986), 259–78; and "The Flow and Composition of German Migration to Pennsylvania, 1727–1775," *Pennsylvania Magazine of History and Biography* 105, no. 3 (1981): 249–78. Her book, *Trade in Strangers: The Beginnings of Mass Migration to North America* (University Park, PA, 1999), expands on these two essays and adds a chapter on Irish immigration. Farley Grubb has also explored German immigration. Much of his work has emphasized the revolutionary era, but his article "German Immigration to Pennsylvania, 1709–1810," *Journal of Interdisciplinary History* 20, no. 3 (1990): 417–36, is particularly pertinent. In this essay he analyzes the social makeup of migrants, showing that most Germans traveled as families. A. G. Roeber has written exhaustively on the German settlers with a focus on their cultural beliefs and values. See esp. A. G. Roeber, *Palatines, Liberty, and Property: German Lutherans in Colonial British America* (Baltimore, 1993). Aaron Fogleman's *Hopeful Journeys: German Immigration, Settlement, and Political Culture in Colonial America, 1717–1775* (Philadelphia, 1996) adds an important analysis on life in Germany. The Irish experience is best captured by Patrick Griffin, *The People with No Name: Ireland's Ulster Scots, America's Scots Irish, and the Creation of a British Atlantic World, 1689–1764* (Princeton, NJ, 2001); see p. 92 for some migration figures and p. 200 on the historiographic debate on the total size of the 1729 migration. Other important works on the Scots-Irish are R. J. Dickson, *Ulster Emigration to Colonial America, 1718–1775* (London, 1966); James Leyburn, *The Scotch-Irish: A Social History* (Chapel Hill, NC, 1962); and the classic work, Henry Ford, *The Scotch-Irish in America* (Princeton, NJ, 1915). For population statistics, see Randall Miller and William Pencak, *Pennsylvania: A History of the Commonwealth* (University Park, PA, 2002), 61. For the estimated German population, see Joseph Illick, *Colonial Pennsylvania: A History* (New York, 1976), 123; and Shepherd, *History of Proprietary Government in Pennsylvania*, 50. Alan Tully makes a similar estimate in *William Penn's Legacy*, 5.

3. This final statistic—that half the population was non-Quaker or non-English—comes from compiling data from the above-cited studies. Here is my rationale. In the decade between 1710 and 1720, the total population of the colony increased from 24,000 to 31,000, a growth of approximately 30 percent. In the decade following (1720 to 1730), that number grew from 31,000 to 52,000, or a surge of 70 percent. Of that 52,000, an estimated 15,000 to 20,000 were German and at least 6,000 were Irish, meaning a high estimate of 26,000 is viable. Quotation from *PCM,* 3: 299.

4. The story of Henry Hawkins is derived from Griffin, *A People with No Name*, 111–12; James Merrell, "Reading Andrew Montour," in *Through a Glass Darkly: Reflections on Personal Identity in Early America* (Chapel Hill, NC, 1997), 21–22; and Jack Marietta and G. S. Rowe, *Troubled Experiment: Crime and Justice in Pennsylvania, 1682–1800* (Philadelphia, 2006), 148. The deposition of Hawkins that provides the narrative can be found in James B. Whisker, *Pennsylvania Workers in Brass, Copper and Tin: 1681–1900* (Lewiston, NY, 1993), 23–24.

5. Deposition in Whisker, *Pennsylvania Workers*, 23–24.

6. Ibid. Note, in the deposition, Davenport's first name is Jonas. Later, in other sources, it will be Jonah. I have chosen to reflect the original use in each case, meaning that later in the book, I refer to Jonah Davenport, who I believe is the same person as the Jonas Davenport who Hawkins knew.

7. Deposition in Whisker, *Pennsylvania Workers*, 23–24.

8. Ibid.

9. On Davenport and James Logan, see Griffin, *A People with No Name*, 112.

10. For a brief but incisive discussion on the cultural heritage of this group, see Griffin, *A People with No Name*, 1–9. For details on the establishment of these settlements, see Tully, *William Penn's Legacy*, 5–7, 13. Tully points out that while the Land Office continued to work, settlers were hesitant to pay quitrents given the uncertainty that existed within the Penn family. Illick, *Colonial Pennsylvania*, 166–67, and Ford, *Scotch-Irish in America*, 266–67.

11. For the German push westward, beyond Philadelphia, see Rodger Henderson, *Community Development and the Revolutionary Transition in Eighteenth-Century Lancaster County, Pennsylvania* (New York, 1989), 6–7; Illick, *Colonial Pennsylvania*, 166–67; Shepherd, *History of Proprietary Government in Pennsylvania*, 50–51; Wokeck, "Flow and Composition"; and esp. Fogleman, *Hopeful Journeys*, map 3.1, 84. For a study on one of these groups, see Stephanie Graumann Wolf, *Urban Village: Population, Community, and Family Structure in Germantown, Pennsylvania, 1683–1800* (Princeton, NJ, 1976), describing a settlement founded by Francis Daniel Pastorious, a representative for German Quakers seeking land in Pennsylvania. Patrick Gordon to the Board of Trade, Dec. 6, 1727, Penn Miscellaneous Papers (hereafter PMP), Penn and Baltimore Family Correspondence, Historical Society of Pennsylvania (hereafter HSP), Philadelphia. See James Lemon, *The Best Poor Man's Country: A Geographical Study of Early Southeastern Pennsylvania* (Baltimore, 1972), 43–49, for settlement patterns.

12. Tully, *Forming American Politics*, 36; Nash, *Quakers and Politics*, 181; Beeman, *Varieties of Political Experience in Colonial America*, 205–6.

13. According to the Statutes at Large of Pennsylvania, it appears the oath was first passed when William Keith requested it in 1724, but it was not enforced until 1727 when German immigrants began to arrive in large numbers. "An Act Proscribing the Forms of Declaration of Fidelity," Chapter CCLXXXI, *Statutes at Large of Pennsylvania from 1682 to 1801* (Harrisburg, 1896), 3: 427–31. For historians on the oaths of allegiance, see Wokeck, "Flow and Composition," 3–4, and *Trade in Strangers*, 116. For the text of the first oath, see "Names of Foreigners Who Took the Oath of Allegiance to the Province and State of Pennsylvania, 1727–1775," *PA Archives*, Second Series, 17: 3. The decision to create an oath of allegiance can be found in "Governor's Council at Philadelphia, September 14, 1727," PMP, Penn and Baltimore Papers, 2: 1725–39, HSP. Historians often refer to the statements German immigrants had to make as "oath," which may not be accurate. Quakers were opposed to taking oaths, and although these statements of allegiance have acquired the appellation "oaths," the text did not require its taker to "swear" any allegiance, only to declare. Fogleman, *Hopeful Journeys*, 20; Wokeck, *Trade in Strangers*, 116.

14. Patrick Griffin, "The People with No Name: Ulster's Migrants and Identity Formation in Eighteenth-Century Pennsylvania," *William and Mary Quarterly* 58, no. 3 (2001): 587–614; and *People with No Name*, chap. 4, esp. 102–103. See also Beeman, *Varieties of Political Experience in Colonial America*, 205–7; and Silver, *Our Savage Neighbors*, 5. See also Franz, "Paxton: A Study of Community Structure and Mobility," 48–51; Sally Schwartz, *A Mixed*

Multitude: The Struggle for Toleration in Colonial Pennsylvania (New York, 1987) chap. 3. See Lemon, *Best Poor Man's Country,* 43–49, for settlement patterns.

15. The best biography of James Logan is Frederick Tolles, *James Logan and the Culture of Provincial America* (New York, 1957). See also Edwin Bronner, "Village into Town," in *Philadelphia: A 300-Year History,* ed. Russell Weigley (Philadelphia, 1982), 40–43; and sections in Illick, *Colonial Pennsylvania,* esp. 109–11, 167–68. Frank Eshleman, "Assessment Lists and Other Manuscript Documents of Lancaster County Prior to 1729," *Lancaster County Historical Society Journal* 20 (1916): 153–94; and Leyburn, *Scotch-Irish,* 191–92. Tully shows that by the 1740s, the westernmost county had more taxables than many of the original eastern ones. See Tully, *William Penn's Legacy,* 93, Table 1. See also Rose Beiler, *Immigrant and Entrepreneur: The Atlantic World of Caspar Wistar, 1650–1750* (University Park, PA, 2008), 114.

16. Ford, *Scotch-Irish in America,* 272–73.

17. Quotation from Ford, *Scotch-Irish in America,* 272.

18. I have found surprisingly little literature on popular conceptions of Native Americans in Great Britain. See Dagmar Wernitznig, *Europe's Indians, Indians in Europe: European Perceptions and Appropriations of Native American Cultures from Pocahontas to the Present* (Lanham, MD, 2007), for some treatment of the issue.

19. A series of letters and depositions provide the core of this narrative. The bulk of these sources can be found in "At a Council, September, 27, 1727," in *PCM,* 3: 284–87. Other treatments of the Thomas Wright murder can be found in *Lancaster County Indians: Annals of the Susquehannocks and Other Indians,* 291–92; I. Daniel Rupp, *History of Lancaster County* (Lancaster, 1844), 197–8; and Merrell, *Into the American Woods,* 95.

20. The location of Snaketown comes from the reports surrounding the incident. Subsequent work by archaeologists and historians has failed to pinpoint its location. For a discussion about its possible location that takes issue with where it was reported at the time, see a letter to the editor by a local resident of Lancaster County, in *Notes and Queries, Historical, Biographical and Genealogical, Relating to the Interior of Pennsylvania,* ed. William Henry Egle (Harrisburg, PA, 1894) 1: 19–20.

21. "At a Council, September 27, 1727," *PCM,* 3: 285–87.

22. Ibid. Griffin, in *People with No Name,* 111–12, makes note of Burt as a gunsmith.

23. "Thomas Wright," in Craig Horle et al., *Lawmaking and Legislators in Pennsylvania* (Philadelphia, 1997), 2: 1086–95.

24. "At a Council, September 27, 1727," *PCM,* 3: 285–87.

25. Ibid.

26. For a discussion of the council and their makeup, see Tully, *William Penn's Legacy,* 79–103, esp. 80–84. For evidence on a quorum, see "A Message from the Governor to the Assembly, November 8, 1755," *PCM,* 6: 684–85.

27. On Patrick Gordon's governorship, see Klein and Hoogenboom, *History of Pennsylvania,* 53–56. Klein and Hoogenboom note that Gordon brought "more harmony" to the colony's politics than anyone since William Penn. J. St. George Joyce makes similar statements in *Story of Philadelphia* (Philadelphia, 1919), 111–12. Alan Tully's *William Penn's Legacy* likewise argues for harmony in Pennsylvania's politics during this administration. Herbert Cummings, in *Scots Breed and the Susquehanna* (Pittsburgh, 1964), 9–12, studies Gordon's role in the crisis of 1728. A good but jaded biographical background of Gordon is Charles Penrose Keith, *Chronicles of Pennsylvania* (Philadelphia, 1917), 2: 686–88. Gordon's speech can be found in "At a Council, August 2, 1726," *PCM,* 3: 254–56.

28. "At a Council, September 27, 1727," *PCM*, 3:284–87.

29. Ibid.

30. Merrell, *Into the American Woods*, 158–67; and John Smolenski, "The Death of Sawantaeny," in *Friends and Enemies in Penn's Woods*, ed. Pencak and Richter , 104–28. The murder of Sawantaeny and events leading to it are also discussed at length in Eric Hinderaker, *Elusive Empires: Constructing Colonialism in the Ohio Valley, 1673–1800* (New York, 1997), 124–26. Quotation from "At a Council Meeting, September 27, 1727," *PCM*, 3: 285–87

31. "At a Council Meeting, September 27, 1727," *PCM*, 3: 286.

32. For more on Penn's initial laws regulating the Indian trade, see "Conditions or Concessions to the First Purchasers," July 11, 1681, *PWP*, 2: 98–101.

33. "An Act for Continuing a Friendly Correspondence with the Indians," 1711 and 1715, *The Statutes at Large of Pennsylvania from 1682 to 1801* (Harrisburg, PA, 1896), 2: 365–68 and 3: 60–63. I have found only one mention of this law by historians of Pennsylvania. See Shepherd, *History of Proprietary Government in Pennsylvania*, 109.

34. "America and West Indies: December 1718, 1–10," *Calendar of State Papers Colonial, America and West Indies: 1717–1718* 30 (1930), 397–404, http://www.british-history.ac.uk/report.aspx?compid=74049.

35. "At a Council, September 27, 1727," *PCM*, 3: 286. And "Speech to the Assembly" in "At a Council, August 2, 1726," *PCM*, 3: 255.

36. "At a Council, September 27, 1727," *PCM*, 3: 284–87.

37. "At a Council, September, 27, 1727," *PCM*, 3: 284–87.

Chapter 3. The First Frontier Crisis

1. The following is based on LeTort's statement to the council that was recorded in "At a Council, April 18, 1728," *PCM*, 3: 312–15. See Merrell, *Into the American Woods*, 158–62, for a detailed discussion of this event.

2. "At a Council, April 18, 1728," *PCM*, 3: 312–15; Merrell, *Into the American Woods*, 158–62.

3. John Wright to James Logan, May 3, 1728, *Lancaster County Indians: The Annals of the Susquehannocks and Other Indians* (Lancaster, PA, 1908), 295; and John Wright to James Logan, Hempfield, May 2, 1728, *PA Archives*, First Series, 1: 213.

4. "Petition of Frontier Inhabitants to Governor," Apr. 29, 1728, *PA Archives*, First Series, 1: 209–10, and "Petition of the Inhabitants of Colebrookdale," May 10, 1728, *PA Archives*, First Series, 1: 213–14. The first petition appears to have been received on May 6, 1728. See "At a Council Held at Philadelphia," May 6, 1728, *PCM*, 3: 302; and Merrell, *Into the American Woods*, 161, 279. Signatures reproduced in *PA Archives*, Sixth Series, 14: 262–63.

5. "At a Council, June 6, 1701," *PCM*, 2: 31. For discussion of the 1701 petition, see James Whisker, *The American Colonial Militia: The Pennsylvania Colonial Militia* (Lewiston, NY, 1997), 2. Whisker also notes that there is evidence that Pennsylvania had a standing militia from its founding. I suspect he is right but only to a certain extent. It is likely that the colony had some body to perform a role at official functions, not as a formal defensive institution. For more on the use of *frontier* in official records, see Appendix 2 "Graphing Frontiers."

6. "At a Council, May 10, 1728," *PCM*, 3: 302–3.

7. "At a Council, May 15, 1728," *PCM*, 3: 303–7; "Petition of the Inhabitants of Colebrookdale," May 10, 1728, *PA Archives*, First Series, 1: 213–14.

8. "At a Council, May 15, 1728," *PCM*, 3: 303–7.

9. Merrell, *Into the American Woods,* 160–66.

10. Hints of this divide can be found in Merrell, *Into the American Woods.* More recently, historians like David Preston in *Texture of Contact* gave a rosier view of early contact moments in Pennsylvania, arguing that it was a period of cohabitation and coexistence.

11. "At a Council, May 15, 1728," *PCM,* 3: 303–7.

12. Ibid.

13. The following narrative is pieced together from "An Examination of Walter Winter" and "An Examination of John Winter" in *PA Archives,* First Series, 1: 218–20. In the *PCM,* Winter's last name is "Winters." I have relied on the spelling in the deposition, believing it better reflects how John and Walter referred to themselves.

14. "An Examination of Walter Winter" and "An Examination of John Winter," *PA Archives,* First Series, 1:218–20.

15. Ibid.

16. Ibid.; Samuel Nutt to the Governor, May 11, 1728, *PA Archives,* First Series, 1: 215–16.

17. George Boone to the Governor, May 12, 1728, *PA Archives,* First Series, 1:217–18.

18. Some historians, hoping to cast regular colonists in a good light, have recently argued that on a daily and personal level, colonists and Indians often coexisted in harmony. In the story of the Winters' murders, there are some shards of evidence that support this contention. See Preston, *Texture of Contact.* While Peter Silver's *Our Savage Neighbors* and Patrick Griffin's *American Leviathan* are less forgiving of colonists and their attitudes toward Indians, they both hold that racial attitudes toward Indians only truly crystallize in the midst of the Revolution. I would believe they were present—perhaps latent during peacetime—much earlier.

19. "At a Council, May 15, 1728," *PCM,* 3: 304.

20. "Instructions for the Apprehension of the Murderers," *PA Archives,* First Series, 1: 217; "At a Council, May 15, 1728," *PCM,* 3: 303–7.

21. "At a Council, May 15, 1728," *PCM,* 3: 303–7. See also "An Examination of Walter Winter" and "An Examination of John Winter," *PA Archives,* First Series, 1:218–20.

22. "At a Council, May 15, 1728," *PCM,* 3: 303–7.

23. Ibid. Instructions to Scull and Zadusky and Instructions to Smith and Skolehoven, *PA Archives,* First Series, 1: 222–24.

24. On Penn and the mixed juries, see "Conditions or Concessions to the First Purchasers," July 11, 1681, *PWP,* 2: 98–101; editor's note, *PWP,* 2: 127–28.

25. An Act for Continuing a Friendly Correspondence with the Indians," *The Statutes at Large of Pennsylvania from 1682 to 1801* (Harrisburg, PA, 1896), 3: 60–63 and 3: 451.

26. Ibid.

27. For an example of how the law can serve as a guide for understanding race, see the discussion over legal codes passed in Virginia in T. H. Breen and Stephen Innes, *"Myne Owne Ground": Race and Freedom on Virginia's Eastern Shore, 1640–1676* (New York, 1982), 24–28. The 1705 Virginia Slave Codes are often used to demonstrate the way racial categories can become codified in law. The law declared all non-Christians imported into the colony would be bound to slavery and that masters had the power to punish their slaves with death. In other words, the protections of the state—who receives them and who does not—are important markers of racial subjugation, even if other codes that signify discrimination are not. The Slave Codes of 1705 specifically placed slaves outside of the state's protection and instead placed them under the sole control of their masters, who could determine their fate with no

fear of state interference. James Merrell discusses the growing divide between settlers on the ground and Indians and suggests that during this period racial categorization was forming on the social level in many colonists' and Indians' minds. Merrell, *Into the American Woods*, 167–75.

28. "At a Council at Philadelphia," May 15, 1728, *PCM*, 3: 303–307. One of the appointed commissioners, Mordecai Lincoln, was the great-great-grandfather of Abraham Lincoln. "Abraham Lincoln in Pennsylvania," http://www.phmc.state.pa.us/ppet/lincoln/page2 .asp?secid = 31.

29. Warrant to Arrest Murderers, *PA Archives*, First Series, 1: 221; "A Proclamation," May 16, 1728, *PCM*, 3: 307–8.

30. "At a Council, May 17, 1728" and "At a Council, May 20, 1728," *PCM*, 3: 308–13.

31. *Votes of Assembly*, 3: 1887; "At a Council, May 17, 1728" and "At a Council, May 20, 1728," *PCM*, 3: 308–13.

32. Background and details on the treaty can be found in "At a Council, May 17, 1728" and "At a Council, May 20, 1728," *PCM*, 3: 308–13, and "At a Council Held at Conestogoe, May 27, 1728," *PCM*, 3: 313–15. For the Ganawese, see C. Hale Sipe, *The Indian Wars of Pennsylvania* (Harrisburg, 1929), 53.

33. "At a Council, May 20, 1728" and "May 26, 1728," *PCM*, 3: 309–13.

34. Ibid.

35. Tawenna, described as a chief in the meeting, has largely stayed out of the historical record. For works that uncovered parts of his life, see Merrell, *Into the American Woods*, 166–67; Charles Keith, *Chronicles of Pennsylvania from the English Revolution to the Peace of Aix-la-Chapelle, 1688–1748* (New York, 1917), 716; and Charles Hanna, *The Wilderness Trail* (New York, 1911), 81. For the best summary of the 1701 treaty, see Jennings, *Ambiguous Iroquois Empire*, 236–39. Jennings also mentions Tawenna as a Conestoga chief on p. 305, fn. 43. The Indians' reply can be found in "At a Council at the Indian Town of Conestogoe, May 27, 1728," *PCM*, 3: 313–14.

36. "At a Council at the Indian Town of Conestogoe, May 27, 1728," *PCM*, 3: 313–14.

37. Similar arguments about Indians' legal status in Pennsylvania can be found in Smolenski, "The Death of Sawantaeny," 104–28.

38. "At a Council at the Indian Town of Conestogoe, May 27, 1728," *PCM*, 3: 313–14.

39. *American Weekly*, May 23, 1728, and May 30, 1728, report on the treaty and the events surrounding it.

40. For a response from Native American leaders, see "At a Council, June 3, 1728," *PCM*, 3: 315–16. Quotation on 315.

41. Frank Diffender, *Historical Papers of the Lancaster County Historical Society* (Lancaster, PA, 1907), 11: 293; and Henry Frank Eshleman, *Lancaster County Indians* (Lancaster, PA, 1908), 308.

42. The third man, Morgan Herbert, was convicted, but his sentence was commuted because it was determined that he took no part in the actual murder of the Indians. See "Council Held at Philadelphia," Aug. 6, 1728, *PCM*, 3: 326–27; "Recommendation to Mercy," *PA Archives*, First Series, 1: 225–26; *Boston Gazette*, issue 451, July 8–July 15, 1728; and *Boston Newsletter*, issue 81, 1728. The record of the case can be found in George Smith, *History of Delaware County* (Media, PA, 1862), 238–39. Gordon reported that Herbert was tried two days later as an accomplice and convicted. His appeal for clemency was endorsed by the three

justices of the peace who oversaw his trial. As far as I can tell, the records of the court case have since been destroyed. James Merrell does not cite them, and the Chester County archives claim to have no record of the case. I consider their reprinting in the *History of Delaware County* to be accurate as all of the other information and sources can be verified. For execution information, see Negley Teeters, *Scaffold and Chair: A Compilation of Their Use in Pennsylvania, 1682–1962* (Philadelphia, 1963), 62–63, 227. The council played an extremely active role in setting up the trial, determining the best time and location so that Indians could witness it if they wished. "A Council Held at Philadelphia," May 15, 1728, and "A Council Held at Philadelphia," May 17, 1728, *PCM*, 3: 303–305.

43. Reports on Indian complaints can be found in the following: John Wright and Samuel Blunston to Governor Gordon, Oct. 30, 1732, *PA Archives*, First Series, 1: 363–65; and John Wright and Samuel Blunston to the Governor, December 30, 1732, *PCM*, 3: 470–72 . Deposition of Tobias Hendricks, *PA Archives*, First Series, 1: 362. Hendricks testifies that Parnel and four others actually lived on the land on which Cresap now lived. John Wright, Tobias Hendricks, Samuel Blunston to Peter Chartier, Nov. 19, 1731, *PA Archives*, First Series, 1: 299.

44. For discussions of county creation and the importance of the county as a political and legal institution in Pennsylvania, see Alan Tully, *William Penn's Legacy*, 103–15, and Bockelman, "Local Government in Colonial Pennsylvania." For an overview of the process in Cumberland County, especially in the creation of a county seat, see Judith Ridner, *A Town In-Between: Carlisle, Pennsylvania, and the Early American Mid-Atlantic Interior* (Philadelphia, 2010), 27–43; "Council Minutes," Feb. 6, 1729, *PCM*, 3: 343–44; *Votes of the Assembly, PA Archives*, Eighth Series, 3: 1923.

45. *Votes of the Assembly, PA Archives*, Eighth Series, 3: 1923.

46. For discussion of these illegal settlements, see Captain Civility to the Governor, 1730, *PA Archives*, First Series, 1: 271–72; John Wright and Samuel Blunston to Governor Gordon, Oct. 30, 1732, *PA Archives*, First Series, 1: 363–65; Deposition of Tobias Hendricks, *PA Archives*, First Series, 1: 362; John Wright, Tobias Hendricks, Samuel Blunston to Peter Chartier, Nov. 19, 1731, *PA Archives*, First Series, 1: 299. Samuel Blunston to Robert Charles, Oct. 3, 1731; Governor Gordon to Governor Ogle, Apr. 18, 1732, in *PA Archives*, First Series, 1: 295, 321–24; John Wright and Samuel Blunston to Governor Gordon, Dec. 30, 1732, in *Minutes of the Provincial Council of Pennsylvania*, 10 vols. (Harrisburg, PA, 1838–52), 3: 504–506; John Wright, Tobias Hendricks, and Samuel Blunston to Peter Chartier, Nov. 19, 1731, *PA Archives*, First Series, 1: 299; *The Kittochtinny Historical Society: Papers Read Before the Society from February 1899 to February 1901* (Chambersburg, PA, 1903), 89; Robert McMeen, "The Scotch-Irish of the Juniata Valley," in *The Scotch-Irish in America: Proceedings of the Scotch-Irish Congress* (Nashville, TN, 1897), 8: 115; Dutrizac, "Local Identity and Authority," 36.

47. Details on this incident can be found in H. Frank Eshelman, *Lancaster County Indians: Annals of the Susquehannocks and Other Tribes of the Susquehanna Territory from About the Year 1500–1763, the Date of Their Extinction* (Lancaster, PA, 1909), 316–19; "Inquisition on Three Indians Murdered" and Joshua Lowe to the Governor, Sept. 5, 1730, *PA Archives*, First Series, 1: 267–69.

48. "Inquisition on Three Indians Murdered" and Joshua Lowe to the Governor, Sept. 5, 1730, *PA Archives*, First Series, 1: 267–69. but esp. Lowe to Governor, *PA Archives*, First Series, 1: 268–69.

49. Captain Civility to Governor Gordon, Sept. 28, 1730, *PA Archives*, First Series, 1: 271–72.

Chapter 4. Pennsylvania's Apogee

1. For a more extensive discussion of the name, see Patrick Spero, "The Conojocular War: The Politics of Colonial Competition, 1732–1737," *Pennsylvania Magazine of History and Biography*, 136, no. 4 (Oct. 2012): 365–403.

2. Samuel Blunston to Robert Charles, Oct. 3, 1731, *PA Archives*, First Series, 1: 295.

3. The biographical background on Blunston comes from "Samuel Blunston," Horle et al., *Lawmaking and Legislators in Pennsylvania*, 2: 220–31.

4. John Wright and Samuel Blunston to Patrick Gordon, Dec. 30, 1732, *PCM*, 3: 470–72, quotation on 470.

5. Samuel Blunston to Robert Charles, Oct. 3, 1731, *PA Archives*, First Series, 1: 295.

6. Ibid.

7. Baltimore claimed that his 1632 charter granted the land to his family, which stated Baltimore had all land on the Delmarva Peninsula that was *hactenus inculta*—that is, all lands "hitherto uncultivated." The Penns, however, argued that the Lower Counties had not been unoccupied lands, but land controlled by the Swedes and then the Dutch. If that was the case, then the land was transferred to the Crown when the Dutch ceded all land in North America to the English, and Penn's charter entitled him to this territory. For detailed analyses of the legal negotiations dating back to William Penn, see Walter B. Scaife, "The Boundary Dispute Between Maryland and Pennsylvania," *Pennsylvania Magazine of History and Biography* 9 (1885): 241–71; Shepherd, *History of Proprietary Government in Pennsylvania*, 117–46; Tansill, "Pennsylvania-Maryland Boundary Controversy"; Fisher, *Making of Pennsylvania*, 318–46; Wainwright, "Missing Evidence," 227–35, and "Tale of a Runaway Cape: The Penn-Baltimore Agreement of 1732," *Pennsylvania Magazine of History and Biography* 87 (1963): 251–69; Tully, *William Penn's Legacy*, 3–17; and Dunn and Dunn, eds., *PWP*, 379–438, 494–500.

8. For Cresap's biography, see Kenneth Bailey, *Thomas Cresap, A Maryland Frontiersman* (Boston, 1944), and Lawrence Wroth, *The Story of Thomas Cresap: A Maryland Pioneer* (Columbus, 1928). The reference to Cresap's early relationship with the Washington family can be found in J. M. Toner, ed., *The Journal of Colonel George Washington* (Albany, NY, 1893), 31–32. For hints that he was a Catholic, see Frederic Godcharles, *Pennsylvania: Political, Governmental, Military, and Civil* (New York, 1933), 1: 137.

9. John Wright and Samuel Blunston to Patrick Gordon, Dec. 30, 1732, *PCM*, 3: 470–72, quotation on 471; Deposition of Tobias Hendricks, *PA Archives*, First Series, 1: 362. Hendricks testified that Parnel and four others actually lived on the land on which Cresap now lived.

10. James Logan quotation from Dutrizac, "Local Identity and Authority," 36.

11. Samuel Blunston to Robert Charles, Oct. 3, 1731, *PA Archives*, First Series, 1: 295.

12. Deposition of Thomas Cresap, Jan. 29, 1731/2, *PA Archives*, First Series, 1: 311–13.

13. Ibid.

14. For the argument about Cornish and Cresap, see Governor Ogle to Patrick Gordon, Feb. 2, 1731/2, and Governor Gordon to Ogle, Feb. 21, 1731/2, *PA Archives*, First Series, 1: 313–15.

15. Quote from Petition of Ross and Carroll, *PA Archives*, First Series,1: 333–35, quotation on 334; Governor Gordon to Governor Ogle, Apr. 18, 1732, *PA Archives*, First Series, 1: 321–24.

16. Governor Gordon to Governor Ogle, Apr. 18, 1732, *PA Archives*, First Series, 1: 321–24.

17. Governor Gordon to Governor Ogle, Apr. 18, 1732, *PA Archives*, First Series, 1: 321–24.

18. The best account of these negotiations is Wainwright, "Tale of a Runaway Cape," 251–93.

19. See Wainwright, 'Tale of a Runaway Cape," esp. 257–63 for information on the map.

20. For the details of the proprietor's negotiations, see Wainwright, 'Tale of a Runaway Cape," and Tully, *William Penn's Legacy*, 5–11.

21. The best biography of the Penns, especially of Thomas, is Lorett Treese's *The Storm Gathering*.

22. See Wainwright, "Tale of the Runaway Cape," for the details of the proprietor's negotiations. Treese, *Storm Gathering*, is a biography of the Penn brothers and explores their financial state. Tully, *William Penn's Legacy*, 5–11; Shepherd, *History of Proprietary Government in Pennsylvania*, 32, 132. Shepherd describes the eight years of negotiations between the two sides after 1724 as "a series of empty promises." John and Richard Penn's Instructions to Thomas Penn, May 20, 1732, and John Penn to Thomas Penn, July 20, 1732, NV-211, pp. 54–58, ser. 1, Penn Family Papers, HSP.

23. For biographical background, see "Charles Calvert," *Oxford Dictionary of National Biography*, http://www.oxforddnb.com/view/article/75619, accessed Nov. 25, 2013; "Thomas Penn," *Oxford Dictionary of National Biography*, http://www.oxforddnb.com/view/article/21855, accessed Nov. 25, 2013; and Treese, *Storm Gathering*.

24. Journey to the New Town in Maryland, Receipt, 1732, NB-011, folder 6, ser. 3, Penn Family Papers, HSP. Not all the funds went to entertainment of Marylanders; some also paid for the travel and lodging of his commissioners. The report was published as *Articles of Agreement* (London, 1735), with the commissioner's report affixed. Letter from Pennsylvania Commissioners for Newcastle to Maryland Commissioners, Mar. 28, 1733, NB-003, folder 9, ser. 7, Penn Family Papers, HSP. Wainwright, in "Tale of a Runaway Cape," details the publication of this document, along with all other legal documents printed during the dispute. It also contains the Logan quotation on 265.

25. John Wright and Samuel Blunston to Governor Gordon, Dec. 30, 1732, *PCM*, 3: 470–72. The best explication of this strategy was published in the *Pennsylvania Gazette*, Feb. 3, 1737.

26. "Deposition of Joshua Low, Dec. 28, 1732," in *PA Archives*, First Series, 1: 356.

27. "Substance of Answer of Dutch to Governor of Maryland, 1736," in *PA Archives*, First Series, 1: 492–94, details the Germans' migration and reasons for allying with Cresap before switching their loyalties to Pennsylvania.

28. Thomas Penn to Samuel Blunston, Jan. 10, 1734, box NB-011, folder 20, ser. 3, Penn Family Papers, HSP, formerly Penn Manuscripts Unbound, HSP. Samuel Blunston to Thomas Penn, Jan. 30, 1734, in *PA Archives*, First Series, 1: 410–12; and Thomas Penn to Samuel Blunston, Feb. 4, 1733, box NB-011, folder 10, ser. 3, Penn Family Papers, HSP, discuss Hamilton's instructions. Please note that Blunston and Penn often corresponded in Old Style, meaning that February 4, 1733, is probably 1734. The content of the letter also seems to imply that it was written after the January 29, 1734, raid on Cresap's home. Except for that one letter, the citations above have been updated to reflect New Style dating.

29. Samuel Blunston to Thomas Penn, Jan. 30, 1734, *PA Archives*, First Series, 1: 410–11

30. Ibid. For details on the raid, see the following depositions: William Glasspill, Feb. 15, 1734, and Michael Dooling, Feb. 15, 1734, *PA Archives*, First Series, 1: 412–14.

31. Samuel Blunston to Thomas Penn, Jan. 30, 1734, *PA Archives*, First Series, 1: 410–11; William Glasspill, Feb. 15, 1734; Michael Dooling, Feb. 15, 1734, *PA Archives*, First Series, 1: 412–14.

32. Thomas Penn to Samuel Blunston, Feb. 4, 1734, NB-011, folder 10, ser. 3, Penn Family Papers, HSP. Though dated 1733, I believe this letter is in the Old Style, as are many of the

letters in this correspondence. All dates reflect the New Style form. Penn stated the behavior of Emerson's men "was very wrong" and wanted to know if "his master gave him any such directions." Samuel Blunston to Thomas Penn, Feb. 24, 1734, Lancaster County Papers, HSP.

33. Samuel Blunston to Thomas Penn, Feb. 12, 1734, vol. 1, p. 1, Lancaster County Papers, HSP.

34. Warrant for the Arrest of John Hendricks, Feb. 21, 1734, NB-025, folder 39, ser. 1, Penn Family Papers, HSP; and deposition of Robert Gordon, Feb. 5, 1734, NB-025, folder 21, ser. 1, Penn Family Papers, HSP; Samuel Blunston to Thomas Penn, Feb. 12, 1734, vol. 1, p. 1, Lancaster County Papers, HSP; Samuel Ogle to Nicholas Macublin (Justice of the Peace), Feb. 21, 1734, NB-025, folder 39, ser. 1, Penn Family Papers, HSP; Warrant for the arrest of Minshall and Hendricks, Feb. 19, 1734, NB-025, folder 39, ser. 1, Penn Family Papers, HSP. Though many of these dates are 1733 on the primary sources, the date refers to 1734.

35. Samuel Blunston to Thomas Penn, Feb. 12, 1734, vol. 1, p. 1, Lancaster County Papers, HSP; James Steel to Samuel Blunston, Feb. 13,1734, James Steel Letterbook, 1730–41, p. 65, Logan Family Papers, 1664–1871, HSP (hereafter cited as James Steel Letterbook).

36. *Maryland Archives, Proceedings of the Council 1732–1753*, pp. 70–77; Deposition of George Soldner, *Archives of Maryland, Proceedings of the Council, 1732–1753* (Baltimore, 1908) (hereafter *Archives of Maryland*), 84; Deposition of Jacob Herrington, Oct. 18, 1735, *Archives of Maryland*, 84–85; Samuel Blunston to Thomas Penn, July 22, 1734, Lancaster County Miscellaneous Collection, HSP; Samuel Blunston to [Thomas Penn], May 12, 1734, Lancaster County Miscellaneous Collection, HSP. Samuel Blunston to Thomas Penn, Mar. 10, 1735, vol. 1, p. 3, Lancaster County Papers Collection, HSP; John Hendricks and Joshua Minshall to Thomas Penn, May 6, 1734, Penn-Bailey Collection, HSP; Samuel Blunston to Thomas Penn, May 12, 1734, Lancaster County Collection, HSP. Dutrizac estimates the conflict affected two hundred households, a large number for the 1730s, in "Local Identity and Authority," 37; Thomas Penn to Samuel Blunston, Apr. 3, 1734, NB-011, folder 22, ser. 3, Penn Family Papers, HSP.

37. Samuel Blunston to Thomas Penn, May 12, 1734, Lancaster County Papers, vol. 1, p. 3, HSP; Deposition of Jacob Herrington, Oct. 18, 1735, *Archives of Maryland*, 84–85; Thomas Penn to Samuel Blunston, Apr. 3, 1734, Penn Manuscripts Unbound, HSP.

38. For details on these warrants, also known as the "Blunston Licenses," see Thomas Penn to Samuel Blunston, Apr. 3, 1734, NB-011, folder 22, ser. 3, Penn Family Papers, HSP; Samuel Blunston to Thomas Penn, Mar. 18, 1734, vol. 1, p. 3, Lancaster County Papers, HSP; Thomas Penn to Samuel Blunston, May 1, 1735, NB-011, folder 32, ser. 3, Penn Family Papers, HSP; Thomas Penn to Samuel Blunston, Apr. 3, 1734 NB-011, folder 22, ser. 3, Penn Family Papers, HSP; Thomas Penn to Samuel Blunston, Aug. 8, 1734, NB-011, folder 25, ser. 3, Penn Family Papers, HSP; Samuel Blunston to Thomas Penn, Aug. 13, 1734, vol. 1, p. 7, Lancaster County Papers, HSP; and Thomas Penn to Ferdinand Paris, Feb. 12, 1736/37, NB-003, folder 17, ser. 7, Penn Family Papers, HSP. Paris was the attorney for the Penns.

39. Discussions of shifting can be found in Governor Gordon to Governor Ogle, Feb. 17, 1732/33, in *PA Archives*, Fourth Series, 12 vols. (Harrisburg, PA, 1900–1902), 1: 509–13; Governor Gordon to Lord Baltimore on Mar. 28, 173[3], *PCM*, 3: 494–500, esp. 495; Governor Gordon to Lord Baltimore, Feb. 17, 1732/33, in *PA Archives*, Fourth Series, 1: 506–509; Samuel Blunston to Thomas Penn, July 22, 1734, Samuel Blunston to Thomas Penn, Jan. 2, , and Thomas Penn to Samuel Blunston, Jan. 10, 1735, all in Lancaster County Papers, HSP; Shepherd, *History of Proprietary Government in Pennsylvania*, 117–46.

40. While we may never know why some Germans enlisted with Maryland and others with Pennsylvania, these Maryland Germans all appear to be laborers without homes or wives, and many may have been recent arrivals, such as Michael Rysner who appears on arrival records for 1732. Michael Tanner, however, the leader of the group who chose to be with Penn, arrived in 1727 and appears to have had a family. Deposition of Jacob Loughman, Oct. 18, 1735, *Archives of Maryland,* 82–84, is the account of a German man. The depositions of George Soldner, Michael Risner, and Philip Crever all imply that they worked with Cresap for wages and perhaps housing. See *Archives of Maryland,* 84–87; List of Foreigners Imported in the Ship Dragon . . . Sept. 30, 1732, *PA Archives,* Second Series, 17: 68–69; "At a Council, September 27, 1728," *PCM,* 3: 284.

41. For the Scots-Irish speech, see James Anderson to William Allen, Address to the Proprietor, June 26 and 30, 1733, NV-089, p. 29, ser. 6, Penn Family Papers, HSP.

42. "The Petition of Jacob Fleegar and Frederick Fleegar, December 15, 1766," Miscellaneous Correspondence, Pennsylvania Historical and Museum Commission, Roll 1; William Findley, *History of the Insurrection in the Four Western Counties of Pennsylvania* (Spartanburg, SC, 1984), chap. 1.

43. Jenny Wright, wife of John Wright and neighbor and close friend of Samuel Blunston, also served as an emissary and news carrier. See, for instance, Samuel Blunston to Thomas Penn, Jan. 13, 1737, vol. 1., p. 29, Lancaster County Papers, HSP. For examples of the roles Esther and Jenny played, see also Thomas Penn to Samuel Blunston, Apr. 18, 1736, NB-011, folder 43, ser. 3, Penn Family Papers, HSP.

44. It is likely that the ferry was auctioned off and the proprietor purchased it. The last mention of Emerson being alive was in a letter Penn wrote to Blunston, dated Apr. 18, 1736. In May, Penn sent Blunston a copy of the grant he had given Emerson and advised him to put the property up for sale, along with the terms of service in the grant. Penn then advised Blunston to "bid on my account," so he could still own the valuable land and dole it out to one of his loyal tenants (Thomas Penn to Samuel Blunston, May 6, 1736, NB-011, folder 44, ser. 3, Penn Family Papers, HSP). The property attracted numerous bidders, and Penn eventually spent more than he wished (Samuel Blunston to Thomas Penn, May 10, 1736, NB-025, folder 9, ser. 1, Penn Family Papers, HSP). For specific details on Penn's plans for the land, see James Steel to Dr. [Samuel] Chew, winter 1737, James Steel Letterbook, p. 131. The handling of Emerson's land provides further evidence of proprietary power in these western areas and among those vested in the institution of the proprietor. In his letter to Chew, Steel wrote, "Some time after the Death of John Emerson who had the Grant of a Plantation within our Proprs Mannor of Conestogo, the Same being taken in Execution and Sold by the Sheriff to pay his debts, was purchased for the Proprs use as lying within a large quantity of rich Land, and thereupon a Tenant was Settled to keep the plantation in Order and for that purpose two Servant men were purchased here the last fall and Sent up with the Tenant who also had their Indentures with them." Later, after Ross established himself, he found a number of stray horses with Emerson's mark. When he asked Steel for advice on what to do with them, Steel advised him to sell them as "for in England (and I suppose the same in Ireland) all Strays & c. are the property of the Lord of the Manor where they are found and it must at least, if not more be so to the Proprs of a large province, Vested with such Extensive powers as the King was pleased by his Royal Charter to Grant" (James Steel to John Ross, Sept. 14, 1737, James Steel Letterbook, 1730–41, p. 160). W. Murray, "The Case Relating to the Dispute Between

Lord Baltimore and the Penns," *Register of Pennsylvania* 2 (1828): 209–16; James Steel to John Ross, Apr. 8, 1737, James Steel Letterbook, 1730–41, p. 139; James Steel to John Ross, [June 5], 1737, James Steel Letterbook, p. 149.

45. Samuel Blunston to James Logan, undated (likely Jan. 1737, improperly dated 1732 in the source), in *PA Archives*, First Series, 1: 316–20.

46. For the public pronouncement in which the German settlers explicitly rejected Maryland for its behavior, see *Archives of Maryland*, 28: 100–101; and "Substance of Answer of Dutch to the Governor of Maryland, 1736," *PA Archives*, First Series1: 492–94. Blunston recounts the constant harassment both sides received in Samuel Blunston to Thomas Penn, May 3, [1736], vol. 1, p. 21, Lancaster County Papers, HSP.

47. *Archives of Maryland*, 28: 100–101. Murray, "Dispute Between Lord Baltimore and the Penns." The "mildness" quote comes from Pennsylvanian sources, though I suspect it was something the Germans likely said given the text of their petition. Their petition says that Pennsylvania's government was preferable to Maryland's, comparing it to Maryland's, which they cast as arbitrary. For "mildness" quote, see George Reeser Prowell, *History of York County* (Chicago, 1907), 1: 53.

48. Proclamation of James Logan, Sept. 17, 1736, in *Pennsylvania Gazette*, Sept. 23, 1736; James Logan to Daniel Dulany and Edmund Jennings, Dec. 10, 1736, box 50, folder 22, ser. 3, Cadwalader Family Papers, HSP. A detailed description of the events can be found in Samuel Blunston to Thomas Penn, Sept. 8, 1736, vol. 1, p. 9, Lancaster County Papers, HSP; and Deposition of William Downard, Dec. 2, 1736, in *PA Archives*, First Series, 1: 513. Maryland's reaction can be found in *Archives of Maryland*, 28: 99–108; "At a Council Held at Philadelphia, December 10, 1736," *PCM*, 4: 120–24, quotation on 122.

49. Ibid.

50. Samuel Blunston to Thomas Penn, Sept. 8, 1736, vol. 1, p. 9, Lancaster County Papers, HSP.

51. Ibid.

52. Ibid.

53. Thomas Penn to unknown, Apr. 18, 1736, and Thomas Penn to Samuel Blunston, Apr. 18, 1736, NB-011, folders 42 and 43, ser. 3, Penn Family Papers, HSP. Jennings, *Ambiguous Iroquois Empire*, 321–22; Jennings, " 'Pennsylvania Indians' and the Iroqouis," in Daniel K. Richter and James H. Merrell, eds., *Beyond the Covenant Chain: The Iroquois and Their Neighbors in Indian North America, 1600–1800* (Syracuse, NY, 1987), 82.

54. For more on the Iroquois in this period, see Jennings, *Ambiguous Iroquois Empire* and Richter and Merrell, *Beyond the Covenant Chain*.

55. Jennings, *Ambiguous Iroquois Empire*, 321–22.

56. Susan Klepp, "Encounter and Experiment: The Colonial Period," in Miller and Pencak, *Pennsylvania: A History of the Commonwealth*, 75.

57. James Logan to Samuel Smith [the sheriff of Lancaster County], undated, James Logan Letterbook, HSP; James Logan to Thomas Penn, Dec. 28, 1736, *Pennsylvania Archives: Papers Relating to Provincial Affairs in Pennsylvania, 1682–1750* (Harrisburg, PA, 1891), 218–19; Samuel Blunston to Thomas Penn, Dec. 26, 1736, in Penn-Bailey Collection, HSP; Samuel Blunston to Thomas Penn, Dec. 10, 1736, vol. 1, p. 27, and Jan. 9, 1737, vol. 1, p. 23, Lancaster County Papers, HSP. In one letter, Blunston asked for Jennings twice: see Samuel Blunston to Thomas Penn, *PA Archives*, First Series, 1: 316–20.

58. For details of the raid, see *PA Archives,* First Series, 1: 504–610; and Deposition of George Aston, Dec. 3, 1736, in *PA Archives,* First Series, 1: 510. The details on Cresap's wife's condition come from an undated deposition in the Lancaster County Papers, vol. 1, p. 27, at the HSP.

59. Deposition of George Aston, Dec. 3, 1736, in *PA Archives,* First Series, 1: 510.

60. Samuel Blunston to Thomas Penn, Dec. 10, 1736, vol. 1, p. 27, Lancaster County Papers, HSP.

61. Samuel Blunston to Thomas Penn, Jan. 13, 1737, vol. 1, p. 29, Lancaster County Papers, HSP; Samuel Blunston to Thomas Penn, Dec. 26, 1736, 12 at night, NB-025, folder 9, ser. 1, Penn Family Papers, HSP.

62. James Logan to Daniel Dulany and Edmund Jennings, Dec. 10, 1736, box 50, folder 22, ser. 3, Cadwalader Family Papers, HSP. Quotation from Samuel Ogle to Pennsylvania government, May 26, 1737, *PCM,* 4: 219.

63. Blunston was right. A number of settlers from Chester County did enlist and join Maryland by settling on the western side of the river. See Dutrizac, "Local Identity and Authority," 46. For quotations, see Samuel Blunston to Thomas Penn, undated [late Nov./early Dec., 1736?], Lancaster County Papers, HSP; and Samuel Blunston to Thomas Penn, Jan. 9, 1737, vol. 1, p. 23, Lancaster County Miscellaneous Papers, HSP.

64. Samuel Blunston to Thomas Penn, Jan. 9, 1737, vol. 1, p. 23, Lancaster County Miscellaneous Papers, HSP.

65. For an account of the ongoing strife and militarization, see James Steel Letterbook, HSP. Samuel Blunston to Thomas Penn, Jan. 16, 1737, and Jan. 9, 1737, vol. 1., p. 23, Lancaster County Papers, HSP. Blunston also requested twenty cartouche boxes to save ammunition and theoretically costs. Cartouche boxes are weatherproof cases in which gunpowder is carried. Such professional outfitting suggests just how seriously Blunston and others took the conflict. Deposition of Daniel McKenny, Apr. 15, 1737, Philadelphia, vol. 1, p. 23, Lancaster County Papers, HSP. Thomas Penn to Samuel Blunston, Jan. 20, 1737, NB-011, folder 38, ser. 3, Penn Family Papers, HSP. James Steel to John Ross, 5-4-1737 (June 5, 1737), James Steel Letterbook, p. 149, HSP. Samuel Blunston to Thomas Penn, Jan. 27, 1737, vol. 1, p. 35, Lancaster County Papers, HSP; Samuel Blunston to Thomas Penn, Apr. 12, 1737, vol. 1, p. 33, Lancaster County Papers, HSP. For the levels of militiamen, see the following letters: Samuel Blunston to Thomas Penn, July 1, 1737, and Aug. 19, 1737, vol. 1, p. 33, Lancaster County Papers, HSP.

66. Samuel Blunston to James Logan, undated (likely Jan. 1737, improperly dated 1732 in the source), *PA Archives,* First Series 1: 316–20.

67. Earlier, Blunston worried that Penn had grown displeased with the cost of maintaining the Germans. See Samuel Blunston to Thomas Penn, Jan. 13, 1736, vol. 1, p. 9, Lancaster County Miscellaneous Papers, HSP; Penn's quote comes from his response to Samuel Blunston, Jan. 20, 1737, box NB-011, folder 38, ser. 3, Penn Family Papers, HSP.

68. Samuel Blunston to Thomas Penn, Jan. 1, 1737, NB-025, folder 9, ser. 1, Penn Family Papers, HSP; and Samuel Blunston to James Logan, undated (likely Jan. 1737, improperly dated as 1732 in the source), *PA Archives,* First Series, 1: 316–20; Beiler, *Immigrant and Entrepreneur,* 127–28.

69. James Logan to Samuel Smith, undated, Logan Letterbooks, HSP; Thomas Penn to Ferdinand Paris, Feb. 12, 1736[7], NB-003, folder 17, ser. 7, Penn Family Papers, HSP.

70. For details on this decision, see the Minutes of the Court at Kensington, May 25, 1738, reprinted in *Archives of Maryland,* 28: 145–49, and the Minutes of the King's Court at

Hampton, Aug. 18, 1737. A transcribed copy of the latter can be found in the Penn Miscellaneous Papers, Penn and Baltimore Family, HSP. It is dated November 22, 1737, and witnessed by John Ross (the Maryland Ross) in Annapolis. James Steel wrote Blunston about the ex parte decision in Dec. 1, 1737, but gave him no details on the actual content of the proclamation. James Steel to Samuel Blunston [Dec. 1], 1737, James Steel Letterbook, 126–27, HSP. After Cresap's house was burned, Ogle had sent off a number of depositions painting the affair in as bad a light as possible. The king ordered all arrests and all other actions to cease, and told all parties to respect the jurisdiction and allegiances of all settlers in the region, a return to the status quo before the 1732 Agreement. The Penns were not present at the hearing, which only made Baltimore's claims all the more powerful. Penn expressed frustration that the decision was made without any representation, but he also expressed some relief because the "expence for defending" the western side had become "more than any advantage that may accrue." Thomas Penn to Samuel Blunston, Dec. 3, 1737, Penn Manuscripts Unbound, Box 12, HSP.

71. Francis Jennings used the term "Long Peace" in at least two of his works, but emphasized it most in "Miquon's Passing: Indian-European Relations in Pennsylvania, 1674 to 1755" (Ph.D. diss., University of Pennsylvania, 1965), 462, and in *The Founders of America: From the Earliest Migrations to the Present* (New York, 1994), 215. For other prominent examples of its use, see Richter, *Facing East*, 152–58, which uses the phrase to describe the general state of early-eighteenth-century North America; and Merrell, *Into the American Woods*, 35–37.

72. Richard Peters's report to Lieutenant Governor James Hamilton, Provincial Council Minutes, July 31, 1750, *PCM*, 5: 437–51. For a historian's treatment of this episode, see Preston, *Texture of Contact*, 139–42, and Ridner, *A Town In-Between*, 31–32, and corresponding footnotes. Alan Tully chronicles the shift in the proprietors' stance toward untitled land in *William Penn's Legacy*, 13–15.

73. Report of Commissioners and Petition of Little Cove, July 25, 1750, *PCM*, 5: 453–54; Message of the Governor to Assembly, Aug. 8, 1750, *PCM*, 5: 454–55. Judith Ridner provides additional details on the way colonists tried to use the rivalry between the two colonies to their advantage in *A Town In-Between*, 31–32. She notes that some settlers threatened to leave the area if Carlisle was made the county seat.

Chapter 5. Becoming a Frontier Country

1. The treaty was convened after a group of Iroquois, in what would become western Pennsylvania, had a dust-up with settlers from Maryland and Virginia, who the Iroquois accused of intruding on their territory. Details on the events that precipitated the treaty can be found in Merrell, *Into the American Woods*, 167–75.

2. William Armor, *Lives of the Governors of Pennsylvania* (Philadelphia, 1872), 141–44.

3. George Thomas, Lancaster, June 25, 1744, *PCM* (Harrisburg, PA), 4: 699–700.

4. Ibid.

5. Ibid.

6. Ibid.; Warren Hofstra, *Planting of New Virginia: Settlement and Landscape in the Shenandoah Valley* (Baltimore, 2005), 48; "Lieutenant Governor Clarke to Governor Gooch, June 16, 1743," *Documents Relative to the Colonial History of the State of New York* (Albany, NY, 1855), 6: 31–32.

7. The Native quote is from Canassatego, an Onondagan, spoken to Conrad Weiser at a treaty in Shamokin in 1749 attended by over 280 Indians from a variety of nations. "Treaty Minutes," read at a Council Meeting, Philadelphia, Aug. 16, 1749, *PCM*, 5: 398–400, quotation

on 400. *Zeisberger's Indian Dictionary* contained a Delaware word for *frontier*, but like Canassatego's use, we cannot be sure of its particular meaning.

8. Petition of Thomas and Richard Penn to His Majesty, undated, Penn Miscellaneous Manuscripts, Penn and Baltimore Papers, HSP. Even though the petition is undated, its authorship provides an insight into the period it was written. Because it was signed by Thomas and Richard, it was likely authored after 1746, when their brother John died. The discussion of the French as a rival suggests that it was before the Seven Years' War, after which the French power was removed from North America. It is likely that this petition came at some time in the 1750s, when the proprietors considered building a trading post at what today is Pittsburgh.

9. "At a Council, Held in Philadelphia, July 31, 1744," *PCM,* 4:739.

10. Ibid.

11. This and the preceding paragraph are based on a variety of works on the Seven Years' War. See esp. Alfred Cave, *The French and Indian War* (Westport, CT, 2004), 4–15; Matthew Ward, *Breaking the Backcountry: The Seven Years' War in Virginia and Pennsylvania, 1754–1765* (Pittsburgh, 2003), see esp. 5–6, 268; Eric Hinderaker, *The Two Hendricks: Unraveling a Mohawk Mystery* (Cambridge, MA, 2010), 224–28; and Fred Anderson, *Crucible of War: The Seven Years' War and the Fate of Empire in British North America, 1754–1766* (New York, 2000), esp. 25–29, 37–66, 94–107.

12. *Pennsylvania Gazette,* May 9, 1754. Timothy Shannon, *Indians and Colonists at the Crossroads of Empire: The Albany Congress of 1754* (Ithaca, NY, 2002), 4–8.

13. On Hendrick, see Hinderaker, *Two Hendricks,* esp. 220–30. On the Albany Congress, see Shannon, *Indians and Colonists.*

14. Benjamin Franklin to William Shirley, Dec. 4, 1754, *Papers of Benjamin Franklin,* 4: 443; Shannon, *Indians and Colonists,* 194–203.

15. Shannon, *Indians and Colonists,* 194–203.

16. Ibid.

17. The best account of this war is Anderson, *Crucible of War.* For Pennsylvania-specific studies, see Preston, *Texture of Contact;* Ward, *Breaking the Backcountry;* Silver, *Our Savage Neighbors;* Davidson, *War Comes to Quaker Pennsylvania;* and William Hunter, *Forts on the Pennsylvania Frontier, 1753–1758* (Harrisburg, PA, 1960).

18. Anderson, *Crucible of War.*

19. See especially David Preston's account of the war and its aftermath in *Texture of Contact.*

20. For a recent reassessment of the Armstrong "victory," see Daniel Barr, "Victory at Kittanning? Reevaluating the Impact of Armstrong's Raid on the Seven Years' War," *Pennsylvania Magazine of History and Biography,* 131, no. 1: 5–32.

21. This lower estimate is based on tax data from 1751–1752, found in Samuel Hazard's *Register of Pennsylvania,* 5: 115. Based on those numbers, Lancaster, York, and Cumberland had 7,825 taxables, while Philadelphia, Bucks, and Chester had 14,313, or about a third of the total taxable population. The higher estimate is based on 1760 data that shows the four counties of Lancaster, Cumberland, Northampton, and Berks had 12,427 taxables while the original counties had 16,221. For the Civil War comparison, see Ward, *Breaking the Backcountry,* esp. 58, 268 fn. 11.

22. Such talk of areas and the people within them *becoming* frontiers because of successful invasions was not confined to Pennsylvania. In Virginia in 1755, George Washington concluded "the inhabitants are in a miserable situation by their losses, and so apprehensive of

danger" that "the Blue Ridge will soon become our frontier." Examples from other colonies and times abound. William Trent to Colonel James Burd, Oct. 4, 1755, *PCM*, 7: 64; George Washington to Robert Dinwiddie, Apr. 7, 1756, *The Writings of George Washington from the Original Manuscript Sources*, ed. John Fitzpatrick (Washington, DC, 1931), 1: 300–304; "Petition of Cumberland County, August 7, 1755," *PA Archives*, First Series, 2: 385; "Petition of Bethlehem," 1757, *PA Archives*, First Series, 3: 164; "Governor Denny to ?," Easton, July 21, 1757, *PA Archives*, First Series, 3: 235. Later examples of people worrying about "becoming a frontier" can be found in Colonel Lochry to President of Congress, Sept. 8, 1777, *PA Archives*, First Series, 5: 599. He writes that "the Allegeny Mountain will soon become the frontier." Samuel Hunter to the Commanders of the Militia in Berks County, Fort Augusta, July 9, 1778, Papers of the Provincial Delegates, 5: 32, HSP. Hunter expressed concern that "Sunbury will be the frontier in less than twenty four hours."

23. "The Petition of the Few Remaining Inhabitants of Lower Smithfield," *PA Archives*, First Series, 3: 174–75; "A Petition of the Remaining Inhabitants of the County of Cumberland, August 21, 1756," *PA Archives*, First Series, 2: 757–58.

24. "A Letter from Justice Adam Reed to Edward Shippen, *PCM*, 7: 303–4; William Trent to Colonel James Burd, Oct. 4, 1755, *PCM*, 7: 64. For the desperation of war, see Silver, *Our Savage Neighbors*.

25. "A Brief Narrative of the Incursions and Ravages of the French and Indians in the Province of Pennsylvania," *PCM*, 6: 767–68.

26. James Smith, *A Remarkable Account* (Lexington, KY, 1799), 85.

27. Rhoda Barber, Journal of Settlement at Wright's Ferry on the Susquehanna River, 1830, HSP.

28. Conrad Weiser to Governor Morris, Reading, Oct. 30, 1755, *PCM*, 6: 656–59; "Petition of the Subscribers, Inhabitants of Derry Township," *PA Archives*, First Series, 3: 159.

29. John Armstrong to General Forbes, Carlisle, July 9, 1758, *PA Archives*, First Series, 3: 448.

30. John Armstrong, William Buchanan, and [William?] Smith to James Burd, Carlisle, Nov. 2, 1755, Edward Shippen Thompson Collection, Pennsylvania Historical and Museum Commission (hereafter PHMC); "Alterations in the Return of the United Brethren Residing in Bethlehem, 1757," July 26, 1757, Journal of John Van Etten, *PA Archives*, First Series, 3: 222–35, see esp. 233; James Read to Richard Peters, Reading, July 27, 1757, *PA Archives*, First Series, 3: 245; Conrad Weiser to Richard Peters, Heidelberg, Oct. 4, 1757, *PA Archives*, First Series, 3, 283–84.

31. Jennings, "Miquon's Passing," 462; Merritt, *At the Crossroads*, 174; Anderson, *Crucible of War*, 164–67, 205–7, 274–80. See esp. Silver, *Our Savage Neighbors*.

32. Ward, *Breaking the Backcountry*; Anderson, *Crucible of War*, chap. 14.

33. Anderson, *Crucible of War*, 163; Hunter, *Forts on the Pennsylvania Frontier*, 176; "A Letter from Bohemia, Cecil County, November 3, 1755," *Pennsylvania Gazette*, Nov. 20, 1755; [Patrick Work?] to Major James Burd, Fort Halifax, May 10, 1757, John Harris Papers, PHMC; *The Acts of Assembly of the Province of Pennsylvania* (Philadelphia, 1755), 277.

34. James Smith, *An Account of the Remarkable Occurrences in the Life and Travels of Colonel James Smith* (Lexington, KY, 1799). For an example of another captivity narrative, see Beverly Bond, Jr., ed., "The Captivity of Charles Stuart, 1755–1757," *Mississippi Valley Historical Review* 13 (1926–1927): 58–81.

35. It should be noted this refers only to the experience of Indians in the Ohio Country. Eastern Delawares experienced hardship during the war because of disrupted harvest. As Anderson describes, their experience could be called "desperation." Anderson, *Crucible of War*, 164.

36. Smith, *An Account*, 27–28.

37. Monday, Aug. 23, 1758, Journal of Joseph Shippen, PHMC; Silver, *Our Savage Neighbors*, 41–42.

38. This analysis is influenced by the work of Gregory Evans Dowd, *War Under Heaven: Pontiac, the Indian Nations, and the British Empire* (Baltimore, 2002). Dowd finds similar patterns as I describe, although his work emphasizes the growth of pan-Indianism in the 1760s.

39. Message of the Assembly to the Lieutenant Governor, *Pennsylvania Gazette*, Dec. 11, 1755.

40. Smith, *An Account*, 5–6. For the most powerful expression of this viewpoint, see Charles Thomson, *An Inquiry into the Causes of the Alienation of the Delaware and Shawnese Indians from the British Interest* (London, 1759).

41. The controversy surrounding the Friendly Association has persisted in historical analysis. William Hunter has argued that the Friendly Association in effect created these issues before the Indians themselves did. Using the example of Shingas, a western Delaware chief, he points out that "some . . . [were] in no way affected by the 'Walking Purchase.'" His interpretation argues that the Virginian loss in 1754 forced Indians to move from a position of neutrality to an alliance with France and that some, such as Shingas, represented people who felt the "discontent of any dispossessed people." Fred Anderson offers a similar analysis of the loss of the Delaware Indians. He recounts how Captain Jacobs, a Delaware chief, came to Philadelphia before allying with the French to ask for ammunition and support from the British. Rebuffed because of the impasse in the government, Anderson concludes this event pushed them into the French fold. Anderson, *Crucible of War*, 269. For other discussions of the Friendly Association, see also, Silver, *Our Savage Neighbors*, 99–103; Davidson, *War Comes to Quaker Pennsylvania*, 190.

42. Historians have tended to place greater emphasis on pan-Indian cooperation during later movements in the Ohio Country, usually as they relate to Pontiac's Rebellion and the Ohio Indians' rejection of the Treaty of Fort Stanwix as negotiated by the Iroquois in 1768. The origins of these later movements have much in common with the experiences of the 1750s. For arguments about Pontiac's Rebellion and the Treaty of Fort Stanwix, see Dowd, *War Under Heaven*, and Michael McConnell, "Peoples 'In Between': The Iroquois and Ohio Indians, 1720–1768," in *Beyond the Covenant Chain*, ed. Richter and Merrell, 93–114. Bond, ed., "Captivity of Charles Stuart," 58–81. I have some difficulty in using this speech by Shingas because of the context it was given. Shingas was speaking to his recent captives, perhaps in an effort to make them feel more comfortable.

43. Bond, ed., "Captivity of Charles Stuart," 58–81.

44. Anderson, *Crucible of War*, 205–7, 268–70, 275–76.

45. Ibid.

46. Fort Pitt Collection, PHMC; Charles Thomson, *An Inquiry into the Causes of the Alienation of the Delaware and Shawnese Indians from the British Interest* (London, 1759).

47. On Forbes, see Anderson, *Crucible of War*, chap. 28.

Chapter 6. Frontier Politics

1. West's biography is based on "William West," in *Lawmaking and Legislators in Pennsylvania*, ed. Craig Horle et al., 2: 1055–64.

2. Ibid.

3. For Hamilton, see "James Hamilton," in Armor, *Lives of the Governors*, 148–55. For more on Virginia's surveyor that West met, see Alan Kullikof, *From British Peasants to Colonial American Farmers* (Chapel Hill, NC, 2000), 147.

4. For what many took as a rejection of western Pennsylvania as part of Pennsylvania, see "Message of the Assembly to the Lieutenant Governor," Isaac Norris, Mar. 9, 1754, *PCM*, 5: 764; Hunter, *Forts on the Pennsylvania Frontier*, 206. For details on the Assembly's treatment of West, see "William West," in *Lawmaking and Legislators in Pennsylvania*, 2: 1055–64.

5. Bernard Bailyn, *The Origins of American Politics* (New York, 1968), 117–19; Tully, *Forming American Politics*, 149–50. For taxables, see Samuel Hazard, *The Register of Pennsylvania* (Philadelphia, 1830), 5: 115. See Beeman, *Varieties of Political Experience in Colonial America*, 212–15, for Pennsylvania's relative inaction. For comparison, New York's colonial legislature passed on average over twenty laws in some years, and Virginia's legislature averaged thirty.

6. *Votes of the Assembly*, *PA Archives*, Eighth Series, 4: 3446–47. "A Message from the Governor to the Assembly," *Pennsylvania Gazette*, Nov. 13, 1755.

7. Richard Jackson, *An Historical Review of the Constitution and Government of Pennsylvania* (London, 1759). There is some debate over the authorship of this work. Thomas Jefferson claimed it was Franklin's work, but most bibliographers now credit Richard Jackson.

8. Davidson, *War Comes to Quaker Pennsylvania*, 111; Tully, *Forming American Politics*, 149. "A Message to the Governor from the Assembly," *PCM*, 7: 742–48; [Joseph Galloway or Benjamin Franklin], *A True and Impartial State of the Province of Pennsylvania* (Philadelphia, 1759), 56.

9. The controversy is covered in many works, but for the political dimensions of it see especially. Davidson, *War Comes to Quaker Pennsylvania*, 147–65, and Tully, *Forming American Politics*, 149–59.

10. Though Franklin is credited with this line, and may have in fact written it, it was nonetheless first delivered by the speaker of the Pennsylvania Assembly. "Message of the Assembly to the Governor, November 11, 1755," *PCM*, 6: 695; *Votes of the Assembly*, *PA Archives*, Eighth Series, 4: 3446–47. The statement was subsequently republished on the title page of *An Historical Review of the Constitution of Pennsylvania*, written by Richard Jackson, where it received wider notice. Jackson also penned a defense of Assembly actions that mirrored the argument made by the Assembly, writing, that a militia could create "a vast number of new relations, dependences, etc., . . . under the control and subject to the dominion of our proprietor, and their governors. . . . The common men would be influenced by their officers and directed by them in their choice of representatives; so that not only the Quakers, but every man who had the virtue and spirit to oppose such arbitrary and unjust proceedings, would be excluded from that important trust." See also Tully, *Forming American Politics*, esp. 149–51.

11. The best account of this debate is Davidson, *War Comes to Quaker Pennsylvania*, 91–196. For total expenditures, see Hunter, *Forts on the Pennsylvania Frontier*, 197–99. Notably, the "gift" the proprietor gave was not as charitable as it seems. The £5,000 was to come from the collection of back taxes owed to him.

12. "A Message to the Governor from the Assembly, September 28, 1757," *PCM*, 7: 742–48, quotation on 746.

13. The story of Grubb's statement was well known throughout Pennsylvania. See the *Pennsylvania Gazette*, June 10, 1756, for a discussion of its truthfulness. For a biography of Grubb, see "Nathaniel Grubb," in *Lawmaking and Legislators in Pennsylvania*, 2: 409–12.

14. For a list of petitions from 1754, see *PA Archives*, First Series, 2: 236. The archives are replete with petitions, and correspondence to the governor suggests that even more petitions were submitted than printed. See Ward, *Breaking the Backcountry*, 102, and "Governor Denny to ?," Easton, July 21, 1757, *PA Archives*, First Series, 3: 235. For an extensive analysis of the language used in these petitions of desperation, see Silver, *Our Savage Neighbors*, especially 73–124.

15. Beeman, *Varieties of Political Experience in Colonial America*, 58. Beeman notes from the 1720s onward, "the [Pennsylvania] assembly concerned itself with the full range of regulatory functions" and "became somewhat more active in promoting economic development, both in terms of regulation of particular trades and in regulating the monetary system of the colony." At the same time, he concludes that from 1760–1756 almost half of all laws "dealt with the routine . . . matters . . . of the colony." By placing its legislative activity within a comparative framework, Beeman concludes such activity was "sparse" and believes the record of inactivity had much to do with "Quaker pacifism," which "made moot the elaborate set of laws and obligations involved with militia service."

16. "Letter from John Elder to Richard Peters, Paxton, Oct. 9, 1755," *PCM*, 6: 704–5.

17. "A Council Held at Philadelphia," Nov. 24, 1755, *PCM*, 5: 729–35. The story of the wagonload of corpses is taken from John Dunbar, *The Paxton Papers* (The Hague, 1957), 11, and especially the eyewitness accounts recorded in John Watson, *Annals of Philadelphia and Pennsylvania, In Olden Time* (Philadelphia, 1850), 165. Peter Silver gives the most recent assessment of it in *Our Savage Neighbors*, 77–78.

18. To the Representatives of the Freemen of the Province of Pennsylvania, in Assembly met: A Remonstrance by the Mayor, Aldermen, and Common-council of the City of Philadelphia, in Behalf of the said City [Nov. 25, 1755], in Copies of Several Public Papers, which have passed in the Province of Pensilvania in the Month of November, 1755, ser. 4, NV-176, p. 81, Penn Family Papers, HSP; *Pennsylvania Gazette*, Jan. 1, 1756. Oral history is recounted in Watson, *Annals of Philadelphia and Pennsylvania*, 165. Petition, Nov. 12, 1755, Penn Manuscripts, Assembly and Provincial Council, 81. 9, HSP.

19. *Pennsylvania Gazette*, June 10, 1756. The quote was discussed in explicit and veiled terms through numerous pamphlets published after the Paxton Boys incident in 1764. See Dunbar, *Paxton Papers*. Daniel Clark to Major [?], Harris's Ferry, Derry Township, Feb. 22, 1757, Harris Papers, PHMC. Letter from Edward Biddle to James Biddle, Reading, *PCM*, 6: 705.

20. "William Allen," *Lawmaking and Legislators in Pennsylvania*, 2: 231–80; "William Plumstead," *Lawmaking and Legislators in Pennsylvania*, 3: 1063–74; "Thomas Yorke," *Lawmaking and Legislators in Pennsylvania*, 2: 1105–7. See also *PCM*, 7: 290–93. For "chiefs of the frontiers," see "Samuel Weiser to Richard Peters, October 14, 1756," *PA Archives*, First Series, 3: 10–11.

21. For West's 1756 mission, see "William West," *Lawmaking and Legislators in Pennsylvania, 1055–1064* and "At a Council, April 21, 1756," *PCM*, 7: 96.

22. Ibid.

23. For John Stanwix, see "John Stanwix," *Lawmaking and Legislators in Pennsylvania*, 3: 1320; Richard McMaster, "Searching for Community: Carlisle, Pennsylvania 1750s–1780s," in Warren Hofstra, ed., *Ulster to America: The Scots-Irish Migration Experience, 1680–1830* (Knoxville, TN, 2012), 88; William Nester, *First Global War: Britain, France, and the Fate of North America, 1756–1775* (Westport, CT, 2000), 67.

24. "Morris to the Assembly, August 12, 1755," *PCM*, 6: 545; "Morris to Assembly, September 24, 1755," *Papers of the Governors*, 1: 495–503; "A Message from the Governor to the Assembly," *Pennsylvania Gazette*, Nov. 13, 1755; "Governor to Assembly, November 13, 1755," *Papers of the Governors*, 1: 516–17; "Letter to the Mayor and Corporation of Philadelphia," *Papers of the Governors*, 1: 532–33.

25. "A Message to the Governor from the Assembly, November 5, 1755," *PCM*, 6: 676–77.

26. "Report to Lord Loudon," *PCM*, 7: 449.

27. "At a Council, Whitehall, March 3, 1756," *PCM*, 7: 275–77.

28. "Petitions of the Inhabitants of Cumberland County," July 15, 1754, *PCM*, 6: 130. For additional petitions, see 129–31. Note the governor at this time was Morris's predecessor, James Hamilton.

29. "Morris to Thomas Penn, November 22, 1755," *PCM*, 6: 738.

30. "Message of Lieutenant Governor Robert Morris to the Assembly, Nov. 8, 1755," *PCM*, 6: 684–85; "A Council Held in Philadelphia," Aug. 22, 1755, *PCM*, 6: 590–91; "A Council Held in Philadelphia," Aug. 29, 1755, *PCM*, 6: 601. For his successor feeling the same pressure, see *PCM*, 7: 278.

31. "A Message to the Assembly, November 8, 1755," *PCM*, 6: 684.

32. Message of Lieutenant Governor Robert Morris to the Assembly, Nov. 8, 1755, *PCM*, 6: 684–85; "A Council Held in Philadelphia," Aug. 22, 1755, *PCM*, 6: 590–91; "A Council Held in Philadelphia," Aug. 29, 1755, *PCM*, 6: 601.

33. For "chiefs of the frontiers," see "Samuel Weiser to Richard Peters, October 14, 1756," *PA Archives*, First Series, 3: 10–11.

34. "Journal of Christian Frederick Post," in *Two Journals of Western Tours*, 1: 18, 197, https://archive.org/stream/twooojournalsofwespostrich#page/no/mode/2up.

35. Ibid.

36. Letter dated Carlisle, Feb. 28, 1760, in John Pritts, *Mirror of Olden Time Border Life* (Chambersburg, PA, 1849), 365; Deposition of Peter Title, Mar. 4, 1760, and Deposition of Richard Davis, Mar. 4, 1760, in *PA Archives*, First Series, 3: 705–6. For the illegal tavern, see *Cumberland County, Pennsylvania, Quarter Session Dockets, 1750–1785* (Baltimore, 2000), 28. I use Title here as the name, though it also appears as Tittel.

37. Anderson, *Crucible of War*, 162–64; Depositions of Tittel and Davis, *PA Archives*, First Series, 3: 705–6. Captain Jacobs reportedly had a relative that was seven feet tall, to whom Doctor John may be referring. He may also be referring to whites he killed that were bigger than Jacobs, although that does not make much sense in the context of the exchange. It would be unlikely he would claim settlers were bigger than Jacobs.

38. In 1784, John Ewing was sent to survey the southern boundary of Pennsylvania and traveled along the communication line created during the Seven Years' War that ran from Philadelphia to Fort Pitt. In his journal, he recounts how Bloody Run got its name: "John Paxton keeps a Tavern at ye Warriors Mt or Bloody Run; so called from the Murder of a

Number of People sent to Scout Provisions to Mr. Buchanan who was surveying ye Roads to Bedford in ye Year 1755." The permanence of this story, conveyed orally, speaks to the lasting effect of the culture of loss and death felt in these areas. John Ewing Memorandum Book, PHMC. For Braddock's field, see, for instance, Ebenezer Denny, *Military Journal of Major Ebenezer Denny* (Philadelphia, 1859), 116–18. Merrell, *Into the American Woods*, 302–6, esp. 304.

39. "At a Council," Feb. 26, 1760, *PCM*, 8: 455; Deposition of John Loughry, Carlisle, May 5, 1760, and Francis West to James Hamilton, Lt. Governor, Carlisle, May 7, 1760, *PA Archives*, First Series, 3: 731–32.

40. Pritts, *Mirror of Olden Time*, 364; Francis West to Governor Hamilton, Mar. 7, 1760, *PA Archives*, First Series, 3: 707.

41. Francis West to Governor Hamilton, Carlisle, Mar. 7, 1760, *PA Archives*, First Series, 3: 707; Feb. 21, 1760, *Votes of the Assembly, PA Colonial Records*, Eighth Series, 6: 5099–5100; Council at Philadelphia, Feb. 26, 1760, *PCM*, 8: 455–56; Deposition of John Loughry, Carlisle, May 5, 1760, and Francis West to James Hamilton, Lt. Governor, Carlisle, May 7, 1760, *PA Archives*, First Series, 3: 731–32.

42. "A Proclamation of Governor Hamilton, 1761," *PA Archives*, First Series, 4: 65. A letter believed to be from Francis West was first produced in Samuel Hazard, *Hazard's Register of Pennsylvania* (Harrisburg, PA, 1829), 4: 309, and reproduced in numerous other accounts of the event.

43. Deposition of John Loughry and Francis West to Governor Hamilton, May 7, 1760, *PA Archives*, First Series, 3: 731–32. "A Council Held at Philadelphia," May 4, 1762, *PCM*, 7: 709; "A Council Held at Philadelphia," May 6, 1760, *PCM*, 3: 712–13.

44. For more on the violence in Pennsylvania and its comparison to violence in neighboring colonies, especially New York, see Preston, *Texture of Contact*. For the idea of Pennsylvania as a "countryside," see Silver, *Our Savage Neighbors*.

Chapter 7. The Permanent Frontier

1. [James Burd?] to [?]. Fort Augusta, Dec. 28, 1756, Edward Shippen Thompson Collection, PHMC, State Archives, Harrisburg, PA. Fort Augusta was probably the most important fort in Pennsylvania. Sitting on the Susquehanna, it served as a strategic midpoint for forts to the west and east. However, its presence was extremely controversial to Indian allies of Pennsylvania, who claimed it sat on unpurchased lands. Fort Augusta was the largest fortification built on the Pennsylvania frontier and held, at some points, over four hundred men. Hunter, *Forts on the Pennsylvania Frontier*, 481–95.

2. For the best overview of this moment, see Jack Sosin, *Whitehall and the Wilderness: The Middle West in British Colonial Policy, 1760–1775* (Lincoln, NE, 1961); Colin Calloway, *The Scratch of a Pen: 1763 and the Transformation of North America* (New York, 2006); and Dowd, *War Under Heaven*.

3. Few historians have ever found much to commend about Amherst's tenure as commander-in-chief over North America. For some typical summaries, see Dowd, *War Under Heaven*, esp. 70–78; Calloway, *Scratch of a Pen*, 69–76; Ward, *Breaking the Backcountry*; and esp. William Nester, *"Haughty Conquerors": Amherst and the Great Indian Uprising of 1763* (Westport, CT, 2000). For evidence of the Indians' awareness of the changed power dynamics, see George Croghan to Board of Trade, Croghan Papers, Cadwalader Collection, Series IV, Box 5, 4, HSP. For Penn quote, see John Penn to Thomas Penn, Nov. 15, 1763, ser. 1, NV-032,

p. 208, Penn Family Papers, HSP. On the pan-Indian movements, see esp. Dowd, *War Under Heaven*. For Delaware quote, see Richard Middleton, *Pontiac's War: Its Causes, Course, and Consequences* (New York, 2012), 86.

4. Ward, *Breaking the Backcountry*, 224–25; Nester, *"Haughty Conquerors,"* quotation on victories on p. x; John Armstrong and Thomas Wilson to Colonel Shippen, Carlisle, June 20, 1763, *PA Archives*, First Series, 4: 108. See also Dowd, *War Under Heaven*, chap. 4; and Richter, *Facing East*, 191–201. For the numbers killed, see Richard White, *Middle Ground: Indians, Empires, and Republics in the Great Lakes Region, 1650–1815* (New York, 1991), 288, fn. 38.

5. John Penn to Thomas Penn, Nov. 15, 1763, ser. 1, NV-032, p. 208, Penn Family Papers, HSP; "An Act for Granting to His Majesty the Sum of Twenty-Four Thousand Pounds for the Defense and Protection of This Province and for Other Purposes Therein Mentioned," *Statutes at Large of Pennsylvania from 1682–1776* (Harrisburg, PA), chap. DV, 311–19; and "An Act for Granting His Majesty the Sum of Fifty-Five Thousand Pounds . . .," chap. DXIII, 344–67; Nester, *"Haughty Conquerors,"* 156–58; Franz, "Paxton: A Study of Community Structure and Mobility," 105–6.

6. Thomas Gage to Henry Bouquet, Mar. 1764, New York, Papers of Thomas Gage, PHMC; Nester, *"Haughty Conquerors,"* 156; John Armstrong to Governor of Pennsylvania, July 17, 1764, *PA Archives*, First Series, 4: 193.

7. The fullest accounts of the Paxton Boys can be found in Brooke Hindle, "March of the Paxton Boys," *William and Mary Quarterly* 3, no. 4 (1946), 461–86; and Silver, *Our Savage Neighbors*, 177–90. The historiography of the Paxton Boys' Rebellion and its aftermath on the politics of Pennsylvania is long and extensive, beginning first with Francis Parkman's *Pontiac's Conspiracy* (New York, 1929). There are a number of influential articles and essays that deal with the rebellion. See Hindle, "March of the Paxton Boys"; Peter Butzin, "Politics, Presbyterians and the Paxton Riots, 1763–1764," *Journal of Presbyterian History* 51 (1973), 70–86; James Crowley, "The Paxton Disturbances and Ideas of Order in Pennsylvania Politics," *Pennsylvania History* 37, no. 4 (1970), 317–39; James Kirby Martin, "The Return of the Paxton Boys and the Historical State of the Pennsylvania Frontier, 1764–1774," *Pennsylvania History* 38, no. 2 (1971), 117–33; Alison Olson, "The Pamphlet War over the Paxton Boys," *Pennsylvania Magazine of History and Biography* 123, nos. 1–2 (1999), 31–54; Krista Camenzind, "Metonymy, Violence, Patriarchy, and the Paxton Boys," in *Friends and Enemies in Penn's Woods*, ed. Pencak and Richter, 201–20. The rebellion has also been a central event in a number of monographs. See Hutson, *Pennsylvania Politics*; Richter, *Facing East*, 201–14; Silver, *Our Savage Neighbors*, 179–90; Griffin, *American Leviathan*, esp. 46–50, 65–67, 153–154, and 171; and Merrell, *Into the American Woods*, 284–88. For a recent work that explores various fraudulent sources created in the nineteenth century that have influenced historical interpretations, see Jack Brubaker, *Massacre of the Conestogas: On the Trail of the Paxton Boys in Lancaster County* (Charleston, SC, 2010). The following account is based on these accounts and the primary sources cited below.

8. For biographies of John and Richard Penn, see Treese, *Storm Gathering*, and Horle et al., *Lawmaking and Legislators in Pennsylvania*, 3: 63–71.

9. Hindle, "March of the Paxton Boys," and Silver, *Our Savage Neighbors*, 174–90.

10. Hindle, "March of the Paxton Boys," and Silver, *Our Savage Neighbors*, 174–90. See also *Declaration and Remonstrance*, in John Dunbar, *The Paxton Papers* (The Hague, 1957), 101–10, and Kenny, *Peaceable Kingdom Lost*.

11. Ibid.

12. John Harris to James Burd, Mar. 1, 1764, vol. 6, p. 95, Shippen Family Papers, HSP.

13. Henry Melchior Muhlenberg, Feb. 5, 1764, *The Journals of Henry Melchior Muhlenberg* (Philadelphia, 1982); John Harris to James Burd, Mar. 1, 1764, vol. 6, p. 95, Shippen Family Papers, HSP. For details on the route, see *An Historical Account of the Late Disturbances Between the Inhabitants of the Back Settlements of Pennsylvania and the Philadelphians* (Philadelphia, 1764), reprinted in Dunbar, *Paxton Papers*, 125–28. The exact number of marchers remains unclear, but the numbers certainly exceeded 200. Joseph Shippen speculated there were 700. This estimate is given credence by two German pastors who met with the marchers. Their reports stated a first wave consisted of 250 people and a second group of 400 that arrived later. The marchers themselves stated they had 1,500 total expected. Joseph Shippen to James Burd, Feb. 9, 1764, vol. 6, p. 87, Shippen Family Papers, HSP, and Muhlenberg, Feb. 6, 1764, and Feb. 7, 1764, *Journals*. Much of the following story is taken from the accounts of Henry Muhlenberg, who offers a rare, incisive, and historically accurate version. The fullest accounts of the Paxton Boys can be found in Hindle, "March of the Paxton Boys," 461–86, and Silver, *Our Savage Neighbors*, 177–90. Hindle did not have access to Muhlenberg's *Journals*, which offer new insights on the march and especially the negotiations that happened in Germantown. Many of Muhlenberg's other details are confirmed by Hindle's account. Not much information exists on Pastor Brycelius, although Patricia Bonomi discusses him in *Under the Cope of Heaven: Religion, Society, and Politics in Colonial America* (Oxford, 2003), 176.

14. Muhlenberg, Feb. 1, 1764, *Journals*; J. Schlosser to Thomas Gage, Jan. 31, 1764, Papers of Thomas Gage, PHMC. Schlosser and Gage had a long-running correspondence on how the British Army should act. Both agreed that they must defend the Indians, but Gage made it clear that they had to work under civil control and not independently.

15. Muhlenberg, Feb. 5–6, 1764, *Journals*.

16. John Penn to Thomas Penn, undated letter following June 16, 1764, letter, ser. 1, NV-032, pp. 296, 238, 236, Penn Family Papers, HSP. For Gage, see various correspondences written during the episode, in the Thomas Gage Papers, Clements Library. For a more easily accessed example, see Thomas Gage to Lord Halifax, May 12, 1764, *Correspondence of General Thomas Gage*, ed. Clarence Edwin Carter (New Haven, CT, 1931), 1: 26; Muhlenberg, *Journals*, Feb. 1, 1764; John Ewing to Joseph Reed, Philadelphia, 1764, in *Life and Times of Thomas Smith*, ed. Burton Alva Konkle (Philadelphia, 1904), 34–36. Muhlenberg, Feb. 1–8, 1764, *Journals*; John Penn to Thomas Penn, undated, letter following letter dated June 16, 1764, ser. 1, NV-032, pp. 296, 238, 236, Penn Family Papers dated June 16, 1764, HSP. The near accidental killing of the Germans became a point of parody in subsequent accounts of the march.

17. Muhlenberg, Feb. 1–8, 1764, *Journals*.

18. Ibid.

19. Ibid.

20. The exact number of marchers remains unclear, but the numbers certainly exceeded 200. Joseph Shippen speculated there were 700. This estimate is given credence by two German pastors who met with the marchers. Their reports stated a first wave consisted of 250 people and a second group of 400 that arrived later. The marchers themselves stated they had 1,500 total expected. Joseph Shippen to James Burd, Feb. 9, 1764, Shippen Papers, 6, HSP, and Muhlenberg, Feb. 6, 1764, and Feb. 7, 1764, *Journals*. Evidence of William Brown's attendance can be found in the *Declaration and Remonstrance* recently acquired by Lancasterhistory.org.

21. Muhlenberg, Feb. 6, 1764, and Feb. 7, 1764, *Journals*.

22. Muhlenberg, Feb. 6, 1764, and Feb. 7, 1764, *Journals*.

23. The best details on the pamphlet war can be found in Olson, "Pamphlet War," and in Dunbar, *Paxton Papers*, 1–51.

24. *Declaration and Remonstrance*, in *Paxton Papers*, 106–8.

25. "Apology," *Paxton Papers*, 195.

26. The "continuall warre" perceived by Virginia's legislature hints at this reasoning, though Nathaniel Bacon made it explicit when he led a band of frontier settlers opposed to the government's frontier policies in 1676. These rebels, like the Paxton Boys, complained that the government's policy, which called for a chain of nine forts, was too defensive and too static to properly protect frontiers. Bacon promised to fight an offensive war against "all Indians in general for they were all enemies." For "continuall warre," see William Hening, ed., "Act I" and "Act XI," 1679, *Statues at Large . . . of Virginia, 1660-1682*, ed. William Waller Hening, Vol. 2 (New York, 1823), 433 and 448. In 1702, Cotton Mather recounted how, during "the time of our Indian Wars," a group of "furious English people . . . clamoured for the extirpation of the praying [converted] Indians . . . as well as the Pagan Indians that were in hostility against us" because a strand of popular sentiment had come to view all Indians as one and the same. Pennsylvanians, who had experienced a distinctive "long peace" during the colony's first several decades, had not shared this experience with their fellow colonists, but by 1763, the Paxton Boys and their supporters had come to express similar views. Nathanial Bacon quoted in Eric Hinderaker and Peter Mancall, *At the Edge of Empire: The Backcountry in British North America* (Baltimore, 2003), 50. Cotton Mather, *Magnalia Christi Americana: Or the Ecclesiastical History of New England* (Boston, 1702), 182. I believe Kathy Brown in *Good Wives, Nasty Wenches, and Anxious Patriarchs: Gender, Race, and Power in Colonial Virginia* (Chapel Hill, NC, 1996) and Jill Lepore in *The Name of War: King Philip's War and the Origins of American Identity* (New York, 1998) both uncover a similar process happening at earlier times and in different places.

Recently, a growing number of historians have tried to argue that the Paxton Boys were not motivated by racial antagonisms, or at least race was not central to their acts. I believe otherwise. For two prominent examples of this argument, see Silver, *Our Savage Neighbors*, and Griffin, *American Leviathan*. Preston in *Texture of Contact* does not discuss race directly, but his treatment of interactions between whites and Native Americans does create a much different picture of intercultural relations, often privileging the ways regular people could get along with one another on a daily basis. While I acknowledge the presence of cross-cultural exchange and interaction, I am more concerned with the rise of violence that broke down these relationships and proved more determinative in the course of history.

27. Benjamin Franklin, *Narrative of the Late Massacres* (Philadelphia, 1764), in *Paxton Papers*, 55–76, quotation on 63.

28. Smith and Gibson, *Declaration and Remonstrance*, in *Paxton Papers*, 104.

29. Many writers used the metaphor of the body to describe the role frontiers played. Frontiers represented the limbs of the metaphorical body politic. See Walter Raleigh, *The Cabinet-Council Containing the Cheif [sic] Arts of Empire and Mysteries of State* (London, 1658); Julius Caesar, *Commentaries* (London, 1655); and Jean Balzac, *Aristippus* (London, 1659). Benjamin Franklin, *Narrative of the Late Massacres* (Philadelphia, 1764), in *Paxton Papers*, 55–76, quotation on 63.

30. The shortest yet most incisive summary of Radical Whig thought can be found in Bernard Bailyn, *Origins of American Politics* (New York, 1967), 38–52. A longer discussion can be found in Bernard Bailyn, *The Ideological Origins of the American Revolution* (Cambridge, MA, 1992), 55–93. For more on the legitimate use of violence, see Pauline Maier, *From Resistance to Revolution: Colonial Radicals and the Development of American Opposition to Britain, 1765–1776* (New York, 1991). For quotations, see Smith and Gibson, *Declaration and Remonstrance*, in *Paxton Papers*, 104; Barton, *Conduct*, in *Paxton Papers*, 267, 278–79, 296–97.

31. Smith and Gibson, *Declaration and Remonstrance*, in *Paxton Papers*, 99–111, esp. 105–6.

32. Ibid., esp. 104, 108–9; Conrad Weiser to Governor Denny, Heidelberg, Oct. 27, 1757, *PA Archives*, First Series, 3: 313–14.

33. See, for instance, Maier, *From Resistance to Revolution*, and Bailyn, *Ideological Origins* and *Origins of American Politics*.

34. Barton, *Conduct*, in *Paxton Papers*, 296–97.

35. "Apology of the Paxton Volunteers," in *Paxton Papers*, 193–94.

36. Ibid. Such a viewpoint seemed to have wider salience, with John Ewing likewise writing to a friend in London that the Conestoga "never were subjects to his Majesty; were a free, independent state, retaining all the powers of a free state." Much of this language was paraphrased from the *Declaration and Remonstrance*, in *Paxton Papers*, 193–95, 201. John Ewing to Joseph Reed, Philadelphia, 1764, in *Life and Times of Thomas Smith*, ed. Konkle, 34–36.

37. The quotation about "what nation under the sun" comes from "Apology of the Paxton Volunteers," HSP and is not founded in the printed Dunbar, *Paxton Papers*.

38. John Penn to Thomas Penn, undated letter following letter dated June 16, 1764, ser. 1, NV-032, pp. 296, 238, 236, Penn Family Papers, HSP.

39. John Penn to Thomas Penn, Sept. 1, 1764, ser. 1, NV-032, pp. 252–56, Penn Family Papers, HSP; Rhoda Barber, Journal of Settlement at Wright's Ferry on the Susquehanna River, 1830, HSP.

40. Benjamin Franklin, *Cool Thoughts on the Present Situation of Our Public Affairs* (Philadelphia, 1764), accessible at http://www.franklinpapers.org/franklin/framedVolumes.jsp?vol=11&page=153b.

41. Ibid.

42. The best analysis on the failure of the change for government is Hutson, *Pennsylvania Politics*.

43. John Penn to Thomas Penn, Dec. 15, 1765, Thomas Penn Letterbooks, Incoming Correspondence, Reel 9, HSP.

44. John Penn to Thomas Penn, Dec. 15, 1765, ser. 1, NV-033, p. 23, Penn Family Papers, HSP; Armstrong quotation from Tully, *Forming American Politics*, 157.

45. The best summary of this election can be found in Hutson, *Pennsylvania Politics*.

Chapter 8. The British Empire's Frontier Crisis

1. For good overviews of this shift, see Sosin, *Whitehall and the Wilderness*; Michael McConnell, *A Country Between: The Upper Ohio Valley and Its Peoples, 1724-1774* (Lincoln, NE, 1992) and Anderson, *Crucible of War*.

2. Robert Rogers, Rogers Estimates, American Philosophical Society (hereafter APS), Philadelphia, PA.

3. Thomas Penn to Governor Hamilton, Jan. 9, 1762, Thomas Penn Correspondence, APS.

4. Calloway, *Scratch of a Pen*, 92–111, esp. 92.

5. Calloway, *Scratch of a Pen*, 92–111, esp. 96; Dowd, *War Under Heaven*, 177–203, quotation on 177. Although some scholars tend to see the proclamation as limiting Native rights, most agree that the line was an attempt by the British to impose order on lands acquired in the peace treaty with France and to create a legal framework to facilitate lawful expansion. In other words, if historian Gregory Evans Dowd is correct in concluding that the line "denied Native sovereignty," it did at least provide Native people with a façade of rights, even if only to create the means through which expansion would happen. The best eighteenth-century proponent for Dowd's point of view might have been George Washington, who said "I can never look upon that proclamation in any other light . . . than a temporary expedient to quiet the minds of the Indians and must fall of course in a few years especially when those Indians are consenting to our occupying the lands." The key to understanding Washington's view of the line is expressed in the phrase "Indians consenting." Consent in this sense held a legal meaning rooted in Lockean political theory in which consent without coercion was just and provided Indians with ownership of the land. Washington, however, simply assumed that Indians were giving and would continue to give lands to Britain. George Washington to William Crawford, Sept. 21, 1767, *The Washington–Crawford Letters*, ed. C. W. Butterfield (Cincinnati, OH, 1877), 1–5.

6. Ward, *Breaking the Backcountry*, 2, 186–215, esp. 202; Col. Stanwix to Richard Peters, Carlisle, July 25, 1757, *PA Archives*, First Series, 3: 239; Sosin, *Whitehall and the Wilderness*, especially chap. 5.

7. Sosin, *Whitehall and the Wilderness*. See also Richter, *Facing East*, and "Native Americans, the Plan of 1764, and a British Empire That Never Was," in *Cultures and Identities in Colonial British America*, ed. Robert Olwell and Alan Tully. Ward, *Breaking the Backcountry*; Calloway, *Scratch of a Pen*, 243–45; Dowd, *War Under Heaven*, 177–78. Gage to Henry Bouquet, Mar. ?, 1764, Papers of Thomas Gage, PHMC.

8. The Black Boys were once a prominent part of popular historical knowledge and discussion. In the 1930s, popular historical fiction writer Neil Swanson wrote *The First Rebel: Being a Lost Chapter of Our History and a True Narrative of America's First Uprising Against English Military Authority* (New York, 1939). The book was the basis for an early John Wayne film, *Allegheny Uprising* (1939). The book is based on the records of the *PA Archives* but adds dialogue and description that is fictionalized. In the 1960s and 1970s, two complementary articles came out on the Black Boys. One examined the rebellion within the context of group action, while the other examined whether or not the Black Boys were part of the Revolutionary Movement. Eleanor Webster, in "Insurrection at Fort Loudon in 1765: Rebellion or Preservation of Peace," *Western Pennsylvania Historical Magazine* 47 (1964), 5–39, explores the motivations; and Stephen Cutcliffe, in "Sideling Hill Affair: The Cumberland County Riots of 1765," *Western Pennsylvania Historical Magazine* 59 (1976), 39–54, takes a more sociological view of their mobilization, informed by the work of Pauline Maier. Alden Vaughan also briefly discusses the Black Boys in his essay on frontier mobilization, "Frontier Banditti and the Paxton Boys' Legacy, 1763–1775," *Pennsylvania History* 52 (1984), 1–29. More recent attention has been paid to the Black Boys, this time focusing more on their relations with imperial policy and Indian relations. See esp. Dowd, *War Under Heaven*, 204–11. Dowd takes a sympathetic view

of the Black Boys, specifically arguing against equating them with the Paxton Boys' Rebellion, a linkage that he argues too many historians have automatically assumed. Griffin, in *American Leviathan*, takes a different tack, arguing the Black Boys symbolized a stateless society. For a literary exploration of the Black Boys, particularly James Smith who wrote an autobiography in which the episode played a prominent role, see Ed White, *The Backcountry and the City: Colonization and Conflict in Early America* (Minneapolis, 2005).

9. William Johnson to George Croghan, Johnson Hall, Apr. 3, 1765, ser. 4, box 202, folder 32, Cadwalader Family Papers, HSP; George Croghan to [Thomas Gage?], Fort Pitt, Mar. 12, 1765, ser. 4, box 201, folder 26, Cadwalader Family Papers, HSP. For a transcription of the April 3 letter, see *The Papers of Sir William Johnson* (Albany, NY, 1953), 11: 667.

10. The best account of the drivers' experience can be found in a number of depositions from the drivers themselves, held in the Papers of Thomas Gage. The depositions follow a letter dated Mar. 11, 1765, written by Thomas Barnsby to Thomas Gage reporting on the disturbances. See the Deposition of Elian Davison, Mar. 8, 1765, and the Deposition of Robert Allison, Mar. 8, 1765, all found in Papers of Thomas Gage, PHMC.

11. Grant wrote a long letter detailing the events from his perspective in a letter to Thomas Gage dated Sept. 16, 1765, Papers of Thomas Gage, PHMC. For information on the sergeant's search and arrests, see "Deposition of Leonard McGlashan," Aug. 20, 1765, *PA Archives*, First Series, 4: 233–36. The prisoner exchange can be found in Thomas Barnsby to Thomas Gage, Mar. 11, 1765, and in "A Copy of a Letter from Lieutenant Charles Grant to Colonel Bouquet," Mar. 9, 1765, Papers of Thomas Gage, PHMC, and Deposition of Lieutenant Charles Grant, *PA Archives*, First Series, 4: 220–22.

12. Quote from Thomas Barnsby to Thomas Gage, Mar. 11, 1765, Papers of Thomas Gage, PHMC.

13. Smith, *An Account*. Evidence corroborating Smith's story can be found in the Records of the Revolutionary Government, Record Group 27, State Archives, Harrisburg, PA, and Hand Papers, David Library of the American Revolution (hereafter DLAR), Washington Crossing, PA.

14. Deposition of Lieutenant Charles Grant, *PA Archives*, First Series, 4: 220–22. There is no record of the destruction of the powder in the *PA Archives*, but information can be found in William Trent to Joseph Shippen, Mar. 13, 1765, Shippen Papers, HSP, and the proceedings of the Governor's Conference, Deposition of Robert Callender, Mar. 28, 1765, Deposition of Robert Allison, Apr. 1, 1765, Deposition of Robert Brownson, Apr. 3, 1765, and Deposition of James Maxwell, Apr. 3, 1765, in the Papers of Thomas Gage, PHMC; John Reid to Thomas Gage, Carlisle, June 1, 1765, Gage Papers, Clements Library, University of Michigan, Ann Arbor, MI (hereafter Gage Papers, Clements Library).

15. Josiah Davenport to Indian Commissioners, Mar. 27, 1765, case 14, box 10, folder 3, Simon Gratz Autograph Collection, HSP; John Armstrong to George Croghan, Mar. 26, 1765, Carlisle, ser. 4, box 201, folder 2, Cadwalader Family Papers, HSP. It is not clear that the "Paxtonians" were the same Paxton Boys. During episodes like this, it became commonplace for people to link organized groups to well-known past groups.

16. Josiah Davenport to Indian Commissioners, Mar. 27, 1765, case 14, box 10, folder 3, Simon Gratz Autograph Collection, HSP; John Armstrong to George Croghan, Mar. 26, 1765, Carlisle, ser. 4, box 201, folder 2, Cadwalader Family Papers, HSP. See also "Extract of a Letter from Colonel Reid to General Gage, June 1, 1765," in *PCM*, 9: 268–69.

17. Thomas Gage to John Reid, June 9, 1765, and Thomas Gage to Governor John Penn, June 16, 1765, Papers of Thomas Gage, PHMC; William Johnson to John Penn, Apr. 12, 1765, *PA Archives*, First Series, 4: 215–16; John Penn to Thomas Penn, Mar. 16, 1765, ser. 1, NV-033, pp. 5–7, Penn Family Papers; John Armstrong to George Croghan, Mar. 26. 1765, Carlisle, ser. 4, box 201, folder 2, Cadwalader Family Papers, HSP; John Penn to Thomas Gage, June 27, 1765, Philadelphia, *PA Archives, Papers of the Governors*, Fourth Series, 3: 303–4; Nathan McCullock, Lt, to George Croghan, Mar. 7, 1765, box 202, folder 35, ser. 4, Cadwalader Family Papers, HSP.

18. Thomas Gage to John Reid, June 9, 1765, and Thomas Gage to Governor John Penn, June 16, 1765, Papers of Thomas Gage, PHMC; William Johnson to John Penn, Apr. 12, 1765, *PA Archives*, First Series, 4: 215–16; John Penn to Thomas Penn, Mar. 16, 1765, NV-033, pp. 5–7, ser. 1, Penn Family Papers, HSP; John Armstrong to George Croghan, Mar. 26. 1765, Carlisle, box 201, folder 2, ser. 4, Cadwalader Family Papers, HSP; John Penn to Thomas Gage, June 27, 1765, Philadelphia, *PA Archives, Papers of the Governors*, Fourth Series, 3: 303–4.

19. Petition from Cumberland County, [Mar. 1765], *Papers of Henry Bouquet* (Harrisburg, PA, 1951–1994), 6: 777–79.

20. Ibid.

21. Ibid.

22. The proceedings in Carlisle can be found in the Papers of Thomas Gage, PHMC. The first mention of the conference came in a letter by John Penn to Thomas Gage dated Mar. 22, 1765. Subsequent letters and depositions suggest he arrived on or about Mar. 27 and stayed through the first week of April. Reports on the proceedings can be found in John Armstrong to George Croghan, Mar. 26, 1765, ser. 4, box 201, folder 2, Cadwalader Family Papers, HSP; Croghan correspondence cited here and Josiah Davenport to Indian Commissioners, Mar. 27, 1765, at the HSP. The depositions taken, which may give the fullest accounting of the initial attack, can be found following a letter Penn wrote Gage dated June 28, 1765, in the Gage Papers, Clements Library. See especially the Deposition of William Smith, Apr. 3, 1765, for the defense of the Black Boys.

23. William Johnson to John Penn, June 7, 1765, *PA Archives*, First Series, 4: 227. Davenport to Indian Commissioners, Mar. 27, 1765, Papers of the Indian Commissioners, HSP. Davenport reports meeting with John Harris, who told Davenport to be ready to encounter resistance from settlers if he traveled west. Thomas Gage to John Penn, July 5, 1765, Papers of Thomas Gage, PHMC; James Smith to Commander Escorting Party, June 12, 1765, *PA Archives*, First Series, 4: 228; "A List of Loading Belonging to Mr. John Gibson," June 1, 1765, *PA Archives*, First Series, 4: 224–25. Throughout July and August, reports of inspections by the Black Boys can be found in a number of depositions and letters. See, for instance, Deposition of Henry Prather, Sept. 12, 1765, and Deposition of Thomas Romberg, Sept. 12, 1765, *PA Archives*, First Series, 4: 37–39. Deposition of Lieutenant Charles Grant, *PA Archives*, First Series, 4: 220–22. The report on the trial is in John Penn to Thomas Gage, June 28, 1765, Gage Papers, Clements Library.

24. John Reid to Thomas Gage, June 4, 1765, Papers of Thomas Gage, PHMC.

25. Lieutenant Charles Grant to General Thomas Gage, Aug. 24, 1765, *PA Archives*, First Series, 4: 281. John Reid also observed that "since Governor Penn's inquiry into that matter the rioters have become more daring and insolent." John Reid to Thomas Gage, June 1, 1765, and John Reid to Thomas Gage, June 4, 1765, Papers of Thomas Gage, PHMC. John Armstrong to George Croghan, Mar. 26, 1765, ser. 4, box 201, folder 2, Cadwalader Family Papers,

HSP. Lieutenant Charles Grant to Thomas Gage, Aug. 24, 1765, *PA Archives*, First Series, 4: 232. John Penn to Thomas Gage, Philadelphia, Feb. 10, 1766, Penn Correspondence, HSP, and *PA Archives, Papers of the Governors*, Fourth Series (Harrisburg, PA, 1900), 3: 310–11.

26. Thomas Gage to John Reid, June 9, 1765, and Thomas Gage to Governor John Penn, June 16, 1765, Papers of Thomas Gage, PHMC; William Johnson to John Penn, Apr. 12, 1765, *PA Archives*, First Series, 4: 215–16; John Penn to Thomas Penn, Mar. 16, 1765, ser. 1, NV-033, pp. 5–7, Penn Family Papers, HSP; Nathan McCulloch to George Croghan, Bedford, Mar. 7, 1765, Gage Papers, Clements Library; John Reid to Thomas Gage, Fort Loudon, June 4, 1765, Charles Grant to Thomas Gage, Sept. 16, 1765, and Henry Bouquet to Thomas Gage, Philadelphia, Mar. 20, 1765, Gage Papers, Clements Library.

27. For the removal of William Smith from office, see John Penn to Thomas Gage, Philadelphia, Feb. 10, 1766, Penn Correspondence, HSP, and *PA Archives, Papers of the Governors*, Fourth Series (Harrisburg, PA, 1900), 3: 310–11.

28. "A List of the Justices for Cumberland County," *PCM*, 8: 637; John Armstrong to George Croghan, Mar. 26, 1765, box 201, folder 2, ser. 4, Cadwalader Family Papers, HSP; William Smith to Charles Grant, Nov. 14, 1765, Fort Smith, Gage Papers, Clements Library.

29. John Armstrong to George Croghan, Mar. 26, 1765, box 201, folder 2, ser. 4, Cadwalader Family Papers, HSP; Charles Grant to Thomas Gage, Fort Loudon, Aug. 24, 1765, *PA Archives*, First Series, 4: 231–33. Petition from Cumberland County, [Mar. 1765], *Papers of Henry Bouquet* (Harrisburg, PA, 1951–1994), 6: 777–79, succinctly conveys this belief in the settlers' own words.

30. Extract of a letter from Lieutenant Charles Grant to Colonel John Reid, Nov. 22, 1765, *PA Archives*, First Series, 4: 246–47; Extract of a Letter from Captain William Grant to Colonel John Reid, Nov. 25, 1765, *PA Archives*, First Series, 4: 247–48; and Thomas Gage to John Penn, New York, Dec. 13, 1765, Gage Papers, Clements Library. Details on the transfer of the guns can be found in "Obligation of James Smith and Samuel Owens," Nov. 18, 1765, *PA Archives*, First Series, 4: 245; "Receipt for Guns Captured," Nov. 10, 1765, *PA Archives*, First Series, 4: 245; "Obligation of Jonathan Smith," Nov. 18, 1765, *PA Archives*, First Series, 4: 246; and John Penn to William Smith and John Reynolds, Dec. 18, 1765, vol. 1, p. 151, Lancaster County Papers, HSP.

31. John Ross to Benjamin Franklin, May 20, 1765, Philadelphia, Read Manuscripts, HSP, also available at http://franklinpapers.org/franklin/framedVolumes.jsp?vol = 12&page = 138a; Thomas Gage to John Reid, June 24, 1765, Papers of Thomas Gage, PHMC. John Penn to Thomas Penn, Mar. 16, 1765, ser. 1, NV-033, pp. 5–7, Penn Family Papers, HSP. John Penn argued that if the Assembly had "paid any regard to my recommendation . . . and framed a militia law, all the late mischief And disturbance might have been prevented, such a law being absolutely necessary to aid the civil powers, and indeed the only natural defence and support of government," in John Penn to Thomas Gage, June 28, 1765, Papers of Thomas Gage, PHMC. John Penn to Thomas Penn, Mar. 30, 1768, ser. 1, NV-033, pp. 130–132, Penn Family Papers, HSP.

32. [James Burd?] to Joseph Shippen, Fort Augusta, Jan. 19, 1764, Shippen Papers, HSP; Franklin, *Cool Thoughts*, http://franklinpapers.org/franklin/framedVolumes.jsp?vol = 12& page = 138a.

33. William Johnson to George Croghan, Johnson Hall, Apr. 8, 1765, ser. 4, box 202, folder 32, Cadwalader Family Papers, HSP.

34. Thomas Gage to William Fauquier, New York, June 2, 1765, and William Fauquier to Thomas Gage, Williamsburg, July 6, 1765, Gage Papers, Clements Library; John Penn to Thomas Penn, Sept. 12, 1766, ser. 1, NV-033, pp. 80–84, Penn Family Papers, HSP.

35. John Penn to Thomas Penn, Sept. 12, 1766, Penn Papers, Thomas Penn Correspondence, HSP.

36. Stump first appears in the historical record in a proclamation by Penn to remove himself from property beyond the line of settlement. "A Proclamation," in *Pennsylvania Gazette*, Oct. 2, 1766. Deposition of William Blyth, Jan. 19, 1768, Gage Papers, Clements Library. The historiography on the Stump murder is not as extensive as those on the Paxton Boys and Black Boys. For the most exhaustive account of the affair, see Linda A. Ries, "The Rage of Opposing Government: The Stump Affair of 1768," *Cumberland County History* 1 (Summer 1984): 21–45. See also G. S. Rowe, "The Frederick Stump Affair, 1768, and the Challenge to Legal Historians of Early Pennsylvania," *Pennsylvania History* 49, no. 4 (1982): 259–88; and Marietta and Rowe, *Troubled Experiment*, chap. 5. Recent works that have dealt with Frederick Stump are Merrell, *Into the American Woods*, 304–305; Griffin, *American Leviathan*, 82–83; and esp. Silver, *Our Savage Neighbors*, 154–59.

37. Blyth Deposition, Gage Papers, Clements Library; List of Indians Murdered, vol. 6, p. 195, Shippen Family Papers, HSP.

38. "A Proclamation," in *Pennsylvania Gazette*, Jan. 28, 1768.

39. "Extract of a Letter from Carlisle, Containing a Full Account of the Taking and Rescue of Frederick Stump," *Pennsylvania Gazette*, Feb. 11, 1768; Receipt for 100 Pounds to William Patterson, Aug. 6, 1764, vol. 6, p. 107, Shippen Family Papers, HSP; William Patterson to Joseph Shippen, Carlisle, Jan. 23, 1768, Shippen Papers, HSP. For a transcription, see also I. D. Rupp, *History and Topography of Northumberland, Huntingdon, Mifflin, Centre, Union, Columbia, Juniata, and Clinton Counties* (Lancaster, 1846), 518.

40. William Patterson to Joseph Shippen, Carlisle, Jan. 23, 1768, Shippen Papers, HSP. For a transcription, see also I. D. Rupp, *History and Topography of Northumberland, Huntingdon, Mifflin, Centre, Union, Columbia, Juniata, and Clinton Counties* (Lancaster, 1846), 518.

41. Shippen to Burd, Lancaster, Jan. 26, 1768, Shippen Papers, HSP.

42. William Patterson to Joseph Shippen, Carlisle, Jan. 23, 1768, Cumberland County Historical Society; Receipt for 100 Pounds to William Patterson, Aug. 6, 1764, vol. 6, p. 107, Shippen Family Papers, HSP; Edward Shippen to James Burd, Lancaster, Jan. 26, 1768, vol. 6, p. 197, Shippen Family Papers, HSP; Edward Shippen Jr. to James Tilgham, Feb. 2, 1768, vol. 6, p. 196, Shippen Family Papers, HSP; Thomas Gage to John Penn, Jan. 26, 1768, Gage Papers, Clements Library.

43. "To Messieurs Hall and Sellers, As the Affair of Frederick Stump," *Pennsylvania Gazette*, Mar. 3, 1768; Edward Shippen Jr. to James Tilgham, Feb. 2, 1768, vol. 6, p. 196, Shippen Family Papers, HSP.

44. "As the Affair of Frederick Stump Appears," *Pennsylvania Gazette*, Mar. 13, 1768; Cumberland County Court Records, PHMC.

45. William Allen to Thomas Penn, Feb. 25, 1768, and William Allen to Thomas Penn, Oct. 12, 1768, Penn Papers, HSP.

46. "Message of the Assembly," Joseph Galloway, Jan. 13, 1768, in *Votes of the Assembly, October 14, 1767-September 26, 1776*, 14.

47. "A Message of the Assembly to the Governor," *Pennsylvania Gazette*, Feb. 4, 1768; John Penn to Thomas Penn, Feb. 8, 1768, ser. 1, NV-033, pp. 130–32, Penn Family Papers, HSP.

48. George Croghan to Colonel Wilkins, Philadelphia, Mar. 1768, Cadwalader Collection, folder 29, HSP.

49. Inquisition, Cumberland County Court Records, PHMC; ser. 1, NV-033, pp. 130–132, Penn Family Papers, HSP. George Croghan to John Penn, Mar. 27, 1768, ser. 4, box 201, folder 29, Cadwalader Family Papers, HSP; George Croghan to Colonel Wilkins, Philadelphia, Mar. 1768, Cadwalader Collection, folder 29, HSP.

50. For South Carolina, see Richard Maxwell Brown, *The South Carolina Regulators* (Cambridge, MA, 1963). For North Carolina, see Marjoleine Kors, *Breaking Loose Together: The Regulator Rebellion in Pre-Revolutionary North Carolina* (Chapel Hill, NC, 2002).

51. Griffin, *American Leviathan*, chaps. 1–3.

52. John Penn to William Johnson, May 23, 1765, *Papers of William Johnson*, 11: 746–47; Thomas McKee to William Johnson, June 1, 1765, *Papers of William Johnson*, 11: 759–61.

53. The Petition of a Number of the Late Inhabitants of Juniata, *Papers of William Johnson*, 4: 751–52.

54. Dowd, *War Under Heaven*, 233–36, 263–65; Griffin, *American Leviathan*, 88–89.

Chapter 9. Independent Frontiers

1. McConnell, *A Country Between Us*, 260. McConnell relies on estimates George Croghan made, which were likely correct given the numbers of people who registered on tax rolls after counties were created.

2. For Croghan's self-regulating community, see George Wilson to Arthur St. Clair, Aug. 14, 1771, in *The St. Clair Papers*, ed. William Henry Smith (Cincinnati, OH, 1882) (hereafter *St. Clair Papers*), 257–59; William Crawford to James Tilgham, Aug. 9, 1771, *PA Archives*, First Series, 4: 424–25. For an example of these resolves in action, see the Deposition of Thomas Woods, *PA Archives*, First Series, 4: 435. Thomas Woods, justice of the peace for Bedford County, went into the settlement to eject a settler but was beaten off by a crew of about twenty-five men. R. L. Hooper to Arthur St. Clair, July 10, 1772, Arthur St. Clair to Joseph Shippen, July 18, 1772, *St. Clair Papers*, 1: 264–67. George Croghan to David Sample, Apr. 4, 1774, *PA Archives*, First Series, 4: 483. Later, in a letter to Lord Dunmore, he expressed his belief that Virginia had rights to the land—as long as it recognized his deeds—and complained of "Mr. Penns Agents . . . forcible entrys on my Lands, by which means I have been deprived the use of my property." George Croghan to Lord Dunmore, Apr. 9, 1774, ser. 4, box 201, folder 33, Cadwalader Family Papers, HSP. For Vandalia, see Sosin, *Whitehall and the Wilderness*, and James Corbett David, *Dunmore's New World: The Extraordinary Life of a Royal Governor in Revolutionary America* (Charlottesville, VA, 2013), chap. 3. For the Penn quote, see John Penn to Thomas Penn, Aug. 3, 1772, ser. 1, NV-034, p. 35, Penn Family Papers, HSP.

3. Dowd, *War Under Heaven*, 233–36. See also Sosin, *Whitehall and the Wilderness*; Griffin, *American Leviathan*, 88–89; and Brendan McConville, *The King's Three Faces: The Rise and Fall of Royal America, 1688–1776* (Chapel Hill, NC, 2006), 220–48

4. See Sosin, *Whitehall and the Wilderness*, chap. 9, and also Griffin, *American Leviathan*, chaps. 3 and esp. 4.

5. The Connecticut conflict is well known in Pennsylvania history. One of the best recent accounts is Paul Moyer, *Wild Yankees: The Struggle for Independence Along Pennsylvania's Revolutionary Frontier* (Ithaca, NY, 2007). Moyer, like many chroniclers, tends to focus on the Connecticut side of the story, especially in the early years. My analysis focuses on how Pennsylvania as a colony defending its territory reacted. Richard Peters to Thomas Penn, Jan. 13,

1761, Philadelphia, ser. 4, NV-017, p. 155, Penn Family Papers, HSP; James Hamilton to Thomas Penn, Nov. 21, 1762, Philadelphia, ser. 1, NV-184, p. 184, Penn Family Papers, HSP.

6. Moyer, *Wild Yankees* provides the best recent analysis of the company and its background.

7. James Hamilton to Thomas Penn, Nov. 21, 1762, Philadelphia, Penn Letterbooks, HSP.

8. Moyer, *Wild Yankees*, 21–31; Oscar Jewell Harvey, *A History of Wilkes-Barre* (Wilkes-Barre, PA, 1909), 1: 425–34. John Penn to Thomas Penn, Nov. 6, 1768, Philadelphia, ser. 1, NV-033, p. 180, Penn Family Papers, HSP.

9. John Penn to Thomas Penn, Mar. 10, 1770, Penn Correspondence, HSP; Hugh Williamson to John Penn, Mar. 24, 1770, Wyoming, *PA Archives*, First Series, 4: 366–67; for hints that the lottery was corrupted, see Edmund Physick to Thomas Penn, Apr. 19, 1769, Penn Papers, HSP.

10. Edmund Physick to Thomas Penn, Apr. 19, 1769, ser. 6, NV-086, pp. 9–13, Penn Family Papers, HSP.

11. Ibid.

12. Ibid.

13. Moyer, *Wild Yankees*, 23; James Kirby Martin, "The Return of the Paxton Boys and the Historical State of the Pennsylvania Frontier, 1764–1774," *Pennsylvania History* 38, no. 2 (1971), 125–28.

14. "Agreement Entered into at Wyoming, 1769," *PA Archives*, First Series, 4: 350–54.

15. Isaac Chapman, *A Sketch of the History of Wyoming* (Wilkes-Barre, PA, 1830), 99. See "Connecticut Lands in Pennsylvania," Letter from Windsor, CT, Mar. 13, 1754, *PA Archives, Documents Relating to the Connecticut Settlements*, Second Series, 18: 166–67. The full letter is Governor Wolcott to Hamilton, Windsor, March 13, 1754, *PCM*, 5: 771–73, particularly quotation on 772.

16. John Penn to Thomas Penn, Mar. 10, 1770, Penn Correspondence, HSP.

17. John Penn to Thomas Penn, Jan. 1, 1770, NV-023, p. 113, ser. 1, Penn Family Papers, HSP; Edmund Physick to Thomas Penn, Mar. 13, 1770, NV-033, pp. 206–10, ser. 1, Penn Family Papers, HSP.

18. Edmund Physick to Thomas Penn, Mar. 13, 1770, NV-033, pp. 206–10, ser. 1, Penn Family Papers, HSP.

19. John Penn to Thomas Penn, Mar. 6, 1771, Penn Correspondence, HSP.

20. John Penn to Thomas Penn, May 22, 1770, Penn Correspondence, HSP; Richard Hockley to Thomas Penn, Feb. 29, 1772, ser. 1, NV-034, p. 5, Penn Family Papers, HSP.

21. Edmund Physick to Thomas Penn, Mar. 13, 1770, NV-033, pp. 206–10, ser. 1, Penn Family Papers, HSP; John Penn to Thomas Penn, Jan. 1, 1770, NV-023, p. 113, ser. 1, Penn Family Papers, HSP.

22. John Penn to Thomas Penn, May 22, 1770, Penn Correspondence, HSP; Arthur St. Clair to John Penn, Ligonier, Jan.15, 1775, *American Archives*, 1: 266. William Egle, "Minutes of the Susquehanna Company," *Documents Relating to the Connecticut Settlement in Wyoming, PA Archives*, Second Series, 18: 76, 87.

23. Egle, "Minutes," *Documents, PA Archives*, Second Series, 18: 91 for quotation; the charter runs from 79–92.

24. Moyer, *Wild Yankees*, 39–41.

25. Details on the 1771 incident can be found in *History of Luzerne, Lackawanna, and Wyoming Counties* (New York, 1880), 37–39, and Pennsylvania Council's Executive Minutes,

Pennsylvania State Archives, Harrisburg, PA, reel B12; *PCM*, 9: 750–72. The details noted above are drawn primarily from the Deposition of Asher Clayton, Aug. 22, 1771, and the Deposition of Joseph Morris, Aug. 22, 1771, both of which were first found in the Provincial Council Executive Minutes held at the Pennsylvania State Archives, Harrisburg. For the 1774 incident, see Henry Bradsby, *History of Luzerne County: With Biographical Sketches* (Chicago, 1893), 44.

26. Griffin, *American Leviathan,* 92–94.

27. The fort was abandoned in October 1772. The remains were sold to Alexander Ross and Captain William Thompson for fifty pounds sterling New York money. They dismantled the fort and sold what they could. George Croghan to [Thomas Gage?], undated, ser. 4, box 202, folder 7 Cadwalader Family Papers, HSP. John Penn to Assembly, Jan. 29, 1773, *PA Archives, Minutes of the Council of Pennsylvania,* First Series, 10: 68–69. David M'Clure, *Diary of David McClure: Doctor of Divinity, 1748–1820* (New York, 1899), 83–85.

28. M'Clure, *Diary of David McClure,* 84–85, 100–101.

29. Ibid. Gage quotation in Griffin, *American Leviathan,* 94.

30. George Croghan to [Thomas Gage?], undated, ser. 4, box 202, folder 7, Cadwalader Family Papers, HSP; M'Clure, *Diary of David McClure,* 84–85, 100–101.

31. John Penn to Thomas Penn, Sept. 12, 1766, Thomas Penn Letterbooks, Incoming Correspondence, HSP. George Wilson to Arthur St. Clair, Aug. 14, 1773, *St. Clair Papers,* 1: 257–59. Wilson was referring specifically to the rejection of Pennsylvania authority by those in the Redstone Creek region, but they were also aware of those who believed the land was Virginia's.

32. For more on Michael Cresap, see Robert Parkinson, "From Indian Killer to Worthy Citizen: The Revolutionary Transformation of Michael Cresap," *William and Mary Quarterly* 63, no. 1 (Jan. 2006), 97–122.

33. Connolly seems to have met Dunmore through a connection to George Washington, who had land interests around Fort Pitt. Connolly's appointment was made sometime in the fall of 1773 after meeting Dunmore, who had traveled to Fort Pitt to survey the geography. Connolly's connections to Croghan and Semple are discussed in Charles Dahlinger, "Fort Pitt," *Western Pennsylvania Historical Magazine* 4, nos. 4–5 (1922), esp. 33–38. The article notes that Semple owned the tavern that Washington stayed at when he traveled to the region in 1770. Historians have frequently remarked on Dunmore's intentions, but Thomas Wharton gives perhaps the best contemporary view in a letter to George Croghan, "There remains no doubt that L D_____ Excursion to the Western Side of the Ohio, is more from a private than public View, & thou may depend on it (but keep it to thyself) that He intends if possible to obtain from the Shawnese a Part of their _____, then its supposed Hostilities will Cease; I have been told that Dr. C____ gave Him this Advice, as his LdS____p is determined to settle his Family in America." Thomas Wharton to George Croghan, Sept. 30, 1774, ser. 4, box 203, folder 37, Cadwalader Family Papers, HSP. For historians' views, see Volwiller, *George Croghan*; Griffin, *American Leviathan,* 97–124; and White, *The Middle Ground,* 356–65. Daniel P. Barr, "Contested Ground: Competition and Conflict Along the Upper Ohio Frontier, 1744–1784" (PhD diss., Kent State University, 2001), 229–89, offers the most exhaustive analysis of the event. For Dunmore's biography, also see the *Oxford Dictionary of National Biography.* The best study of John Connolly, an exceedingly interesting character, is Douglas MacGregor's "John Connolly: An American Loyalist" (MA thesis, Indiana University of Pennsylvania,

2000). MacGregor also has an essay forthcoming in Pencak, ed., *Pennsylvania's Revolution*, on the American Revolution in the area around Fort Pitt.

34. Arthur St. Clair to John Penn, Feb. 2, 1774, *American Archives*, Series 4, 1: 266. An advertisement posted on Jan. 1, 1774, called for all men to muster with the Virginia militia. A copy of the advertisement can be found in *St. Clair Papers*, 1: 272 fn. 2, and Joseph Spear to Arthur St. Clair, Feb. 23, 1774, *American Archives*, 1: 269. Reports of the blank commissions came primarily from Pennsylvanians; see Thomas Smith to Joseph Shippen, Apr. 7, 1774, *American Archives*, Series 4, 1, 207. Lord Dunmore to John Connolly, June 20, 1774, ser. 4, box 202, folder 4, Cadwalader Family Papers, HSP. That the officers in the Virginia militia had distinctive dress is shown in a deposition taken Dec. 24, 1774, when Samuel Whitesill described encountering the Virginia militia led by William Christy and Simon Girty "who seemed to be officers, from their dress." Deposition of Samuel Whitesill, Dec. 24, 1774, *St. Clair Papers*, 1: 351–52 fn. 2. Dahlinger, "Fort Pitt," 35–36. Connolly's decision to build a ducking stool meant to punish and embarrass women, a blatant show of patriarchal power, undoubtedly was another means by which Virginia hoped to convince unallied settlers of its power. Connolly also was likely trying to establish order over Fort Pitt, and rampant prostitution was a frequent complaint visitors made when they visited the town. Pennsylvania had a whipping post, and lashings were given out but no reference has been found to a ducking stool. Alexander S. Guffey, "First Courts in Western Pennsylvania," *Western Pennsylvania Historical Magazine* 7, no. 1 (1924), 145–77.

35. Aenas Mackay expressed his "surprise at the . . . the courts of law first sitting at Hanna's. Pray may I ask you the question, Where is the conveniency for transacting business on these occasions, as there is neither houses, tables, nor chairs? Certainly the people must sit at the roots of trees and stumps and in the case of rain the lawyers' books and papers must be exposed to the weather." Aenas Mackay to Arthur St. Clair, Mar. 3, 1773, *St. Clair Papers*, 1: 269–70. For details on these behind-the-scenes shenanigans, see Arthur St. Clair to Joseph Shippen, Jan. 15, 1774, *St. Clair Papers*, 1: 274–76.

36. Aenas Mackay to John Penn, Apr. 4, 1774, *PA Archives*, First Series, 4: 484–86; Thomas Smith to Joseph Shippen, *PA Archives*, First Series, 4: 618–20. As demonstrated in Konkle, ed., *Life and Times of Thomas Smith*, the *PA Archives* date of 1775 for the letter is inaccurate, and it was written sometime around April 1774; see *Life and Times*, 52–55.

37. Kenneth Bailey, *Thomas Cresap: Maryland Frontiersman* (Boston, 1944), and Robert G. Parkinson, "From Indian Killer to Worthy Citizen: The Revolutionary Transformation of Michael Cresap," *William and Mary Quarterly* 63, no. 1 (2006), 97–122. For reports of these rumors, see Arthur St. Clair to Joseph Shippen, Sept. 24, 1771; George Croghan to Arthur St. Clair, June 4, 1772; and Arthur St. Clair to Joseph Shippen, July 18, 1772, all in *St. Clair Papers*, 1: 260–67; and George Wilson to Major Luke Collins, July 9, 1772, *PA Archives*, First Series, 4: 454–55.

38. Speech, *St. Clair Papers*, 1: 280–81, fn. 2.

39. Arthur St. Clair to Joseph Shippen, July 18, 1772, Bedford, *St. Clair Papers*, 1: 265–67.

40. Mar. 3, 1774, *Virginia Gazette*.

41. Petition of the Inhabitants Settled on the Waters of Ohio, May 13, 1774; Assembly Message to Governor, *American Archives*, 1: 275–76.

42. Petition of the Inhabitants Settled on the Waters of Ohio, May 13, 1774, *American Archives*, Series 4, 1: 275; Advertisement of John Connolly, June 18, 1774, *PA Archives*, First Series, 4: 475; John Connolly to Arthur St. Clair, July 19, 1774, *PA Archives*, First Series, 4: 548.

43. Arthur St. Clair to John Connolly, July 22, 1774, *PA Archives*, First Series, 4: 549–50.

44. Alexander Withers, *Chronicles of Border Warfare* (Cincinnati, OH, 1912), 134–36; Griffin, *American Leviathan*, 108–10. There is a document from April 1774 that makes it appear that Lord Dunmore sent explicit instructions to incite a war with Indians. "Immediately commit some depredations" were his exact words. I came across the letter at the Pennsylvania State Archives, when Jonathan Stayer, one of their resident archivists, gave me a copy of the letter that the State Archives had acquired in 1938. The document came from the Columbus Genealogical Society. There has been some dispute about the validity of this missive. Therefore, the document's authenticity is tough to determine. Its content does seem to jive with events happening in the areas. Its handwriting is similar to eighteenth-century script, and language and spelling used conform to eighteenth-century standards. But because of the uncertainty surrounding its authenticity, I have not included these data in the text of the book. The index card that came with the image states it was taken from the Mss. Sec, Misc. Copies, 1550–1778. The instructions came from Alexander McKee in a letter dated Apr. 4, 1774, Williamsburg, VA.

45. Augustine Prevost, "Turmoil at Pittsburgh, The Diary of Augustine Prevost, 1774," *Pennsylvania Magazine of History and Biography* 85, no. 2 (1960), 111–62.

46. Arthur St. Clair to John Penn, May 29, 1774, *St. Clair Papers*, 1: 296–302. St. Clair to the Six Nations and Delaware, May 1774, *PA Archives*, First Series, 4: 500–501. Although St. Clair acknowledged the Shawnee appear "threatening," he hoped to "keep the path open" with these Indians. Arthur St. Clair to John Penn, June 16, 1774, *PA Archives*, First Series, 4: 519–20. Smith, *Narrative*, 73; Narrative of Spencer, Draper Manuscripts, 23CC, DLAR. For the belief that Dunmore tried to divide colonies, see Konkle, ed., *Life and Times of Thomas Smith*.

47. Arthur St. Clair to John Penn, May 29, 1774, *St. Clair Papers*, 1: 296–302. St. Clair to the Six Nations and Delaware, May 1774, *PA Archives*, First Series, 4: 500–501. Although St. Clair acknowledged the Shawnee appear "threatening" he hoped to "keep the path open" with these Indians. Arthur St. Clair to John Penn, June 16, 1774, *PA Archives*, First Series, 4: 519–20. Smith, *Narrative*, 73; Narrative of Spencer, Draper Manuscripts, 23CC, DLAR. For the belief that Dunmore tried to divide colonies, see Konkle, ed., *Life and Times of Thomas Smith*.

48. Pension Report of Samuel Hammond, Draper Manuscripts, 8DD, David Library of the American Revolution.

49. Pension Report of Samuel Hammond, Draper Manuscripts, 8DD, DLAR; William Preston to Edward Johnson, Aug. 2, 1774, Preston Papers, Virginia Historical Society, Richmond, VA; William Fleeming to Nancy Fleeming, Sept. 27, 2774, Virginia Papers, Draper Manuscripts, 2ZZ, DLAR. Virginia Assembly to Lord Dunmore, May 13, 1774, *Journals of the House of Burgesses*, 6. For an article that shows Virginia's ability to incorporate new areas, see Richard Beeman, "The Political Response to Social Conflict in the Southern Backcountry: A Comparative View of Virginia and the Carolinas During the Revolution," in Ronald Hoffman and Thad Tate, ed., *An Uncivil War: The Southern Backcountry in the American Revolution* (Charlottesville, VA, 1985).

50. Petition from Westmoreland County, June 14, 1774, *PA Archives*, First Series, 4: 518. See the subsequent petitions, often signed by many of the same people, in *St. Clair Papers*, 1: 317–19, fn. 1. Arthur St. Clair to John Penn, June 16, 1774, *PA Archives*, First Series, 4: 519–20. Arthur St. Clair to John Penn, July 22, 1774, *American Archives*, 1: 677.

51. Virginia Assembly to Lord Dunmore, May 13, 1774, *Journals of the House of Burgesses*, 6.

52. The militias began in late May 1774. Details can be found in Arthur St. Clair to John Penn, May 29, 1774, and George Croghan to Arthur St. Clair, June 4, 1774, *St. Clair Papers*, 1: 302–4. See John Connolly to George Croghan, June 2, 1774, and June 3, 1774, both in ser. 4, box 201, folder 17, Cadwalader Family Papers, HSP; George Croghan to John Connolly, June 3, 1774, ser. 4, box 201, folder 33, Cadwalader Family Papers, HSP; Lord Dunmore to John Connolly, June 20, 1774, ser. 4, box 202, folder 4, Cadwalader Family Papers, HSP. George Croghan to Michael Cresap, undated, 1774, ser. 4, box 201, folder 33, Cadwalader Family Papers, HSP. Arthur St. Clair to John Penn, June 12, 1774, *St. Clair Papers*, 1: 306. St. Clair recounts how an "idle report of Indians" in a war party sent hundreds of families fleeing. He "took to horse" to stop people from heading east but found it "impossible to persuade the people."

53. Lord Dunmore to George Croghan, June 20, 1774, ser. 4, box 202, folder 4, Cadwalader Family Papers, HSP; Devereux Smith to John Penn, Feb. 14, 1775, *PA Archives*, First Series, 4: 612; Boyd Crumrine, *Virginia Court Records in Southwestern Pennsylvania; Records of the District of West Augusta and Ohio and Yohogania Counties, Virginia, 1775–1780* (Baltimore, 1974); "Virginia Entries," *PA Archives*, Third Series, 3; Arthur St. Clair to John Penn, Aug. 25, 1774, *St. Clair Papers*, 1: 340–43. Deposition of George Ashton, Aug. 24, 1774, *PA Archives*, First Series, 4: 571–73.

54. The cessation of quitrents appears in a resolution in *Proceedings of the Provincial Conference of Committees* (Philadelphia, 1776), 9. The *Votes of the Assembly* also record that the tax collector, Samuel Kinkead, did not collect any taxes.

55. Votes of the Assembly, *PA Archives*, Eighth Series, 8: 7095–96.

56. James Tilghman to Thomas Penn, Mar. 31, 1774, ser. 1, NV-034, p. 123, Penn Family Papers, HSP.

57. See especially the exchange between Penn and Dunmore in March 1774. Lord Dunmore to John Penn, Mar. 3, 1774, Williamsburg, and John Penn to Lord Dunmore, Mar. 31, 1771, *American Archives*, 1: 253–60.

58. Lord Dunmore to John Penn, Mar. 3, 1774, Williamsburg in *St. Clair Papers*, 1: 285–87.

59. See Schwartz, *Jarring Interests*, for an account of New York's border conflicts. Belleseiles, *Revolutionary Outlaws: Ethan Allen and the Struggle for independence on the Early American Frontier* (Charlottesville, VA, 1995) also covers the conflict between New Hampshire and New York.

60. [Benjamin Franklin], "Rules by Which a Great Empire May Be Reduceds to a Small One," published in numerous newspapers. See, for example, *Pennsylvania Gazette*, Dec. 15, 1773, and *New York Journal*, Jan. 27, 1774.

61. "July 8, 1775," *Journals of Continental Congress*, 2: 167. Griffin, *American Leviathan*, 94, draws similar conclusions about the empire, arguing that without the willingness to use force in the west, "there was no saving the west." I do not agree that force against settlers was necessary to implement policy. Sufficient and powerful state-building could have sufficed. There were numerous plans and proposals meant to address the problem of order in the west. The problem was that the empire lacked the will and means to adapt to the new demands, in part because the imperial crisis in the east made addressing the west all the more difficult.

Chapter 10. Creating a Frontier Government

1. Beeman, *Varieties of Political Experience in Eighteenth Century America*, esp. 289.

2. David Hackett Fischer, *Paul Revere's Ride* (New York, 1994), 299–300. "Proceedings of the Provincial Conference," *The Proceedings Relative to Calling the Conventions of 1776 and*

1790 (Harrisburg, PA, 1825), 35–45; Edward Burd to Jasper Yeates, July 6, 1776, MG 207, folder 28, LancasterHistory.org, Lancaster, PA. Language of foreign mercenaries was pervasive, and its most famous usage probably can be found in the Declaration of Independence, which accuses King George of "transporting large Armies of foreign Mercenaries to compleat the works of death, desolation, and tyranny."

3. *Votes of the Assembly, Pennsylvania Archives,* Eighth Series, 8: 7237–39.

4. *St. Clair Papers,* 1: 363–65. "Association of Freeman and Inhabitants of Lancaster," Gratz Collection, case 1, box 16, HSP. For the committee's founding, see *PCM,* 10: 279–82, and enlistment oath at *PCM,* 10: 295–96. For the best analysis of the structure of revolution in Philadelphia, see Steven Rosswurm, *Arms, Country and Class: The Philadelphia Militia and the "Lower Sort" During the American Revolution* (New Brunswick, NJ, 1989); and Richard Ryerson, *The Revolution Has Now Begun: The Radical Committees of Philadelphia, 1765–1776* (Boston, 1978). Accounts of committees forming can be found in nearly all the essays in John Franz and William Pencak, eds., *Beyond Philadelphia: The American Revolution in the Pennsylvania Hinterland* (University Park, PA, 1998), as well as Ryerson, *The Revolution Has Now Begun.* Although Ryerson's emphasis is on Philadelphia, the function of the committees is well chronicled.

5. *St. Clair Papers,* 1: 363–65.

6. James Burd to Jasper Yeates, Sept. 19, 1775, Yeates Correspondence, HSP.

7. "Association of Freemen and Inhabitants of Lancaster," May 1, 1775, Gratz Collection, case 1, box 16, HSP. For a transcription, see *PA Archives,* Second Series, 13: 291–92; Rhoda Barber, Journal of settlement at Wright's Ferry on the Susquehanna River 1830, HSP; Edward Shippen to Delegates in Philadelphia, June 3, 1775, box 7, folder 9, Jasper Yeates Papers, HSP.

8. Edward Shippen to Delegates in Philadelphia, June 3, 1775, box 7, folder 9, Jasper Yeates Papers, HSP. See also the Minutes of the Lancaster County Committee in the Peter Force Collection, Series 7, Van Pelt Library, University of Pennsylvania.

9. David Freeman Hawke, *In the Midst of Revolution* (Philadelphia, 1974), 150; James Allen, Diary, May 15, 1776, HSP.

10. Thomas Gilpin, *Exiles in Virginia* (Philadelphia, 1848); Treese, *Storm Gathering,* 171–201.

11. "Minutes of the Provincial Convention," *The Proceedings Relative to Calling the Conventions of 1776 and 1790* (Harrisburg, PA, 1825), 45–64.

12. Edward Burd to [?], Mar. 15, 1776, Reading, Shippen Papers, 7, HSP; "Minutes of the Committee of Safety," June 30, 1775, and July 18, 1775, *PCM,* 10: 279, 295.

13. Edward Burd to [?], Mar. 15, 1776, Reading, Shippen Papers, 7, HSP; Thomas Smith to Arthur St. Clair, Aug. 22, 1776, Philadelphia, *St. Clair Papers,* 1: 373–74.

14. Thomas Smith to Arthur St. Clair, Aug. 22, 1776, Philadelphia, *St. Clair Papers,* 1: 373–74. Thomas Smith to Arthur St. Clair, Aug. 3, 1776, Philadelphia, *St. Clair Papers,* 1: 370–72, quotation on 371. Opposition to the new office holding can be found in Edward Shippen to Jasper Yeates, Sept. 13, 1776, box 7, folder 14, Jasper Yeates Papers, HSP; David Freeman Hawke, *In the Midst of Revolution* (Philadelphia, 1961), 192.

15. "An Act Obliging the Male White Inhabitants of This State to Give Assurances of the Same," *The Statutes at Large of Pennsylvania from 1682 to 1801,* 110.

16. The account of these events can be found in the following: Robert Galbraith to Thomas Smith, Sept. 29, 1777, Bedford, and Deposition of Robert Galbraith, Sept. 29, 1777, *PA*

Archives, First Series, 5: 638; "Committee of Correspondence of Bedford to President Wharton," Oct. 2, 1777, *PA Archives, War of Revolution,* Second Series, 3: 130–33; Robert Galbraith to Thomas Wharton, Yorktown, Oct. 31, 1777, *PA Archives,* First Series, 5: 730–31; Warrant for Arrest of Thomas Smith, Lancaster, Nov. 17, 1777, *PA Archives,* First Series, 6: 12–13. Such events were common in this moment. For another example, see also the case of Michael Hooffnagle, who also refused to relinquish Westmoreland County's records, even though he was an ardent patriot. For the account of this affair, see Circular of Council, Lancaster, Dec. 12, 1777, *PA Archives,* First Series, 6: 88–89; "Minutes of the Council of Safety," Mar. 21 and 22, 1777, *Minutes of the Supreme Executive Council* (hereafter *SECM*), 11: 186–88. In 1776, the *Provincial Council Minutes* were renamed the *Minutes of the Supreme Executive Council.* Although some histories state the records were returned, I have found no record of the books' discovery. "Minutes of the Council of Safety," July 26, 1777, *SECM,* 11: 252–53; "Minutes of the Council of Safety," Feb. 28, 1778, *SECM,* 11: 432–33; Deposition of Jeremiah Loughead, July 26, 1777, *PA Archives,* First Series, 5: 452–53. Several local histories of Westmoreland relate this story. Some report the records were found, and one refers to a letter Thomas Wharton sent to George Washington to personally intercede in the matter. I have not located this letter or evidence of the return of the books. For these stories, see Edgar Hassler, *Old Westmoreland: A History of Western Pennsylvania During the Revolution* (Pittsburgh, 1900), 178; and John Boucher, *A Century and a Half of Pittsburg and Her People* ([New York], 1908), 1: 117–18.

17. James Cannon to Robert Whitehill, Apr. 9, 1777, Whitehill Papers, Cumberland County Historical Society; Information on the constitutions sent to Bedford can be found in Konkle, ed., *Life and Times of Thomas Smith,* 89.

18. Quote from James Cannon to Robert Whitehill, Apr. 9, 1777, Whitehill Papers, Cumberland County Historical Society; Information on the constitutions sent to Bedford can be found in Konkle, ed., *Life and Times of Thomas Smith,* 89.

19. Robert Galbraith to President Wharton, Feb. 6, 1778, *PA Archives,* First Series, 6: 238–39; Robert Galbraith to Thomas Wharton, May 16, 1778, Bedford, *PA Archives,* First Series, 6: 511–12; Minutes of Supreme Executive Council, Dec. 18, 1778, *SECM,* 11: 645–46; Konkle, ed., *Life and Times of Thomas Smith,* 122–33; Minutes of Council, Aug. 17, 1778, *SECM,* 11: 554–55; Minutes of Council, Nov. 28, 1778, *SECM,* 11: 629–30.

20. See John Nevill to the Committee of Safety, Fort Pitt, June 13, 1776, *Virginia Magazine of History and Biography* 16, no. 1 (1908), 53; "Order for Capt. John Nevill to Take Possession of Fort Pitt," 1776, *Virginia Magazine of History and Biography* 18 (1910), 33; Quote from John Campbell to Committee of Correspondence at Hanna's Town, undated, post-1775, Miscellaneous Correspondence, Roll 1, PHMC.

21. For the Delaware as the fourteenth state, see C. H. Sipe, *The Indian Wars of Pennsylvania* (Harrisburg, 1929), 568–69; Lorraine Williams, "Caught in the Middle: New Jersey's Indians and the American Revolution," in *New Jersey and the American Revolution,* ed. Barbara Mitnick (New Brunswick, NJ, 2005), 102. Patrick Henry to George Morgan and John Nevill, Williamsburg, Mar. 19, 1777, *Papers of Patrick Henry,* 46–47; "Minutes of Council of Virginia, Expedition to Pluggy's Town, March 12, 1777," *PA Archives,* First Series, 5: 258–59.

22. George Morgan and John Nevill to Patrick Henry, Fort Pitt, Apr. 1, 1777, in William Wirt Henry, *Patrick Henry: Life, Correspondence, and Speeches* (New York, 1891), 2: 54–57; and in *PA Archives,* First Series, 5: 285–88.

23. Ibid.

24. General Edward Hand to Jasper Yeates, Fort Pitt, Oct. 2, 1777, Edward Hand Papers, Draper Collection, DLAR. The first reports of the Indians of the Ohio Country all taking sides with the British began arriving in Fort Pitt in late July 1777. See Arbuckle to Edward Hand, Fort Randolph, July 26, 1777, Hand Papers, DLAR, and a letter from David Zeisberger to George Morgan, July 7, 1777, *PA Archives*, First Series, 5: 446–47. For the history of warfare in the area during the revolution, see Walter Dunn, *Choosing Sides on the Frontier in the American Revolution* (Westport, CT, 2007), and Griffin, *American Leviathan*.

25. See, for example, "An Account of the Number of Militia, Waggons, and Horses, and Flour, etc, wanted from each County in the State," *PA Archives*, Second Series, 3: 426–27. Edward Hand to Jasper Yeates, Fort Pitt, Mar. 7, 1778, Hand Papers, Draper Collection, DLAR. Petition to Continental Congress, May 12, 1778, Bedford County Militia Records, MG-147, PHMC. Supreme Executive Council to President Wharton, Philadelphia, Sept. 8, 1777, *PA Archives*, First Series, 5: 590.

26. Edward Hand to Geo Woods, David Espy, Benjamin Elliot, Fort Pitt, June 28, 1778, Bedford County Militia Records, MG-147, PHMC.

27. Ibid.

28. For the various militia acts in Virginia, see *Statutes at Large of Virginia*, ed. William Hening, 9–10: chaps. 1, 4, 6, 12; Patrick Henry to William Fleeming, Williamsburg, Feb. 19, 1778, Henry Papers, Section 1, Virginia Historical Society, Richmond, VA.

29. For the various militia acts in Virginia, see *Statutes at Large of Virginia*, ed. William Hening, 9–10: chaps. 1, 4, 6, 12; Patrick Henry to William Fleeming, Williamsburg, Feb. 19, 1778, Henry Papers, Section 1, Virginia Historical Society, Richmond, VA.

30. William Irvine to General George Washington, Fort Pitt, Apr. 20, 1782; Council to William Irvine, Philadelphia, Dec. 17, 1781; William Moore to William Irvine, Philadelphia, Jan. 7, 1782; William Irvine to ?, Fort Pitt, Apr. 20, 1782; Notes from Meeting, Apr. 5, 1782, all Irvine Papers, Draper Collection, DLAR.

31. William Irvine to ?, Fort Pitt, Apr. 20, 1782, Irvine Papers, Draper Collection, DLAR. At a meeting of the officers and principal inhabitants of Washington County at Catfish Camp on Thursday the 22nd August, 1782; and William Irvine to Major Scott and Washington County Militia, Ft. Pitt, Apr. 18, 1782, both Irvine Papers, Draper Collection, DLAR.

32. Marshel to William Irvine, Washington County, Apr. 4, 1782, Irvine Papers, Draper Collection, DLAR.

33. The fullest account of the massacre and its repercussions can be found in Silver, *Our Savage Neighbors*, 265–81.

34. Ibid.

35. Historians Patrick Griffin and Peter Silver each argue that the Gnadenhutten massacre marked the creation of a new racial paradigm on the frontier in which Euro-Americans viewed Indians en masse as subhuman and a distinct race. Silver writes that the massacre demonstrated "a powerful postwar distaste for Indians as Indians, a feeling that in this instance was by itself so clearly pivotal and indiscriminate as to be worth labeling racist." Griffin finds that the Gnadenhutten massacre showed that "settlers now conceived Indians as innately inhuman, irredeemable." Silver, *Our Savage Neighbors*, 273, and Griffin, *American Leviathan*, 171. For Williamson's subsequent career, see Silver, *Our Savage Neighbors*, 278.

36. Dunn, *Choosing Sides*, 143.

37. For a good summation of the back and forth see Dunn, *Choosing Sides*, 126–27; Ordinances of Convention, William Hening, ed., *Statutes at Large*, 9: 9–151, see 118 and 262.

38. "Virginia Delegates in Congress to the Speaker of the Pennsylvania Convention, July 15, 1776, in *The Papers of Thomas Jefferson, Volume 1, 1760-1776*, ed. Julian P. Boyd (Princeton: Princeton University Press, 1950), 465–66 ; Marie Kimball, *Thomas Jefferson: War and Peace, 1776–1784* (Westport, CT, 1980), 90–91; James Mitchel and Henry Flanders, eds., *Statutes at Large of Pennsylvania*, 9: 569–72.

39. Edward Hand to Jasper Yeates, Fort Pitt, Aug. 28, 1777, Hand Papers, Draper Collection, DLAR; George Rogers Clark, *Memoirs*, in *Conquest of the Country Northwest of the River Ohio, 1778–1783*, ed. William English (Indianapolis, 1896), 469.

40. Henry, *Patrick Henry*, 206; Kimball, *Thomas Jefferson: War*, 92; John Boucher, *History of Westmoreland County, Pennsylvania* (New York, 1906), 2: 65.

41. "Resolutions and State Papers," *Statutes at Large of Virginia*, ed. Hening, 519–37.

42. Ibid.

43. Moyer, *Wild Yankees*, 32; Samuel Hunter to the Commanders of the Militia in Berks County, Fort Augusta, July 9, 1778, vol. 5, p. 32, Letters of Members of the Pennsylvania Provincial Congress, HSP. President Wharton to Edward Hand, Philadelphia, Aug. 22, 1777, *PA Archives*, First Series, 5: 540–42; Supreme Executive Council to Lieutenants of Certain Counties, *PA Archives*, First Series, 5: 541–42; William Moore to William Irvine, in Council, Philadelphia, Sept. 4, 1782, Irvine Papers, Draper Collection, DLAR.

44. Quote from William Moore to William Irvine, in Council, Philadelphia, Sept. 4, 1782, Irvine Papers, Draper Collection, DLAR; For other discussions of the western and northern areas being connected in official thinking, see Supreme Executive Council to Lieutenants of Certain Counties, *PA Archives*, First Series, 5: 541–42.

45. Articles of Confederation, http://avalon.law.yale.edu/18th_century/artconf.asp.

46. For the Trenton Decree, see Moyer, *Wild Yankees*, 35–36, 41–42. For the actual records of the court, see *Journals of Continental Congress, 1774–1789* (Washington, DC, 1922), 24: 6–32.

47. Henry Martyn Hoyt, *Brief of a Title in the Seventeen Townships in the County of Luzerne: A Syllabus of the Controversy Between Connecticut and Pennsylvania* (Harrisburg, 1879), 46–47.

48. Joseph Reed to George Bryan, Trenton, Dec. 3, 1782; Dec. 13, 1782; Dec. 20, 1782; Dec. 25, 1782, in *Life and Correspondence of Joseph Reed*, ed. William Bradford Reed (Philadelphia, 1847), 2: 388–91.

Conclusion

1. "Daniel Drake," in *Recollections of the Early Republic: Selected Autobiographies*, ed. Joyce Appleby (Boston, 1997), 29–58.

2. Crevecoeur, *Letters*. "Daniel Drake," in *Recollections of the Early Republic*, ed. Appleby, 29–58, quotations on 34–35.

3. "Daniel Drake," in *Recollections of the Early Republic*, ed. Appleby, 29–58.

4. The most complete recent history of these mobilizations is Terry Bouton, *Taming Democracy: "The People," the Founders, and the Troubled Ending of the American Revolution* (New York, 2007), esp. parts 2 and 3.

5. Bouton, *Taming Democracy*, esp. 145–67, quotations on 117 and 148.

6. Ibid., 145–67, quotations on 118 and 148. Bouton sees these rings as distinctive to the early republic and this moment. I see them as rooted in the colonial past.

7. The best recent account of the Whiskey Rebellion is in Thomas Slaughter, *The Whiskey Rebellion: Frontier Epilogue to the American Revolution* (New York, 1986). See also Bouton,

Taming Democracy, 216–43, and Griffin, *American Leviathan,* 222–39. For accounts from participants, see William Findley, *History of the Insurrection in the Four Western Counties of Pennsylvania* (Philadelphia, 1796), and Hugh Henry Brackenridge, *Incidents of the Insurrection* (New Haven, CT, 1972). Quotation from Slaughter, *Whiskey Rebellion,* 146.

8. Slaughter, *The Whiskey Rebellion;* Bouton, *Taming Democracy,* 216–43; Griffin, *American Leviathan,* 222–39.

9. Slaughter, *Whiskey Rebellion,* esp. chap. 8, quotation on 195.

10. Alexander Hamilton, "Federalist Number 8," in Charles Kessler, ed., *The Federalist Papers* (New York, 1999), 61.

11. The best background material can be found in Gordon Wood, *Empire of Liberty: A History of the Early Republic, 1789–1818* (New York, 2009), 217–23; and Rodger C. Henderson, "Findley, William," *American National Biography Online,* Feb. 2000, http://www.anb.org/articles/03/03-00170.html.

12. Wood, *Empire of Liberty,* 217–23, and Henderson, "William Findley."

13. The following summary of Findley's arguments can be found in Findley, *History of the Insurrection,* chap. 1.

14. Findley, *History of the Insurrection,* 24.

15. Ibid., 21–23.

16. Ibid., 21, 30–32.

17. Ibid., 124–25, and Slaughter, *Whiskey Rebellion,* 3, 55–56, 177, 181–82.

18. Hinderaker, *Elusive Empires,* part 3. For the best synthesis on early federal and Federalist Indian policy, see David Andrew Nichols, *Red Gentleman and White Savages: Indians, Federalists, and the Search for Order on the American Frontier* (Charlottesville, VA, 2008).

19. For Fries' Rebellion, see Paul Douglas Newman, *Fries's Rebellion: The Enduring Struggle for the American Revolution* (Philadelphia, 2005).

20. Brackenridge, *Incidents of the Insurrection,* 41–43. The quotation comes from a newspaper essay Brackenridge published in the *National Gazette* on February 2, 1792. The article appeared on the front page of the newspaper.

21. February 2, 1792, *National Gazette.*

22. For some early accounts of memory being passed down, see Merrell, *Into the American Woods,* 304. For travelers' accounts in the 1780s and 1790s, see John Ewing Memorandum Book, PHMC, and Ebenezer Denny, *Military Journal of Major Ebenezer Denny* (Philadelphia, 1859), 116–18; Slaughter, *Whiskey Rebellion,* 62. Fisher Ames, *The Speech of Mr. Ames* (Boston, 1796).

23. Andrew Jackson, "Second Annual Message, December 6, 1830," in *The Early American Republic: A Documentary Reader,* ed. Sean Patrick Adams (Malden, MA, 2008), 160; and James Richardson, ed., *A Compilation of Messages and Papers of the Presidents,* vol. 3: 1083.

24. On Roosevelt, see Richard Hofstadter, ed., *Turner and the Sociology of the Frontier* (New York, 1968).

Coda

1. Turner, "The Significance of the Frontier in American History," in *The Frontier in American History,* ed. Ray Allen Billington (New York, 1962), 1.

2. See the collected anthology *Turner and the Sociology of the Frontier,* edited by Richard Hofstadter (New York, 1968), for the distillation of this debate and page 5 for the quotation. For discussions on the safety valve, an often overlooked element of his thesis today, see Fred

Shannon, "A Post-Mortem on the Labor-Safety-Valve Theory," 172–86; Norman Simler, "The Safety-Valve Doctrine Re-evaluated," 187–200; and George Murphy and Arnold Zellner, "Sequential Growth, the Labor-Safety-Valve Doctrine, and the Development of American Unionism," 201–24, all in *Turner and the Sociology of the Frontier*, ed. Hofstadter; and Ellen Von Nardroff, "A Resources and Sociopsychological Safety Valve," in *The Frontier Thesis: Valid Interpretation of American History?* ed. Ray Allen Billington (New York, 1966), 51–63.

3. For "ethnocentric" and "English-speaking," see Patricia Limerick, *The Legacy of Conquest: The Unbroken Past of the American West* (New York, 1987), 21. For "gender bias," see Fredrika Teute and Andrew Cayton, eds., *Contact Points: American Frontiers from the Mohawk Valley to the Mississippi* (Chapel Hill, NC, 1998), 3. For "shibboleth," see Stephen Aron and Jeremy Adelman, "From Borderlands to Borders: Empires, Nation-States, and the Peoples in Between in North American History," *American Historical Review*, 104, no. 3 (1999): 814. For a thoughtful and still up-to-date review of the historiography, see Gregory Nobles, "Breaking into the Backcountry: New Approaches to the Early American Frontier, 1750–1800," *William and Mary Quarterly*, 46, no. 4 (October 1989): 641–70. Patricia Nelson Limerick was Turner's most vocal critic in the 1980s and 1990s. See esp. Limerick, *The Legacy of Conquest*, esp. 20–32.

4. Aron and Adelman, "From Borderlands to Borders," 814–41.

5. "Border-land, n." OED Online, June 2015, Oxford University Press. http://proxy.library.upenn.edu:2179/view/Entry/21625?redirectedFrom=borderland& (accessed June 26, 2015).

6. For an attempt to redefine the frontier for historians in the 1990s, see Teute and Cayton, eds., *Contact Points*, 1–16. Aron and Adelman, "From Borderlands to Borders," 814–41, quotation on 814. For the development of "borderlands" as an analytical concept, see Aron and Adelman, "From Borderlands to Borders." They define *frontier* as a "zone of intercultural penetration," while they treat *borderlands* as specific areas of imperial contestation. The historiography, however, has often conflated the distinction they tried to draw. Today, the use of *borderlands* by historians is just as likely to mean "an area of intercultural penetration" as it is an area of contestation. For Limerick's reconsiderations, see Patricia Nelson Limerick, "Turnerians All: The Dream of a Helpful History in an Intelligible World," *American Historical Review* 100, no. 3 (June 1995), 697–716. For the "f-word," see Kerwin Lee Klein, "Reclaiming the 'F' Word, or Being and Becoming Postwestern," *Pacific Historical Review* 65, no. 2 (1996): 179–216.

7. James Merrell, "Second Thoughts on Colonial Historians and American Indians," *William and Mary Quarterly* 69, no. 3 (July 2012): 451–512.

8. For two essays that chronicle the etymology of the word *frontier*, see Fulmer Mood, "Notes on the History of the Word Frontier," *Agricultural History* (April 1948): 78–82; and John Juricek, "American Usage of the Term 'Frontier' from Colonial Times to Frederick Jackson Turner," *Proceedings of the American Philosophical Society* 110, no. 1 (1966): 10–34. My thesis was developed independent of these essays but builds off a similar theme: the term *frontier* had meanings far different from Frederick Jackson Turner's usage. Juricek concludes that "the old 'border' sense of the 'frontier' was common in American until the early nineteenth century. In colonial and early national times, when Anglo-Americans spoke about frontiers, they usually were referring to the more or less fortified outer edges of the colonies, states, or nations." While I largely agree with this conclusion, I believe that the military connotations of the term had a far larger social and political resonance within eighteenth-century colonial culture than Juricek shows. I also think the role of an area for invasion is more pronounced than a "border" area implies.

9. Data compiled from *Pennsylvania Gazette,* accessed through Accessible Archives, http://www.accessible.com/accessible/index.html.

10. "Proposal by the Board of Trade of Great Britain Concerning the Defense of Carolina," *Colonial and State Records of North Carolina,* 2: 393–94, http://docsouth.unc.edu/csr/index.html/document/csr02-0200. For newspaper, see "From a Book Intitled, the Annals of Europe for the Year, 1739," *Boston Evening-Post,* Oct. 14, 1754.

11. "For "frontier by both sea and land," see *Journal of the Honourable House of Representatives for 1739* (Boston, 1739), 182; "Speech of Jonathen Belcher, February 22, 1733," *Boston News-letter,* Feb. 28, 1733/1734. For examples of eastern and western, see the legislative proceedings for virtually any year during the 1740s and 1750s. This eastern frontier referred primarily to areas outside of Boston and probably primarily the area that would become Maine. For instance, in the legislative proceedings of 1745, a committee specifically referred to Georgetown as the "most eastern and northern parts of the eastern frontier." *Journal of the Honourable House of Representatives* (Boston, 1745), and in 1740, the speech of Jonathan Belcher, *Boston Evening Post,* June 30, 1740; "A State of the Province of Georgia, Attested upon Oath, in the Court of Savannah, Nov. 10, 1740," in *Tracts and Other Papers Relating Principally to the Origin, Settlement, and Progress of the Colonies in North America from the Discovery of the Country to the Year 1776* (Washington, DC, 1836), ed. Peter Force, 1: 16; James Madison, "Federalist No. 41," in *The Federalist Papers,* ed. Charles Kessler (New York, 1999), 229

12. For more on how print can help foster and reflect a sense of national belonging, see Benedict Anderson, *Imagined Communities: Reflections of the Origin and Spread of Nationalism* (New York, 1991).

13. *Several laws & orders made at the General Court, held at Boston for election the 3d. of May 1676* (Cambridge, MA, 1676); *Several laws and orders made at the sessions of the General Court held at Boston the 13th of October 1675. As also at the sessions of Court held at Boston, the 3d. of November 1675* (Cambridge, MA, 1675).

14. Ibid. For other uses of interior, see the petition from the *Pennsylvania Votes of Assembly,* Eighth Series, 7: 5582.

15. "Act II, 'ffronteers to be seated with ffowre able men,' 1664," *Statutes at Large . . . Virginia,* ed. William Hening (Richmond, 1810), 2: 209; "Act I" and "Act XI," 1679, *Statues at Large . . . of Virginia, 1660–1682,* ed. Hening (New York, 1823), 2: 433, 448.

16. "Letter from the Lords Proprietors of Carolina to the Albemarle County General Assembly," Oct. 21, 1676, *The Colonial and State Records of North Carolina* 1: 228–30; *American Weekly Mercury,* Oct. 20, 1720 (Philadelphia).

17. *American Weekly Mercury,* Oct. 20, 1720 (Philadelphia).

18. King George II, "Proclamation," 1732, in *Tracts and Other Papers Relating Principally to the Origin, Settlement, and Progress of the Colonies in North America,* 1:6.

INDEX

ACKNOWLEDGEMENTS

One of the first books that got me interested in revolutionary Pennsylvania was Charles Lincoln's *The Revolutionary Movement in Pennsylvania, 1760–1776* (Philadelphia, 1901). The book is now often overlooked in the historiography of the American Revolution, but it remains a useful model. Lincoln's arguments were original for his time and the research that buttressed those arguments is still impressive. It is a book worth reading more than a century after its publication.

I first discovered Lincoln's work as I conducted undergraduate research on the Paxton Boys' Rebellion. As I began to prepare the final draft of this manuscript, I was drawn to Lincoln's study yet again. Despite many years and multiple readings, I discovered something new. A passage of the preface resonated like it never had before: "Errors, both of fact and of judgment, have undoubtedly crept into this study, and for these the indulgence of the reader is asked. The purpose of the work has been to show the interdependence of the colonial and national revolutions, and if this has been done the author is content." Lincoln's words gave me a level of reassurance necessary to send off the manuscript to the publisher. Despite untold hours spent editing and fact-checking, I had been hesitant to submit the manuscript until it was perfect. Reading Lincoln's humble request, the request of a historian I had long admired and whose work had inspired the manuscript, reminded me that no one is perfect. Therefore, I ask you, the reader, for the same indulgence. My purpose in this work has been to demonstrate the centrality of frontiers to the politics of colonial and revolutionary Pennsylvania, and that colonial competition over land played a large role in the political development of colonial Pennsylvania. Moreover, I hope to show that the fusion of these two issues created a crisis of governance on the verge of American independence that influenced the course and consequence of the Revolution.

Hundreds of people have helped make this book better, from librarians and archivists who helped me find materials, to institutions that provided financial support that made my research and writing possible, to colleagues and peers who helped me refine my arguments, to friends who provided social sustenance, to family members who provided every measure of support, and to many others. I owe them all an incredible debt of gratitude.

Several institutions provided significant support at crucial stages of this project. The David Library of the American Revolution, Virginia Historical Society, William L. Clements Library, and Pennsylvania State Archives all provided me with research fellowships. Their support provided me with access to materials that strengthened several of the core arguments of this book.

I was also lucky to receive several long-term fellowships, which provided me with the time necessary to write. The University of Pennsylvania provided me with five years of funding through a Benjamin Franklin Fellowship. The McNeil Center for Early American Studies and The State Society of the Cincinnati of Pennsylvania provided me with a fellowship, as I transitioned from researching to writing. The Doris Quinn Foundation and the David Library of the American Revolution provided me with funds to finish writing.

I also had the incredible honor to receive a two-year postdoctoral fellowship at the American Philosophical Society through a grant from The Pew Charitable Trusts. The fellowship provided me with time to revise the manuscript and the opportunity to begin the time-consuming and painstaking digital research necessary to create the maps and graphs included in this book and published as a digital supplement at mappingfrontiers.com. Charles Greifenstein supervised my work there, but, more than that, he served as the person I could go to when I wanted to talk history and writing. Martin Levitt, Librarian at the Society, sat with me for countless hours talking about management and the future of libraries and archives.

After my postdoc, I had the great pleasure to assume an assistant professor position at Williams College. The students at Williams made me appreciate the importance of writing. At Williams, I had students who would do the reading; they just wanted whatever they read to be engaging. I am a much-improved historian because of my experience in the classroom at Williams. The College itself provided generous research support throughout my time there, including a year's sabbatical leave. They also helped me receive a Hellman Grant, which provided funds for undergraduate students, led by one of the best undergraduate students I had, Nate Thompson ('15), to compile data used to create the maps for this book and its website. Devyn Spence Benson, Justin Crowe, Sara Dubow, Susan Dunn, James McAllister, Nicole Mellow, Scott Wong, and Jim Wood were supportive colleagues, and the Leadership Studies Program and the History Department made my time at Williams wonderful.

The David Library of the American Revolution has nurtured this project from its inception and has been truly an intellectual and professional home throughout. The Library's vast collection served as a foundation for this study, and it was during my time there as a fellow conducting research that I realized what my project was really about. I finished writing the first draft as the Historian at the Library, a staff position. I revised the manuscript as a member of the board. I then returned to the Library as a Scholar-in-Residence during my sabbatical from Williams, and it was then that I put the final touches on the book and sent it off to the press. Moreover, during my time as a staff member and as a member of the board of trustees, the Library has played a central role in my professional development. On a personal note, the Library has been my family's second home. Our oldest daughter learned to crawl on the front porch; our second daughter's first memories are from the year we spent living in the Farmhouse next-door to Meg McSweeney, the chief operating officer, and Marcel; and our son was born that year, too. Fellow board members Yvette Taylor-Hachoose, Jim Linksz, Sandra Miller, Norval Reece, Nancy Spears, and Francine Stone provided me with mentorship in the management of nonprofits. We confronted some of the major issues independent research libraries face in the twenty-first century, and I am grateful for the opportunity they provided me. Meg, Francine, and Nancy became great friends who always prodded me to move along with the book, even as we worked on many other exciting ventures.

As the book moved to page proofs, I returned to the American Philosophical Society as the Librarian. Keith Thomson provided moral support and wisdom, while Abby Shelton provided incredible support on all matters. Merrill Mason, Molly Roth, and John Wolfe made my transition to the APS smooth, and my other colleagues have made it a great place to be.

Several individuals played important roles in the development of this book as mentors. At the University of Pennsylvania, Rick Beeman's scholarship encouraged my own interests in political history. He also helped introduce me to the world of public history. Mike Zuckerman remains a confidant whose advice on matters of both scholarship and life has helped

guide me through the years. Bill Pencak, who passed away before the com-
pletion of this book, encouraged me and read drafts of several portions.
Peter Silver, James Merrell, and Andrew Cayton took part in a manuscript
workshop at Williams that proved transformative. The book is much better
and very different because of their feedback. Richard Dunn helped found
the McNeil Center (then the Philadelphia Center) and served as Executive
Officer at the American Philosophical Society with his wife Mary. I am in
awe of his legacy, and I am grateful for the conversations he and Mary have
had with me over the years about the profession and my work. I met Brendan McConville late in this project's life, but he has been instrumental in
pushing me to get it done—and in serving as a friend to talk to about all
sorts of matters.

Bob Lockhart at Penn Press showed a great interest in this project from
an early stage. He provided editorial criticism of revised chapters even
before I agreed to publish with Penn Press. The rest of the Penn Press
editorial team was also very helpful. I especially appreciate the diligence
paid to the maps and images used in the text. Outside reviewers solicited
by the Press helped me refine the manuscript.

Friends and colleagues helped in all sorts of ways, large and small, professional and personal. John Kenney has been a true friend who not only
read a lot of my stuff, but, more important, was a partner-in-crime in grad
school and beyond. Kyle Roberts has provided a strong shoulder to lean on
since graduate school. Nicole Maurantonio has been a great friend. Juan
Jose Ponce and Clemmie Harris were good comrades, as was Brian Rouleau.
I have benefited from the scholarship of Drew Lipman, whose work on very
different frontiers nonetheless influenced my own work, and it was good to
have a fellow proud Bay Stater in the City of Brotherly Love. Carl Robert
Keyes has also been a great friend with whom I have shared many a memo-
rable weekend. Frank Fox, a fellow scholar of revolutionary Pennsylvania,
has read and provided feedback on more drafts of my material than he
probably cares to remember. Frank's mentorship in matters of career was
just as helpful as his encouragement to continue my research. During my
time at the McNeil Center, I enjoyed the fine fellowship of Zara Anishan-
slin, Bill Campbell, Bill Carter, Michael Carter, Jo Cohen, Ken Cohen,
Simon Finger, Robb Habberman, Adam Jortner, Brian Murphy, and Chris-
tina Snyder, among many others.

My friends outside of academia always asked me "How is the Paxton
Boys' Rebellion doing?" As I gave them the latest update, many of them